Greek and Roman Slaveries

Blackwell Sourcebooks in Ancient History

This series presents readers with new translations of the raw material of ancient history. It provides direct access to the ancient world, from wars and power politics to daily life and entertainment, allowing readers to discover the extraordinary diversity of ancient societies.

Published

In Preparation

Greek and Roman Slaveries

Eftychia Bathrellou
University of Lisbon
Lisbon, Portugal

Kostas Vlassopoulos
University of Crete
Rethymno, Greece

WILEY Blackwell

Registered Office
John Wiley & Sons, Inc., 111 River Street, Hoboken, NJ 07030, USA

Editorial Office
111 River Street, Hoboken, NJ 07030, USA

For details of our global editorial offices, customer services, and more information about Wiley products visit us at www.wiley.com.

Wiley also publishes its books in a variety of electronic formats and by print-on-demand. Some content that appears in standard print versions of this book may not be available in other formats.

Library of Congress Cataloging-in-Publication Data
Names: Bathrellou, Eftychia, author. | Vlassopoulos, Kostas, 1977- author.
Title: Greek and Roman slaveries / Eftychia Bathrellou, Kostas Vlassopoulos.
Description: Hoboken, NJ : John Wiley & Sons, 2022. | Includes bibliographical
   references and index.
Identifiers: LCCN 2021021140 | ISBN 9781118969298 (paperback) |
   ISBN 9781118969328 (pdf) | ISBN 9781118969335 (epub)
Subjects: LCSH: Slavery--Rome--History. | Slavery--Greece--History.
Classification: LCC HT863 .B38 2022 | DDC 306.3/6209495--dc23
LC record available at https://lccn.loc.gov/2021021140

Cover image: © Museo Archeologico Nazionale di Reggio Calabria
Cover design by Wiley

Set in 10/13pt StoneSerif by Integra Software Services Pvt. Ltd, Pondicherry, India

SKY10034073_040622

To the memory of
Gerasimos Vlassopoulos (1949–2018),
Stavros Bathrellos (1950–2016),
and Metaxia Anaplioti (1937–2018),
who encouraged us to keep walking in the paths we had taken,
whatever the odds.

Contents

List of Figures and Maps

Figures

Front cover: Inscribed terracotta tile, first century BCE/first century CE: Museo Archeologico Nazionale di Reggio Calabria; su concessione del Ministero della Cultura n. 8 del 24/3/2021 – Museo Archeologico Nazionale di Reggio Calabria.

Map

Note to the Reader

Editions of Greek and Latin literary texts, inscriptions, and papyri

All translations are our own. Unless otherwise specified, we have translated what is considered the standard edition of the Greek and Latin literary texts. For papyri, we have translated the text appearing in papyri.info, while for inscriptions we have translated the text indicated in their reference number unless otherwise specified.

Signs used in the book

***	indicates that something of the original Greek or Latin text has been lost in transmission.
†	indicates that the transmitted Greek or Latin text is problematic, and the exact wording of the original cannot be recovered.
[…]	indicates that (i) text has been omitted by us or (ii) text has been lost through damage to the inscription or papyrus.
[aaa]	lost text restored by the modern editor.
<aaa>	text erroneously omitted in the transmitted Greek or Latin text but added by the modern editor.
(aaa)	text added by us to facilitate understanding.

Names of persons, places, and peoples

We have used assimilated English forms of names of persons, places, and peoples whenever we judged them recognizable relatively widely (e.g. Attica, Rhodes, Lacedaemonians, the philosopher Socrates).

Names of ancient authors: We have followed the style of the *Oxford Classical Dictionary* both for the authors of the sources and for authors mentioned in them.

Other persons' names: In translations of Latin sources, we have kept the Latin form of persons' names, whatever the names' origin. With one exception (source 12.2), in translations of Greek sources, we have transliterated people's names of Greek origin but used the Latin form of Latin names.

Place names: We have used Greek transliterations of toponyms in the Eastern Mediterranean and Latin forms of toponyms in the Western Mediterranean, the northern Balkans, and northern Europe.

Names of peoples: For the names' roots, we have followed the same policy as with place names, so that the people can be connected with the corresponding toponym relatively easily. But we have tended to use assimilated English endings throughout (e.g. Achaeans, Kilikians, Dacians).

Acknowledgements

This book has had a very long gestation, from the early 2010s, when it was conceived, until its final delivery almost a decade later. We would like to thank Wiley Blackwell and its staff for their original invitation to contribute this volume to the Blackwell Sourcebooks in Ancient History series, as well as for their patience over the years; we hope that the final product has made the long journey worth its salt!

Much of the final work for this book was done in lockdown conditions because of the COVID-19 pandemic, and we are grateful to colleagues and friends who gave us access to material we would not otherwise be able to consult in such circumstances. We would particularly like to thank Angelos Chaniotis, Eleanor Dickey, Kyriaki Konstantinidou, and the staff at the Library of the Faculty of Letters at the University of Lisbon for providing us with materials and going out of their way to help. Kostas Vlassopoulos would like to thank the Department of History and Archaeology, University of Crete, for the research leave in spring 2020, alongside with the Center of Hellenic Studies in Washington, DC, for the Spring Fellowship during the same period; in combination, they provided the time and facilities for completing this volume. We would also like to express our gratitude to the following scholars and friends for their help and generosity in terms of finding the texts and images that appear in this volume: Elizabeth Fentress, Harriet Flower, Pavlina Karanastasi, Stephanie Maillot, Monica Trümper, Mantha Zarmakoupi, and Gabriel Zuchtriegel. We would also like to thank the British Museum, the Leiden Rijksmuseum, the Museo Archeologico Nazionale di Reggio Calabria, the National Archaeological Museum of Athens, and the Parco Archeologico di Pompeii for permission to reproduce the images included in this volume. Special thanks also go to Margherita Maria Di Nino for her help in our communication with Italian cultural authorities and to Timothy Duff and Fotini Hadjittofi, who always found time to discuss translation issues with us; Timothy

Duff also read and improved large parts of our text, for which we are very grateful. Needless to add, all remaining errors and other shortcomings are our own responsibility.

Finally, we would like to thank our families and friends, whose company and friendship supported us when writing this book and gave us joy: Katerina Arampatzi, Stamatis Bathrellos, Nikos and Vassiliki Boutsika, Apostolos Delis, Vanessa Hillebrand, Eleni Kalamara, Aleka Lianeri, Dunja Milenkovic, Christos Roussis, Vassiliki Stavrou, and Anastasia Theologou.

The years during which we prepared this book were sadly marked by the death of many of our loved ones. This book is dedicated to the memory of our fathers, Gerasimos Vlassopoulos and Stavros Bathrellos, and of EB's great aunt Metaxia Anaplioti; their sagacity and their love guided us, gave us strength, and to a great extent shaped our lives.

Abbreviations

AJA	*American Journal of Archaeology.*
AJP	*American Journal of Philology.*
An.Ep.	*L'Année épigraphique.*
Arch.Eph.	*Ἀρχαιολογικὴ Ἐφημερίς.*
AS	*Ancient Society.*
AT	*Antiquité Tardive.*
BASP	*Bulletin of the American Society of Papyrologists.*
BCH	*Bulletin de Correspondance Hellénique.*
BHG	F. Halkin, *Bibliotheca Hagiographica Graeca*, Brussels, 1957[3].
BICS	*Bulletin of the Institute of Classical Studies.*
BNJ	*Brill's New Jacoby*, Berlin, 2008–2019.
CA	*Classical Antiquity.*
CEL	P. Cugusi, *Corpus Epistolarum Latinarum*, I–III, Florence, 1992–2002.
Chambry	É. Chambry, *Ésope Fables*, Paris, 1927.
CIL	*Corpus Inscriptionum Latinarum*, I–XVII, Berlin, 1862–.
CJ	*Classical Journal.*
CMG	*Corpus medicorum Graecorum*, Berlin, 1908–.
CP	*Classical Philology.*
C.Pap.Gr.	M. M. Masciadri and O. Montevecchi, *Corpus Papyrorum Graecarum, I: I contratti di baliatico*, Milan, 1984.
CQ	*Classical Quarterly.*
CRRS	*Corpus der Römischen Rechtsquellen zur Antiken Sklaverei*, I–X, Stuttgart, 1999–.
Dodone	E. Lhôte, *Les lamelles oraculaires de Dodone*, Geneva, 2006.
EAD	*Exploration Archéologique de Délos.*
EAM	T. Rizakis and G. Touratsoglou, *Ἐπιγραφὲς Ἄνω Μακεδονίας*, Athens, 1985.
EKM	L. Gounaropoulou and M. B. Hatzopoulos, *Ἐπιγραφὲς Κάτω Μακεδονίας: Ἐπιγραφὲς Βέροιας*, Athens, 1998.
ERH	*European Review of History – Revue européenne d'histoire.*

FD	*Fouilles de Delphes.*
FGrH	F. Jacoby, *Die Fragmente der Griechischen Historiker*, I–III, Leiden, 1923–1958.
G&R	*Greece & Rome.*
Goukowsky	P. Goukowsky, *Diodore de Sicile Bibliothèque historique: Fragments, tome iv: livres xxxiii-xl*, Paris, 2014.
Grauf.	R. Marichal, *Les graffites de la Graufesenque*, Paris, 1988.
Hausrath–Hunger	A. Hausrath and H. Hunger, *Corpus fabularum aesopicarum*, 1.1–1.2, Leipzig, 1970^2 and 1959^2.
I.Amyzon	J. Robert and L. Robert, *Fouilles d'Amyzon en Carie, I. Exploration, histoire, monnaies et inscriptions*, Paris, 1983.
I.Aph.	J. Reynolds, C. Roueché and G. Bodard, *Inscriptions of Aphrodisias*, 2007, available at http://insaph.kcl.ac.uk/iaph2007.
I.Bouthrôtos	P. Cabanes and F. Drini, *Corpus des inscriptions grecques d'Illyrie méridionale et d'Épire. 2.2: Inscriptions de Bouthrôtos*, Athens, 2007.
I.Ephesos	*Die Inschriften von Ephesos*, I–VIII, Bonn, 1979–1984.
I.Iznik	S. Şahin, *Katalog der antiken Inschriften des Museums von Iznik (Nikaia)*, Bonn, 1979–1982.
I.Leukopetra	P. M. Petsas, M. B. Hatzopoulos, L. Gounaropoulou and P. Paschidis, *Inscriptions du sanctuaire de la Mère des Dieux autochthone de Leukopétra (Macédoine)*, Athens, 2000.
I.Lindos	C. Blinkenberg, *Lindos. Fouilles et recherches, 1902–1914. Vol. II, Inscriptions*, Copenhagen and Berlin, 1941.
I.Magnesia	O. Kern, *Die Inschriften von Magnesia am Maeander*, Berlin, 1900.
I.Miletos	P. Herrmann et al., *Inschriften von Milet*, I–VI, Berlin and New York, 1997–2006.
I.Oropos	V. C. Petrakos, *Οι επιγραφές του Ωρωπού*, Athens, 1997.
I.Philippi	P. Pilhofer, *Katalog der Inschriften von Philippi*, Tübingen, 2009.
I.Priene	W. Blümel and R. Merkelbach, *Die Inschriften von Priene*, I–II, Bonn, 2014.
I.Rhegion	L. D'Amore, *Iscrizioni greche d'Italia: Reggio Calabria*, Rome, 2007.
I.Smyrna	G. Petzl, *Die Inschriften von Smyrna*, I–II, Bonn, 1982–1990.
I.Sultan Daği	L. Jonnes, *The Inscriptions of the Sultan Daği*, I, Bonn, 2002.
IC	M. Guarducci, *Inscriptiones Creticae*, I–IV, Rome, 1935–1950.
ID	*Inscriptions de Délos*, I–VII, Paris, 1926–1972.
IG	*Inscriptiones Graecae*, I–XIV, Berlin, 1877–.
IGDO	L. Dubois, *Inscriptions grecques dialectales d'Olbia du Pont*, Geneva, 1996.
ILS	H. Dessau, *Inscriptiones Latinae Selectae*, I–III, Berlin, 1892–1916.
Ima. Ita.	M. H. Crawford et al., *Imagines Italicae: A Corpus of Italic Inscriptions*, I–III, London, 2011.
Inscr. It.	*Inscriptiones Italiae*, Rome, 1931–.
JBL	*Journal of Biblical Literature.*
JHS	*Journal of Hellenic Studies.*
JJP	*Journal of Juristic Papyrology.*
JRA	*Journal of Roman Archaeology.*

JRS	*Journal of Roman Studies.*
K-A	R. Kassel and C. Austin, *Poetae Comici Graeci*, I–VIII, Berlin, 1983–2001.
Kühn	K. G. Kühn, *Claudii Galeni opera omnia*, I–XX, Leipzig, 1821–1833.
MBAH	*Münstersche Beiträge zur Antiken Handelsgeschichte.*
P.Brem.	U. Wilcken, *Die Bremer Papyri*, Berlin, 1936.
P.Brux.	G. Nachtergael, *Papyri Bruxellenses Graecae*, I, Brussels, 1974.
P.Cair.Zen.	C. C. Edgar, *Zenon Papyri, Catalogue général des antiquités égyptiennes du Musée du Caire*, I–V, Cairo, 1925–1940.
P.Herm.	B. R. Rees, *Papyri from Hermopolis and other Documents of the Byzantine Period*, London, 1964.
P.Lips.	L. Mitteis, *Griechische Urkunden der Papyrussammlung zu Leipzig*, Leipzig, 1906.
P.Oxy.	*The Oxyrhynchus Papyri*, I–LXXXIII, London, 1898–.
P.Tebt.	*The Tebtunis Papyri*, I–IV, London, 1902–1976.
P.Turner	P. J. Parsons et al. (eds.), *Papyri Greek and Egyptian Edited by Various Hands in Honour of Eric Gardner Turner on the Occasion of his Seventieth Birthday*, London, 1981.
P.Ups.Frid.	B. Frid, *Ten Uppsala Papyri*, Bonn, 1981.
P.Wisc.	P. J. Sijpesteijn, *The Wisconsin Papyri*, I, Leiden, 1967.
P&P	*Past & Present.*
PBSR	*Papers of the British School at Rome.*
PdP	*La Parola del Passato.*
PG	J. P. Migne, *Patrologiae cursus completus, series Graeca*, Paris, I–CLXI, 1857–1886.
PMG	D. L. Page, *Poetae melici Graeci*, Oxford, 1962.
PSI	*Papiri greci e latini*, I–XVII, Florence, 1912–2018.
RIB	R. G. Collingwood and R. P. Wright, *The Roman Inscriptions of Britain, I, Inscriptions on Stone*, Oxford, 1965.
SB	F. Preisigke et al., *Sammelbuch griechischer Urkunden aus Ägypten*, I–XVIII, Strasbourg, 1915–1993.
SCI	*Scripta Classica Israelica.*
SEG	*Supplementum Epigraphicum Graecum.*
SGDI	H. Collitz et al., *Sammlung der griechischen Dialekt-Inschriften*, II, Göttingen, 1899.
Sigalas	A. Sigalas, *Des Chrysippos von Jerusalem Enkomion auf den heiligen Theodoros Teron*, Leipzig, 1921.
Tab.Vind.	A. Bowman and J. D. Thomas, *The Vindolanda Tablets*, London, 1994.
TAM	*Tituli Asiae Minoris*, I–V.3, Vienna, 1901–2007.
TAPA	*Transactions of the American Philological Association.*
TPSulp.	G. Camodeca, *Tabulae Pompeianae Sulpiciorum*, Rome, 1999.
UPZ	U. Wilcken, *Urkunden der Ptolemäerzeit: ältere Funde*, I–II, Berlin, 1927–1957.
Walton	F. R. Walton, *Diodorus Siculus Library of History. Volume XII: Fragments of Books 33–40*, Cambridge MA, 1967.
ZPE	*Zeitschrift für Papyrologie und Epigraphik.*
ZSS	*Zeitschrift der Savigny-Stiftung für Rechtsgeschichte: Romanistische Abteilung.*

Introduction

Slavery was a ubiquitous and fundamental phenomenon of Greek and Roman societies. Slaves constituted a substantial proportion of the population of ancient communities. They worked in practically all sectors of ancient economies, as agricultural workers, artisans, traders, servants, performers, managers, and even civil servants. Their exploitation allowed their masters to live as they wished; the domination of slaves shaped the formation of households, relations of gender, constructions of identity, and cultural practices. Slavery was used as a powerful tool to think about hierarchy, power, religion, and the good life. There is hardly any aspect of ancient history, literature, or archaeology that does not involve, in one way or another, slaves and slavery. Consequently, a sourcebook on ancient slavery has immense value for those interested in the study of Classics, ancient history, and classical archaeology.

The volume at hand is not the first slavery sourcebook. There exist two older sourcebooks on ancient slavery; one in English, by Thomas Wiedemann, that covers both Greek and Roman slavery,[1] and one in German, by Werner Eck and Johannes Heinrichs, that focuses on the Roman imperial period.[2] Both are still valuable works, and we have tried as far as possible to avoid duplicating their contributions and their selection of texts.[3] Instead, our sourcebook tries to present different texts and new topics and uses an alternative, interactive format. We have tried to design a sourcebook that is both user-friendly and at the same time an introduction to the sources and scholarship on Greek and Roman slaveries. Each chapter is preceded by an introduction, which lays out the wider issues examined in the chapter. Each source is accompanied by a small introduction, setting the

---

[1] Wiedemann 1981.
[2] Eck and Heinrichs 1993.
[3] For other important collections of sources on ancient slavery, see Scholl 1990; *CRRS*.

Greek and Roman Slaveries, First Edition. Eftychia Bathrellou and Kostas Vlassopoulos.
© 2022 John Wiley & Sons, Inc. Published 2022 by John Wiley & Sons, Inc.

context and providing necessary information, references to relevant scholarly literature, and a series of questions, which aim to help readers to analyze and debate each source. To help readers focus on how a source illuminates the issues under examination, we have limited the information we offer to the absolutely necessary. We have tried to ensure that each source and question can be studied productively solely on the basis of the evidence provided in the sourcebook. At the same time, by offering bibliographical suggestions, we have tried to make each source a window to the wider scholarship and an opportunity to explore further the issues that each source raises.[4] All translations of sources are our own, specifically made with the readership of this volume in mind.

This sourcebook includes a substantial number of sources that are relatively unknown or have never been examined in connection with slavery. We have also made a serious effort to include some of the material and visual evidence for ancient slaves and slavery and to examine some issues using more than one types of evidence. Nevertheless, we deeply regret that our linguistic limitations meant that we have only included sources written in Greek and Latin. The study of ancient slaveries needs to move beyond the usual focus on Greek and Roman slaveries and engage seriously with slavery in Mesopotamia, Syria, Anatolia, Egypt, the Punic world, Italic societies (Etruscans, Oscans), and temperate Europe.[5] We cannot achieve this wider aim in this work; hence, this is a sourcebook of Greek and Roman slaveries rather than *ancient* slaveries. But we have tried to use Greek and Roman sources as evidence for other slave systems (Anatolian, Jewish, Celtic, Germanic, Sarmatian) and to point out consistently their similarities with and differences from the better-known Greek and Roman slave systems. We also emphasize the diversity of these systems. The study of Greek slavery usually focuses on classical Athens, while that of Roman slavery is usually geared toward republican and imperial Rome and Italy. Other areas and periods, like the Hellenistic and early imperial Eastern Mediterranean, or late antiquity, are often ignored in synthetic, non-specialist surveys. We have tried to maintain a chronological and geographical balance, from the archaic period to late antiquity and including the whole of the Mediterranean and its adjacent areas, within the limits of the available evidence.

Finally, our selection of sources has been guided by our selection of topics. We have obviously included important topics that have always generated important research, such as the brutality of slavery, the economic exploitation of slaves, and the practices of manumission and the conditions of freedpersons. At the same time, we wish to present new topics, perspectives, and approaches, which have been at the forefront of innovative research in the last fifteen years. Earlier approaches tended to see slavery from a unilateral and top-down perspective, as a relationship defined exclusively by the masters. This meant that slavery was approached as a static institution, while slaves were largely seen as passive objects of domination and exploitation. We have adopted a processual approach, which explores the variety of economic, social, political processes and contexts within

---

[4] For the voluminous scholarship on ancient slavery, see the search engine at http://sklaven.adwmainz. de/index.php?id=1584.
[5] Lewis 2018; Vlassopoulos 2021a.

which slavery was employed for a variety of purposes; at the same time, while masters played a major role in the historical configuration of slavery, the agency of enslaved persons and other groups and factors (the state, religious groups, voluntary associations) was also significant. The involvement of various processes, contexts, and agents generated important contradictions and conflicts, as well as both widespread diversity and convergent tendencies. We thus devote chapters to the various slaving strategies of masters and the dialectical relationships between masters and slaves, free and slave, and the communities of enslaved persons. In addition, we attempt a systematic comparison of ancient slave systems while also exploring how they changed in the course of the 1500 years of ancient history. Finally, while slavery is usually approached as a socioeconomic phenomenon, recent work has put at the forefront its cultural and political aspects. We have thus devoted substantial space to the geopolitical setting of ancient slave systems and the role of slaves within cultural and religious processes.

All these various factors and topics were, of course, interrelated, and this means that the sources we have selected can be profitably juxtaposed and examined from a variety of viewpoints. We have included extensive cross-references to enable readers to explore sources in different contexts than those we have placed them; the detailed index is also a tool for using the sourcebook in multiple and alternative ways. We hope that this volume adequately reflects the diversity and richness both of the ancient evidence for slavery, as well as its modern scholarly study.

1

What Is Slavery?

What is slavery? Modern scholarship has largely focused on two definitions: slaves were human property,[6] and slavery is a form of social death: the violent domination of dishonored outsiders without acknowledged kinship links (natal alienation).[7] There is no shortage of ancient sources that support these two definitions (1.1, 1.11–2, 1.14). On this basis, scholars have constructed a stereotype of slaves as outsiders acquired through trade or war (1.2) who lived and worked under the direct control of their masters.

We aim to assess the advantages and limits of these approaches by examining servile groups like the Spartan helots and the Cretan *woikeis*, who were native inhabitants with their own families, working the land and surrendering a part of the harvest to their masters. Were such groups really slaves, or should they be interpreted as persons in an intermediate state "between slavery and freedom," as serfs or dependent peasants (1.3)? Or should we rather see them as slaves with peculiar characteristics, as a result of the peculiar histories of the societies in which they lived (1.4–9)? If so, slavery was not a uniform institution across ancient societies but a complex and contradictory phenomenon affected by a variety of economic, political, social, and cultural processes.[8] Social death was undoubtedly a constant threat that slaves faced and a harsh reality for many of them, but how should we account for cases in which masters (1.18) or states (1.15) honored their slaves? How should we interpret sources in which slaves present themselves as honorable persons (1.17) or honor their fellow-slaves (1.16)? Natal alienation was undoubtedly part of the slave condition, but how should we account for the evident significance of slave families for how slaves acted (1.13)?

---

[6] Andreau and Descat 2011.
[7] Patterson 1982.
[8] Lewis 2018.

Greek and Roman Slaveries, First Edition. Eftychia Bathrellou and Kostas Vlassopoulos.
© 2022 John Wiley & Sons, Inc. Published 2022 by John Wiley & Sons, Inc.

If property and social death emphasize the power of masters over slaves, we also need to take into account the role of slave agency. Should we see slavery as a relationship unilaterally defined by the masters or rather as an asymmetrical negotiation of power involving, masters, slaves, and other groups and agents?[9] In this respect, we explore a variety of issues: the negotiations that were inherent in the master–slave relationship (1.19, 1.21–2), the slaves' quest for emotional fulfillment and support and its impact on how slavery operated as an institution (1.20, 1.25), the significance of the intervention of the state and other third parties in relations between masters and slaves (1.23–4), and the conjunctures that slaves could take advantage of to enhance their conditions (1.26).

Finally, we move beyond property and social death to examine other ways (modalities) of conceptualizing slavery that existed in ancient societies, even in the text of the same author: as domination, an instrumental relationship, an asymmetrical relation of benefaction and reward, and so on (1.27). Although some sources can describe enslaved persons as natural slaves (1.28), it was also possible to conceive of slavery as an extreme form of bad luck, from which it was legitimate to seek to escape (1.30). These diverse modalities were partly complementary and partly contradictory;[10] we shall explore their consequences for how slavery operated in the various ancient societies.

PROPERTY AND DOMINATION: "CHATTEL SLAVES" AND OTHERS

1.1   Aristotle, *Politics*, 1253b23–1254a17:[11] Greek Philosophical Treatise (Fourth Century BCE)

Literature: Garnsey 1996: 107–27; Millett 2007; Vlassopoulos 2011a.

Because property is part of the household, so the art of acquiring property is part of household management – for both living and living well are impossible without the necessaries. Now, as a specific art would have to have its own proper tools, if its work is to be accomplished, so is the case with the person practicing household management. Tools can be inanimate or animate. For example, for the helmsman, the helm is an inanimate tool, while the lookout man an animate one (for when an art is concerned, an assistant is a kind of tool). Accordingly, a possession is a tool for maintaining life; property is a multitude of tools; a slave is a kind of animate possession; and every assistant is like a tool before tools. For if every tool could accomplish its own task when ordered or by sensing in advance what it should do [...], then master-builders would not need assistants, nor would masters need slaves.

---

[9] Harper 2011.
[10] Vlassopoulos 2021a.
[11] Unless otherwise specified, we have translated what is considered the standard edition of the Greek and Latin literary texts.

"Possessions" are spoken of in the same way as "parts." A part is not merely a part of another entity but also is wholly of that other entity. The same is true of a possession. This is why a master is just the master of his slave, not "his slave's" without qualification, but a slave is not merely the slave of his master but also wholly his. It is clear from these considerations then what the nature and the essential quality of a slave are. For anyone who, while being human, is by nature not of himself but of another, is by nature a slave; now, a human being is of another when, while being human, he happens to be a possession.

- Property, tool, nature: how does Aristotle use these concepts to characterize slavery?

- What does he mean when he claims that the master is just the master of the slave, but the slave belongs to the master completely?

- Under what conditions does Aristotle think that slavery would be superfluous?

1.2 *Digest*, 1.5.3–4: Collection of Latin Juristic Texts (Sixth Century CE)

The *Digest* is a collection of excerpts from the works of republican and early imperial Roman jurists made during the reign of the emperor Justinian in the sixth century CE.

Literature: Lambertini 1984; Cavallini 1994; Garnsey 1996: 23–34; Welwei 2000; Lenski 2016.

Gaius, *Institutes*, Book 1: Certainly, the most important division in the law of persons is the following: all men are either free or slave.
     Florentinus, *Institutes*, Book 9: Freedom is one's natural ability to do what one pleases unless this is prevented by force or by law. Slavery is an institution of the law of nations[12] whereby a person is subjected against nature to the ownership (*dominium*) of another. Slaves (*servi*) are thus named because commanders tend to sell captives, and thus to pre*serve* them, rather than kill them. They are, indeed, said to be *mancipia* because they are *captured* from the enemy by force (*manus*).

- What is freedom according to these passages?

- What is the cause of slavery?

- What conception of slavery underlies these passages? How does it relate to the view expressed in 1.1?

---

[12] See 1.11.

1.3 Pollux, *Onomastikon*, 3.83: Greek Thesaurus
(Second Century CE)

Literature: Lotze 1959; van Wees 2003; Paradiso 2007; Lewis 2018: 143–6.

> Between free men and slaves are the helots of the Lacedaemonians, the *penestai* of the Thessalians, the *klarôtai* (i.e. "those belonging to the allotted land") and *mnôitai* of the Cretans, the *dôrophoroi* (i.e. "tribute-bearers") of the Mariandynoi,[13] the *gymnêtes* (i.e. "unarmed") of the Argives and the *korynêphoroi* (i.e. "club-bearers") of the Sikyonians.[14] But those helots who are released to freedom are called *neodamôdeis* (i.e. "new members of the community") by the Lacedaemonians.

- Which groups are enumerated in this passage? In which parts of the Greek world are they located?
- How are these groups characterized? On what grounds?
- Do the passages below by Strabo (1.6) and Plutarch (1.7–8) support such a characterization?
- Did these groups exist when Pollux was compiling his thesaurus? Cf. 1.6.

1.4 Thucydides, 5.23: Greek Historiography
(Late Fifth Century BCE)

Thucydides lists the terms of the alliance agreed between the Athenians and the Lacedaemonians in 422/1 BCE, after the signing of the "peace of Nikias," a peace treaty that ended the first ten years of the Peloponnesian war.

Literature: Vlassopoulos 2011a.

> The Lacedaemonians <and the Athenians> will be allies for fifty years under the following terms: If any enemies invade the land of the Lacedaemonians and harm the Lacedaemonians, the Athenians are to help the Lacedaemonians in the most effective way possible, as far as they can. [...] And if any enemies invade the land of the Athenians and harm the Athenians, the Lacedaemonians are to help <the Athenians> in the most effective way possible, as far as they can. [...] And these things are to be done in a just, prompt and honest manner. Also, if the slaves revolt, the Athenians are to help the Lacedaemonians with all their power, as far as they can.

---

[13] A people on the south coast of the Black Sea; cf. 3.29.
[14] Sikyon and Argos are cities in the northern Peloponnese.

- What is the exception in this list of reciprocal obligations for Athenians and Spartans?

- Who are the people referred to as slaves? How does this compare with Pollux's definition in 1.3?

- Why is there no reciprocal obligation for the Spartans to help the Athenians in the case of a slave revolt? What does this imply about differences between the Athenian and Spartan slave systems?

1.5 Thucydides, 8.40.2: Greek Historiography (Late Fifth Century BCE)

In 412/1 BCE, in the course of the Peloponnesian War, the Chians asked for Spartan help to revolt from the Athenians, who then tried to reconquer the island. On the slaves of Chios, cf. 9.24, 11.6.

Literature: Luraghi 2009; Lewis 2018: 139–41.

> The Chians had many slaves – a greater percentage than any other city, except that of the Lacedaemonians. And because they were so many, the punishments they used to receive for their offences were harsher. So, when the Athenian forces seemed firmly established with a fortified base, the majority of the slaves immediately deserted to them and, as they knew the land well, it was they who caused the greatest harm.

- Who are the slaves in Lacedaemon, who are compared with the slaves in Chios?

- Does this description of the servile groups of Sparta differ from the way they are described in 1.3?

- What makes possible the description of helots in such divergent ways?

- Should we prefer one description to another?

- How are Chian slaves treated? Why?

- If Athenian chattel slaves were unlikely to revolt (1.4), how do Chian chattel slaves compare? How can we explain such divergence?

1.6 Strabo, *Geography*, 8.5.4: Greek Geography (End of First Century BCE/Early First Century CE)

Ancient authors tried to account for the origins of the helots. Here Strabo reports the views of Ephorus, a fourth-century BCE historian: according to his account, originally the Spartans were equal with the other communities of Laconia.

Literature: Vidal-Naquet 1986.

> Ephorus says that (king) Agis, son of Eurysthenes, withdrew the equality and commanded everyone to pay tribute to the Spartans. All the others obeyed, but the Heleians, who had the city of Helos – and were called Helots – revolted. They were defeated totally in war and were condemned to be slaves on specified terms: namely, that their owner was not allowed to manumit them or to sell them outside the border. And this war was called the war against the Helots. We may almost say that it was those around Agis who established the helot system that persisted until the time of the Roman rule. For the Lacedaemonians held these men in a way as public slaves, having assigned to them some houses to live in and special services to perform.

- How are the origins of the helots explained?
- What conditions modified the slavery of the helots? What do you think were the reasons for such conditions?
- How does Strabo try to conceptualize the peculiar slavery of the helots? With what does he compare them?

1.7   Plutarch, *Spartan Sayings* 239d–e: Greek Collection of Sayings (Late First/Early Second Century CE)

Literature: Hodkinson 2008; Luraghi 2009.

> Lycurgus[15] was thought to have secured for the citizens a fine and blessed good: abundance of leisure. For it was absolutely forbidden to touch manual work; moreover, there was no need at all of money-making, which involves painstaking accumulation, or of business activity, because Lycurgus had rendered wealth wholly unenviable and dishonorable. The helots worked the land for the Spartans, paying to them a part of the produce (*apophora*), which was regularly set in advance. A curse was in place against anyone who rented out the land for more, so that the helots might serve gladly since they were making some gain, and the Spartans themselves might not try to get more.

- In which way did the Spartans benefit from the agricultural work of their helots? How did it differ from other forms of employing slaves in agriculture? Cf. 4.2–6.
- How does Plutarch explain the reason for this arrangement?
- Do you accept Plutarch's explanation? What other explanations can you think for this arrangement?
- Does this arrangement make helots completely different from chattel slaves? Cf. 12.18–9.

---

[15] The legendary founder of Spartan social and political order.

1.8   Plutarch, *Life of Lycurgus*, 28: Greek Biography
(Late First/Early Second Century CE)

Literature: Luraghi 2002; Luraghi and Alcock 2003.

> In other respects, too, the Spartans used to treat the helots harshly and cruelly, to the point that they would force them to drink great amounts of unmixed wine and introduce them to the communal messes, thus demonstrating to the young what it meant to be drunk. And they would order them to sing songs and dance dances ignoble and ridiculous and abstain from the songs and dances of the free. This is why they say that later, during the invasion of Laconia by the Thebans,[16] when the Thebans would order the helots they captured to sing the songs of Terpander, Alcman, and Spendon the Spartan, they used to refuse, saying that their masters would not wish it. So those who say that in Lacedaemon the free man is freest, while the slave is most a slave, have correctly gauged the difference.

- How did the Spartans try to humiliate the helots?
- Why did the Spartans enforce such practices on the helots?
- What example does Plutarch cite to show the effects of such practices on slaves?
- Does Plutarch think that helots were "between slave and free"? Cf. 1.3.
- What do you think?

1.9   Aristotle, *Politics*, 1264a17–22: Greek Philosophical Treatise
(Fourth Century BCE)

Aristotle draws attention to the vagueness of Plato's *Republic* about whether the ideal of communal property would apply to all the classes in the ideal city or to the guardians only.

Literature: Lewis 2018: 147–65.

> If everything is common to all in the same way as among the guardians, then in what way will the farmers be different from the guardians? Or what benefit will there be to those who submit themselves to their rule? Or on what consideration will they submit themselves to the guardians' rule unless the guardians think of a clever idea similar to that of the Cretans? For the Cretans have allowed to their slaves everything they allow to themselves, with only two exceptions: they forbid them to use the gymnasia and possess weapons.

---

[16] In 369 BCE the Thebans invaded Laconia and Messenia, ultimately liberating the Messenian helots.

- What activities are prohibited to Cretan slaves? Why?

- Does this necessarily mean that Cretan slaves were better treated than Spartan helots?

- Does the description "between slave and free" (see 1.3) fit Cretan slaves better than helots?

1.10 Ps.-Xenophon, *Constitution of the Athenians*, 1.11–2:[17] Greek Political Treatise (Probably Fifth Century BCE)

This text, while critical of Athenian democracy, attempts to offer a sociological analysis of why the Athenian system works and is difficult to overthrow.

Literature: Vlassopoulos 2007; Canevaro 2018.

> If anyone is also surprised at the fact that here they allow their slaves to live in luxury and, some of them, magnificently, they could be shown to be doing this too with good reason. For where there is a naval power, it is necessary for financial reasons to be slaves to the slaves – so that we may receive the payments (*apophora*) the slaves make – and then to let them free. "But in Lacedaemon, my slave would have been in fear of you!" But if your slave is in fear of me, there will be a risk that he might even give his money so as not to be in danger. Where there are wealthy slaves, it is no longer useful that my slave should be in fear of you. This is why we established equality of speech between slaves and free men and between metics and citizens.

- How does the author describe the condition of slaves at Athens?

- How does he explain the peculiar condition of Athenian slaves?

- Do you find his explanation credible? What is the author's agenda?

- Why would a Spartan helot fear a free man who is not his master more than an Athenian slave would?

- Can we say that Spartan helots behaved more slavishly than Athenian slaves?

- Can we say that some Athenian slaves worked and lived as independently as most Spartan helots?

- In the light of this and the above passages, does it make sense to posit a single categorical distinction between helots and chattel slaves?

---

[17] Greek text: Marr and Rhodes 2008.

SOCIAL DEATH

1.11   Social Death and Roman Law

Civil law was the law applying to Roman citizens; the law of nations refers to rules common to all human communities; natural law was law according to nature. On the Digest, see 1.2.

Literature: Buckland 1908: 397–418; Wieling 1999: 1–30; Bodel 2017.

—————   1.11.a   *Digest*, 50.17.32: Collection of Latin   —————
Juristic Texts (Sixth Century CE)

Ulpian, *On Sabinus*, Book 43: As far as the civil law is concerned, slaves are regarded as nobodies. However, this is not the case with natural law because as far as natural law is concerned, all human beings are equal.

—————   1.11.b   *Digest*, 50.17.209: Collection of Latin   —————
Juristic Texts (Sixth Century CE)

Ulpian, *On the Lex Iulia et Papia*, Book 4: We compare slavery closely with death.

———   1.11.c   *Paul's Views (Pauli Sententiae)*, 4.10.2: Latin   ———
Juristic Text (Third Century CE)

For the *senatus consultum Claudianum* (SCC), see 11.22. According to this law, a free woman who entered a union with a slave could lose her free status and become a slave.

Under the *senatus consultum Claudianum*, a daughter who is a slave or a freed-woman cannot inherit her mother's estate if the latter dies intestate. For neither slaves nor freedpersons are acknowledged as having a mother who is a Roman citizen.

- What does Ulpian compare slavery with? Why?
- What are the rights of slaves according to civil law?
- Does Roman law recognize slave kinship?
- How do these passages use the distinction between natural law, civil law, and the law of nations with regard to slavery?

1.12 *P.Herm.* 18, 1–12: Papyrus with Record of Official Proceedings in Greek, Egypt (323 CE?)

Literature: Wolff 1966; Straus 2004a: 14–15.

> [...] when [...] were about to become consuls [for the third time], on the eighth day before the Ides of December, on the 9th day of the month Choiak.
> When Firmus came forward and presented Patricius, the advocate, Clematius said: "Firmus, who came forward, has a slave called Patricius. Firmus has brought him here so that he be questioned on his status."
>
> The officials[18] said to Patricius, "Are you slave or free?" He responded: "Slave." The officials said to him, "Whose slave?"
> He replied, "Firmus's."
> The officials said to him, "From which place did he acquire you?"
> He replied, "From Reskoupos."
> The officials said to him, "From whom?"
> He responded, "From Nikostratos."
> The officials said to him, "Is your mother a slave?"
> He replied, "Yes."
> The officials said to him, "What is her name?"
> He replied, "Hesychion."
> The officials said to him, "Do you have siblings?"
> He replied, "Yes, one. His name is Eutychios."
> The officials said to him, "Is he a slave, too?"
> He replied, "Yes."

- What kind of questions do the officials ask to establish the identity of the slave?
- What questions do they ask concerning his family? What does this imply?
- What question concerning his family do they *not* ask? What does this imply about natal alienation?

1.13 Ammianus Marcellinus, *History*, 28.1.49: Latin Historiography (Fourth Century CE)

Ammianus here delineates the persecution in Rome of members of the senatorial rank through trials under the emperor Valentinian I. Fausiana was a widow of senatorial rank, accused of adultery with two men of the same rank, Abienus and Eumenius. Anepsia was also a widow of senatorial rank. Simplicius of Emona was at the time (*ca.* 374–5 CE) in charge of the persecution.

---

[18] In the original Greek, these officials are specified as holding the office of *hypomnêmatographos*, literally "recorder of deeds".

Literature: Harper 2011: 69–78, esp. 72.

> But after Fausiana was convicted, they (i.e. Abienus and Eumenius) were en-
> listed among the accused and summoned with edicts to appear in court.
> They took themselves off into deeper concealment. Of the two, Abienus was
> hiding for a long time in the house of Anepsia. However, as unexpected
> events often aggravate pitiable misfortunes, a man called Sapaudulus, a slave
> of Anepsia, stricken by pain because his spouse (*coniunx*) had received a beat-
> ing, denounced the matter to Simplicius, after reaching him in the night.
> Public attendants were sent and, when they were pointed out to them, the
> attendants dragged them away from their hiding place.

- Why did Sapaudulus reveal the secret of his mistress?
- What political conditions allowed Sapaudulus to take his revenge? What are
  the implications of this for the exercise of slave agency?
- What were the consequences of slave family for this particular mistress?
- What can we learn from this story about the significance of kinship for slaves?

1.14 Ps.-Plutarch, *On the Education of Children*, 8f–9a: Greek Moral Philosophy (Late First/Early Second Century CE)

Literature: Golden 1985; Klees 2005.

> I also state that children should be guided toward honorable practices through
> admonitions and reasoning – not, by God, through beatings and blows. For
> these measures seem rather more fitting to slaves rather than to the free.
> Children end up dull and shudder at hard work, partly from the pain of the
> blows, partly from the outrage they suffer. It is, instead, praise and rebuke
> that are most beneficial for the free – praise because it urges toward what is
> good, rebuke because it keeps one away from what is disgraceful.

- By what means should free children be trained? How should slaves be trained?
- How can we explain the different treatment of free and slave?

1.15 *IG* I³ 1390: Greek Inscription on Theater Seat, Athens (450–400 BCE)

In the ancient world, the privilege of sitting in the first row at the theater was a
major indication of honor, reserved for magistrates, priests, and benefactors of the
community and bestowed on prominent foreigners. The theater of Dionysus in
Athens had inscriptions on the marble seats, reserving them for particular categories of people. Ancient cities possessed public slaves who performed many
important tasks as civil servants.

Literature: Kamen 2013: 19–31; Ismard 2017: 57–79.

> (Seat) of the (slave) assistants of the Council.

- To what people does this inscription refer?
- Why do you think the Athenians conferred this honor on these slaves?
- Can we learn something about slavery from this inscription?

1.16 *SEG* XL 1044: Greek Funerary Inscription, Gordos, Lydia (69–70 CE)

This funerary text uses the language of honorific inscriptions, a common feature of epitaphs from Roman Lydia. All the names recorded are Greek. Because the style is largely elliptical, we have added the assumed words in round brackets, to assist comprehension.

Literature: Martin 2003; Zoumbaki 2005.

> In the year 154, on the eighth day of the last third of the month Artemisios.
> Elikonis honored Amerimnos, her husband [...]; Amerimnos (honored) his father; Terpousa (honored) her own son; his grandmother Nikopolis (honored him); Alexandros and Demetria and Terpousa (honored) their brother; Aigialos, his foster father, (honored him); Gamos (honored) his in-law. All his kinsmen and fellow slaves honored Amerimnos.
> Farewell.

- What kind of inscription is this?
- What kind of community is presented here honoring Amerimnos? What forms of kinship are evident? Cf. 7.12.
- Are these people slaves? How can we know?
- Is the master of these people mentioned? If not, what are the implications?
- What do you think about the use of the vocabulary of honor by this group of slaves?

1.17 *CIL* VI, 6308 (Latin Text After Caldelli and Ricci 1999): Latin Funerary Inscription, Rome (First Half of First Century CE)

The deceased was buried in the columbarium of the slaves and freedpersons of the aristocratic Statilii Tauri (see 4.9, 10.16). For columbaria, see 7.17.

Literature: Caldelli and Ricci 1999; Borbonus 2014.

> Jucundus, [freedman?] of Taurus, litter-bearer. So long as he was alive, he was a man, and defended both himself and others. So long as he was alive, he lived honorably.
>
> This is offered by Callista and Philologus.

- What was Jucundus' legal and work status?
- How is he described in his epitaph?
- What was the role of honor in Jucundus' life?

1.18   *P. Turner* 41, 1–20: Papyrus with Petition in Greek, Oxyrhynchos, Egypt (Mid-Third Century CE)

Literature: Llewelyn 1992: 55–60, 1997: 9–46.

> Aurelia Sarapias, also called Dionysarion, daughter of Apollophanes, also called Sarapammon, formerly *exegêtês* of Antinoopolis, acting without a guardian, in accordance with the *ius liberorum*.[19] I own a slave, formerly my father's, Sarapion by name, who I thought would commit no wrongdoing because he was part of my patrimony and had been entrusted by me with our affairs. This man, I don't know how, at the instigation of others, adopted an enemy's attitude toward the honor and the provision of the necessities for life I was giving him. He stealthily took from our household some clothes I had prepared for him and some other stuff, which he helped himself to from our belongings, and secretly ran away. When it came to my ears that he was at Chairemon's, in the hamlet of Nomou, I requested [...].

- What are the names of the mistress and the slave? Can we draw any conclusions from this?
- How is Sarapion described?
- Why did Sarapias not expect him to betray her and flee?
- Why does Sarapias think that Sarapion was ungrateful? What did she offer her slave?
- What do you think of the employment of the term honor in this context?
- How does Sarapias explain Sarapion's change of behavior? How credible do you find her explanation? What other explanations can you think of?
- What can we learn about "the mind of the master class" from this petition?

---

[19] According to this law, women with a certain number of children were allowed to act without a guardian. See also 10.17.

SLAVERY AS AN ASYMMETRICAL NEGOTIATION

1.19 Herodas, *Mimiambs*, 5:[20] Greek Verse Mime (First Half of Third Century BCE)

Herodas' mimiambs are poems of a dramatic form, written in a type of iambic meter associated with invective poetry. They are influenced by comedy and the mime and were probably not only read but also performed, possibly to a fairly learned audience. For many societies, the theme of sexual relations between a mistress and her slave is an object of satire.

Literature: Fountoulakis 2007; Parker 2007; Todd 2013.

Bitinna: Tell me, Gastron. Is *this* so overfull, that it is no longer enough for you to move my legs, but you've been coming on to Menon's Amphytaia?

Gastron: I to Amphytaia? Have I seen the woman you speak of?

Bitinna: You spin out excuses all day long.

Gastron: Bitinna, I'm a slave. Do whatever you want with me but don't suck my blood day and night.

Bitinna: You! You can't hold your tongue either! – Kydilla, where is Pyrrhias? Call him to me.

Pyrrhias: What is it?

Bitinna: Bind this man! Are you still standing there? Untie first the rope from the bucket. Fast! – If I don't make an example of you to the whole country with my beatings, don't count me a woman. – Isn't he, rather, like the proverbial Phrygian, who is the better for a beating? – I am the one responsible for this, Gastron, I, who set you up among men. But if I erred back then, you won't find Bitinna a fool now, as you think – not anymore. – Come, you, by yourself! Take his cloak off and bind him.

Gastron: No, no, Bitinna, I beseech you as your suppliant.

Bitinna: Take it off, I say. You must realize that you are a slave and that I put down three minae for you. I wish the day that brought you here had never dawned. – Pyrrhias, you'll be sorry. I see you doing everything but binding him. Tie his elbows together tightly; saw them off with the rope.

Gastron: Bitinna, let me off this error. I'm human. I erred. But if you catch me again doing something not to your liking, have me tattooed.

Bitinna: Don't try to make up to me like this. Do it to Amphytaia, with whom you roll about and [...].[21]

Pyrrhias: I've bound him fast for you.

Bitinna: See to it that he doesn't untie himself without your noticing. Take him to the executioner's, to Hermon, and tell him to strike a thousand blows into his back and a thousand to his belly.

---

[20] Greek text: Cunningham 2002.
[21] The end of this sentence has not survived in its entirety.

Gastron: Will you have me killed, Bitinna, without first examining whether this is true or false?

Bitinna: When you yourself just said, with your own tongue, "Bitinna, let me off this error?"

Gastron: I wanted to cool off your anger.

Bitinna: You, are you still standing staring? Aren't you taking him where I'm telling you to? – Kydilla, crush the snout of this rogue. – And you, Drechon, do me the favor and follow wherever this man here might lead you. – Slave girl, give a rug to this cursed fellow, to cover his unmentionable ... tail, so that he won't become a spectacle walking naked through the market-place. – For the second time, Pyrrhias, I'm telling you once more: you are to tell Hermon to inflict a thousand here and a thousand there. Have you heard? If you stray from what I say by one iota, you yourself will pay both the principal and the interest. Go on now. And don't take him by Mikkale's but by the direct road. – Just as well I remembered: Slave girl, call them, run and call them, before they get far.

Kydilla: Pyrrhias! You wretch! You deaf one! She's calling you. Ah! But you look as if it is a grave-robber you pull to pieces – not your fellow-slave. Look how violently you are now dragging him to be tortured! Ah, Pyrrhias! It is you whom Kydilla will see, with these very two eyes, in five days, at Antidoros', rubbing your ankles with those Achaean chains that you recently shed.

Bitinna: Hey, you. Come back here, keeping this man bound exactly as when you were taking him away. Call me Kosis the tatooer and ask him to come here, bringing needles and ink. – In one go, you must turn ... colorful. – Gag him and hang him, like the ... honorable Daos!

Kydilla: No, mummy. Let him off now. I beg you. As your Batyllis may live, and you may see her entering her husband's house and take her children in your arms. This one error... .

Bitinna: Kydilla, don't give me grief, or I will run out of the house. Shall I let *him* off? This seventh-generation slave? And which woman won't justly spit on my face when she sees me? No, by the Lady Tyrant, our goddess! But since he, although human, does not know himself, he will now find out, with this inscription on his forehead.

Kydilla: But it is the twentieth, and the Gerenia festival is in four days.

Bitinna: I'll let you off the hook now. And be grateful to this girl here, whom I cherish no less than Batyllis, as I reared her in my own arms. But when we have poured our honeyless libations to the dead, you will then celebrate a second "honeyless" festival.

- What is the relationship between Gastron and Bitinna? Why does Bitinna want to punish Gastron?
- How does Gastron attempt to avoid punishment?
- How does Kydilla try to get Gastron off the hook? What does her strategy tell us about master–slave relations?
- How are relationships among slaves depicted in this passage?

- What is the relationship between Kydilla and Bitinna? How do both sides use their relationship to present their arguments and achieve their aims?

- To which genre does the passage belong? What is the point of presenting a mistress that has sexual relationships with her slave?

- Can we use this passage to understand slavery as an asymmetrical negotiation between masters and slaves?

1.20 Galen, *How to Detect Malingerers (Quomodo simulantes morbus deprehendi)*, pp. 114,14–115,14 Deighgräber and Kudlien[22] (XIX.4–5 Kühn): Greek Medical Treatise (Late Second/Early Third Century CE)

Literature: Schlange-Schöningen 2003: 255–90, 2006.

I must now recall what has already been said, namely that experience together with resourcefulness can detect those who make false claims, including those who pretend to be suffering from severe pain. When another man claimed that he had extremely severe pain in his knee – this man was a slave, one of these who run beside their master in his journeys – I noticed that his pain was a sham. What made me suspicious was both the fact that his master would set out that day and the character of the lad; he was the kind who are capable of shamming in such things. I also asked one of his fellow-slaves who disliked him whether the lad had a liaison with some woman, which would naturally make him wish to stay put when the master set off on a longer journey, into the country, away from home. And this was indeed the case. These things I found out using common resourcefulness. However, there was a huge swelling on the lad's knee, who would astound a lay man but would be obvious to one with specialist experience as caused by thapsia.[23] This is the result of medical experience, not something that a layperson can resolve with his resourcefulness. Another result of medical experience was the discovery that the lad had not previously suffered or done anything that was capable of suddenly causing such a swelling. For he had not run more than normal, nor had he been wounded by someone else, nor had he got hurt by leaping over a ditch. Moreover, there were no signs of blood excess in his body, nor had his earlier regimen included excessive consumption of food and drink or a sedentary lifestyle. On top, when we asked him what type of pain he felt, he was slow to respond, did not give a straight answer and contradicted himself. So, when his master went out, I put a drag on his knee, which does not at all extinguish pain but is capable of cooling the heat produced by thapsia. After one hour, I had him admitting that he felt no pain at all.

- What is the job of the malingering slave? Are you surprised that the master calls a famous doctor like Galen for such a slave?

---

[22] *CMG* V 10,2,4.
[23] A poisonous plant.

- Why does Galen suspect that the slave is lying?
- What does he suspect the reason to be?
- How does he try to find out the truth? Does he ask the master?
- What can we learn about slave life and relations among slaves from this passage?
- Are the slaves mere instruments for the purposes of their masters?
- How does acknowledging slave agency change our understanding of slavery?

1.21 Galen, *The Doctrines of Hippocrates and Plato* (De placitis Hippocratis et Platonis), V.7.64–66, pp. 352,20–354,2 De Lacy[24] (V.497–98 Kühn): Greek Medical Treatise (Late Second/Early Third Century CE)

Galen is here commenting on Plato, *Republic*, 440c1–d3, which illustrates via an example that the spirited part of the soul is an ally of the rational part of the soul. The Platonic example consists of the opposing reactions of two men to harsh treatment: one of them believes that he is in the wrong, while the other believes that he is being wronged.

Literature: Schlange-Schöningen 2003: 255–90, 2006.

The man who thinks that he is suffering justly, because he himself committed some wrong first, endures his punishment all the more nobly the nobler he is by nature. The other man, who thinks that he is being wronged, gets angry, rages and fights on the side of what seems to him to be just. We can observe these things happening every day among our slaves, too. Those who are caught thieving or doing things of that sort do not get angry when they are being whipped or starved or dishonored by their masters. But those who think that they suffer, or have suffered, such punishments wrongly, their spirit always turns savage inside them and craves vengeance on the one who is wronging them.

- Which forms of punishment for slaves are presented in the passage?
- What criterion determines whether slaves accept punishment or not, according to Galen? Do you believe Galen?
- How might the principle of just punishment have affected the unilateral right of masters to punish their slaves?

1.22 Aulus Gellius, *Attic Nights*, 1.26.3–9: Latin Miscellany of Learned Material (Second Century CE)

Aulus Gellius here reports part of the answer given to him by Lucius Calvinus Taurus, a contemporary Platonist philosopher, when he asked him whether wise men ever got angry. Plutarch, another Platonist, was an influential philosopher and biographer.

---

[24] *CMG* V 4,1,2.

Literature: Harris 2001: 317–36; Klees 2005; Hunt 2016; Lenski 2016.

"This is what I think," Taurus said, "about getting angry. But it would do no harm to hear, also, what our Plutarch, an extremely learned and wise man, thought. Plutarch," he said, "once gave orders that a slave of his, a worthless and insolent fellow but with ears filled with philosophical works and arguments, be stripped of his tunic for I don't know what offence, and whipped. The beating had started, and he kept protesting that he had not done anything deserving flogging – he had not been guilty of anything wrong or criminal. In the end, amid the flogging, he began to shout – no longer making complaints, groans, and laments but serious and reproachful arguments: that Plutarch's behavior was improper for a philosopher; that it was shameful to get angry; that Plutarch had often lectured on the evil of anger and had even written a very fine book *On Lack of Anger*, and that it was not compatible with anything of what was written in the book that he, submitting and yielding to anger, punished him with many blows.

"Then Plutarch spoke, calmly and mildly. 'Oh you who deserve to be under the whip, do I now seem angry to you? Is it from my face, or from my voice, or my complexion or, even, from my words that you perceive I've been seized by anger? I think that neither my eyes are fierce, nor is my face wild, nor am I shouting uncontrollably, nor am I raging to the point of foaming around the mouth or turning red, nor am I saying words to be ashamed of or regret, nor am I trembling or gesticulating because of anger. For, in case you don't know it, all these things are the typical signs of anger.' And, turning at the same time toward the one who was whipping the slave, he said: 'Meanwhile, while this fellow and I are arguing, you continue your task.'"

- How does the slave initially attempt to avoid punishment? How does this relate to 1.21?
- What is the second argument that he uses? Does it work?
- How is Plutarch's emotional state portrayed in this passage? Can we learn something about masters' mentality from Plutarch's response?
- How does this master–slave negotiation relate to that described in 1.19?
- What conclusions should we draw from the fact that the slave has learned some of his master's philosophy?
- What conclusions can we draw about slave agency from this passage?
- How does this passage illustrate both the asymmetry and the negotiation that slavery involves?

1.23   *Digest*, 1.6.1–2: Collection of Latin Juristic Texts (Sixth Century CE)

On the Digest, see 1.2.

Literature: Härtel 1977; Knoch 2017: 111–18.

> Gaius, *Institutes*, Book 1:
>
> Slaves are under the power (*potestas*) of their masters. This power is derived from the law of nations, for we can observe that equally among all nations masters have had power of life and death over their slaves. Whatever acquisition is made via the slave is made by the master. In our times, however, no man who is a subject of the Roman Empire is permitted to act against his slaves with excessive brutality and without a cause acknowledged by the laws. For, through an enactment of the divine (emperor) Antoninus, one who kills his own slave without cause is to be punished in the same way as one who has killed the slave of another. But even excessive harshness of masters is also curbed via an enactment of the same emperor.
>
> Ulpian, *On the Duties of the Provincial Governor*, Book 8:
>
> If a master acts brutally against his slaves or forces them to indecency and disgraceful violation, the tasks of the governor are stated in the rescript addressed by the divine Antoninus Pius to Aelius Marcianus, the governor of the province of Baetica. The terms of this rescript are the following: "It is certainly proper that the power (*potestas*) of the masters over their slaves be unimpaired and that no man's rights be taken from him. However, it is in the interest of the masters not to deny relief to those who justly implore for help against brutality or starvation or intolerable insult. For this reason, investigate the complaints of the slaves of the household of Julius Sabinus who fled and took refuge at my statue. If you find that they have been treated more harshly than is fair or subjected to infamous insult, order that they be sold on the condition that they may not come back under the power (*potestas*) of their present master. And if he should fraudulently evade my decision, he should know that I will pursue the punishment of this offence more severely." Also, the divine (emperor) Hadrian ordered the banishment from Rome for a five-year period of one Umbricia, a married woman of good family, because she had treated her female slaves in the most savage way for extremely trivial reasons.

- What powers do masters have to punish their slaves? Cf. 5.1.
- How did Roman emperors limit the masters' right to punishment?
- How is this limitation justified?
- How did the slaves of Julius Sabinus attempt to escape their cruel master? Cf. 6.14–5.

1.24 Libanius, *Orations*, 47.21: Greek Epideictic Oratory (Fourth Century CE)

Libanius uses an analogy in order to persuade the emperor of the need to prevent tenants of agricultural land around Antioch in Syria from requesting help from people other than the owners of the land they cultivate.

> Nor is it right that a slave who demands justice for wrongs he has suffered should look to someone else and present himself before someone who has no proper authority over him and beg for that man's help, thereby bypassing his master. For he would no longer belong to his master entirely but would surrender a large share of himself – both of his goodwill and his labor – to the person who assisted him. It is indeed right that he receive justice, but he should receive it through his master. The result of a slave's securing justice through someone else is often that the master could be deprived of his slave, becoming the object of the slave's contempt because of the other man's assistance.

- Why should slaves ask only their masters for help?
- What was the danger if they asked other people for help? How does this relate with 1.23?
- What implications does this passage have for slavery as a relationship? Did it involve only masters and their slaves?

1.25 Gerontius, *Life of Melania*, 10: Saint's Life in Greek (Fifth Century CE)

A little before the sack of Rome by the Visigoths in 410 CE, the extremely wealthy Roman aristocrats Melania the Younger and her husband Pinianus are planning to liquidate their property to donate the money to the Church. Cf. 11.14.c, on the reaction of some slaves to the Visigothic invasion.

Literature: Roth 2005; Harper 2011: 192–5; Vlassopoulos 2018a.

> And while Melania and Pinianus were making these plans, the enemy of truth, the devil, raised a most challenging trial for them. He felt envy at the young couple's godly fervor and suborned Severus, the brother of the blessed Pinianus, and he convinced the slaves of Melania and Pinianus to say: "By no means are we being put up for sale! If we are forced, rather than being put on the market, we will have your brother Severus as our master, and he will buy us himself." This disturbed them greatly, seeing their slaves in their estates around Rome revolting.

- How do the slaves react to the news of their being put on the market? Why? What difference would it make to them?
- What proposal do they make? Why?
- How do the wishes of Severus and the slaves fit in together?
- What does the intervention of Severus tell us about the factors that shape slavery as a negotiation?

1.26   Aristophanes, *Clouds*, 1–7: Greek Comedy (Late Fifth Century BCE)

This comedy was written in Athens during the course of the Peloponnesian War. The speaker is an old Athenian man.

Literature: Hanson 1992; Demont 2007.

> Oh dear, oh dear! Oh, king Zeus, what a piece of work this night has been! Unending. Won't day ever come? Yet, I heard a cock crow long ago. But the slaves are snoring. They wouldn't have done this before. Oh war, be damned, for the many evils you've brought. For now, I can't even punish my slaves.

- Why can the speaker not punish his slaves as he used to?
- Is this comic exaggeration? Cf. 11.11.c.
- Which factors can affect slavery apart from slaves and masters?
- How can these factors affect slavery as an asymmetrical negotiation?

MODALITIES OF SLAVERY

1.27   Artemidorus, *The Interpretation of Dreams*: Greek Dream Book (Second Century CE)

Literature: Annequin 1987, 2005; Kudlien 1991; Pomeroy 1991; Vlassopoulos 2018a; Thonemann 2020.

> 1.48: To dream that one's own feet are on fire is a bad sign for everyone equally and signifies loss and destruction of what one has, including one's children and slaves. For, similar to slaves, children submit to their parents and serve them like slaves. This point is missed by many dream interpreters, who hold that feet signify only slaves.
>
> 1.62: If a slave competes in a sacred contest, wins, and receives a garland, he will be proclaimed free. For these achievements are characteristic of free men.
>
> 1.78: Having sex with one's own slave, male or female, is good. For slaves are the possessions of the person who has had the dream. They thus signify that he will get pleasure from his possessions, which naturally happens when they increase in quantity and value. To be penetrated by a slave is not a good sign for it signifies that one will be harmed by the slave and become the object of the slave's contempt.
>
> 2.8: Rain, hurricane, and stormy weather bring on dangers and harm. Only to slaves, poor men, and those who are in difficulty do they foretell relief from their present troubles. For great storms are followed by fair weather.

2.9: Being struck by lightning will result in the manumission of those slaves who are not in a position of trust, but slaves who are trusted and honored by their masters or who own many possessions will lose the trust, the honor, and the possessions.

2.12: Seeing a tame lion wagging its tail and approaching harmlessly could be a good sign and bring benefits: to a soldier from his king, to an athlete from his bodily vigor, to a citizen from a magistrate, to a slave from his master. For the lion resembles them in power and strength.

3.28: A mouse signifies a slave. For mice too live with us, are fed on the same food as us, and are cowardly. It is therefore good to see many mice inside one's house, especially if they are joyful and having fun. For they foretell much merriment and further acquisition of slaves.

4.30: Together with their other effects, slaves (in dreams) can also be references to the body of their masters. One who sees in his dream his slave suffering from fever will probably fall ill himself. For the relationship of the slave to the man who has the dream is analogous to that of the body to the soul.

- With what other categories of people are slaves associated in each passage? Are they different or the same?
- What conceptions of slavery are present in these various passages?
- Are these various conceptions of slavery compatible with each other?

1.28 Herodotus, 4.1–4.4: Greek Historiography (Fifth Century BCE)

The fourth book of Herodotus is devoted to the Scythians, a major power in the north coast of the Black Sea. After reporting a Scythian expedition against the Medes in the Near East, Herodotus narrates the consequences of the long absence of the Scythians from home.

Literature: Harvey 1988; Hunt 1998: 42–52.

After 28 years away from their own land and upon their return home after such a long time, the Scythians were met by a task no less laborious than their war against the Medes, for they found a substantial army opposing them. To be more specific: the wives of the Scythians, as their husbands had been away from them for a long time, were having relations with the slaves. [...] From these slaves and the Scythian wives, a generation of youths was reared, who, when they learnt of their origins, were opposed to the Scythians returning from the land of the Medes. First, they dug a wide trench, stretching from the Taurian mountains to lake Maiotis, at the point where it is broadest, and thus cut off the land. Then, when the Scythians attempted to invade, they camped opposite them and started fighting them. As they met in battle many times and the Scythians could not manage to gain the upper hand in this manner, one Scythian said the following: "What are we doing,

Scythians? We are fighting against our own slaves, so we get killed and thus become fewer, and we kill them and will thus rule over fewer men in the future. Therefore, I think that we should now leave aside spears and bows, and each one should take his horse whip and draw near them. Until now, they have seen us bearing arms and thought of themselves as the same as us and of the same origin. But when they see us bearing whips rather than arms, they will learn that they are our slaves. When they realize this, they will not stand their ground." The Scythians heard this and proceeded to do it. The others, shocked at what was going on, forgot the battle and started to flee. This then is how the Scythians ruled over Asia and, when driven out again by the Medes, it was by such means that they returned to their own land.

- How did the Scythians overcome the resistance of the sons of their slaves?
- Did the children of the Scythian women and the Scythian slaves grow up as slaves?
- If not, why did the stratagem of the Scythians work on these young men, according to the passage? What does this imply about how masters thought of slaves?
- What conception of slavery is evident in this passage? Cf. 1.1.

1.29   Xenophon, *Memorabilia*, 1.3.10–11: Greek Collection of Socratic Conversations (First Half of Fourth Century BCE)

Socrates is commenting on the behavior of Kritoboulos, son of his friend Kriton of Alopeke.

Literature: Brock 2007; Vlassopoulos 2011a.

"You should now consider Kritoboulos a most reckless man, capable of anything; he would do a somersault into a ring of knives or jump into fire."

"What did you see him do," Xenophon said, "that makes you condemn him like that?"

"Didn't he dare," Socrates said, "to kiss Alcibiades' son, who is extremely beautiful and exactly in the bloom of youth?"

"Well, if such is his reckless deed," Xenophon said "I think that I too would endure this danger!"

"Wretched man," Socrates said. "What do you think would happen to you if you kissed someone beautiful? Wouldn't you immediately become slave, from free, and waste much in harmful pleasures and have no time to pursue beautiful and honorable things but be forced instead to concern yourself with things you wouldn't care for even if mad?"

- How is slavery understood in this passage?
- Should we dismiss this use of slavery as metaphorical and, hence, historically insignificant?

1.30 Dio Chrysostom, *Oration 15* (Excerpted):[25] Greek Epideictic Oratory (Late First/Early Second Century CE)

Literature: Panzeri 2011.

As it happens, I was present lately when two men had a dispute over slavery and freedom. [...] The one man, finding his arguments outmatched and himself at a loss, turned to abuse, as often happens in such cases, and taunted the other with not being a free man. The taunted man very gently smiled and said: "My good man, how can one tell who is a slave and who is a free man?"

The first man said: "By Zeus, I do know, of course, that I and all these here are free men, while you have nothing to do with freedom." [...]

The other stood up and [...] asked him how he knew this about the two of them. The first man said: "Because I know that my father is an Athenian, if anyone is, while yours is a slave of so and so," mentioning his name. [...] "And I also know that your mother is a fellow-slave of your father." [...]

The other responded: "Come now, by the gods, if I do agree with you that my parents are such as you say, how can you know about their slavery? Did you also have precise knowledge of their parents and are prepared to swear that they were both born to slave people and that so were those before them and everyone from the beginning of the line? For, clearly, if there has been one free man among a kin-group, it is no longer possible rightly to consider his descendants as slaves. It is impossible, my good man, that any kin-group existing from all eternity, as they say, does not have countless members who have been free and no fewer who have been slaves." [...]

The first man responded: "Let us then leave aside arguments related to one's kin-group and ancestors, since you consider these so difficult to determine." [...]

And the other said: "But, in the name of the gods, what actions and experiences of mine do you know of, that make you say you know I am a slave?"

"I know that you are kept by your master, that you attend him and do whatever he orders you to do, and that you take a beating if you don't obey."

"But you thus also make sons their fathers' slaves," the other said, "for poor sons often attend their fathers and walk with them to the gymnasium or to dinner; also, they are all kept by their fathers, often take beatings from them and do whatever their fathers command them to do. Moreover, on the basis of showing obedience and taking a beating, you can go on and claim that a school-master's pupils are his slaves and that gymnastic trainers or any other teachers are their pupils' masters. For they too give orders and beat those who disobey."

"No, by Zeus!" the first man said, "for gymnastic trainers and other teachers cannot imprison their pupils, nor sell them nor throw them into the mill; masters, however, are allowed to do all these things."

"Well, perhaps you are not aware of the fact that among many communities, and extremely well-ordered ones at that, fathers are allowed to do to

---

[25] Greek text: von Arnim 1893–96.

their sons all these things you mentioned, including selling them, if they so wish, and even more terrible than these: that is, they are allowed to kill them, without trial or without even bringing any accusations at all against them. Yet these men are not their fathers' slaves but their sons. And if I was as much of a slave as could be," he said, "and had been one justly from the beginning, what prevents me being as much of a free man as anyone else from now on? Or what prevents you from the opposite fate? That is, if you had been born to manifestly free parents, to be now more of a slave than anyone else?"

"I can't see," the first man said, "how I, a free man, will become a slave, but it is not impossible that you have become free, if your master manumitted you. [...] How, as you claim, can *I* become a slave?"

"Well, countless men, while free, sell themselves, and end up working as slaves by contract – sometimes not at all on reasonable terms, but on the harshest ones."

Up to this point, those present paid attention to the arguments with the idea that they were put forward not so much in earnest as in jest. Afterward, however, they started to be more involved in the rivalry, and it seemed to them odd that it was not possible to name a criterion by which one could indisputably distinguish the slave from the free, but instead, it was easy to question everything and produce counter-arguments constantly. So, they set aside the particular case of that man and his slavery and started to examine who is a slave. And they tended toward the conclusion that the man who is validly possessed by someone else, like another item of his property or another one of his grazing animals, to the degree that he can be used in any way the owner wants, this man is correctly called and is the slave of his owner. Once more, the man who had been bringing counter-arguments in relation to slavery raised the question: what on earth determined the validity of possession? For many long-time owners had been shown to possess houses, or fields, or horses, or oxen unjustly, including even some who had inherited these things from their fathers. Similarly, it was possible to possess a man unjustly.

"For owners acquire slaves, similarly to all the rest of their property by taking them from others, or as gifts, or by purchase, or by inheritance, or by having them born in their own house – those called 'home-born' slaves. Another way of possession, which I think is the most ancient of all, is when men are taken as war captives or through plunder and are thus enslaved. It stands to reason that those who were first enslaved were not initially born slaves but were defeated in war or captured by robbers and were thus forced to be slaves to their captors. So, the most ancient way, which all the rest depend on, is extremely weak and has no strong value. For whenever these men manage to flee again, nothing prevents them from being free, as they were slaves unjustly; consequently, they were not slaves before that either. In fact, there are cases in that not only did they themselves flee from slavery but also enslaved their masters. In this case, too, a shell flips, as they say, and everything becomes the opposite of what it was before."

One of the bystanders said that the captured persons themselves could not perhaps be called slaves, but those born to them, and those of the following generation and the one after that, could fittingly be called slaves.

"But how? For if being captured makes one a slave, then the name of slave would be more fitting to those captured than to their children; if again it is having been born to slaves what makes one a slave, then clearly the children born to men who were free but got captured cannot be slaves. [...] So, if even this way of possession, from which all the others derive, is not just, it is possible that no other such way is just, and no one can be characterized as really and truly a slave. But perhaps to start with, we should not characterize as a slave one for whose body money has been paid or one born to parents characterized as slaves, as is widely thought, but rather one whose behavior is not that of a free man but befitting a slave. For we can agree that many called slaves have the comportment of free men, while many free men behave in ways much befitting a slave." [...]

- At what circumstances does the first man accuse his interlocutor of being a slave? What does this show about the ways slavery is understood?

- How does the man who accuses the other of being a slave understand and define slavery throughout the oration?

- What are the problems of such definitions, according to his interlocutor? What do you think?

- What is the definition of slavery agreed by the bystanders? What are its problems?

- What is the last conception of slavery presented in the oration? No real objections are raised to that in the oration, but what is your opinion?

2

Studying Slavery
The Variety of Evidence and Its Interpretative Challenges

This chapter focuses on the methodological and evidentiary problems that scholars face when they use the various forms of evidence for ancient slavery. One major problem is that of identifying slaves in our sources. In many cases, there is no explicit labeling, and it is necessary to debate the criteria we use to identify slaves or former slaves (2.1–4). In other cases, the evidence is ambiguous and can be interpreted in various ways (2.4–5, 2.9–10); occasionally, we also get explicit identification of individuals as if they were still slaves, although there are reasons to doubt such labels (2.7). Sources can also use concurrently different terms for slaves, thus creating significant problems of interpretation (2.6).

The study of the material and visual culture of slavery has become a burgeoning field in recent years. But identifying slaves in the material and visual record presents problems of its own. What criteria should we use to make such identifications? What role does the depiction of slaves play in ancient objects (2.10, 2.12)? Sometimes epigraphic evidence makes it easy to identify ancient objects as made by or for slaves; consequently, such objects are extremely helpful for understanding the identities, values, and life histories of ancient slaves or former slaves (2.11). In other cases, epigraphic evidence is ambiguous, and the visual evidence becomes crucial for making identifications (2.13). But the most difficult question concerns the identification of slaves in the material record: can we locate slaves in ancient buildings on the basis of space use (2.14–5)?

Finally, is it possible to identify the voice of slaves in the extant ancient sources, given that most sources were written by elite authors, who were

Greek and Roman Slaveries, First Edition. Eftychia Bathrellou and Kostas Vlassopoulos.
© 2022 John Wiley & Sons, Inc. Published 2022 by John Wiley & Sons, Inc.

usually slaveholders? To what extent can we use fictional slaves to reconstruct the lives and views of real slaves (2.16–21)? Can we trust inscriptions that purport to present the slaves' own words (2.22)? How reliable are the statements and narratives of elite authors for understanding slaves (2.23–4)? And when we have texts written by people who had experienced slavery, how useful are they for reconstructing that experience (2.25)? Debating these methodological problems is a necessary first step for studying the wealth of evidence on ancient slavery and slaves.

IDENTIFYING SLAVES IN DOCUMENTARY SOURCES

Literature: Schumacher 2001; Bruun 2014; Maffi 2014; Straus 2016; Chaniotis 2018; Zelnick-Abramovitz 2018.

2.1 *IG* II^2 2940: Greek Dedicatory Inscription, Laureion, Attica (Fourth Century BCE)

Laureion, in southeastern Attica, was the site of the Athenian silver mines, where thousands of slaves used to work (see also 4.10, 7.2, 8.27). Some of the names mentioned below are Greek (Kallias, Artemidoros, Sosias, Hermaios), while others are foreign names, from Paphlagonia (Tibeios, Maes), Phrygia (Kadous, Manes, Attas), Bithynia (Sangarios), and of other imprecise origins (Hermos). The name of the deity honored has not survived fully on the stone and can be restored in various ways, as Men Tyrannos or god Herakles.

Literature: Zoumbaki 2005; Vlassopoulos 2010, 2011b, 2015; Hunt 2015.

The following *eranistai*[26] offered this dedication to [Men Ty]ra[nnos] for good fortune: Kadous, Manes, Kallias, Attas, Artemidoros, Maes, Sosias, Sangarios, Hermaios, Tibeios, Hermos.

- What group is responsible for this dedication?

- How do they describe themselves? Do they identify their legal status?

- Can we draw any inferences on the basis of the dedicators' names? Do these names indicate a single origin or a variety of origins?

- Can we draw any inferences from the find spot of the inscription?

- If these people are slaves, what can we learn about slavery from their collective dedication?

---

[26] *Eranistai*, literally contributors to a collection, refers either to an *ad hoc* group financing something, or to a more permanent association, financed by its members' contributions.

2.2   *IG* XII.1 881: Greek Funerary Inscription, Rhodes, Dodecanese (Hellenistic Period)

All three individuals mentioned in this epitaph have Greek names. Phronimos and Euphronios share the same root.

Literature: Boyxen 2018: 82–93; Lewis 2018: 277–82.

> Phronimos, Galatian. Artemisia, Syrian. Euphronios, *engenês*.[27]

- What are the names and nationalities of the three individuals commemorated in this epitaph?
- Do these three individuals have the same origins? What conclusions can we draw from this?
- Are these three individuals slaves?
- Are there any onomastic links between these three individuals? How can we interpret this? Why are these three individuals commemorated together? What can we infer about their relationship?

2.3   Masters and Fathers

—— 2.3.a   *SEG* XV 787: Greek Dedicatory Inscription, Galatia ——
(First–Third Century CE)

Personal names are often followed by a male name in the genitive case in Greek. In the case of free men, the name in the genitive is that of the person's father. In the case of slaves, it is not always clear whether the name in the genitive is that of their father or their master. Alypos and Limnaios are male names.

Literature: Robert 1955: 28–33; Drew-Bear 1999: no. 609, 374–6.

> Alypos (son *or* slave) of Limnaios, as fulfillment of a vow to Mother Malene, on behalf of his masters, and the livestock and the dogs.

- What is the status of Alypos? How can we establish it?
- Why does Alypos make this dedication? What can we learn about him from this inscription?
- Is Limnaios the name of his father or of his master? Can we tell?
- If Limnaios is the father of Alypos, does this tell us anything interesting about the natal alienation of slaves (cf. 1.11–12)?
- If there are major differences in how often slaves in different societies or periods mention their fathers' name, how do you think we should explain this?

---

[27] A term often used in Rhodian inscriptions to describe slaves born locally.

—— 2.3.b *Polemon* 2 (1934–40) Supplement, 13, 18.27–34: ——
Greek Inscription Recording Manumissions, Thaumakoi,
Thessaly (First Century BCE)

In Thessaly, manumitted women and men had to offer to the city treasury the sum of 15 staters upon their manumission. Whether this was a manumission tax or a fee for registering the manumission is debated by modern scholars. Manumitted slaves had to have a *prostatês* (patron), a role usually undertaken by their former master.

Literature: Zelnick-Abramovitz 2005: 259–62, 2013.

> When Gorgias, (son) of Philiskos, of (the city of) Gyrton, was general, and Astomachos, (son) of Tychaios, was treasurer, the following were manumitted on the third day of the month Aphrios: Armenos of Philodemos and Archiboulos of Agathon (were manumitted) by Philodemos, (son) of Pyrrhandros. And each of them gave the 15 staters.

- What are the names of the two manumitted slaves? What is the name of the manumittor?

- Notice the two personal names in genitive (of X) that follow the names of the slaves. How do they relate to the name of the master?

- Are the genitives after the slaves' names the names of the master, the names of the slaves' father, or the names of their patron?

- If it is the name of the father, what implications does this have about the natal alienation of slaves? If it is the name of the patron, why do these slaves have different patrons?

2.4 *SEG* L 276: Greek Letter Inscribed on Lead Tablet, Athens (Fourth Century BCE)

Literature: Jordan 2000; Harris 2004; Eidinow and Taylor 2010; Vlassopoulos 2018b.

> Lesis is sending this message to Xenokles and to his mother, not to overlook at all that he is perishing in the foundry, but to go to his masters and find something better for him. For I have been handed over to a very wicked man. I'm perishing from being whipped; I'm tied up; I'm treated like dirt – more and more.

- What might the relationship between Lesis and Xenokles be?
- Who are Lesis' 'masters'? How should we understand this term?
- What is he doing in the foundry? How is he treated there?
- Is Lesis a slave? What problems can you envisage for such an interpretation?
- If Lesis is not a slave, how do you envisage his status?

- How does Lesis try to sort out his problems? What connections and networks does he employ?

2.5 *P.Ups.Frid.* 7: Papyrus with Document in Greek, Unknown Provenance, Egypt (275 CE)

Literature: Llewelyn 1992: 60–3.

> Isidoros to Ammonilla. Greetings.
> Since you have been my servant girl (*korasion*) for some time, I give you the authority from now on to go wherever you wish, without any reproach from me. [...]

- What is the relationship between Isidoros and Ammonilla? What term is used to describe Ammonilla?

- What is the point of this document? Why was it written?

- Can we tell if Ammonilla was the slave of Isidoros?

2.6 *IC IV 72 ii2–10*: Inscribed Laws in Greek, Gortyn, Crete (Fifth Century BCE)

The provisions below belong to the famous Gortyn Code. The term *dōlos* (*doulos* in Attic Greek) is a typical Greek term for "slave"; the term *woikeus* (*oiketês* in Attic Greek) is also commonly used for "slaves." The use of both terms in the same legal texts has created a debate between scholars who think they have the same meaning and those who think that *dōlos* refers to slaves, while *woikeus* to a different group of "serfs." The term *apetairos*, which literally means one excluded or banished from a *hetaireia* (that is, an association of "comrades"), seems here to refer to a free man but of a status lower than that of full citizens.

Literature: Link 2001; D. M. Lewis 2013, 2018: 147–65; Gagarin and Perlman 2016: 345–50.

> If he (i.e. a free man) rapes a free man or a free woman, he shall pay 100 staters.[28] If he rapes an *apetairos*, 10 staters. If a *dōlos* rapes a free man or a free woman, he shall pay double. If a free man rapes a *woikeus*, whether male or female, he shall pay 5 drachmas. If a *woikeus* rapes a male or a female *woikeus*, he shall pay 5 staters.

- What fines for rape does this law envisage?

- What status terms are employed in this passage?

- Do *dōlos* and *woikeus* both refer to slaves?

---

[28] 1 stater = 2 drachmas.

- If they refer to different groups, are there provisions for the rape of *woikeus* by a *dōlos*? If not, why?

- If *dōlos* and *woikeus* refer to the same group of people, how can we explain that both terms are used in the same passage?

- What can we learn about the Greek vocabulary of slavery from this text?

2.7 Aeschines, *Against Timarchos*, 54–64: Greek Law-Court Speech, Athens (Mid-Fourth Century BCE)

In this lawsuit against the Athenian politician Timarchos of Sphettos, Aeschines accuses him of not being fit to be a politician because he had lived as a paid male escort and had dissipated his paternal inheritance (cf. 4.33). Athenian sources often refer to freedpersons as if they were still slaves; whether Pittalakos was still a slave when the events described here took place is a matter of debate.

Literature: Fisher 2001: 189–204, 357–62, 2008; Hunter 2006; Kamen 2009; Vlassopoulos 2009.

Among those who spent their time at that gambling house, there was one Pittalakos, a public-slave fellow, a servant of the city. He had plenty of money, and when he saw at the gambling house Timarchos here, he took him up and kept him at his home. And this foul man here did not at all feel ill at ease that he was going to disgrace himself before a public slave, a servant of the city. The only thing he looked to was if he would get a sponsor for his repugnant habits; never did he give a thought to what is fine or most shameful. [...]

At the time when this man was living with Pittalakos, here comes Hegesandros,[29] sailing down from the Hellespont. And I know well you have long been wondering why I have not mentioned him; so well known is what I am going to say. This Hegesandros – whom you know better than I do – arrives. It so happened at the time that, having sailed to the Hellespont as treasurer together with Timomachos of Acharnai, who had been general, he returned here, having made very good use, as word has it, of Timomachos' naivety – with no less than 80 minai of silver. And in a way he was greatly responsible for Timomachos' misfortune. With plenty to spend, he hung out at Pittalakos' – they used to play dice together – and this is where he first saw Timarchos. He liked him, desired him, wished to take him up, to his house – in a way, he thought him to be of a nature similar to his own. First he talked to Pittalakos and asked him to hand Timarchos over to him. As he could not convince him, he approached the man himself. He didn't need to waste many words; Timarchos agreed immediately. For even in the ... business itself, his wickedness and untrustworthiness were terrible – so he should naturally be despised because of these things too.

When Timarchos had got rid of Pittalakos and been taken up by Hegesandros, Pittalakos was, I believe, suffering, as he thought that he had wasted so much money in vain, and was full of jealousy at what was going on. He would spend much time at their house. When he was getting to be a nuisance, behold the

[29] Hegesandros of Sounion and his brother Hegesippos (nicknamed Hair-bun; see later) were prominent Athenian politicians of the time.

great might of Hegesandros and Timarchos! On one occasion, they and some others, whose names I do not wish to mention, got drunk and at night burst into the house where Pittalakos lived. First they started to smash his instruments and throw them out to the street – some shaken knucklebones and dice boxes and other dicing equipment; then they killed the quails and cocks the wretched man loved; in the end, they tied Pittalakos himself onto the pillar and kept whipping him relentlessly for so long that even the neighbors heard his cries.

The following day, Pittalakos, utterly indignant at this, goes to the market-place naked and sits down at the altar of the Mother of the gods. A crowd quickly gathered, as was usual, and Hegesandros and Timarchos feared that their repulsive conduct might be proclaimed to the whole city – an assembly gathering was about to take place. They run to the altar – they and some of their dicing companions. They stood around Pittalakos and were begging him to rise from the altar, saying that the whole thing had been a drunken brawl. And this very one here – back then, he was not, by Zeus, as unpleasant to look at as he is now, but still quite decent – was touching the man's chin in supplication, saying he would do anything he would like him to. Finally, they convince him to rise from the altar, so as to receive some portion of what was just. But once he left the marketplace, they paid no more attention to him.

Aggrieved at this outrage, the fellow brought legal actions against the two men. But when this was coming to trial, behold another instance of Hege-sandros' great might! A man who had not wronged him in anything but, on the contrary, had been wronged by him, a man who was nothing to him but was a public slave, a servant of the city – such a man did Hegesandros try to lead away to slavery, claiming he belonged to him. Pittalakos, now in extreme danger, appeals to a man, and indeed a very decent one. There is one Glau-kon of Cholargos; he removes Pittalakos back into freedom. After this, legal actions were lodged. With time, they handed the case over for arbitration to Diopeithes of Sounion, who was of the same deme as Hegesandros and had had at some point relations with him, when in his prime. After Diopei-thes undertook the case, he kept putting it off time after time, doing a favor to Hegesandros and Timarchos. But when Hegesandros started to appear on your rostrum and was fighting his war against Aristophon of Azenia – that is, before Aristophon threatened him with making before the assembly the same formal accusation I am making against Timarchos – and his brother Hair-bun was one of the regular speakers in the assembly, and in general they had the nerve to be offering you counsel over your relations with other Greek cities, at that time Pittalakos lost confidence in himself, took a good look at who he was and what men he was opposing, and made a correct decision – for the truth must be told: he held his peace and decided to be contented if he should not suffer any further trouble. So, it was then that Hegesandros, who had won this... fine victory without a fight, kept Timarchos here at his house.

- Who is Pittalakos? What do we hear about his professional activities and possessions?

- What conclusions about sexual relations between free and slave can we draw from the sexual relationship between Pittalakos and Timarchos?

- How does Pittalakos attempt to redress the assault against him? How does he involve the free community and his citizen acquaintances in his conflict with Timarchos and Hegesandros?

- How does Hegesandros try to stop Pittalakos' legal challenge? What do you think about his claim?

- Is Pittalakos still a public slave when these incidents take place? If yes, is there anything remarkable about his story?

- If Pittalakos is no longer a public slave, why is he described as if he were?

- What is Aeschines' agenda in telling this story?

- What conclusions should we draw about establishing and challenging status in classical Athens?

2.8 *CIL* VI, 12366: Latin Funerary Inscription, Rome (Second Century CE)

In the Roman world, while slaves were referred to by their own names, accompanied by their master's name in the genitive, freedmen and freedwomen tended to use a name with three or two parts respectively, following the practice of Roman citizens. For the first elements, freedmen usually adopted their patron's *praenomen* and *nomen*, while freedwomen their patron's *nomen*; as their name's last element, freed persons kept the name by which they were known when they were slaves. Cf. 12.29. The names Agapete, Agapetus, Elpis, Philete, and Bostrychus are Greek and are often borne by Roman slaves and freedmen.

Literature: Bruun 2013.

> To the divine spirits: For Gnaeus Arrius Agapetus.
> Arria Agapete, his mother, and Bostrychus, his father, and Elpis, his *mamma*,[30] and Philete (?), his nurse, set this up for a most dutiful son, who well deserved it. He lived three years and 45 days.

- Who is the deceased? Can we establish his status?

- Who are the dedicators? Can we establish their status? How are they related to Agapetus?

- What can we learn about Roman slaves and freedpersons from this passage?

2.9 *CIL* VI, 9983: Latin Funerary Inscription, Rome (First Century CE)

Literature: Joshel 1992.

> Here lies Archelaus, manager (*vilicus*).

- What was Archelaus' legal status upon his death? Can we tell?

---

[30] Term used affectionately of a woman who cared for a small child without necessarily being the child's biological mother or wet-nurse.

FINDING SLAVES AND SLAVERY IN VISUAL AND MATERIAL CULTURE

Literature: Himmelmann 1971; Kolendo 1979; Morris 1998, 2011; Schumacher 2001; Thompson 2003; George 2011; Joshel and Petersen 2014; Osborne 2017; Binsfeld and Ghetta 2019.

2.10   The Iconography of Funerary Monuments

Literature: Reilly 1989; Zanker 1993; Schumacher 2001: 65–90; von Behren 2009; Kampen 2013.

——————   2.10.a   *IG* I^3 1289: Funerary Relief with Greek   ——————
Inscription, Athens (End of Fifth Century BCE) (Fig. 1)

Hegeso, daughter of Proxenos.

Figure 1   Funerary stele, end of fifth century BCE, Athens: National Archaeological Museum of Athens, inv. no. 3624, image provided under CC BY license from Wikimedia Commons.

- Which figure is Hegeso? How is she depicted?
- Who is the other figure? How is she depicted? Can we establish her status?
- What iconographic purpose does the second figure serve?

——————— 2.10.b *I.Smyrna* 64: Funerary Relief with Greek ———————
Inscription, Smyrna, Ionia (Second Century BCE) (Fig. 2)

<The people> honors Diodotos the younger, son of Diodotos.

Figure 2 Funerary stele, second century BCE, Smyrna: Leiden, Rijksmuseum, inv. no. Pb. 75 Smyrna: image provided under CC BY licence by the Leiden Rijksmuseum.

- Who are the two main figures? How are they represented and with what attributes?
- Who are the smaller figures? How are they represented? Can we establish their status?
- What iconographic purpose do the smaller figures serve?

2.10.c *CIL* XIII, 7684: Funerary Stele with Latin Inscription, Antunnacum, Germania Superior (First Century CE) (Fig. 3)

Central pedestal: Firmus, son of Ecco, soldier of the Cohort of the Raeti, of the nation of the Montani, 36 years of age, with 14 (?) years of service. His heir set this up, according to the will.

Left pedestal: Fuscus, his slave.

Figure 3 Funerary stele, first century CE, Antunnacum: image provided under CC BY licence from Wikimedia Commons.

- Who is the central figure? How is he depicted?

- Who is the left figure? How is he depicted?

- Who is the right figure? How is he depicted?

- Why is the slave represented in this monument? Could we identify him without the inscription?

2.11 *SEG* XXXVI 587: Funerary Stele with Greek Inscription, Amphipolis, Macedonia (ca. 100 CE) (Fig. 4)

Literature: Finley 1977; Kolendo 1978; Duchêne 1986; Donderer and Spiliopoulou-Donderer 1993; Rizakis 2002; Bodel 2005.

Aulus Caprilius Timotheos, freedman of Aulus, slave trader.

Figure 4 Funerary stele of Aulus Caprilius Timotheos, *ca.* 100 CE, Amphipolis: image from J. Roger, "Inscriptions de la région du Strymone," *Revue archéologique*, 1945, 24, Figure 8.

- What is the status of the deceased? What is his profession? Do you see any contradiction in these?

- What is represented on the reliefs? Are there any connections between the representations and the content of the inscription?

- What attitude towards the profession of the deceased is suggested by the combination of word and image on this funerary monument?

2.12   The Warren Cup: Roman Silver Vessel (First Century CE) (Fig. 5)

Literature: Clarke 2003:78–91; Butrica 2005: 236–8; D. Williams 2006; Harper 2013: 25–6.

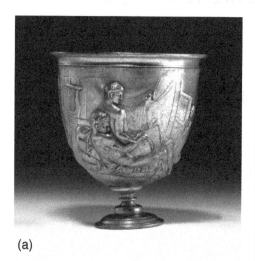

(a)   (b)

Figure 5a–b   The Warren cup: Roman silver vessel, first century CE: British Museum, inv. no. 1999,0426.1.

- How are the two individuals having sex depicted? What differences between them can we observe in terms of age or status?
- What is the third figure doing? How is he depicted?
- How should we interpret his voyeuristic presence in the scene?
- Can we establish the status of the three individuals depicted?
- Can this artistic depiction tell us anything about slavery?

2.13   *CIL* VI, 1958a: Latin Funerary Inscription, Rome (First Half of First Century BCE) (Fig. 6)

Roman freedpersons involved in crafts and trade often achieved wealth, which they tried to convert into social prestige. Roman slaves commonly bore Greek names, which they kept as their *cognomina* after they were manumitted, but free-born Roman citizens could also have Greek names as *cognomina*. Eurysaces is a Greek name.

Figure 6 The funerary monument of Marcus Vergilius Eurysaces, 100–50 BCE, Rome; image provided under CC BY licence from Wikimedia Commons.

Literature: Petersen 2006: 84–122.

> [This is the monu]ment of Marcus Vergilius Eurysaces, baker, contractor. It
> is evident!

- What is depicted on the reliefs of this monument? What can we learn about the identity of the deceased from them?

- How does the deceased identify himself?

- Can we establish whether Eurysaces was a former slave? Apart from his Greek *cognomen*, are there other reasons to assume he had been a slave?

2.14   The Agora of the Italians: Delos, Cyclades (Second Century BCE) (Fig. 7)

The small island of Delos was an important sanctuary, long before becoming the busiest cosmopolitan port of the late Hellenistic Mediterranean and a large slave market (cf. 8.19). Scholars have been debating whether some buildings can be identified as slave markets, and the so-called agora of the Italians has been the prime candidate. The vast unpaved courtyard enclosed 3440 m^2 and could easily hold thousands of people. The porticoes round the courtyard had a second storey, which could house around a thousand persons. Rooms 28–30 housed sweat baths. The propylon (3) has been interpreted as either the entrance to the building or a platform for slave auctions.

Literature: Coarelli 2005; Fentress 2005; Trümper 2009: 34–49.

- What entrances were there for this building? How easy was access to it? Why might this allow us to connect the agora to the slave trade?

- Does the size of the courtyard suggest that the agora was a slave market? How? If not, what other functions can you imagine for this courtyard?

- If the courtyard was used for housing thousands of slaves, what problems can you envisage as emerging?

- How could one access the upper storey of the porticoes? In what way could they facilitate its use as a slave market? What other functions can you imagine?

- Were the baths important for a large slave market? Was the size of the baths sufficient for dealing with thousands of slaves per day?

- To which rooms does corridor 70a lead? Could these rooms be used for the sale of slaves?

- Would slave traders require a specific large-scale building for conducting their business? What other alternatives can you imagine?

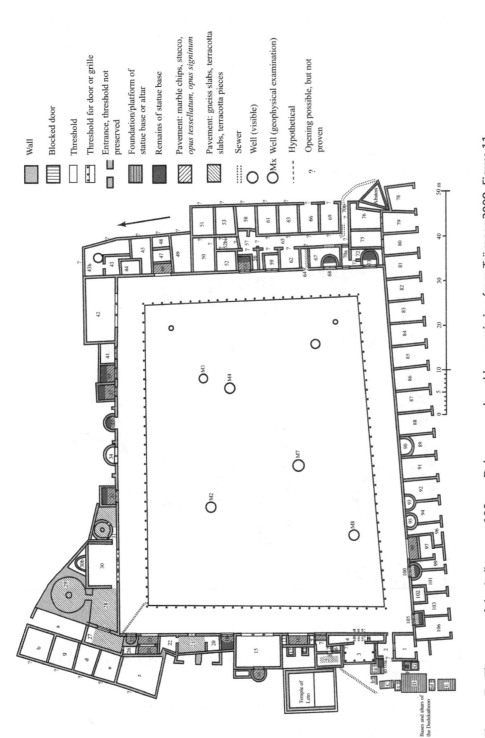

Figure 7 The agora of the Italians, *ca.* 100 BCE, Delos; reproduced by permission from Trümper 2009, Figure 11.

Wall

Blocked door

Threshold

Threshold for door or grille

Entrance, threshold not preserved

Foundation/platform of statue base or altar

Remains of statue base

Pavement: marble chips, stucco, *opus tessellatum, opus signinum*

Pavement: gneiss slabs, terracotta slabs, terracotta pieces

Sewer

Well (visible)

Mx Well (geophysical examination)

Hypothetical

? Opening possible, but not proven

2.15   *SEG* III 672: Greek Graffito on Wall, Delos, Cyclades (Late Hellenistic Period) (Fig. 8)

The following graffito was inscribed in room c of the so-called House of the Lake; on the same wall, there were graffiti showing four transport ships. Antiocheia on the Maeander was a city in Karia in Asia Minor, near the river Maeander. Like most Aegean islands, Delos is relatively treeless and waterless. For Delos' importance for the Hellenistic slave trade, see 2.14, 8.1, 8.19.

Literature: Severyns 1927; Rauh, Dillon and McClain 2008; Zarmakoupi 2016.

> This is the Antiochean land: figs and plenty of water.
> O Maeander Saviour, save us and give water.

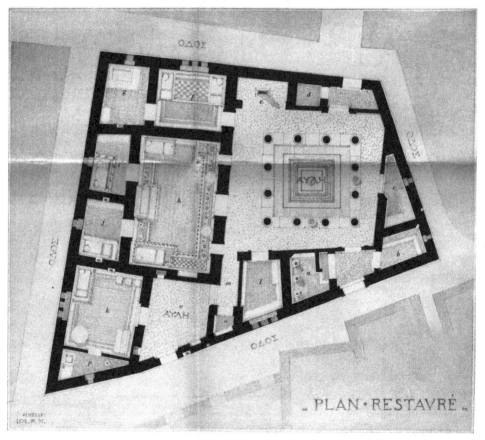

Figure 8   House of the Lake, late Hellenistic period, Delos: reproduced by permission from Zarmakoupi 2016, Figure 4.10.

- What do you think did the author of this graffito want to express?
- Where was it inscribed? Who was likely to use or occupy this room? Is it possible to establish this on the basis of a room plan?

- Can this graffito be attributed to a slave? If yes, why? If not, what other explanations can you think of?

HEARING THE SLAVES' VOICE?

Literature: Fitzgerald 2000; McCarthy 2000; Hunt 2011; Joshel 2011; Akrigg and Tordoff 2013; Bathrellou 2014; Richlin 2017.

2.16   Alciphron, *Letters*, 1.2:[31] Greek Literary Epistolography (Second/Third Century CE)

This passage and the next are not real letters but fictional. Mounychia is a harbor in the Piraeus. Lemnos is an island in north-eastern Aegean, while Rhodes is an island in southeastern Aegean.

Literature: Biraud and Zucker 2018.

> Galenaios to Kyrton: All our labors are in vain, Kyrton. During the day, we get scorched by the sun's heat; in the night, we scrape off the bottom of the sea in the light of torches; and, as the saying goes, we pour our pitchers into the jar of the Danaids. So ineffectual and fruitless is the toil in which we spend our lives. We can't fill our bellies even with sea-nettles or mussels, while our master gathers in both the fish and the coins. Nor is it enough for him to get all this out of us, but he keeps searching the boat, too. And a little while ago, when we sent this boy here, Hermon, from Mounychia to take our catch to the master, he sent orders so that we should also take to him sponges and the sea-wool that grows luxuriantly in Lemnos. The result was that, before he finished making these extra demands, Hermon left behind the fish-basket, fish and all, left us, too, boat and all, and went off on a rowing boat, having mixed with some Rhodian seamen. Thus, the master had to mourn for a slave, while we for a good fellow-worker.

- The name of this letter's writer derives from the Greek word for the stillness of the sea, while that of his addressee from the Greek word for a fish net. What do these names imply about the genre of this text?

- What is the status of addressor and addressee?

- What do we learn about their work?

- How might Galenaios and his fellow-slaves on the boat have hoped to have fared better if they had had a different master?

- How does Hermon manage to escape? What sort of links does he exploit?

- Can we use this text as a realistic depiction of social relations?

---

[31] Greek text: Schepers 1905.

2.17 Alciphron, *Letters*, 2.24–5:[32] Greek Literary Epistolography (Second/Third Century ᴄᴇ)

Salakonis, the name of the female correspondent, means arrogant, and Gemellus, the name of the male correspondent, could have been understood as an allusion to a euphemism for "testicle."

Literature: Biraud and Zucker 2018.

Gemellus to Salakonis:
Why do you act so haughtily, Salakonis you wretch? Didn't I take you up from the workshop, where you had to work beside that lame clothes mender? Didn't I even do it without mother's knowledge? Aren't I keeping you as if you were some heiress to whom I had got married? But you've got on your high horse, you cheap little slave girl, and you never stop giggling and making fun of me. Won't you cease from your arrogance, you wretch? I will show you your lover is your master, and I will have you roast barley in the countryside. Then you will learn by suffering into what misery you drove yourself.

Salakonis to Gemellus:
I can endure anything, except for sleeping with you, master. In the night I did not run away, nor was I hiding under the bushes, as you thought, but I slipped into the trough and lay there, with its curve around me as cover. And since I've decided to end my life by hanging myself, listen to one who speaks openly and clearly; my keenness to die strips away all my fear. I detest you, Gemellus. I loathe your shaggy body and avoid it like a fox; I loathe your foul mouth, which sends forth horrible smells from the bottom of your throat. Be damned to a horrid end, so horrible as you are. Go to some bleary-eyed peasant hag, her life hanging by a … single molar, her body perfumed by … pitch oil.

- What are the respective statuses of Gemellus and Salakonis?
- How are they represented in this text?
- How does Salakonis respond to Gemellus' demands?
- What forms of slave labor are mentioned in the text? What role does sex play among these forms of labor?
- Can we use this text as a realistic depiction of social relations?

2.18 Menander, *The Shield*, 238–45:[33] Greek Comedy (End of Fourth/Early Third Century ʙᴄᴇ)

Daos, the slave of a young Athenian who is believed to have been killed while on military campaign in Asia Minor, returns to Athens, to his master's house, with the booty collected by the master. In this scene, Daos, who had accompanied his

---

[32] See 2.16.
[33] Greek text: Ireland 2010.

master on the campaign, is in conversation with a slave waiter. Hard labor at the mills is often presented as punishment for slaves. The Getai were a Thracian tribe.

Literature: Cox 2013; Konstan 2013; Bathrellou 2014; Harrison 2019.

> **Waiter**: Be damned to perdition then, by Zeus, since you've done such a thing, you idiot. You had so much gold, and slaves, and you've returned bringing them back for your master? And you didn't run away? Where on earth are you from?
>
> **Daos**: From Phrygia.
>
> **Waiter**: A good for nothing! A sissy! Only we, Thracians, are men! Oh Apollo, the Getai are the manly sort! That's why the mills are full of us.

- What does the waiter expect Daos to have done after his master's death on campaign? How does he explain Daos' behavior? If this was a serious conversation and not a buffoonish scene from a comedy, how do you think Daos could have justified his decision?

- What are the ethnic identities of these two slaves?

- How does the waiter present his own ethnic identity? What evidence does he bring in favor of his argument?

- Can we take this dialogue as a realistic representation of how slaves perceived their ethnic identities and conversed with each other? Or is this merely the mirror image of Athenian assumptions about barbarian slaves?

2.19 Menander, *Men at Arbitration*, 538–49 and 557–66:[34] Greek Comedy (End of Fourth/Early Third Century BCE)

The interlocutors here are two slaves: Habrotonon, a musician and *hetaira* working for a pimp, hired temporarily by a young Athenian man, and Onesimos, the valet of that Athenian man. The two are concocting a plan. Habrotonon, whose sexual advances have been rejected by the Athenian, will pretend to be the mother of a baby fathered by him. Then, she will look for the real mother.

Literature: Bathrellou 2012; Cox 2013; Vester 2013.

> **Onesimos**: But you don't mention that you will become free. For as soon as he acknowledges you as the child's mother, he will immediately free you, of course.
>
> **Habrotonon**: I don't know. But I'd like it to happen.
>
> **Onesimos**: Don't you know?! But what thanks will I get for this, Habrotonon?
>
> **Habrotonon**: By Demeter and Persephone, I will regard you as the cause of all I might achieve.
>
> **Onesimos**: But if you stop searching for her on purpose and let it drop, having thus deceived me, what will happen then?

---

[34] Greek text: Blanchard 2013.

> **Habrotonon**: What for, dear? Do I seem to you to have set my heart upon having children? Just let me become free, gods! May this be my reward!
> **Onesimos**: I wish you would get it. [...]
> *(Habrotonon exits; Onesimos remains alone on stage.)*
> **Onesimos**: The woman is full of ideas. When she saw that it'd be impossible to achieve freedom by the way of love and that she's struggling in vain, she goes off on a new tack. I, however, will be a slave all my life – driveling me, senseless, completely incapable of planning such things! But, possibly, I will get something from her, if she succeeds. It would be right. How worthless even my calculations are, wretched me, expecting to receive thanks from a woman! Just let me avoid further trouble!

- What strategies has Habrotonon used to gain her freedom?

- As far as can be judged from this excerpt, is the wish of these two slaves to become free represented in a negative light or sympathetically?

- What would the free audience think in hearing this slave dialogue on freedom? Would such a depiction conflict with ideas about the servile and dishonored nature of slaves?

- Can we take this passage as a realistic depiction of slave mentalities?

2.20 Menander, *Hero*, 15–44:[35] Greek Comedy (Late Fourth/Early Third Century BCE)

Daos and Getas, two male slaves, are friends.

Literature: Harris 2002.

> **Getas**: What are you saying? Are you in love?!
> **Daos**: I am.
> **Getas**: Your master is giving you a double share of grain. That's bad, Daos. You probably eat too much.
> **Daos**: My heart aches when I see this girl who lives with us. A very good girl, of my own station, Getas.
> **Getas**: Is she a slave?
> **Daos**: Just so ... to some extent, in a way. There was a shepherd, his name was Tibeios, and he lived here, in Ptelea.[36] He had been a slave at some point when young. He had these twin children, as he himself used to say: Plangon, the girl I love –
> **Getas**: Now I see.
> **Daos**: And the lad, Gorgias.
> **Getas**: He who is now looking after the sheep here, at your place?

---

[35] Greek text: Sandbach 1990.
[36] An Athenian local community.

Daos: That's the one. Already an old man, Tibeios, their father, took one mina from my master to feed them, and then another (for there was a famine). Then he ... withered away.

Getas: Possibly because your master would not give him a third mina.

Daos: Perhaps. When he died, Gorgias took a little more cash, buried him, performed the usual rites, and came here to us, bringing his sister along. He is staying on here, working off the debt.

Getas: And what of Plangon?

Daos: She works the wool together with my mistress and does some housework too. A girl so ... – Getas! Are you laughing at me?!

Getas: No! By Apollo!

Daos: Getas, she is so much like a free girl; really decent.

Getas: And you? What are you doing for your case?

Daos: I've attempted nothing in secret, by Herakles! But I've spoken to my master, and he's promised to let her l[ive with me], after he discusses it with [her brother].

- What is the family history of Plangon and Gorgias? Are they slaves?
- How do the children of Tibeios try to pay back their debt obligations?
- How does Daos try to sort out his love life?
- How credible is this fictional source for understanding the lives of slaves and their descendants?

2.21 Plautus, *Persian*, 251–71:[37] Latin Comedy (Second Century BCE)

Toxilus, a slave, has asked his good friend Sagaristio, another slave, for a loan. With the money, he wants to buy off from her master, a pimp, the slave girl he is in love with.

Literature: Segal 1968: 102–36; Parker 1989; McCarthy 2000: 122–66; Richlin 2014.

Sagaristio: To splendid and glorious Jupiter, the son of Ops, the highest, the strong, the powerful, who bestows wealth, good hopes, abundance *** I joyously bring a thank-offering. Deservedly so, because they give this abundance of convenience to my friend in a friendly manner, so that I can bring him plenty of money on loan when he needs it. What I couldn't even dream of or think of or believe in, namely, that I would have this opportunity, has now fallen down from heaven, as it were. For my master (*erus*) sent me off to Eretria, to buy trained oxen for him. And he gave me money because, he said, there would be a market there in a week from now. He's stupid; he gave this money to me, whose mind he did know. I will put all this money to another use: "There were no oxen which I could buy." Now, I will both make my friend happy and bring

---
[37] Latin text: de Melo 2011.

much good to myself. What will be of benefit for a long time, I will use up in a single day. There will be whipping on my back. I don't care. Now I will lavish from my purse these trained oxen upon a friend. This is indeed a charming thing to do, to get a good bite out of super-stingy old men, greedy ones, tight-fisted ones, who seal up the salt-cellar with the salt, so that the slave might not get it. It is a virtue to see clearly when occasion suggests so. What will he do to me? He will order that I be beaten with whips, that I be chained in shackles. He can go hang! He shouldn't think that I will entreat him! To hell with him! He can't do anything new anymore to me, anything that I haven't experienced.

- How does Sagaristio treat his master's orders?
- How will Sagaristio use his master's money? Why?
- What punishment does Sagaristio expect? Does he fear it?
- Can we use this comic passage to understand slave mentality?

2.22   *I.Philippi* 416: Latin Funerary Inscription, Philippi, Macedonia (First–Third Century CE)

Literature: Aubert 1993; Gardner 1993: 59–60; Martin 2003: 226–7.

Here lies Vitalis, slave of Gaius Lavus Faustus, also his son, a home-born slave (*verna*), born in the household. He lived 16 years. Manager (*institor*) of the Apriana tavern, well received by the people but snatched away by the gods. "I ask you, travelers, if I ever sold somewhat less than the correct measure, in order to add to my father's gains, forgive (me). I ask the gods above and those below that you preserve my father and mother. And farewell!"

- What is the relationship between the slave and his master?
- What do we learn about the slave's professional activities?
- How does the slave describe himself?
- In whose voice does the text speak? Does this imply that it was composed by the slave himself? Compare with 7.39.
- How useful is this inscription for understanding slavery?

2.23   Phaedrus, *Fables*, 3, Prologue, II. 33–7: Latin Verse Fable (First Century CE)

Literature: Bradley 1984: 150–3; Hopkins 1993; Rothwell 1995; Champlin 2005.

I will now explain briefly why the genre of fables was invented. Because slavery, being at the mercy of everyone and everything, did not dare to say what it wanted, it transferred its true sentiments into fables and avoided censure by jesting with made-up stories.

- Why does the passage present fable as servile discourse?
- Compare with 4.21, 5.18, 7.8, 7.34, 9.19. Do these fables represent a slave point of view?

2.24 Theodoret, *Religious History,* 9.9: Greek Biography of Ascetics (Fifth Century CE)

At this part of his biography of Peter of Galatia, an ascetic active in the early fifth century CE, Theodoret narrates events connected with the relationship between Peter and Theodoret's own mother, a wealthy woman of Antioch.

Literature: Klein 1982.

At another time, my mother took a slave cook who was being perturbed by an evil demon to Peter, and begged for his help. The divine man prayed and ordered the demon to reveal the cause of his power over this creature of God. And he, like a murderer or a robber standing before the court and ordered to speak of his crimes, started to go through everything, forced by fear to tell the truth, although this was not his habit. So, he was saying that in Heliopolis the slave's master had fallen ill and, since he was ill, the mistress was sitting by her husband's side. And the slave girls of the mistress of the house in which they lived were relating the lives of the monks who led philosophical, ascetic lives in Antioch and of the great power they have against demons. Then the slave girls, like children playing and having fun, pretended to be possessed by demons and to have gone mad, while that slave, draped in a coat, pretended to exorcise them in the way of the monks. "During this performance," the demon said, "I was standing by the door and could not bear those boastful stories about the monks. So, I wanted to test the power the slaves impetuously claimed the monks had. With this in mind, I left the slave girls alone and entered this man, wishing to find out how I might be expelled by the monks. But now I have indeed found out and had enough of tests. So, I will immediately come out of him, upon your command." Upon saying these words, the demon started to flee, whereas the slave cook to enjoy his freedom.

- What activities among slaves does the story report?
- What is the relationship between slaves and Christianity as depicted in this passage?
- Who narrates the events which took place at Heliopolis? How does this affect the veracity of the story?

- Can we take this story at face value? Or is this a fantasy of what masters thought slaves might be doing behind closed doors?

- What freedom did the slave cook start to enjoy at the end?

2.25 Saint Patrick, *Confession*, 1, 16–9: Christian Autobiographical Text in Latin (Probably Fifth Century CE)

Saint Patrick was the son of a local dignitary in Roman Britain; after being captured and sold as a slave in Ireland in the early fifth century CE, he managed to escape, before returning to Ireland years later as a Christian missionary. While many later texts about Patrick are legendary, the authenticity of this text is generally accepted.

Literature: Thompson 1985: 16–34; McLuhan 2001; Rio 2017: 30–1; Beavis 2020.

1: I, Patrick, a sinner most ignorant of city ways, the least of all the faithful and most contemptible in the eyes of many, was the son of the deacon Calpurnius, son of the presbyter Potitus, who was from the settlement of †Bannavem Taburniae†. He had a small estate nearby, and I was captured there. I was about 16 years old at the time. I did not know the true God and was taken to Ireland in captivity with so many thousands of people. This we deserved because we had gone away from God and did not keep His commandments; nor did we obey our priests, who used to admonish us for our salvation.

16–19: But after I arrived in Ireland – and so I used to tend the sheep every day and pray many times a day – my love of God set in more and more and so did my awe of Him. And my faith increased, and my spirit was stirred, so that in one day I would say up to a hundred prayers and almost the same at night. I even used to stay out in the forests and on the mountain, and I would rise for prayer before dawn in snow and frost and rain. And I never felt unwell, nor did I show any laziness because, as I can now see, the Spirit was burning inside me at that time. And it was there that one night, in my sleep, I heard a voice telling me: "You fast well. You will soon return to your homeland." And again, after a little time, I heard a prophetic voice saying to me: "Look! Your ship is ready!" And it was not nearby, but about 200 miles away, at a place where I had never been nor did I know anyone. And then, shortly afterward, I fled and left the man with whom I had been for six years. I went "in the power of God," who directed my path to the good and, until I reached that ship, I was in no fear of anything.

The day I arrived, the ship was about to set off from that place. I said that I had the means to sail with them. The captain was not pleased with this and replied harshly and indignantly: "Don't even try to come with us!" When I heard this, I went away from them, to return to the hut where I was staying. On the way, I began to pray and, before I had completed my prayer, I heard one of them crying loudly after me. "Come quickly! These men are calling you!" Immediately I returned to them, and they began to say to me: "Come! We trust and admit you. Show your friendship to us in any way you like'. [...] We set sail immediately. After three days we reached land, and for 28 days we journeyed through deserted wild country. They ran out of food and hunger overtook them. [...]

The captain, who is a pagan, asks Patrick to pray to God for food; he complies.

And, with God's help, this came to pass. Look! A herd of swine appeared on the road in front of our eyes! They slaughtered many of them and stayed there for two nights. They ate well, and their dogs, too, were filled. For many of them had become weak and had been left half dead by the road. After this, they gave their utmost thanks to God, and I became honored in their eyes. And from that day onward, they had food in abundance.

- How does Patrick describe his experience of slavery?

- How realistic is his description of the flight? What elements are left undiscussed? What can we learn about slave flight from this?

- Why does Patrick give more space to describing his escape than his life in slavery?

- What do you think is the purpose of this narrative? How does it affect its historical reliability?

- How useful is this narrative for understanding the experience of slavery?

3

Living with Slavery and Its Consequences

In this chapter, we focus on slaveholders and the consequences of slavery for various aspects of their lives. We commence with exploring the diversity of ancient slaveholders: masters could own from just a few to thousands of slaves (3.1). At the same time, slaveholders included magnates (3.4–5), the middling sort (3.2–3), institutional owners (3.6), and even other slaves (3.6). The diversity of masters had important implications in how slaves were used and for what purposes. Owning slaves defined the identities and practices of ancient slaveholders. It defined their sense of power (3.7) and honor (3.12) and their everyday activities (3.8–9). The proper use of slaves was a major element for projecting images of the self (3.11, 3.14) or criticizing enemies (3.10). Masters conceived slaves as extensions of themselves and their wishes (3.13) and used them to construct relationships with third parties (3.16). In ancient patriarchal societies, owning slaves was a crucial aspect of the intersection between gender and class (3.15).

This brings us to the role of slavery for the structure of ancient households and economies. In the households of slaveholders, relations between husbands and wives and parents and children were affected in important ways by the existence of slaves (3.17, 3.20–1); strategies of reproduction and survival often depended on the role of slaves (3.18–9). The ubiquity of slaves in the living space of ancient households and villas affected everyday life – and is an important aspect of recent scholarship (3.22). Slavery also shaped ancient economies in various ways. It was an important factor in ancient technological developments (3.24), affected the conceptions of work and the work choices of free people (3.23, 3.26), and shaped the labor markets of ancient societies (3.25, 3.27). Finally, slavery was good to think with. Slavery was a means of debating the nature of the ideal society (3.29–30), and the extent of the "moral circle" of ancient communities: the people for whose fate they cared about and the people who were fair game for pursuing various strategies for wealth, power, and glory (3.28, 3.31). Slavery also defined how ancient people, like Christian communities, thought about their relationship with the divine (3.32–3).

Greek and Roman Slaveries, First Edition. Eftychia Bathrellou and Kostas Vlassopoulos.
© 2022 John Wiley & Sons, Inc. Published 2022 by John Wiley & Sons, Inc.

THE DIVERSITY OF SLAVEHOLDERS

3.1   Gaius, *Institutes*, 1.42–4:[38] Latin Juristic Text (Second Century CE)

The *lex* (law) *Fufia Caninia* was passed in 2 BCE and was part of a series of Augustan laws dealing with freedpersons and manumission. Manumission by *vindicta*, by census, or among friends was employed by masters while alive, while manumission by testament took place after their death. For the different methods of manumission in the Roman world, see 10.10, 10.13.

Literature: Buckland 1908: 437–78; Mouritsen 2011: 80–92.

> The *lex Fufia Caninia* has set a certain limit to the number of slaves who are to be manumitted by will. Specifically, one who owns more than two slaves and not more than 10 is permitted to manumit as many as half of them. One who owns more than 10 but fewer than 30 slaves is permitted to manumit up to a third. And one who owns more than 30 but not more than 100 is granted the power to manumit up to a quarter. Finally, one who owns more than 100 but not more than 500 slaves is permitted to manumit not more than a fifth. Nor is <one allowed, even if he owns more than 500 slaves, to manumit any more;> the law prescribes that no one is allowed to manumit more than 100. But if one has only one or two slaves, the law does not apply to this person, and he therefore has unrestricted power of manumission. Nor does this law apply to those who manumit by a procedure other than by will. Therefore, those who manumit by *vindicta*, by the census, or among friends are permitted to set free their whole household (*familia*) unless, of course, a different cause impedes their manumission.

- What categories of slave owners does the law identify, and what rate of manumission is allowed for each category?
- What are the implications of the fact that slave owners could manumit up to 100 slaves in their will? Why would they manumit so many slaves at once?
- What can we learn about patterns of slaveholding from this text?

3.2   Galen, *Affected Places (De locis affectis)*, II.10.21–22, pp. 378,14–380,2 Gärtner[39] (VIII.132 Kühn): Greek Medical Treatise (Late Second/Early Third Century CE)

A grammarian (*grammatikos*) was a teacher of language and literature at intermediate level. Cf. 12.13, on slave owning by teachers at a higher level of education.

---

[38] Latin text: de Zulueta 1946.
[39] *CMG* V 6,1,1.

Literature: Kaster 1988; Schlange-Schöningen 2003: 255–90, 2006.

> Accordingly, a light diet and unmixed wine cause sleeplessness. This is espe-
> cially the case when the unmixed wine happens to be naturally warm or suffi-
> ciently old. Such a thing happened once to us in Pergamon; I had better relate
> it. The child in question was owned by a grammarian. Every day, the teacher
> used to go to the baths accompanied by another slave boy and would leave
> behind in the house the child in question, locking him in. His job was to look
> after the house and prepare the meal. One day, however, he felt extremely
> thirsty; there was no water inside, so he drank a great amount of old wine.
> From that point onward, he was persistently unable to sleep; later his tem-
> perature rose, and he died from lack of sleep and the delirium that befell him.

- Who is the master in this story?

- How many slaves does he have? Are these many or few? What does their
  number imply about the master's wealth?

- How are these slaves employed?

3.3 *P.Lips.* I, 26.1–9: Papyrus with Contract in Greek, Hermopolis, Egypt (300–325 CE)

The beginning of this papyrus is lost. Nearchos and Eudoxios, possibly two
brothers, arrange to divide among themselves property that they previously held
in common.

Literature: Bagnall 1993; Harper 2011: 56–8.

> [...] Nearchos [...] to us, being not yet of age [...] we held this in common.
> Today that we became [of age], we decided to divide these, so that each of us
> may acknowledge that he can exert authority over his own separate share for
> all time. Accordingly, of our own free, independent and unchanging will, we
> agree that our property be divided among ourselves from now for all time, so
> that each one might have full and unchallenged authority, and that I, Near-
> chos, have obtained by lot Eustephios – whose mother is Euthias, a female
> slave born in our house – farmer by profession, and Neilos, a donkey-driver,
> while I, Eudoxios, have obtained by lot Sarapion – whose mother is Silvana,
> a female slave born in our house – weaver of Tarsian fabrics by profession,
> and Eros, a farmer.

- What is the purpose of this document?

- What are the professions of the slaves mentioned?

- What are the origins of these slaves?

- What conclusions may we derive from this document concerning the wealth
  and slaving practices of these two slave-owners?

3.4   Philostratus, *Lives of the Sophists*, 558: Greek Biography (First Half of Third Century CE)

Herodes Atticus was an Athenian notable and intellectual of the second century CE.

(Herodes) mourned these daughters of his in such an extreme manner because he was angry with his son Atticus. He had become ill-disposed toward him because he was – so he thought – stupid, slow at learning his letters, and bad at memorizing. When his son had proven himself incapable of learning his first letters, Herodes had the idea of raising together with him 24 slave boys of the same age named after the letters of the alphabet, so that his son would necessarily practice his letters when using the names of the boys.

- How did Herodes try to help his son to learn the alphabet?
- What can we learn about patterns of slaveholding in the Roman imperial period by comparing Herodes with the grammarian mentioned in 3.2?

3.5   Palladius, *Lausiac History*, 61.5–6: Greek Biography of Ascetics (Early Fifth Century CE)

In this chapter, Palladius narrates the life of Saint Melania the Younger. See also 1.25.

Literature: Roth 2005; Harper 2011: 192–5.

She manumitted those slaves who wished to be manumitted. They were 8,000. The rest did not want to be freed but had chosen to be slaves to her brother. She handed over all those to him for three pieces of money each. Her possessions in the provinces of Spain, in Aquitania, in Tarraconensis and in the provinces of Gallia she sold off. She kept for herself only those in Sicily, Campania, and Africa and obtained their income for the provision of monasteries. Such was her wisdom in relation to the burden of money. Her ascetic practice was as follows: she would eat every other day – initially, in fact, she would eat only on Saturdays and Sundays – and she had appointed to herself a portion of the service of her own slave women, whom she made her fellow ascetics. She has her mother Albina with her, similarly practicing asceticism and also dispersing her own riches for her part. They live in their estates, sometimes in Sicily other times in Campania, together with 15 eunuchs and 60 maidens, some of whom are free, some slave.

- In which regions were the properties of Melania located? What does this show about her wealth?
- How many slaves did she possess?
- Did she liberate all of her slaves? Why?

3.6 *I.Ephesos* 18.c.13–22: Proconsular Edict in Greek, Ephesos, Ionia (First Century CE)

The provincial governor of Asia Paullus Fabius Persicus tries to curb waste in Ephesos and the temple of Artemis.

Literature: Shaner 2018: 23–41.

> Similarly, any free men offering the services of public slaves and, hence, burdening the common treasury with superfluous expenses, should, it is decreed, be released from their posts, and public slaves should be put in their place. Similarly, it is deemed right that those public slaves reported to be buying babies from random people and dedicating them to Artemis, so that their slaves be raised from the revenues of Artemis, should themselves provide for the raising of their own slaves.

- Why does the governor prohibit the use of free men for jobs done by public slaves? What does this tell us about slave ownership in Roman Ephesos?
- How do public slaves acquire slaves?
- What trick do public slaves use to feed their slaves?
- How useful is this source for gauging the extent of slave ownership in Roman Ephesos?

BEING MASTER, BEING MISTRESS

3.7 *PMG* 909: Greek Song, Probably to Be Performed in a Symposion (Uncertain Date; Possibly Fifth Century BCE)

Literature: Tedeschi 1986; Lewis 2018: 157–8.

> My great wealth is a spear and a sword
> and my fine shaggy hide-shield, which guards the skin.
> Thanks to this I plough, thanks to this I harvest,
> thanks to this I tread the vines' sweet grapes,
> thanks to this I am called master of slaves.[40]
> Those who don't have the courage to bear spear and sword
> and the fine shaggy hide-shield, which guards the skin,
> all, crouched down *** my knee ***
> *** prostrate themselves *** calling <me>
> master and great king.

---

[40] Literally "master of a *mnoia*," one of the terms used for groups of slaves in Crete (cf. 1.3, 2.6).

- How does the speaker present himself?
- What is the main source of his power and wealth?
- What forms of wealth and power does he possess?
- How is slavery inscribed in the speaker's representation of identity, power and wealth?

3.8 *The Conversation Book of Conrad Celtes*, Excerpted:[41] Bilingual (Greek and Latin) Conversations for Language Learning (Roman Imperial Period)

The words and phrases in brackets offer to the language learner vocabulary alternatives.

Literature: Dionisotti 1982; Dickey 2015: 140–91.

3–17:
"Nurse / (male nurse) / dress me / and put on my shoes." / It is time / (it is opportune) / before daylight / for us to go early / to school. / In the morning / when I began to be awake / (and I woke up early) / I got up / (I arose) / from sleep / and from the camp-bed (and from bed). This I do first / (this I did first): / I took off my night-clothes / and I took a linen shirt. / [...] Then I awoke / my slave boy. / I said to him: / "Get up, boy! / See if it is already light. / Open the door / and the window." / And he did so. / Then I said to him: / "Give me my stuff, / hand to me my shoes, / fold my finer clothes, / and put / my everyday clothes / aside. / Give me a wrap / and a cape." / "Here they are." / I took the other things, too. / Then I come down / from the bed, / I put on my waist-band, / I put my cape around / my neck. / I get dressed / (I got dressed) / as it is proper / (as it was proper) / for the son of the household / (for a well-born man). / So, I asked for / shoes, / trousers, / socks, / leggings. / I am putting on my shoes. / (I have my shoes on). / I am given water / for my face. / I wash. / (I clean my face.) / When I have washed my mouth / (I rinse) / (I have rinsed), / I dry myself / with a clean towel / (I dried). /"Give me a cloth / (a towel). Dry me. [...]

"Bring / clean water / to my lord brother (Latin: to your master / (my brother)), / so that he too / can go with me / (or with us) / outside / (to school)." And thus, / in order, I commanded / to be given / (to continue to be given) / to us / (to you, to them, to me) / a tunic / (tunics) [...]. / From there, / afterward, / I proceeded from home / outside / (to the lecture hall, / to the bridge, / to the neighborhood, / to the marketplace) / with my slave boy / who carries my case of books / (or my paedagogue, / or my fellow-student). [...] / Finally, I return / to my father's house. / I go to greet / my parents, / (my father, / my mother, / my grandfather, / my grandmother, / my brother, / my sister, / and all my relatives, / my uncle / and aunts, / my nurse / and male nurse, / the steward of the house, all the freedmen (*colliberti*), / the doorkeeper, / the

---

[41] Greek and Latin text: Dickey 2015: 164–91. Instead of writing one line below the other, we have used slashes (/) to mark line-ends in the manuscript preserving this text.

domestic servant, / the neighbors, / all our friends, / the tenant who lives in our house (*incola*), / the steward of the tenement house, / the eunuch). [...] 43–64:

I enter / my father's house; / I take off my clothes, / my finer clothing; / I put on my everyday clothes. / I request / (or ask for, / or myself take)/ water to wash my hands. / Since I am hungry, / I say to my slave boy: / "Set the table, / and put the tablecloth, / and a napkin. / And go / to your mistress/ and bring bread, / and relish, / and a drink of wine / (of beer, / of spiced-wine, / of absinth, / of milk). Tell my mother / that I have to return again / to the teacher's house. / So for this reason, / hurry / bring us / lunch." [...]

Towards the evening:
"Tell / your fellow-slave / that I should have something to eat / after my bath. / Set out a kettle, / and many pots, / prepare dinner, / put coals in the room. / Sweep the house; / bring water. / Cover the bench / (put a covering over the couch, / set up the semi-circular couch, / spread out the coverings), / spread a finer one. / Open the cellar, / bring out wine jars, / and wine, / olive-oil / and fish-sauce, / beer. [...]

"Bring out cups / and a bowl / (cups, drinking cups), / a candelabrum, / decorate the three-leg table, / sprinkle flowers / in the triclinium, / put out coals / and incense, /and have everything ready. / Tell your fellow-slave, 'The cooks should make tasty food, / because I have asked / to dinner / great men / and foreigners.'/

"Get yourself ready / faster, / so that we can bathe earlier. / Bring our things / to the baths / (our change of clothes). / Pick up the sandals / (boots / and shoes). / Set them out carefully / and get a suitable space / so that we can go down more nicely. / You will be told off / if you do not follow. / You go first, / in front, / with the oil-flask. / Why the delay? / You are doing it slowly / (you are slow)." [...] / I entered the anointing-room, / I asked for the oil-flask. / "Give me oil, / anoint me, / and rub / my whole body, / on every side. [...] Give me the strigil, / scrape me down. / Give me the towels, / dry me: / head and shoulders, / chest and tummy, / my arms and my sides, / back and thighs, / knees and shins, / feet and heels, / soles of my feet. / Come! / Get dressed, / with clean and nice clothes. / Give me my clothes, / and dress me." / "Wrap up / your master / and dress him. / Let him come with me." /

"You [plural] are nice and clean!" / "May it be well for you!" [singular] / "May it be well for you! [plural] / Bathe (me) well!" / [...] "You [singular] are nice and clean! / To your good health, master. / We wish you well." / "Collect our stuff / and the other necessary things. / Follow us / (follow me). / Let us go home." A good bath / offers / hot water / (water in good temperature). / I thank / the bath keeper.

- What kind of text is this? What purpose does it serve?

- In what functions are slaves present in this text?

- What can we learn about ancient slavery from the ubiquitous presence of slaves in it?

- Who gives orders to slaves in the earlier parts of this text (i.e. until the dinner preparations)? What is his age? What can we learn from this about the master–slave relationship?

- How is the relationship between masters and slaves represented in this passage? Does it consist solely of commands addressed to slaves?

3.9   Pliny the Elder, *Natural History*, 29.19:[42] Latin Encyclopedic Work (First Century CE)

Pliny here deplores the blind trust of the Roman elite in doctors, who tended to be foreigners and often slaves.

Literature: Blake 2013.

> We walk with another's feet, we see with another's eyes, we make our greetings with the help of another's memory, we even live by another's work. The precious things nature offers and the fundamentals of life are lost to us. We have nothing else to call our own but our pleasures.

- To what uses of slaves does Pliny refer?
- What effects does slavery have on the masters?
- How does slavery, as depicted in this passage, compare with 1.1 and 3.13?

3.10   Cicero, *Against Piso*, 66–67: Latin Deliberative Oratory (ca. 55 BCE)

In this invective, originally delivered in the Roman Senate, Cicero tries to besmirch the reputation of his political enemy, the Roman senator Lucius Calpurnius Piso. Here he presents Piso's enjoyment of luxury, particularly his house arrangements and his banquets, as lacking in both splendor and refinement and unworthy of a member of the Roman elite.

Literature: Garland 1992.

> But do not think that (Piso) pursues luxury of the (refined) sort. For, although every sort of luxury is bad and disgraceful, there is, nonetheless, a type of luxury which is more worthy of a free-born or a free man. There is nothing fine in Piso here, nothing elegant, nothing exquisite, and – to do justice to an enemy– nothing even particularly expensive, except his lusts. No embossed artifacts. Huge cups and, what is more, made in Placentia, so that he might not appear to despise his people. His table piled up not with shellfish or fish but with loads of half-rotten meat. He is attended by dirty slaves – many of whom are old men even. The same man stands in for both cook and steward; no baker in the house; no cellar. His bread from the corner shop, his wine from the barrel.

---

[42] Latin text: Rackham et al. 1938–1963.

- What uses of slaves does Cicero mention?

- What was wrong about Piso's use of slaves?

- What was wrong concerning Piso's non-use of slaves?

- What can this passage tell us about Roman conceptions of mastery and identity?

3.11   Apuleius, *Apology*, 17: Latin Law-Court Speech, Sabratha, Tripolitania (158–9 CE)

Apuleius defends himself from accusations against his private life and the charge that he used magic to seduce and marry Pudentilla, a widow much richer than him. In this excerpt, he addresses one of his accusers, Sicinius Aemilianus.

Literature: Bradley 2012; Lenski 2017.

Whether you have slaves to farm your land or you yourself exchange labor with your neighbors, I neither know nor care. But you know that at Oea[43] I manumitted three slaves on the same day. Your advocate reproached me with this, together with the other things he had been told by you, although shortly before he had said that I had arrived at Oea with only one slave attendant. Well, I'd like you to tell me this: how could I manumit three slaves out of one? Unless this, too, is magic! Should I speak about how blind you are in telling such lies or how accustomed you have become to lying? "Apuleius came to Oea with one slave." And then, after a bit of chatter in between: "Apuleius manumitted three slaves in one day." It would not even have been credible if I had come with three slaves and manumitted all of them. But even if I had done so, why would you think that three slaves are a sign of poverty rather than three freedmen a sign of wealth?

You have actually no idea, Aemilianus, no idea whatsoever, of how to bring accusations against a philosopher. You reproach me for my small household (*famulitii*), which, in fact, I should have simulated for the sake of glory. For I know not only of philosophers, of whom I consider myself a follower, but also of commanders of the Roman people who have gloried in the small number of their slaves. Haven't your advocates read even the following? Marcus Antonius, who had been a consul, had only eight slaves in his house. Carbo, that man who became most powerful politically, one less. Manius Curius, a man so distinguished through many honors, who celebrated a triumph three times at a single gate, this Manius Curius had only two attendants in the camp. So, this man, who had triumphed over the Sabines, the Samnites and Pyrrhus, had fewer slaves than triumphs. And Marcus Cato did not wait for others to praise him, but he himself wrote in a work of his that, when he departed for Spain as consul, he took away from Rome only three of his slaves. Since, when he arrived at the Villa Publica, it appeared to him that he would need more, he ordered that two slaves be bought in the mar-

---

[43] The modern Libyan Tripoli.

ket, from the dealer's platform and took these five to Spain. If Pudens had read this, I think he would have either refrained from this reproach or would have preferred to reprimand me on the grounds that for a philosopher three attendants are too many rather than too few.

- How is slavery used to attack Apuleius? Why?
- How does Apuleius defend himself?
- What role does slavery play in delineating the moral qualities and the virtuous conduct of Roman citizens?

3.12   *Digest,* 47.10.1.3: Collection of Latin Juristic Texts (Sixth Century CE)

On the Digest, see 1.2.

Literature: Saller 1994; Glancy 2002a: 12–4.

Ulpian, *On the Edict*, Book 56: Again, an insult (*iniuria*) is effected against one either personally or through others. An insult is effected against one personally when it happens directly against a head of household, male or female (*paterfamilias/materfamilias*); an insult is effected through others when it happens by consequence, for example, against my children or my slaves or my wife or my daughter-in-law. For insult is directed against us when it is effected against those who are under our power (*potestas*) or in our affection.

- In what ways can the honor of a *pater/mater familias* be insulted?
- How is slavery related to the honor of a *pater/mater familias*?

3.13   Peter of Alexandria, *Canonical Letter*: Church Regulations in Greek (306 CE)

Three years into Diocletian's persecutions of Christians in Egypt, Peter, Bishop of Alexandria, defines how the Church should treat penitent Christians who had fallen away from the Church during the persecutions by sacrificing to the pagan gods or by sending their slaves to do so in their place.

Literature: Vaucher 2018.

Canons 6–7: Concerning those who submitted their Christian slaves in their place. The slaves, since they were as if under the hand of their masters and had themselves in a way been imprisoned by their masters and threatened greatly by them, and since they have come to this and made this slip because of fear of their masters, shall demonstrate the works of penitence for one year. In future, they should learn to do "the will of God" as slaves of Christ (*Eph.* 6:4) and fear Him, keeping in mind especially that "the Lord will reward each one for whatever good they do, whether they are slave or free" (*Eph.* 6:8). The free, however, shall be put under a three-year scrutiny of their penitence because of their dissimulation and because they forced their fellow slaves to sacrifice, hence disobeying the apostle,[44] who wished masters should treat their slaves in the same way, without threatening them. "Since you know," he says, "that he who is both their master and yours is in heaven, and there is no favoritism with him" (*Eph.* 6:9). And if we all have one master who shows no favoritism and since "Christ is all, and is in all," in barbarians and Scythians, in slave and free (*Col.* 3:11), they should examine what they did when they wished to save their own lives. They dragged our fellow slaves toward idolatry, although the slaves too could have escaped, if they had provided them with "justice and equality," as the apostle also says (*Col.* 4:2).

- What is the duration of the penalty imposed by Peter on the slaves?

- What is the duration of the penalty Peter imposes on the masters?

- How do punishments for slaves and masters compare, and how does Peter justify the difference?

- Why did Christian masters send their slaves to sacrifice in their place? Does this tell us anything interesting about how they conceived of slavery?

- How do the masters' views relate to those expressed in 1.1 and 3.9?

- Does Peter's conception of slavery differ from that of the Christian masters, and if so, in what ways?

- What do you think was historically more significant: the actions of the Christian masters, the views of the Christian bishop, or both? Cf. 11.18–21.

3.14 John Chrysostom, *Homilies on Paul's First Epistle to the Corinthians*, 40.5 (*PG* 61.353–4): Christian Sermon in Greek (Fourth Century CE)

The Church Father expands here upon Paul *1 Cor.* 15:34: "Come back to your senses as you ought, and stop sinning," noting that Paul's exhortation can also be applied to the greedy wealthy men of Chrysostom's own times.

Literature: Harper 2011: 51–2; de Wet 2015: 105–13; Ramelli 2016: 165–71.

What does the wealthy man have many slaves for? Just as in clothes and food one should pursue solely what is necessary, so one should do in relation to slaves. So what need is there for them? There is no need. In fact, each master should ideally make use of only one slave; or, rather, even two or

---

[44] St. Paul.

three masters should make use of only one slave. If this seems tough, think of those who have no slave at all and so enjoy more ready attendance. For God made them self-sufficient in ministering to their own needs, or, rather, those of their neighbor, too. If you are not convinced, listen to Paul, who says: "These hands of mine have supplied my own needs and the needs of others" (*Acts* 20:34). The teacher of the world, then, who was worthy of the heavens, was not ashamed to serve tens of thousands; you, however, think it shameful not to take around many herds of slaves. Don't you realize that this more than anything is what puts you to shame? God gave us hands and feet so that we might not need slaves. Nor was the class of slaves introduced because of necessity. If so, God would have formed a slave, too, together with Adam. But it is the price of sin and the punishment of our disobedience. But when Christ came, he put an end to this too. For "in Jesus Christ, there is neither slave nor free" (*Gal.* 3:28). Therefore, possessing a slave is not necessary. But if it is necessary, then a single one will more or less suffice – two at the most. What is the point of having swarms of slaves? For like the sheep traders and the slave dealers, so do the wealthy go about the baths and the marketplace. However, I don't want to be too exact. You can have a second slave, too. But if you gather many, you are doing this not as a humane act but in self-indulgence.

- Why do people have slaves according to the author?
- Does John Chrysostom disapprove of slavery?
- Why does Chrysostom concede one or two slaves to masters but disapproves of their having many slaves? What difference is there between these two uses of slaves?
- Is there an alternative to slavery for Chrysostom?
- What can we learn from this text concerning the large-scale employment of slaves?
- What is the link between ownership of many slaves and being humane?

3.15 John Chrysostom, *Homilies on Paul's Epistle to the Hebrews*, 28.4 (*PG* 63.197–8): Christian Sermon in Greek (Fourth Century CE)

Reflecting on *Hebr.* 11:37–12:3, Chrysostom argues for the value of enduring affliction and urges his contemporaries to contribute to the church whatever possessions they do not need.

Literature: Harper 2011: 342, 2017.

You may also have, if you want, two slaves. But isn't it shameful, one might say, that a free woman be escorted by two slaves only? Get away! It is not being escorted by two slaves what is shameful for a free woman but walking escorted by many. Perhaps you laugh when you hear this. Believe me: this is what is shameful, walking escorted by many. You consider it a great thing to walk escorted by many, like sheep traders or slave dealers. This is delusion and vainglory; the other is dignity and wise discipline. A free woman should not be distinguished by the number of her attendants. What is the connection between virtue and possessing many slaves? This has nothing to do with the soul. What has nothing to do with the soul cannot be an indication of a free woman. When a woman is content with little, then she is truly free. But when she needs a lot, she is a slave worse than a chattel.

- What need was there for a free woman to be escorted by slaves?

- Why could it be thought as shameful for a free woman to be escorted by only two slaves?

- What does this passage imply about patterns of slaveholding?

- According to this passage, how did slavery affect attitudes to gender and behavior?

3.16   Juvenal, *Satires*, 5.49–75: Latin Satirical Poetry (Late First/Early Second Century CE)

The narrator is addressing a poor Roman citizen who has been invited to dinner by his wealthy patron. He disparages the poor man for putting up with his patron's humiliating treatment.

Literature: D'Arms 1991; Garrido-Hory 1997, 1998.

If the belly of the master is on fire from the food and wine, distilled water is ordered, cooler than the snow of the land of the Getae. – Was I complaining just now that the wine poured to you, the clients, was not the same as the wine poured to him?! The *water* you drink is different! – *You* will be given your cup by a Berber messenger boy or by the bony hand of a black man from Mauretania, whom you wouldn't like to run into in the middle of the night, when taken uphill past the monuments on the Via Latina. In front of *him*, the flower of Asia: acquired for a price higher than the wealth of the fiery Tullus and of Ancus[45] and, to put it briefly, higher than all the paltry possessions of the kings of the Romans.

So, since this is how things stand, when you need a drink, try to catch the eye of the Berber Ganymede! A boy bought for so many thousands does not know how to mix a drink for the poor, but his arrogance is suited to his beauty and age. When will the other chap come to you? When will he come at your request, to serve water, hot or cold? Surely he resents serving an old client and that you should ask for things or recline while he is on his feet. The greatest houses are full of proud slaves.[46] Here is another! With what

---

[45] Legendary kings of Rome.
[46] Although part of the transmitted Latin text, this sentence might not have been part of the original.

grumble did he hand you bread that can hardly be broken to pieces! Lumps of already moldy dough, that make your molars shake and into which no tooth can be admitted. But the master is served bread soft and white, made from the finest flour. – Restrain your hand! The bread pan must be respected! But suppose you are a bit naughty: above you stands he who will make you put it back. "Impertinent guest! Be so good as to fill yourself from the normal basket and to recognize the colour of your bread!"

- Which slaves serve which dinner participants and why?
- How are these slaves described?
- What can we learn about Roman attitudes to different ethnicities from this passage? Cf. 8.22.
- How are slaves used to create a hierarchy among dinner participants?

THE HOUSEHOLD AND SLAVERY

3.17   *P.Tebt.* II, 407: Papyrus with Copy of Letters in Greek, Tebtynis, Egypt (199 CE?)

Copy of two letters sent by Marsisouchos to his daughter and to his wife to inform them about the manumission of various slaves.

Literature: Glancy 2002a: 4–5.

Copy: Marsisouchos, son of Marsisouchos, formerly high priest of the most sacred temple of Hadrian at the Arsinoite nome to [...] daughter of Marsi-souchos. Greetings. Because my wish is that, of the property that I made according to [...] my mother, securing the possessions that would [come] to me, including slaves, the slaves should be free under the auspices of Zeus, Earth, and Sun, on account of the companionship and concern that I have for them [...] (namely [...] and Sarapias, together with her offspring Ther-mouthis, and Soteria, together with her offspring Isidora, Dioskoros [...] and Sarapammon), you [will do well] not to wrong them. But if you do not pre-serve this wish of mine, [...] whatever was settled on you and whatever else you acquired, including deeds of sale and security deeds [...], should become the property of the great god Sarapis at Alexandria.
   Year 7, on the 24th day of the month Tybis.
   [...] I wrote the above on my way to the court, the examination being held auspiciously.
   [*Copy of another letter*]: Marsisouchos, son of Marsisouchos, son of Apollonios, formerly high priest of the most sacred temple of Hadrian in the Arsinoite nome, to Berenike, daughter of Didymos, and my wife. Greetings. Because it is my wish that, of the possessions I have in your name (namely, a vineyard at the village [...] and arable land and palm trees at other villages of the division of Polemon, and at Herakleia of the division of Themistos, and

the slaves Euporos, Nikephoros and Holokotteinos), the slaves should be free under the auspices of Zeus, Earth, and Sun, since Euporos and Holokotteinos are offspring [...] registered as offspring of your female slave Epiteuxis, you will do well [...] these letters of mine. Otherwise, you must know that if you do not do this [...], everything that I have placed in your name shall belong to the great [god] Sarapis [at Alexandria]. For, every right to use these [...] at your place, from the sale you have [...]. I myself have given to the persons who are being freed [...], [having paid off] on their behalf all the fees for their manumission [...]. I wrote this on my way to the court [...] from the slave Nikephoros, son of Ta[...], his mother, [...] of Heron from Tebtynis.

- Which slaves does Marsisouchos manumit? Does he mention the same slaves in the two letters?

- Does he expect his wife and daughter to acquiesce to the manumission? Why do you think that the daughter and wife might object?

- How does he try to achieve his aim?

- How does Marsisouchos describe his motive for manumission?

- Why do you think that Marsisouchos might go to such trouble to manumit the slaves?

- How does slavery shape the dynamics of this household?

3.18 *P.Oxy.* L, 3555: Papyrus with Petition in Greek, Oxyrhynchos, Egypt (First/Second Century CE)

Literature: Glancy 2002b; cf. Heinen 2006.

[...] To [...] the *stratêgos*, from Thermouthion, daughter of Ploutarchos, from the city of the Oxyrhynchians.

I have a young slave servant girl, born in the household, whose name is Peina. I loved and looked after her like a daughter, hoping that, when she became of age, I could have someone to look after me at my old age, given that I am a woman who lives alone and has no other help. On the 19th of last month, this girl was crossing the city to have lessons in singing and other things, attended by Eucharion, a freedwoman of Longinus. At the time of the departure from my house, she brought in Peina, her right arm bound up. I asked what had caused this, and she told me that the girl had been knocked down by a slave boy called Polydeukes, who was driving a donkey. The result was that her whole arm has been crushed, and most of it mutilated, while in the rest there are open wounds. At the time, I did not know of the person in charge of your office and, thinking that the injury would heal, I did not file a petition. However, since the injury is untreatable and I cannot bear the pain for my servant girl, as she is in danger of her life while I am despondent about living – when you see it, you will undoubtedly become indignant, too – I have had to flee to you and seek refuge, my protector, and I request to be assisted and to receive [...] from you [...].

- How does Thermouthion describe her relationship to Peina?

- Did Thermouthion have a family? What did she expect from Peina?

- Did slavery provide an alternative means for creating a family and for providing certain of its functions?

- Why would Thermouthion send Peina to learn how to sing? Should we reinterpret her expression of feelings toward Peina in the light of this?

- What other slaves or ex-slaves do we encounter in this text? What are their economic roles?

3.19   *Genesis*, 30:1–13: Biblical Text in Greek – Septuagint[47] (Original Hebrew Possibly Sixth Century BCE)

Jacob married the two sisters Rachel and Leah, having worked for their father Lavan for 14 years. Leah had given birth to four sons for Jacob, while Rachel had not yet conceived a child.

Literature: Martin 1993; Kriger 2011: 313–44; Lewis 2018: 199–222.

Seeing that she could not bear children for Jacob, Rachel envied her sister and said to Jacob: "Give me children. If not, I am going to die." Jacob got angry and said to Rachel: "Can I play God? He withheld from you the fruit of the womb." Then Rachel said to Jacob: "Here is Bilhah, my slave girl. Go in to her. She shall give birth on my knees, and through her I, too, shall have children." And she gave Bilhah, her slave girl, to Jacob as a wife. And Jacob went in to her. And Bilhah, Rachel's slave girl, conceived and bore Jacob a son. And Rachel said: "God has judged my case, heard my voice and given me a son." She accordingly named the boy Dan. And Bilhah, Rachel's slave girl, conceived a second time and bore Jacob a second son. And Rachel said: "God has helped me, and I struggled against my sister and won." And she named the boy Naphthali. Leah saw that she had ceased bearing children and took Zilpah, her slave girl, and gave her to Jacob as a wife. Jacob went in to her, and Zilpah, Leah's slave girl, conceived and bore Jacob a son. And Leah said: "In good fortune." And she named him Gad. And Zilpah, Leah's slave girl, conceived again and bore Jacob a second son. And Leah said: "I am happy because women shall call me blessed." And she called him Asher.

- How did Rachel try to overcome her sterility? How did Leah react to her sister's act?

- What role did slavery play in the formation of this household?

- Did slavery play this role in all ancient societies? Cf. 11.1, 12.22.

---

[47] Greek text: Rahlfs and Hanhart 2006.

3.20 Plautus, *Casina*, 47–57: Latin Comedy (Second Century BCE)

The following lines come from the prologue to the play, which at this point sets out for the audience the background to the plot. Sixteen years earlier, a slave brought to his mistress a baby girl he saw being abandoned. The mistress, wife of the old man and mother of the son mentioned in the passage, raised the girl.

Literature: Rei 1998; McCarthy 2000: 77–121.

> When the girl reached the age when men would fancy her, this old man here fell desperately in love with her, and so did his son, in opposition. Now, each of them, father and son, is preparing his legions against the other, secretly. The father commissioned his manager (*vilicus*) to ask for that girl to become his wife. He is hoping that, if the girl is given to the manager, there'll be ready night watches for himself away from home, unbeknownst to his wife. His son, on the other hand, commissioned his armor bearer (*armiger*) to ask for the girl to become his wife. He knows that, if he achieves this, he will have the object of his love inside his own stables.

- What is the aim of father and son?
- What sort of slaves do the two men use? How do they use them to get what they want?
- How does this passage illuminate slave families?
- What can this passage tell us about how Roman masters used slaves as tools for their aims?

3.21 Dio Chrysostom, *Oration 10*, 12–3:[48] Greek Epideictic Oratory (Late First/Early Second Century CE)

In this fictitious speech, Dio has Diogenes the Cynic philosopher advise a man whose one and only slave has run away: it is not worth pursuing him because it is preferable to live without a slave.

Literature: Edmondson 2011; Golden 2011.

> So, if you have a wife, she would not consider it worthwhile to attend to your needs, seeing that a slave is kept in the house. In fact, her quarrels with him and her own self-indulgence would annoy you. Now, however, she will be less lazy and take better care of you. Moreover, in households that have slaves, the children soon become spoilt, lazier, and more arrogant. This is because there is someone else doing everything for them, and they have someone to look down on. But in households where the children grow up on their own, they become far more manly and stronger and learn to look after their parents from the very beginning.

---

[48] Greek text: von Arnim 1893–96.

- How does slavery affect the relationship between husband and wife?

- How does slavery affect the free children and their relationship to their fathers?

- From what point of view does Dio assess the impact of slavery?

- How useful for the study of slavery do you deem this source, given its rhetorical nature?

3.22   Roman Houses and Villas

Literature: Joshel and Petersen 2014: 162–213.

——————   3.22.a   Sidonius Apollinaris, *Letters*, 2.2.9–11, 13, 19:   ——————
          Latin Epistolography (Fifth Century CE)

In this letter to a friend whom he is inviting to his villa, Sidonius, a Gallo-Roman aristocrat who also became bishop of Clermont, describes his villa Avitacum, in Roman Gaul. He starts with the baths, which include a pool into which water falls from the mouths of six lion heads.

Literature: Samson 2002.

Here, if the owner is surrounded by a crowd of the people of his household (*domestica turba*) or of guests, so little can the exchange of words be heard, because of the roar of the stream as it falls, that the people speak into each other's ears. Thus overpowered by this outside sound, this public conversation assumes the character of a bizarre clandestine meeting. Past these spaces, there appears the front of the women's dining room; next to this there is the store room for the house's provisions, separated from the weaving-room only by a partition like those in military camps. On the east side, a walkway framed by a colonnade overlooks the lake, supported by rounded †pillars†, rather than looking odious with monolithic columns. On the side of the vestibule, there is a roofed long stretch extending inward, not obstructed by partitions, which, although not a †hippodrome†, should rightly, I think, be called an enclosed walkway, because it does not have a view onto anything. At the end of this passageway, however, stealing some of its space, there is a very cool place, where a most talkative chorus of my clients' womenfolk and of nurses spread an ... open feast for the gods and ... sing retreat, when I and my family make for our bedrooms! From the enclosed walkway we come to the winter dining room, which the blazing fire in the vaulted fireplace has often stained with black soot. [...] When the food is eaten up, a lodging space will receive you because it is the least hot and the most summery of spaces. It opens to the north only; it receives daylight, but the sun does not touch it. In between, there is a very narrow side room, where sleepy chamber servants can doze off rather than sleep. [...] The estate [...] spreads out in forests and is full of colors in its meadows, full of flocks in its pastures, the purses of its shepherds full of savings.

- In which spaces of Sidonius' luxury villa and estate do his slaves work? What do they do?

- How else do the slaves use the different spaces of the villa? In whose company do they do so? Why do they choose these spaces, and what can their choices tell us about slave agency?

- How does the master view the slaves' use of space and activities? How is his life affected by them?

────────── 3.22.b   The Archaeology of a Roman Villa: ──────────
Villamagna, Lazio (Early Second–Fifth Century CE)

The imperial estate of Villamagna dates to the early imperial period. It included the residential villa, a winery, baths, and the workers' barracks (Fig. 9a). The barracks were built around 250 CE and remained in use for roughly two centuries; they comprised two wings separated by a 3-m-wide alley. The south wing consisted of a row of 10 rooms and the north of 20, and both had upper stories (Fig. 9b). The rooms had earthen floors and often large storage vessels that probably contained rations, as well as hearths and querns for cooking. Some rooms had infant burials under their floors. The excavated objects were of low value but included large numbers of hairpins and sewing needles.

Literature: Fentress and Maiuro 2011; Fentress, Goodson and Maiuro 2016: 116–79.

- Can we draw any conclusions about the inhabitants from the architectural arrangements of these rooms?

- What were the material conditions of life in these rooms? What conclusions can we draw from this as regards the everyday life of the inhabitants?

- What conclusions can we draw from the finds concerning the inhabitants of the barracks?

- How likely do you think it is that the inhabitants were slaves?

Figure 9   a) Plan of the "villa barracks," second–fifth century CE, Villamagna: reproduced by permission from Fentress, Goodson and Maiuro 2016, Figure 5.75. b) idem, Figure 5.6.

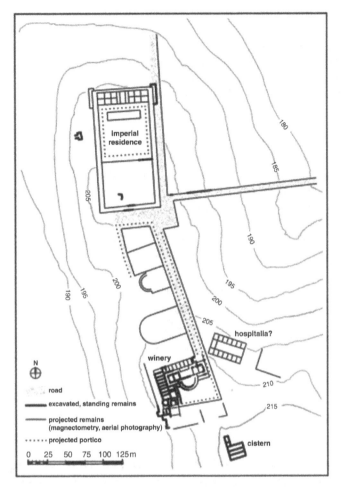

Figure 9 (Continued)

THE ECONOMY AND SLAVERY

3.23 Aristophanes, *Wealth*, 510–26: Greek Comedy (Early Fourth Century BCE)

Poverty is trying to prevent Chremylos from helping Wealth to restore his eyesight. Wealth's cure would result in riches being distributed equally among all just men.

Literature: Garlan 1988: 119–45.

> **Poverty**: If Wealth were to regain his eyesight and distribute himself equally, no one would learn a craft or pursue a mental enquiry. And if these two things disappear, who will wish to be a smith, or do shipbuilding, or sewing, or wheel making, or shoe making, or brick making, or laundering, or tanning? Who will wish to break the land with his plough and reap Demeter's fruits, when it is possible to live idly, without giving a thought to any of these?

Chremylos: You are talking nonsense. The slaves will labor on our behalf over all the things you just listed.

Poverty: And where will you get slaves from?

Chremylos: We will buy them with money, of course.

Poverty: But who will sell them off in the first place, if he, too, already has money?

Chremylos: Some merchant wanting to make profit, who's come from Thessaly, from robbers and slave traffickers.

Poverty: But there won't be any robbers or slave traffickers – according to your logic, of course. For who will want to risk his own life and do this if he is wealthy? Therefore, you will be forced to plough and dig and take up all the other toils yourself and thus lead a much harder life than you do now.

Chremylos: May *you* be the one who suffers this!

- How does Poverty criticize Chremylos' plan for the equal distribution of wealth?
- What role does slavery play in this debate?
- Does Chremylos have a counterargument to Poverty as regards slavery? If not, why?
- Can Chremylos and Poverty imagine a world without slavery? What assumptions about labor and slavery do they share?
- What conception of slavery is presented in this passage?

3.24 *Greek Anthology*, 9.418 = Antipater 82 Gow–Page: Greek Epigram (Late First Century BCE/Early First Century CE)

The Nymphs are water divinities, here a personification of water (cf. 7.19). In some expressions of Greek (and Roman) popular imagination, in an earlier phase in human history, there was no need to work, and human life was free from toil (cf. 3.29).

Literature: Rihll 2008.

Stop the hand that turns the mill, women grinders! Sleep long, even if the cocks' crow announces daybreak. For Demeter ordered the Nymphs to undertake the labors of your hands. They leap on the very edge of the wheel and spin the axle round. He, with his spokes that turn round and round, makes the heavy concave millstones from Nisyros whirl. Once again, we enjoy the ancient way of life, as we learn to feast on Demeter's fruits without labor.

- What technological development does the poem present?
- How important was this development for the lives of slaves (cf. 2.18)?

- Do you think that this technological change had widespread economic effects?
- Did technological changes make slavery less profitable and important?

3.25 Demosthenes, *Against Stephanos I*, 71–2: Greek Law-Court Speech, Athens (Fourth Century BCE)

The speaker, Apollodoros, was the son of Pasion, a slave banker who ultimately became an Athenian citizen; his opponent, Phormion, was also a slave banker who became citizen and married Apollodoros' mother. Rich slave bankers could sometimes afford the benefactions that led to the grant of citizenship.

Literature: Cohen 1992: 61–110; Trevett 1992.

It is right, Athenians, to feel indignation at the past deeds of Phormion, who brought in this man as a witness, when you have seen his shameless ways and his ingratitude. For, I believe, all of you know that if Phormion had happened to be purchased by a cook or some other artisan when on sale, he would have learnt the craft of his master and would be very far from the prosperity he now enjoys. But because my father, who was a banker, acquired him, he educated him in reading and writing, taught him his trade, and put him in charge of a lot of money. As a result, he now enjoys good fortune, having used the luck through which he came to us as the beginning of his current good fortune.

- Why was Phormion lucky?
- What was peculiar about slave bankers?
- What does the passage imply about the possibility of slave social mobility through changing profession?
- What does this passage reveal about human resources and training in ancient economies?

3.26 Xenophon, *Memorabilia*, 2.8: Greek Collection of Socratic Conversations (First Half of Fourth Century BCE)

Literature: Scheidel 1990, 2002; Carlsen 2013: 123–40.

Once, when he saw another friend of his, whom he had not seen for a long time, Socrates said to him: "Where are you coming from, Eutheros?" Eutheros replied: "At the end of the war, Socrates, I returned from abroad, and I am now living here. But since our possessions in other lands have been taken away from us and my father did not leave me anything in Attica, I have been forced to make my living with my own labor now that I have returned home.

It seems to me that this is preferable to asking someone for a loan, especially since I do not possess anything on the basis of which I could borrow money."

"And for how long, in your opinion, will you be able to earn your living with your labor?" Socrates asked.

"Not for long, by Zeus," said Eutheros.

"But when you get older," Socrates said, "you will clearly need money for expenses, but no one will be willing to pay you for your labor."

"You are right," Eutheros said.

"So, it would be best" Socrates said, "to undertake a type of work which can assist you when you get older, too. That is, to approach one of the wealthy, one who needs a person to help him to manage his possessions, supervising works and helping him with the harvest and the preservation of his property – a mutually beneficial arrangement."

"I could hardly tolerate slavery, Socrates," Eutheros said.

"Surely, those who take up leading roles in the cities and manage public affairs are not thought as more slavish because of such tasks, but, on the contrary, as exemplary free men."

Eutheros said: "Socrates, I cannot at all tolerate to have to be held to account by someone else."

"But, Eutheros," Socrates said, "it is very difficult to find a task about which one can avoid being held to account. Not only is it difficult to do something in such a manner that no mistake is made, but it is also difficult to avoid unfair criticism even if one manages to do something perfectly."

- What is Eutheros' current economic condition? How does he make a living?

- What employment does Socrates suggest to Eutheros?

- How does Eutheros react? Why?

- What was Eutheros' economic condition before his current hardship? Would that have affected how he sees paid employment?

- What is more telling for ancient economics, Eutheros' reaction or Socrates' advice (or both)?

- What can we learn about the impact of slavery on labor practices in ancient economies from this passage?

3.27 *P.Brem.* 63, 1–17: Papyrus with Letter in Greek, Possibly from Hermopolis, Egypt (116 CE?)

Literature: Wipszycka 1965: 81–8; Bieżuńska-Małowist 1977: 90; Droß-Krüpe 2020.

Eudaimonis to her daughter Aline. Greetings.

First of all, I wish that you should give birth in good time and receive the news that the baby is a boy. You sailed off on the 29th, and the following day, I finished drawing down.[49] I received the material from the dyer on the 10th of the month Epeiph but with difficulty. I am working with your slave girls as much as is possible. I cannot find women to work with us; they are all working for their own mistresses. Our people marched throughout the whole city striving after higher payment.

- In what work activity is Eudaimonis involved? With whom is she working?
- What labor problem is she facing? How is she trying to sort it out? Why is it difficult to find a solution?
- What can we learn from this text about the role of slavery in the labor market of the Roman Empire?

THINKING WITH SLAVERY

3.28   Plato, *Laws*, 776b–777a: Greek Philosophical Dialogue (Fourth Century BCE)

On helots, *penestai* and the Mariandynoi, see 1.3, 3.29, 8.18.

Literature: Garlan 1988: 149–53; Thalmann 1996.

Athenian: Next, the question of possessions: What sort of possessions should one have so that one's property might be best arranged? In the majority of cases, it is not difficult either to think what they should be or to acquire them, but in the case of slaves, there are all sorts of difficulties. The reason for this is that we speak of slaves in a manner that is, in a way, both correct and incorrect. For what we say about slaves is both consistent and inconsistent with the ways we use them.

Megillos: What do we mean by that? It is not yet clear to us what point you are making, my friend.

Athenian: That is very natural, Megillos. For the helotic system of the Lacedaemonians would create extreme perplexity and strife to nearly all the Greeks; some would deem it good, some not good. – Slavery as practiced in Heraklea, which involves the enslavement of the Mariandynoi, or the nation of the *penestai* in Thessaly, would be less controversial. – If we look at these and all similar examples, what should we do regarding the possession of slaves? What I happened to mention as I was proceeding with my argument, about which you naturally asked what point I was making, is actually the following: we can take it for granted that, presumably, we would all agree that the slaves we possess should be as good and well disposed toward us as can be. And there have been many examples of slaves who were superior to brothers and

---

[49] Probably a reference to the process of spinning wool.

> sons in all forms of virtue and saved their masters, together with their possessions and their whole houses. We presumably are aware of the fact that such things are said about slaves.
>
> **Megillos:** Of course.
>
> **Athenian:** But haven't we also heard the opposite? How there is nothing sound in a slave's soul and that a sensible man should never show any trust to any member of their class? And the wisest of our poets even declared, referring to Zeus: "Far-sounding Zeus deprives men," he says, "of half their share of sense – whomever the day of slavery might pull down."[50] As a result of such considerations and mental distinctions, some show no trust whatsoever in the class of slaves but treat them like beasts, with goads and whips, and thus make the souls of the slaves not thrice but many times enslaved; others, however, do exactly the opposite in every way.

- What contradiction in contemporary perceptions of slavery does the Athenian speaker point out?

- How is the "positive" image of slaves presented? Is this a relatively credible depiction of slaves, or merely the wishful thinking of masters?

- Why was there such a "positive" image of slaves? What purposes did it serve?

- How is the "negative" image of slaves presented? Why was there such an image?

- Why did these contradictory images of slaves coexist?

- Why are helots and *penestai* mentioned in this passage? Were they truly slaves? (Cf. 1.3 and 1.9.)

3.29 Athenaeus, *The Learned Banqueters*, 6.263b–d: Greek Antiquarian Treatise (End of Second Century CE)

Literature: Vogt 1974: 26–38; Finley 1975; Garlan 1988: 126–38; Williams 1993: 116–17; Paradiso 2007; Sells 2013; MacLean 2020.

> Pherecrates[51] says in his *Wild men* (fr. 10 K-A):
>
> No one had a slave back then – no Manes or Sekis –[52] but the women themselves had to toil over all household chores. On top of that, they used to grind the grain at dawn, so the village echoed as they were handling the mill stones.
>
> And Anaxandrides[53] says in his *Anchises* (fr. 4 K-A):

---

[50] Paraphrasing Homer, *Odyssey* 17.322–3.
[51] A fifth-century BCE comic poet.
[52] Names commonly borne by slaves.
[53] A fourth-century BCE comic poet.

> Slaves have no city in any land, my dear man, but fortune takes their bodies everywhere. Many are slaves today, but tomorrow they are demesmen of Sounion;[54] then, the day after that, they … use the marketplace! For god steers everyone's tiller.

And Posidonius, the Stoic,[55] says in book 11 of his *Histories* (*FGrH* 87 F 8):

> Many, unable to govern themselves because of their weak intelligence, offer themselves to the service of more intelligent people; they obtain from them provision for life's necessities, while repaying them in turn with whatever services they are able to offer with their own persons. And it was in this manner that the Mariandynoi submitted themselves to the citizens of Heraklea: they promised to work in perpetuity for them if they provided them with necessities, adding the further condition that none of them should be sold outside the land of the Herakleotes but only within the confines of their own land.[56]

- What society does Pherecrates describe? Why are there no slaves in it?

- How does the speaker in Anaxandrides' play present slavery? What point is he trying to make?

- How does Posidonius explain the origins of the condition of the Mariandynoi?

- What is the wider argument that the case of the Mariandynoi illustrates? What is the conception of slavery that Posidonius presents?

- Are there any differences between the conceptions of slavery presented in the three passages cited by Athenaeus? Are they compatible with each other?

3.30 Crates, *Beasts*, fr. 16 K-A: Greek Comedy (Fifth Century BCE)

Literature: Vogt 1974: 26–38; Finley 1975; Garlan 1988: 126–38; Williams 1993: 116–17; Konstan 2012; Sells 2013; MacLean 2020.

> **A:** So no one will own a male slave, nor a female slave, but an old man will have to look after himself on his own?
> **B:** Not at all. For I will make everything capable of moving itself.
> **A:** And what advantage might this bring?
> **B:** Every little vessel will approach on its own, when someone calls it. "Table, set yourself; get yourself ready on your own! Little grain sack, do the kneading! Ladle, pour! Where is the cup? Go and wash yourself up! Cake, up you go! The pot should be pouring out the beetroot by now. Fish, get a move on!" "But I'm not done yet on the other side." "Well, turn yourself over, won't you, and rub in some salt and olive oil?"

---

[54] An Athenian local community (*deme*); only Athenian citizens could be members of a deme.
[55] See 4.22.
[56] Heraklea was a Greek colony on the south coast of the Black Sea; the Mariandynoi were a population native to the same area.

- Are there any slaves in the society imagined by character B? Why not?

- How does this society without slaves compare with the slave-less society described by Pherecrates in 3.29? How can we explain the difference?

- What assumptions about the role of slavery in contemporary Greek society does the passage depend on?

- What conception of slavery does the passage illustrate? How does it compare with other conceptions of slavery, as seen in passages 1.27–30?

3.31   Polybius, *History*, 2.58.8–13: Greek Historiography (Second Century BCE)

Polybius here criticizes the historian Phylarchus for his depiction of the punishment inflicted on the Arcadian city of Mantineia by the Achaean Confederacy, when the latter sacked Mantineia in 223 BCE. While Phylarchus had presented the punishment as extremely cruel and harsh, Polybius justifies it by pointing out that the citizens of Mantineia had previously betrayed the Achaean Confederacy in a most ungrateful way (given that, according to Polybius, the Achaeans had treated them humanely after they defeated them in 227 BCE) and massacred the Achaean garrison they themselves had asked for.

Literature: Texier 1979; Gaca 2010; Nicholson 2018.

The Mantineans became vengeful killers of those who had let them scot free in the past, although they had conquered them completely and who were guarding their freedom and safety in the present. How angry a reaction does this deserve? What sufferings could be considered as adequate punishment? One might perhaps say: to be sold, together with their wives and children, since they were defeated at war. But the laws of war dictate that this is imposed even upon those who have committed no impious act. Therefore, the Mantineans deserved a greater and more devastating punishment. So, if they suffered what Phylarchus alleges, it is not reasonable that pity is accorded to them by the Greeks; rather, praise and approval should be accorded to those pursuing and punishing their impiety. However, nothing worse befell the Mantineans in this calamity, except for the fact that their properties were plundered and that the free population was sold into slavery. [...]

- What happened to the citizens of Mantineia?

- Does Polybius think that their enslavement was wrong?

- Does Polybius consider enslavement in war as unjust? If not, how does he think about it?

- What conception of slavery does this passage entail?

3.32 *Acts of Thomas*, 2: Greek Apocryphal Christian Text (Third Century CE)

Thomas refuses to obey Jesus and go to India as a missionary; Jesus has other ideas. For actual slave contracts, see 9.12.

Literature: Glancy 2012; de Wet 2018: 8–31.

> When Thomas was considering this and uttering his response, it so happened that a merchant from India was there. His name was Abbanes, and he had been sent by king Gundaphoros with instructions to buy a carpenter and take him to him. The Lord saw him about the marketplace at noon and told him: "Do you want to buy a carpenter?" He replied, "Yes." Then the Lord said: "I have got a slave who is a carpenter and I want to sell him." He said this and showed Thomas to him from afar. He agreed with him the price of three pounds of uncoined silver and wrote a deed of sale saying: "I, Jesus, son of Joseph the carpenter, confirm that I have sold my slave by the name of Judas to you, Abbanes, merchant of Gundaphoros, king of the Indians." When the sale was concluded, the Savior took Judas, also called Thomas, and led him to Abbanes the merchant. When Abbanes saw him, he said to him: "Is that your master?" The apostle responded: "Yes, he is my lord." Abbanes said: "I have bought you from him." And the apostle kept quiet.

- How does Thomas understand his relationship to Jesus?
- Why does Jesus play with the metaphor of slavery? What aim does this metaphor allow him to achieve as regards Thomas?
- What would early Christians think of Christ as a seller of slaves?
- What did Christians mean when they described themselves as "slaves of God"?

3.33 John Chrysostom, *Homilies on Paul's Epistle to the Ephesians*, 22.2 (*PG* 62.157): Christian Sermon in Greek (Fourth Century CE)

After a verse-by-verse commentary on *Ephesians* 6:5–9, Chrysostom is here reflecting upon the passage as a whole, alluding also to *Eph.* 5:22–6:4. Cf. 7.10.

Literature: Harper 2011: 33–8; de Wet 2015: 51–64.

> If one should ask what the origin of slavery is and why it was introduced to human life – for I know that many are interested in such questions and want to find out – I will tell you: It is greediness, vulgarity, and insatiety what has given birth to slavery. For Noah did not have a slave, nor did Abel, nor Seth, nor those after them. This thing is the child of sin, of an outrage against the fathers. Let children hear that they deserve to be slaves if they are undutiful toward their fathers. Such a child has deprived himself of nobility. One who

outrages his father is no longer his son. If one who outrages his father is not a son, then how can one who outrages our true father be his son? He has exited nobility; he has done an outrage to his nature. Moreover, wars and battles have captured men. But Abraham did have slaves, someone says. Yes, but he had not used them as slaves. See how Paul makes everything dependent on the head:[57] the wife – so that, he says, the head might love her; the children – so that he might raise them "in the training and instruction of the Lord" (*Eph.* 6:4); the slaves – "since you know that your own Master, too, is in heaven" (*Eph.* 6:9). So, Paul says, you too should be humane and forgiving because you, too, are slaves.

- What are the causes of slavery according to Chrysostom?

- Did slavery exist at all times? How does Chrysostom's view about the historicity of slavery compare with the passages examined?

- Does Chrysostom's point about slavery as the child of sin assume that every slave deserves to be a slave?

- Is slavery the collective outcome of original sin? Are there other causes of slavery?

- How does Chrysostom try to counter the argument that the patriarchs had slaves? On what conception of slavery is his argument based?

- What is the relationship between slavery and hierarchy that this passage envisages?

---

[57] *Eph.* 5:23: "the husband is the head of the wife as Christ is the head of the church".

4

Slaving Strategies

Ancient societies exhibited a variety of ways in which slaves were employed and of purposes served by these employments. These diverse slaving strategies often co-existed in the same slave system. But while some of them could be compatible with each other, others were deeply contradictory: by using slavery for widely different purposes, they created different kinds of slaves. As a result, these various uses were both fundamental for ancient societies and at the same time created important contradictions and tensions within them.[58]

Slaves could be used in labor processes under the direct control of their masters, either to produce wealth in estates, workshops and mines (4.2–7) or to provide the enormous amount of drudgery required for the everyday maintenance of households and the personal service of their masters (4.8–9). But slaves could also be employed as a source of revenue; such slaves lived and worked on their own but surrendered to their masters a portion of their products or earnings (4.10–2); such slaves were often indistinguishable from free people. Apart from labor and revenue, slaves were used for a variety of other aims. Slaves could create prestige for their masters, advertising their masters' wealth and power through their exotic origins (4.19), their participation in large slave retinues (4.20), or their grave monuments (4.21). Slaves were also used for the gratification of the diverse sensory pleasures. They were thus involved in some of the most important cultural activities of ancient societies, such as music (4.16) or gladiatorial shows (4.18); finally, the use of slaves for the sexual gratification of their masters was undoubtedly one of the most important functions of ancient slavery (4.14–7). Slaves could also be used for their expertise, often requiring high skills of literacy, like scribes and accountants (4.22–4). But it was the use of slaves in positions of trust and authority, as managers, overseers, and agents, that shows one of the most paradoxical slaving strategies (4.25–8).

---

[58] Vlassopoulos 2021a: 58–74.

Greek and Roman Slaveries, First Edition. Eftychia Bathrellou and Kostas Vlassopoulos.
© 2022 John Wiley & Sons, Inc. Published 2022 by John Wiley & Sons, Inc.

Masters often tried to combine these various slaving strategies to achieve their various aims; it is therefore important to explore the portfolios of ancient masters as a means of studying the complementarities and contradictions between the various slaving strategies (4.29–34). A major consequence of this diversity is the emergence of the slaves' economy: economic activities in which slaves operated as autonomous agents (4.35–6) and resources that were largely under the slaves' control (4.37–8).[59] The significance of the slaves' economy for the lives of many ancient slaves is undeniable.

4.1 *Digest*, 50.16.203: Collection of Latin Juristic Texts (Sixth Century CE)

On the Digest, see 1.2.

Literature: Thomas 1999; Ismard 2019: 115–32.

> Alfenus, *Digest*, Book 7: The following was stated in the censorian law for the port customs of Sicily: "No one is to pay harbor duties on slaves one takes home for one's own use." The question arose whether one who sent slaves from Sicily to Rome in order to staff an estate had to pay harbor duties on these people or not. The response was that there were two questions in this formulation. The first question was what "to take home" meant; the second, what "to take for one's own use" meant. [...] What "for one's own use" means is very uncertain. It seems more preferable to assume that the term covers what has been acquired to secure one's subsistence. And so, on this premise, the question arises in relation to slaves: Which of them were acquired for "one's own use"? Are they the treasurers (*dispensatores*), stewards of tenement houses, managers (*vilici*), porters, weavers, also the rural workers, owned in order to cultivate the fields from which the head of household (*pater familias*) obtains the produce through which he can sustain himself? Are they, finally, all slaves whom one has bought in order to have them oneself and use them for some purpose and not in order to sell them? And it appeared that a head of household had "for his own use" only slaves who were charged with tending to his body and his own care and were intended for these roles; in this category, masseurs,[60] bedroom attendants, cooks, personal servants, and others who were required for similar roles were included.

- What slave professions and tasks does the text enumerate? Which slaving strategies are represented here?

- Which slaves are considered to be for the master's own use? On what criteria?

- Would all ancient societies have the same range of slaving strategies as those represented here for Rome?

---

[59] Berlin and Morgan 1991.

[60] We translate "unctores" rather than "iunctores" (harnessers), of the Mommsen–Krueger edition of the Latin text, because we think this makes more sense in the context.

LABOR FOR THE PRODUCTION OF WEALTH

See also 2.16, 3.3, 3.11, 3.22.b, 3.27, 4.1, 5.10, 5.14–5, 5.28, 6.13, 7.7, 7.35, 11.10, 11.11.c, 11.12.b, 12.9, 12.15, 12.19.

4.2   *FD* III 4.77, 6–24: Greek Inscribed Decree, Delphi, Phokis (First Century BCE)

Decree of the citizens of Delphi, honoring king Nikomedes III of Bithynia (cf. 8.20) and his wife Laodike. All names of slaves are Greek.

Literature: Ismard 2017: 35–79.

Because King Nikomedes, son of King Nikomedes, and Queen Lao[dike, daughter of King Mi]thradates, happen to be disposed piously towards the god[61] [and with goodwill] towards the city of the Delphians, when the city sent to them as ambassadors Aristokles, son of Her[akon, and Hybrias], son of Xenon, to request slaves (*sômata*) for the god and for the city, Nikomedes and Laodike acted in a manner worthy of themselves and of their ancestors and promised [the slaves] and also sent them over. They entrusted their ambassador Bias with handing over to the god and to the city 30 slaves, whom Bias delivered [in the first] assembly through the aforementioned magistrates. The city decided to assign [tasks] to them and give to the treasurers Kleon, son of Herys, and Tarantinos, son of [Dromokleides], five slaves for the sacred sheep, whose new names are [...]sion, Phosphoros, Hierokles, Heliodoros, and Ion. For the sacred goats, to give to [... son of ...]sitheos: Menon, Doros, Rhodon, Hippias, and Lykeas. For the [sacred cattle], to give to Theoxenos: Hypatodoros, Onasimos, Nikephoros, Demetrios. Also, for the [sacred] horses, to give to [Eukleides]: Kallias, and to Astoxenos, son of Dionysios: Kerdon, Parnassos, Nymphon [...]. Also to give to Antallos and Herakleides as apprentice boys [...] for building work: Niko[...]. And to give to Euameros as apprentice boy: Olympichos, as baker; and [to ...] as apprentice [boy]: Ophelion, as cook; and to appoint Hermaios as guard of the wrestling school. Also to give to the [temple-attendants]: Leon, Dorimachos, Sophon [...], so that they might serve at the sanctuary; and as potter apprentices: Olympiodoros and Onasagoras.

- How did Nikomedes benefit the god and the city of Delphi? How does the decree characterize his acts?

- In what capacities will the slaves be used?

- What is the point of renaming the slaves?

---

[61] Apollo.

4.3   Varro, *On Agriculture*, 1.17.1 and 3:[62] Latin Agricultural Treatise (First Century BCE)

On Varro's recommendations on the right type of agricultural slaves, see also 5.14.

Literature: Schumacher 2001: 91–107; Joshel 2010: 166–79; J. P. Lewis 2013.

> I will now discuss the means by which farmland is cultivated. Some divide these into two parts, namely men and aids to men, without which it is impossible to cultivate. Others divide them into three parts, namely the speaking component of the *instrumentum*,[63] the component that produces sound but cannot speak, and the mute component. The speaking component includes slaves; the sound-producing but inarticulate component includes oxen; the mute component includes carts. [...] In my opinion, it is more expedient that land which is rough and difficult be cultivated by hired laborers, rather than by slaves, and the same holds true in good land too for heavier farm work, such as when storing the products of vintage or harvest. On the kind of men they should be, Cassius writes the following: that one should acquire laborers who are able to endure hard work, not younger than 22 years of age and with aptitude for agriculture; and that this can be judged on the basis of their response to orders related to other things, and in the case of those of them who are newly acquired, through examination of what jobs they had usually been doing for their previous master.

- Which are the components of the *instrumentum* for cultivating the land, according to Varro and earlier writers?

- Does Varro think that slaves are the only speaking components of the *instrumentum*?

- What other farm workers apart from slaves does Varro enumerate?

- What are the principles by which a landowner should decide whether to use slaves or freemen?

- How should the master decide which workers are suited for agricultural labor?

4.4   "Chained" Slaves

Many modern works on ancient slavery convey images of Romans employing gangs of chained slaves to cultivate their lands. This obviously has important implications for our understanding of Roman slavery. The following texts are the basis of the modern image of Roman chain gangs; the terms employed by Roman authors, which modern scholars translate as chained gangs, are usually *vincti* or *inpediti*. These terms, however, actually refer to slaves who had been chained and confined in the estate prison (*ergastulum*) as punishment for perceived transgressions.

Literature: Roth 2011.

---

[62] Latin text: Traglia 1974.
[63] See 4.6.

—— 4.4.a   *Digest,* 21.1.48.3: Collection of Latin Juristic Texts   ——
(Sixth Century CE)

On the Digest, see 1.2. The Edict of the aedile, which offered provisions and legal remedies for buying and selling, demanded that sellers of slaves notify purchasers of slaves' defects, including any crimes they might have committed.

> Pomponius, *On Sabinus*, Book 23: It is right that the Edict of the aedile should not apply to one who has sold a slave in chains. For it is much more effective to do this than to proclaim that the slave had been put into chains.

- Why did Roman sellers have to inform the buyer that a slave on sale had once been put in chains (i.e. had been a *vinctus*)?
- What assumptions about slaves does this provision assume?

——— 4.4.b   Gaius, *Institutes*, 1.13:[64] Latin Juristic Text   ———
(Second Century CE)

The Augustan legislation on manumission created different statuses for manumitted slaves on the basis of a variety of criteria; cf. 3.1, 10.10–3. The following categories of slaves of Roman citizens are prohibited from gaining citizenship after their manumission.

> Moreover, the *lex Aelia Sentia* stipulates that slaves put into chains for punishment by their masters, or slaves who have been branded, or have been questioned under torture for a wrongdoing and been convicted of that wrongdoing, or slaves consigned to fight with other men or with wild beasts, or cast into a gladiatorial school or into prison and then manumitted by the same master or by another may be free and their status be that of foreigners who have surrendered (*peregrini dediticii*).

- Which groups of slaves are prohibited from becoming citizens? What potential common features do all these groups share?
- On the basis of this law and 4.4.a, how did Romans view "chained" slaves (*vincti*)?

---

[64] Latin text: De Zulueta 1946.

—— 4.4.c   Pliny the Younger, *Letters*, 3.19.5–7: Latin Epistolo- ——
graphy (Late First/Early Second Century CE)

Pliny is considering buying an estate and discusses the advantages and disadvantages of this particular estate and the options available to him.

> Now, my principal dilemma: the land is fertile, its soil rich, with good water supply. It consists of fields, vineyards, and woodlands, whose timber gives a moderate but stable return. However, this fertility of the land is being weakened by inadequate cultivators. For the previous owner often sold the items the tenants (*coloni*) had mortgaged, and while this reduced the debts of the tenants temporarily, it exhausted their resources for the future. This resulted in their debts mounting again. As a result, they will have to be provided with slaves, which will cost more, because good slaves will be needed. For I don't keep chained slaves myself, nor does anyone there.

- What factor affects the cost of slaves that Pliny is considering?
- Why is Pliny refusing to employ *vincti*?

———— 4.4.d   Columella, *On Rural Affairs*, 1.9.4:[65] Latin ————
Agricultural Treatise (First Century CE)

Columella here specifies the ideal physical, intellectual, and moral characteristics of different types of agricultural workers.

> Vineyards do not demand so much tall men as strong and broad-shouldered ones, for a build of this type is better suited to digging and pruning and the other tasks of viticulture. A sound character is less of a requirement in viticulture than in other agricultural activities. This is because the vine worker has to do his work together with others and under supervision; moreover, crooked men tend to have more agile minds, which is a desideratum in this type of work. For viticulture demands of the workers not only strength but also a shrewd acumen. And it is on account of this that many have their vineyards cultivated by chained slaves (*alligati*). However, there is nothing that a sound man of equal quick-wittedness won't do better.

- What kind of slaves are suited for the dressing of vines?
- Why are crooked slaves more quick-witted? What does this imply about slavery? Cf. 5.11.
- Why are chained slaves suited for tending vines?
- Should we then envisage Roman vineyards tended by slave chain gangs?

---

[65] Latin text: Ash, Forster, and Heffer 1941–55.

4.5 Columella, *On Rural Affairs*, 1.7.6–7:[66] Latin Agricultural Treatise (First Century CE)

Literature: Martin 1971; Roth 2007.

But in distant estates, which cannot easily be visited by the head of the household (*paterfamilias*), it is more acceptable for every kind of land to be under free tenants (*coloni*) rather than under managers who are slaves. This is particularly true for land under cereal production; to such land (as also to vineyards or land planted with trees) a tenant can do the least damage, while slaves cause the gravest harm. Slaves hire out oxen and pasture cattle and other livestock poorly. Their ploughing is superficial and careless, and they enter into the accounts many more seeds than they have sown. What they have put into the earth, they don't tend well, to make it grow properly. And what they have brought to the threshing floor, they make less every day during threshing either by fraud or by negligence. For they themselves steal it and do not guard it against the thieving of others. Nor do they enter what is preserved into the accounts reliably. The result is that both the agent (*actor*) and the household are at fault, and the land often gets a bad reputation. Therefore, it is my opinion that an estate of this type be let out, if, as I said, it has to do without the owner's presence.

- Why should tenants be preferred to slaves for far-away lands?

- What acts do slaves commit in such circumstances? Why do slaves commit such acts? What are their motives?

- What can we learn about the relationship between slave workers and managers from this passage? Compare with 7.43.

4.6 *Digest*, 33.7.8; 33.7.12.3 and 5: Collection of Latin Juristic Texts (Sixth Century CE)

On the Digest, see 1.2.

Literature: Veyne 1981; Aubert 2009.

7.8: Ulpian, *On Sabinus*, Book 20: Sabinus states clearly in his books on Vitellius that the *instrumentum* of an estate (*fundus*) includes what has been provided for the purpose of procuring, gathering, and preserving the fruits. For the purpose of procuring, for example, the people who cultivate the land and those who instruct them at work and supervise them, among whom one can include managers (*vilici*) and overseers (*monitores*).

7.12.3, 5: Ulpian, *On Sabinus*, Book 20: The question arises whether a slave who was like a tenant (*colonus*) on the land is included in a legacy of the *instrumentum*. Both Labeo and Pegasus rightly denied this, since the

---

[66] See 4.4.d.

slave was not in the estate as part of the *instrumentum*, although he was accustomed to giving orders to the household (*familia*). [...] Trebatius thinks that the baker and the barber acquired for the needs of the rural household are included in the *instrumentum*. And so is the builder acquired for house restorations, and the women who bake the bread and look after the villa. Likewise, the millers intended for the use of the rural household and the woman working in the kitchen and the housekeeper (*vilica*) if she somehow helps her husband in some duty. Likewise, the women who work the wool to make clothes for the rural household and the women who make condiments for them.

- What jobs do slaves perform in a Roman estate?
- What do the various jobs suggest about the size and activities taking place in a Roman estate?
- What are the slaves' various work statuses?
- Are there differences between the slave tenant and the other slaves? Why is he not considered part of the *instrumentum*? Why would slave tenants be employed?

4.7 Apuleius, *Metamorphoses*, 9.12: Latin Novel (Second Century CE)

The narrator and protagonist of this story is Lucius, a man transformed into an ass (cf. 5.10). At this point in the story, Lucius-ass, recently bought by a mill owner, has just finished his first day working at a mill.

Literature: Thompson 2003: 188–98; Bradley 2012: 59–78.

I started to observe with some pleasure the habits of this disagreeable workshop. Good gods! What poor shadows of men they were... . Their whole bodies covered with livid blow marks, their scarred backs scarcely hidden by their torn rags; some with only a tiny covering cast over their private parts, but all clad in garments so threadbare that their bodies were visible to all. Foreheads branded with letters, half-shaven heads, fettered feet; also, sickly yellow complexions, eyelids gnawed by the smoke-filled darkness of the steamy blackness, making them half-blind. And like boxers who fight having first sprinkled their bodies with dust, they are white with dirty flour.

- What are the working conditions in this mill?
- Why are these slaves branded? Does this explain why they are there? Compare with 2.18 and 5.10.
- What is the narrator's reaction to the lot of these slaves?

WORK FOR HOUSEHOLD MAINTENANCE AND PERSONAL SERVICE

See also 1.17, 1.20, 1.26, 2.5, 2.10, 2.24, 3.2, 3.8–10, 3.14–6, 3.22a, 3.24, 4.1, 5.2, 5.12.

4.8   Seneca, *Letters*, 47.5–8: Latin Moral Philosophy in Epistolary Form (First Century CE)

On this letter, see also 5.12, 10.22, and 11.16.

Literature: D'Arms 1991.

I pass over other cruel and inhumane conduct toward slaves; for we maltreat them as if they were beasts of burden instead of human beings. When we recline for dinner, a slave has to wipe away what we spit; another crouches under <the couch> and gathers what the drunkards have dropped. Another carves the expensive fowl. With confident movements, he guides his expert hand along the breast or the rump and separates out pieces of meat. Unhappy man, whose sole aim in life is the proper carving of poultry… . Unless the one teaching this because of his love for pleasure is more miserable than the one who learns it out of necessity… . Another slave serves the wine: made up like a woman, he wrestles against his years. He cannot flee his boyhood; he is dragged back to it. Although he already has the build of a soldier, his skin is smooth: its hair rubbed out or plucked out. He has to remain sleepless throughout the night, which he divides between his master's drinking and his lust. In the bedroom, he is a man; in the dining room, a boy. Another slave has been instructed to judge the guests. The unhappy man must stand there and look for those who will be invited again the following day – their flattery or their lack of control over their tongue or appetite will earn them the invitation. Add to these the slaves who select and buy the foodstuffs (*obsonatores*): fine is their knowledge of their master's palate; they know what will excite him with its flavor, what will delight him with its appearance, what novelty can rouse him even when he is nauseous, what he is tired of because of having it in abundance, what he craves for this particular day.

- What forms of specialized slave services does Seneca mention in this passage?
- What can we learn about Roman patterns of slaveholding from this description?
- How does Seneca present the slaves who perform these services? What effects do these services have on the slaves?
- Does Seneca approve of such slave services? Why?

4.9   *CIL* VI, 6229: Latin Funerary Inscription, Rome (First Half of First Century CE)

The inscription comes from the collective tomb of the slaves and freedpersons of the aristocratic clan of the Statilii Tauri (see 1.17, 10.16). About 25% of the inscriptions from this tomb mention the dead person's profession or task.

The emperor Augustus established a corps of German bodyguards, which survived until 68 CE. The first Statilian senator was in charge of keeping order in Rome between 16 and 13 BCE.

Literature: Hasegawa 2005: 32–3; cf. Lenski 2009.

> Felix, German, (slave) armor bearer of Taurus the son, is buried here.

- In what capacity did Felix serve his master?
- How should we explain the fact that a profession or task is recorded only for a minority of slaves? Why is it mentioned here? How could it relate to contemporary Roman history?

REVENUE

See also 1.7, 1.10, 2.3a, 2.4, 3.3, 4.32–3, 4.35, 7.20, and 12.12.

4.10 Xenophon, *Ways and Means*, 4.14–5: Greek Treatise on Economic Policy (First Half of Fourth Century BCE)

On slaves at the mines of Laureion, see also 2.1, 7.2, and 8.27.

Literature: Rihll 2010.

> Those of us, you see, who have given thought to this, have heard long ago that Nikias son of Nikeratos once acquired 1000 men working in the silver mines. He hired them out to Sosias the Thracian, on condition that Sosias paid him one obol a day net for each one of them and that he always kept the number of men the same. Hipponikos too had 600 slaves hired out in the same manner, who yielded one mina net per day. Philemonides had 300 slaves, who yielded half a mina, and others had as many slaves, I suppose, as they could afford.

- Why are there such large numbers of slaves in the Laureion mines? Can you imagine similar numbers of concentrated slaves in any other economic field?
- How does Nikias employ his slaves? How does his differ from other slaving strategies?
- Why does Nikias employ his slaves in this way?
- What does the obligation of Sosias to replace slaves imply about mining conditions and the rate of profit?

4.11 *Grauf.* pp. 226–8: Ostracon with Accounts in Latin, Graufesenque, Gaul (First Century ᴄᴇ)

The ostracon has been found in an industrial pottery complex, and the accounts relate to the pottery industry. Written in a very elliptical manner, they record the tasks performed by the slaves of one Atelia and the mule driver of a man called Candidus in the period of one month (between 22/7 and 23/8).

Literature: Strobel 1987; Aubert 1994: 207–11; Gallimore 2010.

Inner side:

(Tally) of the slaves of Atelia, from the 11th day (before the Calends) of August to the 10th day before the Calends of September:
   [Se]cundus and Agileius: 14.5 days at (preparing) clay. [...] of the 30 days, 4 (days) to (the workshop of) Capuries, 11 (days) [...].
   [Onesimus and Ca]llistus: [...] Onesimus to (the workshop of) the Sabri 3 (days); to the workshop of Crau[cina] [...]; [... Calistus]: to (the workshop of) Craucina 3 (days); likewise Onesimus: [...] at wood piling 1 (day); [...] of the 30 days [...] 3 (days).
   Calistus: at polishing [...].
   Vigedos: 3 (days) at the market; [...] at wood piling; [...] at (preparing) clay 3 (days). [...]

Outer side:

Mule driver of Candidus (son or slave) of Urus: 25 days at (preparing) cl[ay], to the m[arket?], to (the workshop of) the Sabr[i] [...]

- What activities did these slaves perform? Where did they perform them?
- Did these slaves work directly for their owners?
- If not, how exactly did the owners profit from the work of their slaves?

4.12 *Acts of the Apostles,* 16:16–9: Greek Biblical Text (First Century ᴄᴇ)

Paul and other Apostles are in Macedonia, trying to convert its inhabitants to Christianity.

Literature: Wendt 2016: 27.

As we were heading for prayer, a slave girl possessed by a spirit of divination came upon us. She used to provide her masters with much income through her soothsaying. She kept following Paul and Silas, crying out and saying: "These men are slaves of the highest God; they show to us the way of salvation." And she did this for many days. Paul got tired of this, turned around

and said to the spirit: "I order you in the name of Jesus Christ to exit her."
And the spirit did so immediately. When her masters realized that it was
their prospects for income that had made their exit, they caught Paul and
Silas and dragged them to the marketplace, to the magistrates.

- What was the profession of this slave?
- In what way did her masters gain from her work?

4.13   *P.Wisc.* I, 5, 1–34: Papyrus with Lease Contract in Greek, Oxyrhynchos, Egypt (185 CE)

Literature: Bieżuńska-Małowist 1977: 88–9; Straus 1977; Hawkins 2016.

Glaukios, son of Pekysis, his mother being Dieus, from the city of the Oxyrhynchians, living in Sento, has hired out to Achillas, son of Harpaesis, his
mother being Tesposiris, from the same city, his female slave Tapontos for
one year, starting on the first day of the present month of Thoth, in order
to work as a weaver. The lessor will present the woman to the lessee on the
following terms: she is not to be absent from the lessee either day or night;
she is to be provided with food and other necessities by Achillas, while her
clothes are to be the responsibility of her master. The hire price for the entire
year is 420 drachmas, which, upon ratification of the lease, I, Achillas, shall
pay to Glaukios in monthly installments at the end of every month, without
delay. The slave Tapontos shall have four days off work in the month of Tybi
and similarly four days in the month of Pachon, a total of eight days, in order to participate in festivals. Nothing will be deducted from the hire price
for these days. However, if she takes more days off work, either because of
festivals or because of illness or of some dire necessity of her master, those
days will be deducted from the monthly payment. If her master needs to use
her for bread making during the night, he shall call for her, without anything being deducted from the hire price.

- In what ways did the master profit from his slave?
- What factors (e.g. gender) would have affected Tapontos' ability to have mul-
  tiple economic functions, profiting simultaneously two people?
- Did Tapontos get any days off work? Why?

GRATIFICATION

Among the various ways in which slaves provided pleasure to the senses, sexual
gratification was particularly important. Alongside some of the sources below, see
also 1.19, 2.12, 2.17, 3.20, 4.8, 4.14, 5.25–6, 6.5, 7.6, 8.26, and 12.22.

Literature: Fleming 1999; Fischer 2010; Harper 2011: 281–325, 2013: 19–79; Cohen 2013, 2015; Green 2015; Kamen and Marshall 2021.

4.14   Horace, *Satires*, 1.2.116–9: Latin Satirical Poetry (First Century BCE)

When your groin swells, if a slave girl or a home-born slave boy is on the spot, then let your passion be released in him or her at once. Would you rather burst with sexual tension? I wouldn't. I like sexual pleasure which is readily available and easy to get.

- What reasons for using slaves for sexual gratification does the passage offer?

- What options were available to men without slaves of their own? What difference did the ownership of slaves make?

4.15   Ps.-Lucian, *Loves (Erôtes)*, 10: Greek Philosophical Dialogue (Second Century CE or Later)

The main subject of this fictional dialogue is whether love affairs with boys are preferable to those with women. In the following passage, the speaker introduces two young men: the Athenian Kallikratidas and the Corinthian Charikles.

Literature: Harper 2013: 26–7.

On that day, I was their host; the following day, Kallikratidas received us, while Charikles did the same the day after. At the banquets, too, I could see clear evidence of each man's disposition. The Athenian was well provided with beautiful boys, and almost all his slaves had not yet grown a beard. They stayed with him until the first dawn appeared on their cheeks, and then, when their cheeks were covered with their first beard, they were sent off as stewards and overseers to his Athenians farms. Charikles was followed by a great troupe of female dancers and musicians, and the whole room was full of women, as in the Thesmophoria. No men were present at all, except, perhaps, a small child or a very old cook, whose age could not give rise to jealous suspicions.

- How did Kallikratidas employ his young slaves? What determined the change of function?

- What was the identity of Charikles' slaves? What were his criteria?

4.16   Galen, *Semen (De semine)*, I.4.29–32, p. 76,12–21 De Lacy[67] (IV.525–6 Kühn): Greek Medical Treatise (Late Second/Early Third Century CE)

Galen here cites a passage of the fifth-century-BCE Greek doctor Hippocrates.

> I will tell you now how I saw semen on the sixth day after ejaculation. A woman of my household owned a valuable female musician who slept with men. It was necessary that she did not become pregnant, so that her price would not be lowered. The musician had heard the kind of things women say to one another: when a woman is to become pregnant, the semen does not come out but stays inside. Hearing this, she understood and always watched for this. When once she did not feel the semen coming out, she informed her mistress. And the word reached me. When I heard what had happened, I ordered her to jump and kick her buttocks. By the time she had jumped seven times, the semen fell to the ground, and there was a noise. When she realized, she kept gazing at it in amazement.

- In what ways did the musician's owner profit from her slave?
- Why would the slave's price be affected by a pregnancy?

4.17   Pliny the Elder, *Natural History*, 7.56:[68] Latin Encyclopedic Work (First Century CE)

> When Antony was one of the Triumvirs, the slave dealer Toranius sold to him as twin brothers two slave boys of exceptional beauty, who had been born one in Asia, the other north of the Alps. So alike did they look. Later, however, the fraud was discovered, as the boys spoke different languages. Antony then rebuked Toranius vehemently, complaining, among other things, of the boys' high price (for he had bought them for 200,000 sestertii). The slave dealer, who was an ingenious man, responded that it was exactly for this reason that he had sold them at such a price. For there would be nothing wondrous in their similarity if they had been produced by the same womb, while finding natives of different nations so similar in appearance should be deemed above any estimate. His response was met with proper admiration, so much so that this proscriber,[69] who had just been raging with threats and insults, reckoned that none other of his possessions was more in accordance with his station.

- Why was Antony willing to pay such a price for these two slaves? Can you think of other explanations apart from sexual gratification?

---

[67] *CMG* V 3,1.
[68] Latin text: Rackham et al. 1938–1963.
[69] i.e. Antony: cf. 5.25, 12.31.

4.18 Gladiators

Literature: Wiedemann 1992: 102–24; Kyle 1998: 76–127.

—— 4.18.a Cicero, *Letters to Atticus*, 4.4a: Latin Epistolography ——
(Second Half of First Century BCE)

Cicero has just asked his friend Atticus, a rich member of the equestrian order, to send him some of his slave scribes. See also 4.23.

> You have bought a magnificent platoon, by God! I hear that your gladiators fight superbly! If you had wanted to hire them out, you would have cleared your expenses with these two shows. But on this later. Do come and, if you love me, arrange for those scribes!

• What investment has Atticus made? How profitable was it?

—— 4.18.b Cicero, *On Behalf of Sestius*, 134: Latin Law-Court ——
Speech (Second Half of First Century BCE)

Cicero is describing how Vatinius, who had testified against Sestius, on behalf of whom Cicero wrote this speech, broke a law forbidding anyone from giving gladiatorial shows within two years of standing, or intending to stand, for office.

> On this issue, judges, I cannot even begin to express my amazement at his temerity. He blatantly acts against the law. And this is done by one who cannot escape conviction because of his agreeable character or be released because of favors owed to him or infringe the laws and the courts with his wealth or his power. What drives this man so that he shows such lack of restraint? It is out of his immense desire for glory, I think, that he obtained a bunch of gladiators (*familia gladiatoria*) – a beautiful group, distinguished, glorious. He had known the enthusiasm of the people, he could envisage the clamorous gatherings that were to take place. Elated with such expectations, burning from desire for glory, this man was unable to keep himself from bringing forward those gladiators, of whom he himself is the most beautiful![70] If he had made this transgression because of this, elated by his enthusiasm to repay the people for the recent kindness of the Roman people to him, still no one would pardon him. But when he adorned with gladiatorial titles men not selected from the market but bought from estate prisons (*ergastula*) and then made some of them *Samnites* some of them *provocatores*[71] by drawing lots, is he not frightened of the outcome of so much license, so much contempt for the laws?

---

[70] The comments on Vatinius' beauty are sarcastic.
[71] *Samnites* and *provocatores* were types of gladiators.

- Which possible motives for buying gladiators are presented here? Cf. the next section on prestige creation (4.19–21).

- What distinction between sources of gladiators does the passage make? Was there a difference in quality between the sources? Why?

- What do the different sources of gladiators tell us about the role of market and punishment in how Roman slavery operated?

——————— 4.18.c *CIL* IV, 2387: Latin Graffito, Pompeii, Italy ———————
(Second Half of First Century BCE)

Such graffiti written on walls announced the outcomes of gladiatorial games.

> Pinna, heavy-armored (*murmillo*), "Thracian,"[72] from the Neronian gladiatorial school, 16 fights, won.
>   Columbus, freedman, 88 fights, killed.

- How many games did Columbus fight? What does this imply?
- What was his status? What does this imply?
- What was Pinna's status?

——————— 4.18.d Symmachus, *Letters,* 2.46: Latin Epistolography ———————
(393 CE)

Symmachus was a prominent Roman aristocrat and man of letters.

Literature: Cecconi 2002: 304–13; Lenski 2011b.

> Symmachus to his brother Flavianus.
>   They say that when Socrates was deprived of things he had desired or aimed at, he judged what had happened as beneficial. Having a sure understanding of his worth and limits, he thought that what chance gave him was better than what he desired. Following the example of this wise man, I put the following on my "things turned out for the good" list. My troop of Saxons was reduced by death – they were of the group decreed to fight for the pleasure of the people – lest my edition of the games be disadvantaged if that troop had been excessively large. For how could a private guard have hindered the impious hands of desperate people, when the very first day of the gladiatorial games saw 29 Saxon necks broken without a noose? So, I am not wasting any more time on this troop (*familia*), who were viler than Spartacus. [...]

---

[72] "Thracians" and *murmillones* were types of gladiators.

- What does Symmachus complain about?
- Where did these gladiators come from?
- What historical event does Symmachus recall?
- How does Symmachus present himself? What does this letter teach us about the mentality of Roman slave-owners?

PRESTIGE CREATION

4.19   Theophrastus, *Characters*, 21.4–5: Greek Collection of Character Sketches (Late Fourth/Early Third Century BCE)

Literature: Diggle 2004: 406–7.

> The man of petty ambition is the kind who, when invited to dinner, contrives to recline by the host himself; he takes his son to Delphi for a haircut; he takes care that his attendant be Ethiopian.

- How does Theophrastus present the owning of an Ethiopian slave?
- What does this imply about the occurrence of black slaves in Athens?
- Is this evidence of a racist attitude toward black slaves?

4.20   Ammianus Marcellinus, *History*, 14.6.16–7: Latin Historiography (Fourth Century CE)

Ammianus here derides the ostentatious displays of wealth at late antique Rome.

Literature: Harper 2011: 43–5; O'Sullivan 2011: 51–76.

> So as not to go on for too long, I leave out the abysmal banquets and the various enticements to pleasures, and I will proceed to the following point. Some gallop through the broad spaces of the city, over upturned paving stones, without fear of danger, with the speed of official messengers – "their heels dented" from spurring their horses, as the saying goes. They drag behind them troops of household members like bands of brigands, not leaving even Sannio at home, as the comic poet says.[73] Many Roman ladies imitate them and run through all quarters of the city with covered heads and in closed litters. And as expert generals place at the front strong units arranged densely, next light-armed troops, behind them javelin throwers, and at the back a reserve – to assist the battle if chance demands it – so do those in charge of the city households, distinguished by the staffs attached to their right hands, arrange their

---

[73] An allusion to Terence *Eunuchus* 780: Sannio has been left behind at his master's house, while all the other slaves, together with the master, besiege the house of a courtesan.

people carefully and diligently. As if a military command had been given, all the weavers march near the front of the carriage; they are joined by the kitchen staff, their faces black from the smoke; after them all the other slaves, indiscriminately, together with plebeian neighbors who can spare the time.

- What is the purpose of these large slave retinues?
- What kinds of slaves are present in these retinues?
- Who commands these retinues? How is hierarchy marked?

4.21 Aesop, *Fables*, 14 Hausrath – Hunger (39 Chambry): Greek Fable Attributed to Aesop

Literature: López Barja de Quiroga 2020.

The fox and the monkey.
 A fox and a monkey were traveling together and started a quarrel over who was better born. Each was going over many arguments. At some point, they arrived at some graves. The monkey looked at the graves and sighed. When the fox asked him why, the monkey showed her the memorials and said, "Shouldn't I cry when I see the stelai of the slaves and freedmen I inherited from my father?" The fox said, "Tell as many lies as you want. For none of these will raise from his grave in order to refute you." In the same way, men who are liars are at their most arrogant when there is no one to refute them.

- Why did the monkey cry at seeing the graves?
- Why does this figure in a contest over good birth? What point is the monkey trying to score with its reaction?
- What does this story suggest about slaves as an instrument of prestige creation?

EXPERTISE

See also 6.27.a, 7.17, 8.28, 10.20, 12.16, and 12.31.

4.22 Seneca, *Letters*, 90.24–5: Latin Moral Philosophy in Epistolary Form (First Century CE)

Seneca reflects upon the views of Posidonius[74] on the contribution of the wise man to technological inventions and the development of various crafts.

---

[74] A late Hellenistic Stoic philosopher; cf. 3.29.

Literature: Rihll 2008.

> They (i.e. technology and arts) were invented by man but not specifically by the wise man. [...] Posidonius says, "It was actually a sage who invented all these things, but as they were too trivial for him to deal with, he assigned them to lowly assistants." This is not so. These things were devised by none other than those who are in charge of them today. We know in fact that some such things were produced within our own memory. For example, the use of windows, which allow the transference of clear light through translucent glass, or vaulted baths and pipes set in the walls, through which heat circulates and the upper and lower parts of the room are kept equally warm. Need I also mention marble, by means of which our temples and houses gleam? Or the rounded and polished masses of stone with which we support colonnades and buildings large enough for crowds of people? Or the shorthand signs, through which even the fastest speech can be taken down, the speed of the hand following that of the tongue? All these things are inventions of the lowliest slaves. Wisdom's seat is loftier: it does not instruct the hand but educates our minds.

- What types of skilled slave labor are mentioned in this passage?
- Are slaves presented as doing only manual labor?
- How does Seneca achieve the trivialization of their contribution?

4.23 Cornelius Nepos, *Atticus*, 13.3–4: Latin Biography (First Century BCE)

Titus Pomponius Atticus was a wealthy Roman of equestrian rank, close friend of Cicero and other powerful Romans of his age. He was a very learned man and occupied himself with business and financial activities, in which he was extremely successful, as well as with literary and philosophical pursuits. See also 4.18.a.

Literature: Forbes 1955; Herrmann-Otto 1994: 288–339.

> He ran a household which was excellent, if the slaves were to be judged by their effectiveness, but barely acceptable, if they were to be judged by their appearance. For the household included extremely learned young slaves, excellent readers, and numerous scribes, so that there was not even an attendant who could not do any of these tasks beautifully. Similarly, the other skilled persons, needed for domestic arrangements, were very good. But none of these had been born or acquired his skills outside the household. This is a sign not only of Atticus' self-control but also of his diligent management.

- What are the main characteristics of Atticus' slaves? How would their skills have been useful to Atticus?
- How do you understand Nepos' emphasis and comments on Atticus' use of slaves born and educated in his house?

4.24 *CIL* XIII, 8355, 9–22: Latin Funerary Verse Inscription, Cologne, Germania Inferior (Fourth Century CE)

This stele also includes, in ll. 1–8, an unfinished epitaph for another young slave: Sidonius, a piper.

Literature: Courtney 1995: 339–40; Fitzgerald 2000: 14–17; Laes 2008: 256–7; cf. Blake 2013.

> This song, this altar, these ashes are the tomb of the slave boy Xanthias, who was snatched away by harsh death. He had already learnt to take down in abbreviation so many letters and words – noting with a hurrying pen what was spoken by a hurrying tongue. Already no one could surpass him in reading; already he had started to be summoned by his master's voice right close to the master's ear, flying along with every dictated word. Alas, he succumbed to hasty death – he who alone would have known his master's secrets.

- What was Xanthias' profession? What skills did he possess?

- Whose voice do we hear in this epitaph? How does this voice present Xanthias? What does this tell us about the master–slave relationship?

- What are the implications of the fact that, if he had lived, Xanthias would have known his master's secrets? How would this affect that master–slave relationship?

MANAGEMENT AND AGENCY

See also 2.9, 2.22, 3.25–6, 5.31, 6.27a, 7.9, 7.43, 12.3, and 12.14.

4.25 *Inscr. It.* X1, 592a–b: Latin Curse Tablet, Pola, Histria (Early Second Century CE)

This curse tablet comes from an area with attested imperial estates in the vicinity. The names and *cognomina* Narcissus, Epaphroditus, Menander, Trophimus, and Hedistus are Greek in origin, and they often indicate slave origins (see 2.8).

Literature: Veyne 1981; Aubert 1994: 136–7; Carlsen 1995: 112–14.

[Mind]ius Narcissus	Vitalis, treasurer
Mindius Maleus	Trophimus, who worked as treasurer
Decidius Hister	
Decidia Certa	Anconius, who worked as manager
Minervius Epaphroditus	Viator, tenant (*colonus*)
Me[nande]r	[Septi]imius (?) Sabinianus
Lu[cifer], treasurer (*dispensator*)	Flavius Hedistus
another Lucifer	Annius Calvo
Amandus, treasurer	Annius Civilis

- Is there a difference in legal status between the people cursed? How can we tell?

- What are the roles assigned to the people with a single name? What context should we imagine for them?

- What do you think is the role of people with double names? How could they be connected to the slaves?

4.26 *Life of Aesop*, Vita G, 9–11:[75] Greek Fictional Biography (First or Second Century CE)

The slave Aesop, who had been unable to speak, has just been granted the ability to speak by the goddess Isis.

Literature: Aubert 1994: 169–99.

Aesop was filled with joy. He then took up his mattock again and started to dig. The overseer of the fields came among the workers and thrashed one of Aesop's coworkers with a stick. Aesop, no longer able to control himself, said, "Hey, you! Why do you beat so bitterly and strike so mercilessly one who has done nothing wrong, while you keep doing wrong every day, without being beaten by anyone?" Zenas, the overseer, said to himself, "What's this? Can Aesop speak?! By the gods! And now that he has started to speak, he attacked no one else but me, the one who talks to him and gives him orders. If I do not concoct something to accuse him of, he is capable of having me removed from my post as manager. For even when he was dumb, he showed me with gestures that 'if my master comes, I will have you removed from the post of manager; I will express my accusations through gestures.' Well, if he threatened to do this with gestures, he will be even more persuasive now that he can speak. It is therefore a good idea to prevent this."

Zenas mounted his horse and started to head fast toward the city. When he arrived at his master's house, he leapt down from the horse. He tied the strap to the ring at the gate, went inside, found his master, and said to him, "My master!"

The master said, "Zenas, why are you upset?"

Zenas said, "Something monstrous has happened on your estate."

The master said, "Might it be that a tree has borne a fruit out of season?"

Zenas said, "No, master."

The master said, "Might it be that a four-footed animal has given birth to a human-like creature, or something like that?"

Zenas said, "No, master."

The master said, "What is it then that you think is monstrous? Tell me the truth."

Zenas said, "That rotten Aesop, the one whom you sent out to the fields to dig, the potbellied one."

The master said, "What? Did he give birth?!"

---

[75]Greek text: Ferrari 1997.

Zenas: "Nothing like that. But he spoke, when he had been dumb before."
The master replied, "Damn you! What? Do you think that this is monstrous?"
Zenas: "Very much so."
The master said, "Why? If the gods got angry with the man and deprived him of his voice for a little while and now they reconciled themselves with him and granted it back to him, do you think this monstrous?"
"Yes, master. For since he started to speak, everything he says exceeds what human nature permits. And he speaks ill of both you and me, uttering slanders and curses that my ears cannot bear hearing. [...]"
The master was shaken and said to Zenas "Go on and sell him."
Zenas said, "Are you kidding, master? Don't you know how ugly he is? Who will wish to buy him and have a dog-faced baboon instead of a man?"
The master said, "So go away and give him to someone as a gift. And if no one wants to take him, beat him to death."
When Zenas received this absolute authority over Aesop, he jumped on his horse again and went to the estate. Zenas said to himself, "My master has given me this absolute power over Aesop: to sell him, give him away, or kill him. What harm has he done to me, that I should kill him? I will sell him." Hence, all the gifts granted to Aesop by the gods kept benefitting him.

- Who is the overseer? What is his status? How is he described?

- What relationships between overseer and slave workers are depicted in this passage?

4.27   *TPSulp.* 45, External Side: Tablet with Contract in Latin, Pompeii, Italy (37 CE)

Literature: Lintott 2002.

In the consulship of Gaius Caesar Germanicus Augustus and Tiberius Claudius Nero Germanicus; on the 6th day before the Nonae of July.
I, Diognetus, slave of Gaius Novus Cypaerus, wrote under the order of my master Cypaerus and in his presence that I have leased to Hesychus, slave of Tiberius Julius Euenus, (who is) freedman of the Emperor, storeroom 12 in the central part of the public Bassian storehouses of the people of Puteoli, in which there has been deposited Alexandrian grain which Hesychus received today from Gaius Novius Eunus as a pledge. Likewise, the space between the columns on the lower part of the same storehouses, where he has deposited 200 sacks of legumes, which he received as a pledge from the same Eunus. From the first day of July, at 1 sesterce every month. Done at Puteoli.

- Who are the contracting parties in this document?

- How many slaves and freedmen appear in this contract?

- In what capacity does Diognetus appear in this contract? What role does he play for his master?

- In what capacity does Hesychus appear in this document?

- Who is the master of Hesychus?

- What economic roles do slaves play in this document? What does this diversity of roles reveal about how the Roman economy operated?

4.28   *TPSulp*. 46, External Side: Tablet with Contract in Latin, Pompeii, Italy (40 CE)

Literature: Lintott 2002; Tran 2013.

> In the consulship of Gaius Laecanius Bassus and Quintus Terentius Culleo. On the third day before the Ides of March.
>   I, Nardus, slave of Publius Annius Seleucus, wrote in the presence of and under the order of my master Publius Annius Seleucus, since he said that he does not know how to write, that I [have leased] to Gaius Suplicius Faustus storeroom 26, which is located in the upper Barbatian properties of Domitia Lepida, in which 13,000 *modii* of Alexandrian grain have been deposited, which my master along with his slaves have measured out. For a fee of 100 sesterces every month. Done at Puteoli.

- In what capacity does Nardus appear in this document? What role does he play for his master? What is his work status?

- Which other slaves appear in this document? What is their work status?

MANAGING A SLAVE PORTFOLIO

4.29   Plutarch, *Life of Crassus*, 2.4–8: Greek Biography (Late First/ Early Second Century CE)

Marcus Licinius Crassus was an important Roman general and politician of the first half of the first century BCE, notorious for his great wealth.

Literature: Forbes 1955.

> In addition, observing those catastrophes which were familiar and endemic to Rome, namely fires and the collapse of buildings, caused by the buildings' size and number, Crassus kept buying slave engineers

and builders. Then, owning more than 500 such slaves, he would buy up those buildings which were on fire, together with their neighboring ones, which their owners would let go for a small price, out of fear and uncertainty. The result was that most of Rome ended up owned by him. Although he had so many craftsmen in his possession, he himself did not build any buildings apart from his own house. Instead, he used to say that those who love building are themselves the cause of their undoing, without any need of rivals. Moreover, although he possessed very many silver mines and extremely valuable rural land together with laborers, yet one would believe that all this was nothing compared with the value of his slaves – so many did he possess and of such ability: readers, secretaries, silver assayers, stewards, table servants. He himself would oversee their training and give his attention to them and instruct them; on the whole, he believed that the management of slaves should very much be the master's concern, since they are the animate tools of household management. And in this Crassus was right, if, as he claimed, he believed that he should govern all the rest through his slaves but govern his slaves by himself. For we can observe that, in relation to inanimate things, household management is economics, but in relation to human beings, household management becomes politics. However, Crassus was not right in the following, namely in refusing to consider or to name as wealthy anyone who was not able to maintain an army from his property.

- To what uses did Crassus put his slaves?
- To what extent was Crassus involved in the management of his slaves? Why?

4.30 Tertullian, *To the Pagans (Ad nationes)*, 1.16.13–19: Christian Apologetic Text in Latin (Late Second/Early Third Century CE)

Tertullian is here arguing for the excess of sexual promiscuity among non-Christians. Along with other evidence, he cites the following event.

Literature: Harper 2013: 100–2.

It was such promiscuity which caused the recent tragedy adjudicated by the city prefect Fuscianus. A young boy of noble origins happened to be neglected by his attendants, he advanced beyond the door and, snatched away by passers-by, left his home. The worthless Greek who had brought him up had from the very beginning corrupted him in the Greek fashion. Afterward, when he came of age, he was brought back to Rome and put on the slave market. His father unknowingly buys him and uses him in the Greek way. From there, as he had relations with the mistress of the household, the master sends the young man to the country and has him chained. The man who looked after him as a boy (*paedagogus*) and his nurse have been in that place for a while, for punishment. The whole case comes back to them. They relate to each other how it had come to this: the man and the nurse that their charge had been lost when still in boyhood; the lad that he, too, had been lost to his boyhood. For the rest, the sequence of events was the same for all; he was born in Rome to a good house; perhaps he also related some signs through which he could be recognized. So, it was by God's will that such a shameful stain has besmirched this world. Their spirit becomes upset about that day; the timing matches the young man's age. Their eyes call to mind something of his features. Some characteristics of his body are being recounted. An earnest effort to make a much-delayed inquiry drives his masters, now clearly his parents. The slave dealer is looked for. Unfortunately, he is found. When the crime is revealed, his parents seek a remedy in the noose. The prefect assigns their goods to their son, who survives wretchedly, not as inheritance but as recompense for outrage (*stuprum*) and incest.

- Which aspects of the slave trade are illustrated by this passage?
- Which slaving strategies are illustrated?
- Does the passage illustrate the precariousness of slave lives? How?
- Why does Tertullian narrate this story? Does his agenda diminish the reliability of his narrative?

4.31 Petronius, *Satyrica*, 53: Latin Novel (First Century CE)

The protagonist in this part of Petronius' parodic novel is Gaius Pompeius Trimalchio Maecenatianus, an extremely wealthy freedman.

Literature: Rose 1967.

A clerk who kept the records (*actuarius*) blatantly interrupted Trimalchio's desire for dance and recited as if reading the city's official records:
"On the 7th day before the Calends of August: On Trimalchio's estate at Cumae, 30 slave boys and 40 girls were born. Taken from the threshing floor to the storehouse: 500,000 *modii* of grain. Tamed oxen: 500.
On the same day: The slave Mithridates was crucified because he spoke ill of the genius of our Gaius.
On the same day: Ten million sesterces were returned to the strongbox, as it was not possible to invest it.
On the same day: There was a fire at the gardens at Pompeii; it started from the house of Nasta, the manager (*vilicus*)".
"What?" asked Trimalchio. "When did I buy gardens at Pompeii?"
"Last year," said the clerk. "This is why they have not yet appeared in the accounts."
Trimalchio flared up: "I forbid that any estates bought on my behalf be entered in my accounts unless I have been informed within six months!"

- What sort of document does Petronius satirize?

- What sort of information is included in this document?

- In what capacities do slaves appear in this document?

- Where precisely can the satirical element be located in Petronius' presentation?

- Can we use this source as evidence for Roman slave management?

4.32 Demosthenes, *Against Aphobos 1*, 9–11: Greek Law-Court Speech, Athens (Mid-Fourth Century BCE)

The speaker here is Demosthenes himself, in a trial against one of his guardians.

Literature: Acton 2014; Porter 2019.

> My father, men of the jury, left two workshops, each doing business on a substantial scale. The one consisted of 32 or 33 knife makers, each worth 5 or 6 minas, or in some cases at least 3 minas; from them he would get an income of 30 minas net per year. The other had 20 couch makers, who were security for a loan of 40 minas and would bring him 12 minas net. He also left about one talent of silver lent out at one drachma, the interest on which would amount to more than 7 minas per year.
>
> All this he left as income-producing assets, as my guardians themselves will admit. Their capital value amounts to 4 talents and 5000 drachmas, while the income they produce is 50 minas per year. Besides those, he left ivory and iron, used as raw material, and wood for the couches, worth about 80 minas; also dye and copper bought for 70 minas. He also left a house worth 3000 drachmas, and furniture, drinking vessels, gold jewelry, and clothes – my mother's trousseau, that is – worth about 10,000 drachmas in total. He also left 80 minas of silver in the house. All this he left at home, but he also left 70 minas in maritime loans, lent out to Xouthos, 2400 drachmas at Pasion's bank, 600 drachmas at that of Pylades, and 1600 drachmas lent out to Demomeles, the son of Demon. He had also lent out a total of about one talent, in various loans of 200 or 300 drachmas each. The capital value of this money amounts to more than eight talents and 50 minas, and, if you check, you will find that the capital value of the whole is about 14 talents.

- What elements does Demosthenes' portfolio consist of?

- How many slaves did Demosthenes' father own?

- What proportion of Demosthenes' wealth was invested in or derived from the slaves?

- How were the slaves employed?

- How do you envisage those workshops functioning? How did the slaves work and where did they live?

4.33   Aeschines, *Against Timarchos*, 97: Greek Law-Court Speech, Athens (Mid-Fourth Century BCE)

On this speech, see 2.7.

Literature: Kamen 2016.

> His father left Timarchos property from which another man would even per-
> form liturgies; this man here, however, did not even manage to preserve it
> for himself. Specifically, a house behind the Acropolis, a piece of marginal
> land at Sphettos, another piece of land at Alopeke; besides, there were slave
> shoe makers, about 9 or 10, each of whom paid in a fee to him (*apophora*) of
> two obols per day, while the manager of the workshop paid in three obols.
> And in addition to those, there was a woman specializing in weaving Amor-
> gos-type garments, who took them to the market, and a man skilled in pat-
> tern weaving. There were also some men who owed him money, and there
> were some furniture and fittings.

- What forms of wealth does the portfolio inherited by Timarchos include?
- How many slaves did Timarchos inherit?
- What were the professions of Timarchos' slaves?
- How do you imagine the shoemaking workshop of Timarchos functioning? How did each slave manage to acquire money for the fee he had to pay in (*apophora*), and how did the manager acquire the money to pay three obols?
- Were the slaves in Timarchos' portfolio exploited in the same way as those in Demosthenes'? What conclusions can we derive from this about the ways owners made money from slaves working at manufacture?

4.34   Diocletian's Price Edict, 31[76] (301 CE)

The edict of emperor Diocletian provided maximum prices for various goods and services. The maximum wage for skilled work was set at 50 denarii a day and half that for unskilled work.

Literature: Scheidel 1996, 2005; Crawford 2010; Harper 2010a; Salway 2010; Groen-Vallinga and Tacoma 2017.

> Concerning the prices of slaves:
>
> A male slave, rural or urban, from 16 to 40 years of age: 30,000 denarii.
> A woman of the aforesaid age: 25,000 denarii.
> Similarly, a man, from 40 to 60 years of age: 25,000 denarii.

---

[76] Latin text: Salway 2010.

> A woman of the aforesaid age: 20,000 denarii.
> A boy or girl from 8 to 16 years of age: 20,000 denarii.
> A male above 60 years of age or less than 8 years of age: 15,000 denarii.
> A female of the aforesaid ages: 10,000 denarii.
>
> For a slave who has been trained in a craft and according to the slave's sex, age, and the type of his or her skills, it shall be proper that the buyer and the seller agree on a price, as long as double the price set for a single one should not be exceeded by any means.

- How many daily wages would it cost an unskilled and a skilled laborer respectively to buy a slave? How cheap were slaves?

- What are the ratios of prices according to gender and age? Do they differ and how?

THE SLAVES' ECONOMY

4.35 Hyperides, *Against Athenogenes*, 6–9:[77] Greek Law-Court Speech, Athens (Second Half of Fourth Century BCE)

Wishing to have sexual access to a slave boy, the speaker, a young Athenian, agrees to arrange for the boy, his brother, and their father Midas to be set free. The three slaves ran a perfume shop for their master Athenogenes. Although the speaker's initial plan was not to buy the slaves for himself – only to supply the money so that their freedom could be obtained – Athenogenes convinced the speaker to buy them off him first. In the following excerpt, the speaker presents Athenogenes' arrangements for the slaves' sale.

Literature: Cohen 2018.

> "However," Athenogenes said, "whatever money Midas and his sons owe – the price of some perfume they owe to Pankalos and to Prokles, and whatever other sum has been paid down for the running of the perfume shop by those frequenting it, as normally happens, you will undertake liability for it. The amounts are quite small and are more than counterbalanced by the stock in the workshop: perfume, scent-boxes, myrrh" – and he went on listing more such words – "from which everything will be easily settled." It was precisely here, it appears, men of the jury, that lay the ruse and the crux of this great fiction. For, if I were to give the money so that they might be freed, I would lose only the money I had given to him but would not suffer any great harm. But if I were to buy them by outright sale (*ônêi kai prasei*),

---

[77]Greek text: Marzi 1977.

having agreed to undertake their debts as if they were of no value – due to my then ignorance – he would afterward set upon me all the creditors and loan contributors, having my agreement in hand. And this is exactly what he did. [...] When this happened, the creditors to whom Midas owed money and the loan contributors approached me and started to negotiate with me. And in three months, all the debts had been declared, and I came to owe, together with the loan contributions, as I said just now, about five talents.

- What is the profession of this family of slaves?
- Why does Athenogenes try to sell them rather than accept money to manumit them?
- How much money had the slaves borrowed?
- Did slaves have the legal right to buy, sell, and borrow?
- What can we learn about the slaves' economy from this passage?

4.36 *P.Oxy.* L, 3597, 1–37: Papyrus with Contract in Greek, Oxyrhynchos, Egypt (ca. 250 CE)

Literature: Cockle 1981; Hengstl 1983; Aubert 1994: 253–5; Mayerson 2000; Schumacher 2001: 122–3; Gallimore 2010.

To Septimius Eudaimon, head of the gymnasium and councillor of the city of the Oxyrhynchians, from Claudianus, his own potter.

I willingly undertake to lease for the present first year your third of the wine jar pottery, including its kilns, chambers, and all equipment, which you own in common with your brothers in your estate near Sennis, for the purpose of making for you 8000 so-called Oxyrhynchite four-*chous* jars, 100 double *keramia*, and 30 two-*chous* jars in the winter production.[78] Your men will provide me at the pottery with black, sandy, and friable earth and all the other necessary material. I shall receive as payment for the making, firing, and coating with pitch of the jars 32 drachmas per 100 jars, that is, a total of 2560 drachmas, 700 of which will be deduced for the dues (*apophora*) I, Claudianus, have to pay to you as my master. I will receive from you the remaining 1860 drachmas as follows: from the current month of Thoth until the month of Tubi, and including the latter, 200 drachmas per month; in Mecheir, 300 drachmas; in Epeiph and Mesore, the remaining 560 drachmas, for stoking. You will also provide me at the pottery with all the fuel necessary for the stoking and for firing the jars, together with the pitch necessary for coating them. You will supervise the coating. You will also supply me continuously all the necessary water for the cistern. In addition to the aforementioned jars, [I shall make] for you 100 more jars, fired and coated

---

[78] Four-*chous* jars had an approximate capacity of 20 liters of wine and double *keramia* 100 liters.

with pitch, and I shall receive two jars of vinegar and one artaba of lentils as extraordinary payment. Upon ratification of this undertaking, I will proceed to the making, firing and coating of the jars, providing myself with potters and every [...]. And I shall hand over the jars in the month of Epeiph on the drying floors of the pottery. They will have been made during the winter production and will be as follows: well fired, coated with pitch from rim to foot, not faulty, well made, without repairs and blemishes. And at the end of the period of the lease, I shall hand over the pottery as regards the part leased to me <clean> from ash and shreds, the right of execution belonging to you as appropriate. The undertaking is valid. I have been asked formally and have given my assent.

- In what ways will Claudianus create revenue for his master?

- Why did Eudaimon lease the pottery to his own slave? What other alternative work relationships between a master and his or her slave can you think? What implications does this have for the slaves' economy?

- How much, of the total of 2560 drachmas payment agreed in this contract, will be Claudianus' payment for his own labor?

- How will Claudianus be able to provide potters for the pottery?

4.37   *Digest*, 15.1.39: Collection of Latin Juristic Texts (Sixth Century CE)

The *peculium* was a Roman legal institution; the male head of household (*paterfamilias*) could set aside various resources and entrust somebody under his authority (including slaves) to use them. The *peculium* functioned as the de facto property of the slave, even though it could be unilaterally revoked by the master.

Literature: Gamauf 2009.

Florentinus, *Institutes*, Book 11: A *peculium* consists of what someone has saved through his frugality or what he has deservingly received from someone for a service he performed, plus what someone's master has wished that his slave kept as his own property (*patrimonium*).

- What were the various sources of the *peculium*?

- What kind of slave activities and relations between slaves and other people are presupposed by the sources of the *peculium*?

4.38 *EAM* 22: Dedicatory Relief with Greek Inscription, Kozani, Macedonia (Second/Third Century CE)

Literature: Roth 2005.

> Chryseros, slave of Philippos, vine dresser, offers this to Zeus Hypsistos as a token of gratitude for the sake of his master. He also sets aside for him (i.e. Zeus Hypsistos) two rows from the vineyards included in his *peculium*.

- What is the profession of this slave?
- What is the reason for his dedication? On behalf of whom does he make it?
- What does he dedicate to Zeus?
- What can we learn from this passage concerning the slaves' economy?

5

Masters and Slaves

Relations between masters and slaves were undoubtedly fundamental to how slave systems operated. In theory, this was a unilateral relationship: masters held all the cards, and slaves had no rights worth speaking of. Masters habitually used violence against their slaves (5.3), even using professionals to torture their slaves (5.4); in most periods and societies, masters faced few obstacles or consequences for inflicting the cruelest punishments on their slaves (5.1). The threat of violence meant slaves were perennially fearful of their masters (5.2). Despite the advantage of force, ruling slaves often proved an intractable problem (5.6). Part of the conundrum was that what masters required was deeply contradictory: slaves who were obedient tools without wills of their own but also able to employ their judgment when necessary for fulfilling their appointed tasks (5.9–10). Given the variety of tasks that slaves performed, violence could prove counterproductive (5.12). Managing human beings and their various needs, even if these were kept to a minimum, had its own requirements (5.11); masters had to try hard to habituate their slaves in the responses they wanted (5.7). Accordingly, most masters usually needed to elicit some goodwill and collaboration from their slaves and reach some kind of accommodation (5.14). Many masters also liked to be seen as benevolent rulers; these factors created openings that slaves could take advantage of (5.5, 5.13). As a result, masters and slaves could opt to see their relationship as one of asymmetrical reciprocity. Masters could reward slaves for their loyal service (5.16–7) and count on such slaves for the most delicate tasks (5.19) or even expect that loyal slaves would put their masters above their fellow slaves (5.18, 5.20).

Given these contradictory tendencies, relations between masters and slaves exhibited a range of outcomes. On the one extreme, violent relationships were common, primarily the brutality of masters but occasionally the violence that slaves were able to inflict on their masters (5.21–2). In many cases, we can see

Greek and Roman Slaveries, First Edition. Eftychia Bathrellou and Kostas Vlassopoulos.
© 2022 John Wiley & Sons, Inc. Published 2022 by John Wiley & Sons, Inc.

exploitation and reward co-existing side by side (5.27). But sex is probably an excellent litmus test for the variety of outcomes: while the casual sexual exploitation of slaves was ubiquitous, in many cases we come across long-standing relationships. These relationships could exhibit all the marks of domination and exploitation (5.24) but also offered slaves opportunities to exert influence over their masters (5.26); they also exhibited the full range of human emotions, like jealousy (5.25). On the other extreme, some slaves could benefit immensely from their close relationship to wealthy and powerful masters. Such slaves and freedmen could become more important than most free persons, gaining honors from cities and communities (5.28, 5.30) and being able to do things that were unthinkable for ordinary slaves or free people (5.29, 5.31).

HIERARCHY AND DOMINATION

5.1 Cassius Dio, *Roman History*, 54.23: Greek Historiography (Third Century CE)

Literature: Syme 1961; Hopkins 1993; Kirbihler 2007; Lenski 2016.

In the same year, Vedius Pollio died. He was a man who in general had done nothing worthy of remembrance. For he had been born to a family of freedmen, belonged to the equestrian order, and achieved nothing brilliant. However, he became most renowned for his wealth and his brutality, and it is for these that he has been given a place in historical accounts. It would be wearisome to relate all the things this man used to do, with one exception. He used to keep in cisterns morays trained to feed on human flesh and to throw in there those slaves of his he wanted to kill. Once, when he was entertaining Augustus, the cup bearer broke a crystal cup; Pollio ordered that he be thrown to the morays, without a modicum of respect for his guest. The slave boy fell before Augustus and supplicated him. Augustus, then, at first tried to persuade Pollio not to do such a thing. But when Pollio did not pay any heed to him, he said, "Bring me all your cups, all those of a similar sort, and any other valuable ones you possess. I want to use them." When they had been brought to him, he ordered that they be smashed. When Pollio saw this, he was vexed. But since he was not angry anymore for the one cup, given the number of all those he had lost, nor was he able to punish his servant for the same thing that Augustus too had done, he kept quiet, though against his will.

- How is Pollio portrayed as a master?

- Are there limits to his power over his slaves?

- How does the slave and Augustus try to change Pollio's decision?

- Did masters in later periods of Roman history have limits on their power? Cf. 1.23.

5.2 Choricius, *Declamations*, 5.60 (= *op.* 20.2.60 Foerster–Richtsteig): Greek Epideictic Oratory (Early Sixth Century CE)

A young man who has excelled in defending his city explains how the enemy's advance and his own devotion to his city expelled any irrelevant thoughts, including those for the girl he desired.

Literature: Harper 2011: 341–2.

> As a fun-loving slave girl talks smart when her mistress is not at home but when the mistress suddenly appears, keeps still, her fear making her control herself, so did my city spring upon my reasoning – like a mistress –, and curbed my desire.

- What does the passage reveal about how slaves behaved in different circumstances?
- Is gender significant for the phenomenon described here?

5.3 Galen, *The Diagnosis and Treatment of the Affections Peculiar to Each Person's Soul (De propriorum animi cuiuslibet affectuum dignotione et curatione)*, 4.7–8, p. 13, 9–18 De Boer[79] (V.17–18 Kühn): Greek Medical Treatise (Late Second/Early Third Century CE)

Galen argues for the need to educate the spirited part of one's soul by giving examples of the problems caused to men when they neglect to do so. Most of his examples are of slave owners not in control of their anger.

Literature: Harris 2001: 317–36; Schlange-Schöningen 2003: 255–90, 2006.

> Others not only throw punches at their slaves but also kick them and gouge their eyes out or stab them with a pen if they happen to have one in hand. I have even known a man who had stricken his slave's eye with a reed pen. Rumor has it that the emperor Hadrian struck the eye of one of his slaves with a pen, and when he learnt that the slave had lost his sight from that eye as a result, summoned him and granted the slave a gift from him in recompense for his eye. The victim kept silent. Hadrian urged him not to be shy and repeated that he should request whatever he wished. The man then requested an eye – nothing else. For what gift could be a true compensation for the loss of an eye?

---

[79] *CMG* V 4,1,1.

- What sort of violent actions against slaves does Galen present?

- The last sentence and the passage's context make it clear that Galen is critical of such actions. Does this show that he does not approve of the use of physical violence against slaves in general?

5.4   *An.Ep.* (1971), No. 88, Col. II, 8–10: Inscribed Regulations in Latin, Puteoli, Italy (Late First Century BCE/Early First Century CE)

The inscription concerns regulations for undertakers, who provided various other services apart from funerals.

Literature: Bodel 2004.

> He who will want to exact punishment on a male or female slave at private expense: as he who will want to exact punishment wishes the punishment to be inflicted, so the contractor will do it. If he wants that the fork-shaped yoke be brought to the cross, the contractor should furnish wooden beams, chains, ropes for the floggers and the floggers. Whoever shall exact punishment should pay four sesterces for each one of those who carry the yoke, for the floggers, and, similarly, for the executioner.

- What details concerning the punishment of slaves does this text provide?

- What are the implications of the fact that the punishment of slaves can be provided as a market service?

- What reasons can you think for masters contracting somebody else to punish their slaves?

5.5   *Philogelos*, 47:[80] Greek Collection of Jokes (Late Antiquity)

Literature: Bradley 1979.

> A *scholastikos*[81] visited his farm after a long time and saw the livestock being put out to graze. When he saw them bleating in their usual way, he enquired why. The steward wanted to tease him and said, "They are greeting you." And he responded, "Bless your heart – and mine! Do give them a holiday for my sake and don't take them out to pasture for three days."

---

[80] Greek text: Thierfelder 1968.
[81] Literally a man with time in his hands, who devotes his leisure to learning. In the collection, where the *scholastikos* is the butt of many jokes, he is presented as a learned fool, whose pedanticism makes him miss what is obvious to common sense.

- What is the point of the joke? On what improper analogy is it based?
- What is the point of the greeting of the animals to the master?
- Why does the master grant them a holiday?
- How does this attitude relate to other attitudes to slaves seen above?
- Can we learn anything about the relationship between slaves and masters from this text?

RULING SLAVES: THE PROBLEM, THE CARROT, AND THE STICK

5.6 Plato, *Laws*, 777b–778a: Greek Philosophical Dialogue (Fourth Century BCE)

Literature: Klees 1975: 142–81; Garlan 1988: 119–200.

Because man is an intractable creature, it is clear that in relation to the necessary distinction, too, that is the distinction in practice between a slave and a free person and master, it looks as if he is not likely to be or become manageable in any way; as a consequence, he is a difficult possession to handle. And this has been historically demonstrated many times: in relation to the frequent revolts of the Messenians; also, in relation to those cities which own many slaves of the same tongue – how much wrong-doing takes place there; or, also, in relation to the deeds of all sorts and the experiences of those called "rovers" (*peridinoi*) – those thieves found on the Italian coast.

If one looks at all these examples, he will be at a loss as to how to act in relation to all such things. So, we are left with only two devices. First, those who are to tolerate better being slaves should not be of the same land nor speak the same language, as much as is possible. Second, we should treat slaves properly, not only for their sake but, rather, for our own good. Proper treatment involves abstaining from any outrageous behavior toward slaves and, if possible, taking greater care to avoid wronging them than we do toward our equals. For the man who respects justice genuinely and not hypocritically and truly hates what is wrong is to be seen most clearly in his treatment of people whom he could easily wrong. The man who, in his dispositions and actions toward slaves, manages to remain untainted by what is unholy and wrong would be most capable of generating the growth of virtue. And one could say the same thing – and rightly so – in relation not only to masters but also to tyrants and to anyone who possesses any kind of power over someone weaker.

It is certainly necessary to punish slaves justly and not to admonish them as if they were free men and thus make them conceited. Any address to slaves should have the form of what nearly amounts to a command. Never should one joke with slaves, whether male or female ones. Many masters tend to behave in such a manner toward their slaves, which is extremely foolish; by making slaves conceited, they tend to make life more difficult, both for the slaves as objects of rule and for themselves as rulers.

- What is the cause of the fact that slaves are difficult to rule?

- Which are the two remedies proposed?

- Why is it important that the slaves are not ethnically homogeneous?

- How should one treat his slaves according to the passage?

- Why does it advise against undeservingly harsh and humiliating treatment of slaves?

5.7 Plutarch, *Life of Marcus Cato*, 21.1–4: Greek Biography (Late First/Early Second Century CE)

The subject of this biography, known as Cato the Censor or Cato the Elder, was a Roman politician and writer, influential in the first half of the second century BCE.

Literature: Astin 1978: 240–66; Bradley 1984: 146–7.

Cato had many slaves in his possession. He used to buy captives, particularly very young ones, who were still capable of being reared and trained like puppies or foals. None of these entered another house, unless under the order of Cato himself or his wife. If a slave was asked about Cato's whereabouts, he would always respond that he had no idea. Slaves were obliged either to be doing their duties in the house or to be asleep. Cato was very pleased with slaves who were prone to sleep. He believed that such slaves were calmer than the wakeful ones and that those who had slept well were better at their tasks than those in need of sleep. Since he thought that the gravest acts of mischief committed by slaves were motivated by sexual desire, he stipulated that his male slaves could have sex with female slaves for a specified sum but were not allowed to approach any other woman. Early in life, when still poor and in military service, he was extremely easygoing in relation to food and considered it most disgraceful to quarrel with a slave because of the demands of the belly. Later, when his situation was improving and he entertained his friends and fellow leaders, he used to whip after dinner slaves who had shown carelessness in serving or preparing dinner. He was always contriving that there would be factions and disagreements among his slaves and was suspicious of and feared their concord. He demanded that those who appeared to have committed a deed deserving death be tried before all the slaves and, if convicted, be killed.

- How did Cato choose his slaves? Why?

- What kinds of behavior did Cato encourage among his slaves? Why?

- What kind of master was Cato, according to the passage?

5.8   Galen, *The Doctrines of Hippocrates and Plato (De placitis Hippocratis et Platonis)*, VI.8.82, pp. 424,33–426,3 De Lacy[82] (V.584 Kühn): Greek Medical Treatise (Late Second/Early Third Century CE)

Literature: Schlange-Schöningen 2003: 255–90, 2006; Hunt 2016; Lenski 2016.

> Even today this is what is habitually done by those who pass judgement on slaves who commit wrongs: they burn, cut, and beat the legs of the slaves who run away; the hands of those who steal; the bellies of gluttons; the tongues of chatterers. To put it simply, they punish the members with which the slaves commit their wicked acts.

- What slave actions are presented as customarily receiving punishment? Do you find Galen's list surprising?

- What sort of punishments does he describe?

5.9   *Life of Aesop*, Vita G, 38:[83] Greek Fictional Biography (First or Second Century CE)

In this passage, whose beginning has not survived, Aesop's master, the philosopher Xanthos, commands Aesop to follow his orders to the letter.

Literature: Hopkins 1993: 10–21.

> [...] "Pick up an oil flask and towels and let's go to the bath."
>   Aesop said to himself, "Masters who are harsh in their demands for service are themselves the cause of their troubles. I will give a lesson to this philosopher, so that he might learn how he should give orders."
>   So, Aesop picked up the stuff mentioned above and, without putting oil in the flask, followed Xanthos to the bath. Xanthos took off his clothes, gave them to Aesop, and told him, "Give me the oil flask."
>   Aesop gave it to him. Xanthos took the flask, found it empty when he tried to pour oil, and said, "Aesop, where is the oil?"
>   Aesop said, "At home."
>   Xanthos asked, "What for?"
>   Aesop responded, "Because you told me 'Pick up an oil flask and towels'; you didn't mention oil. And I was supposed to do nothing more than what I was told. For if I didn't obey this instruction, I would be liable to a beating."
>   Then he kept silent.

---

[82] *CMG* V 4,1,2.
[83] Greek text: Ferrari 1997.

- What order does Xanthos give? Why?

- How does Aesop subvert his master's wishes?

- How does this story relate to 5.10?

- How does this story illustrate an inherent contradiction of slavery?

5.10 Ps.-Lucian, *The Ass*, 42: Greek Novel (Second Century CE?)

Lucius, the narrator and protagonist of this story, is a man transformed into an ass (cf. also 4.7, from a Latin novel, which probably had a common source with this Greek work). At this point in his story, Lucius' owners have been arrested for theft, and the ass, together with the rest of their belongings, is being put up for sale.

Literature: Bradley 2012: 59–78.

The following day, they decided to put my masters' stuff and myself on sale and sold me to a stranger, who lived in the neighboring town and was a baker by trade. He took me, bought 10 medimnoi of wheat, loaded me with it, and drove me back to his town and home on an exhausting journey. When we arrived, he took me to the mill, and there I saw a great number of animals – my fellow slaves; there were also many mill stones, all being turned by the animals, and everything there was full of flour. And on that day, since I was a slave from elsewhere, who had carried a very heavy load and come on an exhausting journey, they let me rest inside; but the following day, they spread a cloth and blindfolded me with it and then harnessed me to the beam of the mill stone and tried to drive me on. On my part, although I knew how to grind, as I had had to do it many times, I pretended not to know. But I had hoped in vain. For many of the men there took up sticks, stood around me, and unexpectedly – since I could not see them – beat me with all their strength. So, all of a sudden, I started to spin like a top from their blows. Thus, I learnt by experience that a slave should do his duty without waiting for his master's hand.

- What happens to Lucius in the milling establishment?

- Why does he compare his experience to slavery? Cf. 4.7.

- What strategy does Lucius initially employ toward his tasks? Does it prove successful?

- What conclusion does Lucius draw about how slaves should behave?

- How does Lucius' attitude compare to that of Aesop in 5.9?

- How did the masters react in each case? Which reaction do you consider more likely to have happened on a regular basis?

- Was violence a successful method under all circumstances to make slaves proactive?

5.11   Libanius, *Orations*, 25.66–7: Greek Epideictic Oratory (Fourth Century CE)

In this work, Libanius argues that no human being is truly free.

Menander, the son of Diopeithes, displayed his good sense (and the fact that he had hence been a slave to his own slaves on a great many occasions) when he said the following, "A house has one slave: its master."[84] For how to keep a slave in both good and bad times is truly a cause of much anxiety. The slave needs only to look at his master's hands, but the master has to stretch his hand forth. And one cannot justify oneself to one's slave by blaming the time of year, or Zeus' anger, or the lack of wind or anything that affects harvests. To the slave the earth bears fruit, even when it doesn't; clothes are weaved, and shoes are made for him while he sleeps. Slaves get married having had to make no plans at all: it is the master's job to provide, the slave's to be strong in bed. When a slave is ill, he has one source of anxiety, his illness; it is someone else who will take care of medicines, doctors, and incantations. When he is dying, he has no fear for his burial. He has someone to bury him: his so-called master but really his slave.

- On what grounds does Libanius endorse the presentation of the master of the household as a slave?
- How credible is this presentation?
- Why is the slave described as carefree? Cf. 10.18.
- Compared with the life of the free poor, do you think slaves lived in better material conditions?
- How credible do you find this description of the master-slave relationship?

5.12   Seneca, *Letters*, 47.2–4: Latin Moral Philosophy in Epistolary Form (First Century CE)

On this letter, see also see also 4.8, 10.22, and 11.16.

Literature: Bradley 2008.

For this reason, I find laughable those who think it shameful to have dinner together with their slaves. Why do they think thus? Only because an extremely arrogant tradition has the master surrounded at dinner by a crowd of standing slaves. He eats more than he can hold, and with immense greed, he loads his belly to the point of swelling and forgetting how to do the work of a belly. As a result, it is a harder task to empty his body than it was to fill

---

[84] Menander, the Athenian comic poet: fragment 506 K-A.

it. The unhappy slaves are not allowed to move their lips, even in order to speak. Every whisper is repressed by the rod; not even chance sounds are exempt from the whip: a cough, a sneeze, a hiccup. A big punishment follows every time a word breaks the silence; they stand about the whole night, mute and hungry. So it happens that those who are not allowed to speak in front of their master make him the topic of conversation. But those who were allowed to speak not only in front of their masters but also with the masters themselves, those whose lips were not sewn together, were ready to stick their necks out for their masters, to turn dangers threatening him onto their own heads. They would speak at banquets but would keep silent when tortured.

- What practices of Roman slaveholders does Seneca condemn?
- What do Roman masters try to achieve by adopting such practices?
- How do such practices affect slaves?
- What is Seneca's recommendation?
- How does this passage illuminate the master–slave dialectic?

5.13   Pliny the Younger, *Letters*, 8.16: Latin Epistolography (Late First/Early Second Century CE)

Pliny is writing to one of his friends. Roman slaves were not legally allowed to own, or bequeath, property.

Literature: Gonzales 2003; Roth 2005.

I have been overwhelmed by the illnesses and deaths of my people – some of them quite young, in fact. Two things console me – consolations by no means equal to the intensity of the pain but consolations nonetheless. First, my readiness to manumit them: those whom I lost when they were already free men I seem not to have lost entirely prematurely; second, that I allow my slaves too to make a sort of will, which I guard as legitimate. They give instructions and make requests as they see fit; I comply as if I had received orders. They can divide, donate, bequeath – in so far as it is inside the household (*domus*), since for slaves the household is a sort of republic, almost like a citizen community (*civitas*). Yet, although I find comfort in these consolations, I am enfeebled and broken by that very humanity which led me to make this concession. But I would not like to become harsher on account of this. Nor am I unaware of the fact that others call occurrences of this kind as nothing other than financial loss and besides see themselves as great and wise human beings. Whether they are great and wise I don't know, but human they are not. For it is part of being human to feel affected by pain but resist it and admit consolation – not to have no need of consolation.

- To whom does Pliny refer as "my people"? How does Pliny react to their death and illness?

- What privileges does Pliny allow his slaves?

- What can we learn from this passage about slave community?

- How do other masters react to slave illness and death?

- Why does Pliny react in a different way? How does he justify his attitude?

- What kind of text is this? What motives might Pliny have to present himself in this way?

5.14   Varro, *On Agriculture*, 1.17.5–7:[85] Latin Agricultural Treatise (First Century BCE)

Literature: Martin 1971; Roth 2005.

One should not acquire slaves of many different nations; this tends to become a principal cause of quarreling in the household. Foremen (*praefecti*) are to be made more eager through rewards, and efforts should be made so that they might have a *peculium*[86] and female companions among their fellow slaves, who might bear them children. Thus, they will become more faithful, with stronger bonds to the estate (*fundus*). It is because of such kinships that slave groups (*familiae*) from Epeiros are highly regarded and of quite large financial value. The goodwill of the foremen should be elicited by some honor being bestowed upon them. The better workers should be consulted as to what work needs to be done, since, when this happens, they do not think that they are looked down upon but rather that they are held in some esteem by the master. They become more devoted to work by being treated in a manner more befitting to free persons, either by more generous food or clothing provisions, by exemption from work, by permission to pasture some livestock of their own on the estate, or by other things of this kind. The result will be that those who have been ordered to do a rather heavy task or have received punishment will find consolation in such things, and their goodwill and positive disposition toward their master will be restored.

- How should masters treat slave foremen?

- Why should masters elicit the goodwill of their agricultural slaves?

- What do you think about the use of the word "honor" in regard to slaves?

- What psychological principle are the masters trying to take advantage of? Do you think this could have worked?

- Would the slaves have interpreted such preferential treatment in the same way as the masters?

---

[85] Latin text: Traglia 1974.
[86] See 4.37.

- What do you think would be the results of allowing slaves to form families or have livestock of their own?

- How does treatment of slaves here differ from that evident in passage 5.12? How would you explain the difference?

RECIPROCITY: LOYALTY, REWARDS, AND OBLIGATIONS

5.15   *Gospel of Luke*, 17.7–10: Greek Biblical Text
(First Century CE)

Literature: Glancy 2000, 2002a: 42–5.

> Jesus said to his pupils, [...] "Which of you, if you own a slave who ploughs the land or tends the flocks, will say to him when he returns from the field: 'Go in and have your dinner immediately', instead of 'Prepare me some dinner, get ready and wait on me until I eat and drink; afterwards you too may eat and drink?' Surely this man won't be thankful to his slave for doing what he was told, will he? So likewise, after you have done all you have been ordered to do, you too should say: 'We are worthless slaves; we have done what we ought to do.'"

- How does Jesus portray the life of a slave? What tasks does the slave perform?

- What does this imply about the employment of slaves?

- Why does Jesus tell this to his pupils? What point is the comparison between his pupils and slaves aiming to drive?

- What conception of slavery does the comparison presuppose? How does it differ from other conceptions of slavery we have examined? Cf. 1.27–30.

5.16   Plautus, *Little Carthaginian*, 129–34, 139–40:
Latin Comedy (Second Century BCE)

Agorastocles, a wealthy young man, tries to coax his slave Milphio to help him to get a girl he is in love with.

Literature: Zelnick-Abramovitz 2005: 39–60; Stewart 2012: 117–55; Giannella 2019.

> **Agorastocles**: Often have I assigned to you, Milphio, many affairs, uncertain affairs, needy ones, affairs helplessly needing counsel, which you, with your wisdom, knowledge, prudence, and sagacity, returned to me in a state of splendor, through your efforts. For these benefactions, I admit that you are owed both your freedom and much grateful gratitude.
> **Milphio**: [...] Now you are flattering me. Yesterday you destroyed three ox hides on my back no problem.

- Why does the master owe gratitude to Milphio?
- How will the master reciprocate these benefactions?
- What model of master–slave relationships does this passage illustrate?
- Are you surprised by slavery been approached from such a perspective?
- How does this passage compare with 5.15?

5.17 *I.Sultan Daği* 11: Greek Funerary Inscription, Sultan Daği, Phrygia (Third Century CE)

"Zeal" and "good will" are attributes usually applied to benefactors in honorific inscriptions.

> Aurelius Leukis, son of Zosimos, erected (this) for his slave Basilike, in her memory, because he was served by her with great zeal and goodwill.

- For whom is this epitaph?
- Who has erected this epitaph? How does he explain his action?
- How does this inscription illuminate the master–slave relationship?

5.18 Aesop, *Fables*, 209 Hausrath – Hunger (282 Chambry): Greek Fable Attributed to Aesop

> The bird hunter and the wild and tame pigeons.
> A bird hunter had spread out his hunting nets and bound some tame pigeons on them. Then he left and stood by waiting to see from afar what would happen. When some wild pigeons came and got entangled in the snares, he ran and tried to catch them. When the wild pigeons were throwing accusations at the tame ones, why didn't they, being of the same stock as them, warn them of the snare, they responded, "In our position, it's better to show precaution in relation to our masters than to do a favor to our relatives." In the same way, slaves should not be blamed for failing their relatives' love because of their regard for their masters.

- What is the complaint of the wild pigeons?
- How do the tame pigeons respond?
- How does this passage conceptualize the master–slave relationship?
- How reliable is this passage for understanding how slaves thought about other slaves?

5.19 Plutarch, *Life of Aratos*, 5.3–6.2: Greek Biography (Late First/Second Century CE)

Aratos of Sikyon, a city in the northern Peloponnese, was a prominent third-century BCE general and politician. As a child and young man, he was an exile. Here, Aratos, still in exile, in the city of Argos, is preparing, together with some other exiles, to invade Sikyon to depose its then ruler, the tyrant Nikokles.

When Aratos was considering seizing some outpost in the Sikyonian land, which he could use as a base in his war against the tyrant, a Sikyonian who had escaped from prison arrived at Argos. He was the brother of Xenokles, one of the exiles. Xenokles brought him to Aratos. He was saying that the inner part of the wall where he climbed over to safety was almost level with the ground, as the terrain was rocky and high at that point, while the wall's outer height was not impossible to master if ladders were used. When Aratos heard this, he sent off two of his own slaves, Seuthas and Technon, together with Xenokles, to reconnoiter the wall. He had resolved to hazard everything in one throw, if he could, secretly and swiftly, rather than end up with a situation where a man with no official political power opposes a tyrant through prolonged warfare and open confrontation. When Xenokles' party returned with measurements of the wall and information that the area was not impassable or difficult, but it would be far from easy to remain undetected once they had got there, because of the dogs of a gardener, which were small but extremely fierce and impossible to silence, he immediately started to work on the plot. [...] As for men, each of Aratos' friends at Argos provided him with 10 † of the few they had, while Aratos himself gave weapons to 30 of his own slaves.

- With what tasks did Aratos entrust his slaves?
- What sort of master–slave relationship does this presuppose?

5.20 *PSI* VI, 667: Papyrus with Letter in Greek, Philadelphia, Egypt (Third Century BCE)

The beginning of this latter has not survived.

Literature: Scholl 1990: no. 73.

[...] I have exhausted myself gathering and carrying wood, and I do not wish to leave from you like the other slave girls, who leave their masters when wronged. I know your ways, namely that you detest wickedness, and I am hence not doing it. Farewell.

- Why did the writer of this letter choose not to flee?

- Why do you think she has written this letter to her master?

CONTRADICTORY RELATIONSHIPS: SLAVERY AND HUMAN INTERACTIONS

5.21   *I.Amyzon 65*: Greek Funerary Verse Inscription, Amyzon, Karia (Second Century BCE)

The inscription is written in elegiac meter and in elevated language.

Literature: Llewelyn 1997: 1–3; Chaniotis 2017.

> Demetrios, son of Pankrates
>
> Demetrios, lamented by all, held by sweet sleep and the nectarous drink of Dionysus. "Slaughtered at the hands of a slave and burnt in a great conflagration together with my halls, I came to Hades, while my father, brothers, and elderly mother received into their bosoms bones and ashes. But my fellow citizens hanged for my sake the one who did this to me; they suspended him alive, a boon to beasts and birds."

- Who killed Demetrios? What circumstances did the killer exploit?

- Who undertook the killer's punishment? Why?

- How was the killer punished? How did punishment relate to crime?

- What kind of text is this? Why are so many details concerning the murder of the deceased mentioned?

5.22   Pliny the Younger, *Letters*, 3.14: Latin Epistolography (First Century CE)

Literature: K. F. Williams 2006; McKeown 2007.

> To an atrocity deserving much more than one letter did his slaves subject the praetorian Larcius Macedo: an arrogant and savage master, who remembered too little – or, rather, too much – that his own father had been a slave. He was taking his bath in his villa at Formiae. Suddenly, he finds himself surrounded by slaves. One takes him by the throat; another strikes him on the face; another on his chest and his stomach, and even – disgusting to relate – batters his private parts. And when they thought that he was lifeless, they threw him down on the hot floor to test whether he was alive. Either because he was unconscious or because he pretended to be so, his body, lying still and outstretched, filled them with confidence that death had occurred. Then, he is taken away, as if paralyzed by heat. His more faithful slaves receive him;

his concubines run to him wailing and shrieking. Thus aroused by the voices and revived by the coolness of the place, he shows he is alive by holding his eyes open and moving his limbs. – Also, by that point it had become safe to do so. – The slaves scatter. Most of them have been arrested; the rest are being sought. The man himself was revived with great difficulty, and then, after a few days, died but not without the consolation of revenge: he was avenged when still alive as murdered men usually are.

You see to how many dangers, to how much abuse, to how many insults we are susceptible. No one can feel secure because he is lenient and gentle, for masters are murdered not through rational judgement but through villainy. But so much for this. What new besides? What? Nothing; otherwise, I would append it: for there is still more space on the page and the holiday permits me to compose more. I will add something in relation to the same Macedo that aptly occurred to me. When he was bathing at the public baths at Rome, something noteworthy and, as his death showed, ominous too took place. A slave of Macedo urged a Roman of equestrian rank to give way by lightly touching him with his hand. He then turned and hit with the palm of his hand not the slave who had touched him but Macedo himself. He hit him so hard that he almost fell down. Thus, the baths were for Macedo the place first of insult and then, in a sort of progression, of death. Farewell.

- What kind of master is Larcius Macedo portrayed as?
- Did all of his slaves behave in the same way? What can this tell us about slave communities?
- How does Pliny explain the actions of the slaves? What conclusion should masters derive from such an event, according to him?
- What stories does Pliny tell about Macedo's past? Why does he provide these details? What aims do they serve?

5.23 *SEG* L 1065: Curse Tablet in Greek, Rome (First–Third Century CE)

The magic words which begin this curse appear in magic books used by specialists, as well as in other curse tablets. Poleitoria is a woman's name.

Literature: Alvar Nuño 2016.

Side A: *Four lines with magical characters are followed by the following text*: Fanchoibikux Petriadê Kratarnadê. Lord messengers, take possession of Claudia Valeria Sophrone and do not allow her to have Poleitoria.

Side B: Arthulailam Semesilam Bachuch Vachaxichuch Menevaichuch Abrasax. Lord gods, take possession of Claudia Valeria Sophrone, who manages the estate prison (*ergastulum*). Let her not take Poleitoria to the prison, to have Poleitoria experience a living death.

- Which persons are mentioned in this curse? What is their relationship?
- What was at stake? What motivated this curse?
- Who might have created this curse tablet?

5.24 Antiphon, *Against the Stepmother*, 14–20:[87] Greek Law-Court Speech, Athens (Late Fifth Century BCE)

The speaker accuses his father's wife, who was his own stepmother and mother of his opponent and half-brother, of having poisoned their father with the help of another woman.

Literature: Bushala 1969; Cohen 2013.

Our house had an upstairs room which was used by Philoneos – a fine man and a friend of our father – every time he spent time in the city. Philoneos had a concubine, whom he was thinking to place in a brothel. The mother of my brother became a friend of this woman. When she perceived that Philoneos was meaning to wrong the woman, she sent for her, and when she came, she told her that she too was being wronged by our father. If that woman was happy to consent, she said she was capable of making both Philoneos love her and my father love herself, mentioning that the plan would be her own, but its execution would lie with that woman. So, she asked her whether she wished to help her; the woman immediately, I believe, promised she would. Sometime later, it so happened that Philoneos had an offering to make to Zeus Ktesios in the Piraeus, and my father was about to sail to Naxos. So Philoneos thought it an excellent idea to both see off my father to the Piraeus, as he was his friend, and, on the same trip, to make the sacrifice and share the sacrificial meal with my father. Philoneos' concubine went with them, because of the sacrifice. When they arrived in the Piraeus, he made the sacrifice, as was expected. Once the sacrifice had taken place, then the woman started to deliberate how she should give them the poison, before dinner or afterward. Upon deliberation, she thought it best to give it after dinner, attending to the counsels of this Klytaimnestra here. [...] After they finished dinner, the two men started to offer libations and burnt frankincense for their safety, as was the custom: the host, because he was offering a sacrifice to Zeus Ktesios, the guest, because he was dining at his companion's and was about to set sail. Philoneos' concubine, pouring the libation precisely while they were praying for things that were not to be fulfilled, poured in the poison. And thinking she was being clever, she gave more to Philoneos, perhaps with the view that the more she gave the more she would be loved by him. For she realized she was being deceived by my stepmother only after evil was already on the way. To our father she poured

---

[87] Greek text: Gernet 1923.

less. And the men, after they finished their libations, held in their hands their own murderer and drank it up – their last drink. Philoneos died immediately; our father fell ill and died 20 days later from the illness. For this, the one who helped and executed has had the just deserts of her actions, although she was not responsible: she was tortured on the wheel and given over to the public executor; but the one who is responsible and conceived of this will have her just deserts if you and the gods will it.

- What was the original relationship between Philoneos and the woman who poured the drug?
- What was the woman's status? Can we determine it?
- What was Philoneos planning to do with this woman? How are his plans described?
- How did the woman attempt to change Philoneos' mind?
- Who helped her and why? What was the other woman's status? Did the two women undertake equal risks? Was their relationship on equal terms?
- How was the woman punished?
- What does this story tell us about master–slave relationships?

5.25 Appian, *Civil Wars*, 4.4.24: Greek Historiography (Second Century CE)

Fulvius was among those proscribed by Octavian, Mark Antony, and Lepidus in 43 BCE.

Literature: Perry 2013.

Fulvius ran away to a female slave of his who had been his concubine, had been manumitted by him, and, in addition, had received a dowry for her marriage. But although she had received so many benefactions, she betrayed him out of jealousy for the woman Fulvius had married after her.

- How did Fulvius treat his former slave?
- How typical was Fulvius' relationship with his freedwoman?
- What motive does Appian attribute to the freedwoman's betrayal?
- How does this story illuminate the master–slave relationship?
- Do you believe Appian's explanation for the slave's betrayal? What other motives can you think of?

5.26 Hyperides, *Against Athenogenes*, 24 and 4–6:[88] Greek Law-Court Speech, Athens (Second Half of Fourth Century BCE)

On this speech, see the introduction to 4.35.

Literature: Cohen 2013; Glazebrook 2014.

> 24: You have to hear what happened. For it will be shown as consistent with the rest of their scheme. Athenogenes kept sending to me the boy, whom I mentioned just now, and the boy used to say that he would not stay with me unless I secured the freedom of his father and brother.
>
> 4–6: In the end, to cut the story short, Antigone[89] later asked me to come and see her once more, and told me that, after a long and hard conversation with Athenogenes, she had just about persuaded him to release for me Midas and his two sons for 40 minas. She kept urging me to produce the money as soon as possible, before Athenogenes changed his mind. So, I collected it from every possible source, including becoming a nuisance to my friends, and I went to Antigone after depositing 40 minas in the bank. She had us meet, Athenogenes and myself, that is; she reconciled us and urged us to treat each other well in the future. I consented to this; Athenogenes took over and said that for what had been achieved I should be grateful to Antigone. "And now," he continued, "it is for her sake that I will show you right away how much I shall do for your benefit. You are about to pay out the money," he continued, "for the freedom of Midas and his sons. I, however, will sell them to you by outright sale. Thus, first of all, no one will give you trouble or try to seduce the boy; second, they themselves will not try any misconduct out of fear; and, most important: under the present arrangement, they could think they owe their freedom to me; but if you buy them by outright sale and afterwards, later, whenever you see fit, you set them free, they will be doubly grateful to you."

- How does the young slave react to the speaker's love interest? How does he try to turn the situation to his advantage?

- What is the motive of the speaker in buying the three slaves?

- How important is the slave family, as illustrated in this passage?

- What argument does Athenogenes use to convince the speaker to buy the slaves himself? Are you surprised by the argument? What does it imply about the relationship between masters and slaves?

---

[88] Greek text: Marzi 1977.
[89] A sex worker facilitating the negotiations between the speaker and Athenogenes.

5.27 *FD* III 6.39–40: Greek Manumission Inscription, Delphi, Phokis (First Century ᴄᴇ)

Literature: Hopkins 1978: 133–71.

6.39 In the archonship of Aristokles son of Philonikos, in the month of Herakleios, when Euangelos son of Megartas and Eukleidas son of Sotas were members of the Council, Aristion son of Eukleidas and Eisias daughter of Kleomantis, with the approval of her son Kleomantis, sold to Apollo Pythios a young female body, whose name is Sostrata, for the price of 300 silver drachmas, and we have received the whole amount. […]

The terms are as follows: Sostrata shall remain with Aristion and Eisias for the whole of their lifetime, giving no reason for reproach and doing everything she is ordered to do. If Sostrata does not do all that she is ordered to do, Aristion and Eisias shall have authority to punish her in any manner they might wish. Whatever children Sostrata might give birth to during the time she remains with Aristion and Eisias shall become free after they have remained with us, except if Aristion and Eisias wish to sell a child as a means against poverty. And Sostrata shall give to Kleomantis a two-year-old baby, and she shall be free, as she entrusted the purchase money to the god, so that she might be free and not liable to seizure by anyone for all time. […]

6.40 In the archonship of Pason, son of Damon, in the month of Ilaios, Aristion and Eisias freed Sostrata from her obligation to remain with them. If something happens to Aristion, Kleomantis and Sostrata shall perform the burial rites and then shall divide what he has left in equal shares among themselves.

- Under what conditions is this slave manumitted?
- What does the obligation of the slave to surrender a baby to the master's son tell us about master–slave relationships?
- How does document 6.40 modify the terms of the original manumission?
- In what ways does Sostrata benefit from the new terms?
- What contradictory aspects of the master–slave relationship are evident in this document?

THE PREPONDERANCE OF THE MASTER–SLAVE RELATIONSHIP OVER OTHER DISTINCTIONS

5.28 Plutarch, *Life of Cato the Younger*, 13: Greek Biography (Late First/Second Century ᴄᴇ)

Cato the Younger (95–46 ʙᴄᴇ) and Pompey (106–48 ʙᴄᴇ) were prominent Roman statesmen of the late Republic. Pompey had conquered Syria and established a new Roman province in the area, thus wielding enormous influence with local communities such as Antioch. By the time of this incident, Demetrios of Gadara was a freedman of Pompey.

Literature: Treggiari 1969; Bellemore 1995.

It is said that, while in Syria, something ridiculous happened to Cato. When he was walking into Antioch, he saw outside, by the city gates, a large crowd of people drawn up on either side of the road. Among them, ephebes with military cloaks and boys had decorously positioned themselves in two separate groups, while some men, priests or magistrates, bore bright garments and garlands. Cato thought it most likely that the city was offering him a reception to honor him and started to get angry at those of his men who had been sent in advance for not having prevented the event. He asked his friends to dismount and started to proceed with them on foot. When they arrived close, the man who was arranging all this and marshaling the crowd, a man already advanced in years, holding a staff in his hand and a garland, advanced and met Cato before the others and, without even greeting him, kept asking where they had left Demetrios and when he would appear. Demetrios had been a slave of Pompey. At that time, the whole world, so to speak, looked to Pompey, so court was paid to Demetrios excessively, as he had great influence with Pompey. Laughter seized Cato's friends, so much so that they were not able to control themselves while walking amidst the crowd. Cato at the time was taken aback and said, "Ah, the cursed city!" and didn't utter another word. But later he, too, used to laugh at this incident, both when he was telling the story and when he would call it to mind.

- What was Cato's expectation when he saw the crowd?
- Whom did the Antiocheans gather to honor instead? Why?
- What can this passage tell us about slavery and power in the late republic?

5.29 *Acts of Peter*, 14:[90] **Christian Apocryphal Text in Latin (Late Fourth Century CE?)**

The Roman senator Marcellus, a very wealthy man who had become a Christian and used to be most generous toward those in need, comes under the influence of Simon Magus. As a result, Marcellus stops supporting the Christian poor. They ask the Apostle Peter to intervene, and he gradually exposes Simon.

Literature: MacMullen 1986; Collon 2012; Lenski 2016: 290–2; cf. Keenan, Manning and Yiftach-Firanko 2014: 508–16.

Marcellus was becoming firmer day by day, through the signs he kept seeing performed by Peter through the grace of Jesus Christ, which He had bestowed

[90] Latin text: Döhler 2018.

on him. And Marcellus attacked Simon, who was in Marcellus' house, sitting in the *triclinium*. He cursed him and said to him: "Oh you greatest enemy and defiler of men, corruptor of my soul and my household, wishing that I flee away from Christ, my lord (*dominus*) and savior." And taking hold of him, he ordered that he be thrown out of his house. The slaves, having been given the power to do so, threw insults at him. Some would box his head, others hit him with sticks, others threw stones, other emptied chamber pots over his head – slaves who had abandoned their master (*dominus*) because of Simon and had been in chains for a long time. Others, fellow slaves, of whom he used to speak badly to their master, taunted him thus: "Now we have repaid you your just deserts, by the will of God, who has taken pity on us and on our master."

- What does Marcellus order his slaves to do?
- Are you surprised that slaves beat up severely a free person without fear?
- How should we explain this?
- Did slaves have reasons of their own to beat Simon?
- What can we learn from this story about the multi-layered character of slave agency?

5.30   *I.Iznik* 1201: Greek Honorific Inscription, Nikaia, Bithynia (First–Third Century CE)

Literature: Horsley 1987: 160–1.

With good fortune.
  In the year 12, the village of the Okaenoi honored Doryphoros, estate manager (*oikonomos*) of the excellent Claudia Eias, with a stele, portraits, seating in the front row and prayers, during his entire life; also, his wife Potamias, for her virtue and her love for her husband. These honors are due to the fact that he has been an outstanding patron for us.

- Who bestows these honors?
- Who are the honorees? What is their status?
- Who is Claudia Eias, and what does her title ("excellent") suggest about her status?
- In what terms does the inscription describe the reason for the honor bestowed?
- Who would you normally expect to be honored in such a context? What does this inscription teach us about the master–slave relationship?

5.31   Diodorus, *Library*, Book 34, Testimonium
1 Goukowsky (=34/35.2.1–3 Walton): Greek Historiography
(First Century BCE)

Literature: Shaw 2001: 2–14.

Diodorus of Sicily says that, whereas the Sicilians had been prospering in every way for 60 years after the defeat of the Carthaginians,[91] the slave war erupted against them for the following reason. Because their wealth quickly rose to great heights and they gained great fortunes, they started to buy up multitudes of slaves. After taking them in herds from the slave pens, they would immediately brand their bodies with marks and other tattoos. The young ones they would use as herdsmen; the others according to the needs of each master. At work they would treat them severely, and they would deem them worthy of little, if any, care, whether in food or in clothing. As a result of this, most slaves would secure their living through thieving, and murders were committed everywhere, since the bandits were dispersed like armies. The governors tried to suppress them, but as they did not dare to punish them, because of the power and authority of the slaves' masters, they were compelled to watch with folded arms the ravaging of the province. As the slaves' masters were Romans of equestrian rank and could decide the cases of provincial governors when they were facing prosecution, they inspired fear to those in office.

- Who were the people who bought countless slaves in Sicily? Where did they find the money?
- How did they employ their slaves?
- How did they choose to manage their slaves? Why?
- How did the slaves react to their lack of provisions?
- Why were the slaves not punished?
- What does this story teach us about the complex facets of master–slave relationships?

---

[91] In 201 BCE.

6

Free and Slave

The distinction between free and slave was fundamental for ancient societies (6.1). The ability of the masters to exercise power over their slaves was reliant on the support provided by free people and political communities (6.2–3, 6.6). Slavery was fundamental for the sexual economy of ancient societies and the distinction between free honorable women and women without honor, who could be sexually exploited (6.5). The free–slave distinction operated in various ways: it determined who could be physically punished and who couldn't (6.7, 6.10) – or who could participate in honorable activities such as athletics (6.9). But making the distinction between free and slave too visible had dangers of its own (6.11).

The community of the free helped masters with recovering their fugitive slaves (6.12) and imposed horrific punishments on recalcitrant slaves (6.13). At the same time, the political community could intervene in the master–slave relationship to enforce its own priorities and interests. This could have negative consequences for slaves (6.16), but it could also offer them significant opportunities by limiting what masters could do to their slaves (6.14–5) or providing places of asylum (6.17). State interests could allow slaves to gain their freedom to enhance the manpower of the community (6.21, 6.23), while competition among the free and civil wars offered slaves both opportunities and dangers (6.24–5). Ancient political systems could have unintended consequences that could benefit slaves: the attempt of democracies to limit the dishonorable mistreatment of their own citizens could end up shielding slaves from mistreatment (6.18–20).

Finally, there were occasions in which the free–slave distinction could be set aside: ancient benefactors could include slaves among those who benefited from their generosity (6.22). But it was rather the slaves and former slaves of powerful masters, like Persian kings (6.26) or Roman emperors (6.27), who illustrate the fact that some slaves could be more important and powerful than many free people in certain ancient societies.

Greek and Roman Slaveries, First Edition. Eftychia Bathrellou and Kostas Vlassopoulos.
© 2022 John Wiley & Sons, Inc. Published 2022 by John Wiley & Sons, Inc.

6.1 *An.Ep.* (1979), No. 384: Latin Curse Tablet, Uley, Britannia (Second–Fourth Century CE)

Side A: Memorandum to the god Mercury from Saturnina, a woman, about the linen cloth she has lost, so that he who obtained possession of it might not find rest before he brings the aforementioned thing to the aforementioned shrine, whether that person be a man or a woman, slave or free.

- Does Saturnina know who has stolen her garment? How does she try to include all possible culprits in her curse? What categories does she use?
- How significant was the distinction between slave and free, according to this text?

6.2 Plato, *Republic*, 578d–579b: Greek Philosophical Dialogue (Fourth Century BCE)

Literature: Garlan 1988: 191–200.

Socrates: Let us look at those individuals in our cities who are wealthy and possess many slaves. These men, Glaukon, resemble tyrants in that they rule over many; the difference is that a tyrant rules over more.
Glaukon: Yes, that is the difference.
S: You do know, don't you, that these men live without fear and without being afraid of their slaves?
G: Yes. What would they be afraid of?
S: Of nothing. But do you understand why?
G: Yes. Because the city as a whole runs to the help of every individual.
S: Well put. However, suppose that some god were to carry off one man who owned at least 50 slaves or more, take him out of the city, along with his wife and children, and place him in a deserted place, together with his other property and his slaves – a place where no free man would run to his help. How terribly, how utterly would he fear for himself, his children, and his wife, that they would be killed by the slaves?
G: I'd think he'd be most fearful.
S: So, wouldn't he be forced to start cajoling some of his slaves and give them many promises and manumit them despite having no wish to do so? And wouldn't he show himself as his slaves' flatterer?
G: It'd be inevitable; otherwise, he'd perish.
S: And what would happen, if the god were to settle many others around him as neighbors, people who would not condone one man being the master of another but instead punish with the gravest punishments such a person, if they came across one?
G: I think he would find himself plagued by all kinds of evils, watched and surrounded solely by enemies.

- How does Plato use the comparison between tyrant and master?

- What enables masters not to be afraid of their slaves?

- What can this passage teach us about the importance of the free–slave dialectic?

6.3   *ILS 9455*: Lead Collar with Latin Inscription, Bulla Regia, Africa Proconsularis (Fourth or Fifth Century CE)

This collar (Fig. 10) was attached to a skeleton found in the abandonment layers of the temple of Apollo in Bulla Regia. Such slave collars date overwhelmingly from late antiquity.

Literature: Ladjimi-Sebaï 1988; Thurmond 1994: 465–6; Leone 1996; Trimble 2016.

> I am Adultera, a prostitute. Hold me because I have run away from Bulla Regia.

Figure 10   Sketch of a lead collar with Latin inscription, Bulla Regia, Africa Proconsularis (fourth or fifth century CE): image from A. Merlin, *Le temple d'Apollon à Bulla Regia*, Paris, 1910, 10, Figure 3.

- What do you think is the purpose of this collar? In what ways could it function?

- Who might the masters of this female slave have been? Are they named? How would they be identified?

- What was the audience for this inscribed collar? What options did the audience have? What does this indicate concerning how slavery operated in ancient societies?

- What effects do you think such collars had on the slaves who wore them?

6.4   *P.Brux.* I, 19, 4–26: Papyrus with Census Declaration in Greek, Arsinoite Nome, Egypt (First Half of Second Century CE)

In Roman Egypt, heads of households were obliged to submit census declarations with all members of their households. The beginning of this document has not survived.

Literature: Keenan, Manning and Yiftach-Firanko 2014: 459–60.

a. Dioskoros, slave of Laberia, daughter of Pasion, from Hellenion, owned by her by 50%; for the other 50%, he has been declared as belonging to Horaiane, her sister. At present a weaver, accounted here as belonging to me; 29 years old, without distinguishing mark.
b. A second Dioskoros, slave of the same woman by the same percentage; for the other 50% he has been declared as belonging to Horaiane, her sister. Unregistered but accounted here among the newborn children of year 1; one year old, without distinguishing mark.
c. Pasion, son of Dioskoros the slave of Laberia, his mother being Alexous, daughter of Hermas. Unregistered, but accounted here among the newborn children of year 1; one year old, without distinguishing mark. As for the rest:
d. Laberia, daughter of Pasion, son of Pasion, her mother being Alexandra, daughter of Pasion [...] from Hellenion; wife of Theon, 32 years old.
e. Isidora, female slave of the above woman and, equally, of her sister Horaiane; 49 years old.
f. Dioskorous, called Sarapous, female slave of the same woman; 23 years old.
g. Alexous, whose father is Hermas, son of Hermas, and whose mother is Tasoucharion, daughter of Syros; she is the wife of the slave Dioskoros; 26 years old.
h. Alexous, daughter of the aforementioned, 8 years old.
i. Taareotis, another daughter of the same people, 6 years old.

- Which slaves are enumerated? What information is recorded about them?
- Who are the owners of these slaves? What arrangement have they adopted in terms of ownership?
- What is the relationship between the slave Dioskoros and Alexous, daughter of Hermas? What is Alexous' status? What is the status of their children?
- What do you think about this marriage? What implications does it have for our understanding of slavery?
- Is this a peculiar Egyptian practice or a widely encountered phenomenon? Compare with 11.26, 12.26–7.

6.5 Philemon, *Brothers*, Fragment 3 K-A: Greek Comedy (Second Half of Fourth/First Half of Third Century BCE)

Solon was an Athenian politician, law-giver and poet of around 600 BCE. His laws came to be seen as the foundation stones of Athenian democracy.

Literature: Glazebrook 2011; Henry 2011.

It was you, Solon, who made an invention for the benefit of all people. They say you were the first person who saw this: the only thing on the side of the people, by Zeus – and life-saving, too. – And it is fitting that *I* am saying this,

> Solon. – Seeing the city full of young men, their nature compulsive and erring against what was not theirs, you bought women and established them at various places, set up and common to all. They stand naked: don't get deceived; look at everything! You happen not to feel very well; you have [...]. The door is open. One obol. Jump inside. There is no affectation whatsoever, nor prattle, nor snap retorts. Instead: the woman you want, the way you want, with no delays. You are coming out: tell her to go to hell – she's nothing to you.

- To which genre does this passage belong? How should we interpret the image it draws?
- What invention is attributed to Solon by the speaker of this comic fragment?
- What is the speaker's opinion of the invention, and how does he justify it?
- How is the slave status of the female prostitutes relevant to the invention's efficacy?

6.6 Tacitus, *Annals*, 14.42–5:[92] Latin Historiography (Early Second Century CE)

The events recorded in this passage took place in 61 CE. The "ancient custom" mentioned is the *Senatus Consultum Silanianum* of 10 CE. Cf. 6.14.

Literature: Bellen 1982; Harries and du Plessis 2013.

> Not long after, the urban prefect Pedanius Secundus was killed by his own slave, either because the slave had been refused his freedom, although a price had been set, or because he was inflamed by desire for a man and could not tolerate his master as a rival. Be that as it may, according to an ancient custom, the whole household (*familia*) that had lived under the same roof had to be led to punishment. Things thus got to the point of sedition, as the people (*plebs*), seeking to protect the very many who had done nothing wrong, quickly assembled and besieged the Senate. In the Senate both those despising excessive severity and those – the majority – who proposed that nothing be changed advocated their cause earnestly. Of the latter group, Gaius Cassius, when it was his turn to express an opinion, spoke in the following manner.
> "[...] A man who had been a consul was killed in his own house from the ambush of his slaves, which no one stopped or revealed, although the decree of the Senate which threatened the whole household to be led to punishment had not yet been at all shaken. Go on and decree impunity, by Hercules! But who will be defended by his rank, when his rank was unable to benefit the prefect of the city? Who will be guarded by a host of his slaves, when 400 did not protect Pedanius Secundus? To whom will his household provide support, when the household did not notice the dangers to us even when in fear? Rather, as some do not blush to make up, was it the case that the murderer avenged the injustices he had suffered, because he had reached

[92] Latin text: Heubner 1994.

an agreement over his own patrimony, or because he had been deprived of a slave he had inherited from his grandfather?! Why don't we then also pronounce that in our opinion the master was murdered justly?! Do you want to seek arguments in an issue which has been considered by men wiser than us? But even if we had to make a decision now for the first time, do you believe that a slave who had summoned the courage to kill his master in such a way, never let slip one threatening word, or never revealed anything in his rashness? Doubtless he concealed his plan! He procured the weapon, while no one else had any idea! Did he really manage to pass the slaves on night duty, open the bedroom doors, carry a light, and do the actual slaughter, without anyone else knowing? Many indications precede a crime. If our slaves reveal them to us, then we can live alone amid many, safe amid an anxious crowd, and last, if we must perish, not go unavenged amid the guilty.

"Our ancestors suspected the spirit of their slaves even when they were born on their estates or in their houses and had conceived an affection for their masters from the start. But now that we keep whole nations amid our households, people of different rites and foreign or non-existent rituals, you won't be able to coerce that medley of people except by fear. 'Some innocent ones will perish.' Yes, but in a stricken army, when one in 10 is beaten with a club, even men who stood firm are chosen by lot to die.[93] There is an element of unfairness in every case of severe exemplary punishment, which is counterbalanced by the advantage gained by the community, as the unfairness concerns only individuals."

As no one on his own dared to speak against the opinion of Cassius, there was a response by the dissonant voices of those who felt pity for the number, age, sex, and the undoubted innocence of most of Pedanius' slaves. Nonetheless the section that was for decreeing punishment prevailed. But it was not possible to conform to the decision, as a great crowd had accumulated and was menacing with stones and torches. Then Caesar censured the people with an edict and had the whole route through which the condemned were led to their punishment surrounded with military guards. Cingonius Varro had proposed that the freedmen who had been under the same roof be deported away from Italy. But this the emperor prohibited, lest an ancient custom that had not been softened by pity should be intensified through cruelty.

- What motives are attributed to the slave who killed Pedanius? What do they reveal about the master–slave relationship?
- What punishment did Roman law detail for the slaves of Pedanius?
- With what arguments does Cassius justify his position?
- Is Cassius only aiming to discourage slaves from killing their masters?
- How do Cassius' arguments help us to understand relations among slaves?
- Is the decision of the Senate evidence of fear – or panic?
- How did the mass react to the execution? How do you explain this?
- Why were there freedmen in Pedanius' house? What does this tell us about elite houses and the condition of freedmen? Cf. 10.16.

---

[93] A reference to the practice of decimation in the Roman army.

MAINTAINING THE FREE–SLAVE DISTINCTION

6.7   *IG* II² 1362: Inscribed Priestly Edict in Greek, Athens (Fourth Century BCE)

Literature: Hunter 1994: 54–84; Arnaoutoglou 2007.

> Gods. The priest of Apollo Erithaseus, on behalf of himself and the demesmen and the Athenian people, proclaims and forbids the cutting or transport of wood, branches with leaves, firewood, and fallen leaves, in and out of the sanctuary of Apollo. Anyone caught cutting or transporting any of the forbidden items away from the sanctuary, if a slave, shall be flogged with fifty lashes, and the priest will deliver him, together with his master's name, to the king archon and to the Council, according to the decree of the Council and the Athenian People. If he is a free man, the priest, together with the demarch, shall fine him 50 drachmas and will deliver his name to the king archon and to the Council, according to the decree of the Council and the Athenian people.

- What acts are prohibited in the sanctuary of Apollo?
- How will the slaves be punished for infractions?
- How will the free be punished?
- What can we learn about the significance of the free/slave distinction from this inscription?

6.8   Galen, *The Therapeutic Method (De methodo medendi)*, IX.4 Johnston and Horsley[94] (X.608 Kühn): Greek Medical Treatise (Late Second/Early Third Century CE)

Galen discusses cases of continuous fever.

Literature: Schlange-Schöningen 2003: 255–90, 2006.

> By way of illustration, I will remind you of two young men whom you have seen with us. One of them was a free man, athletically skilled; the other was a slave. The slave was not untrained, but, of course, he was not particularly good at wrestling but at what befits a slave: that is, he could handle the daily exercises and tasks. The free man got a continuous fever without putrefaction; the slave got a continuous fever with putrefaction.

---

[94] Johnston and Horsley 2011.

- What similarities and differences between the free and slave patient does Galen note?

- To what does he attribute those differences?

6.9 *EKM* 1, Beroia 1, Back Side II. 21–23 and 26–32: Inscribed Law in Greek, Beroia, Macedonia (200–166 BCE)

Law regulating activity in the gymnasium of the city of Beroia, including the duties of the gymnasiarch, the man in charge of the gymnasium.

Literature: Mactoux 1988; Crowther 1992; Gauthier and Hatzopoulos 1993; Golden 2008: 40–67; Roubineau 2018.

> The gymnasiarch shall have authority to whip disorderly boys and boys' attendants (*paidagôgoi*), if the latter are slaves; if the attendants who show lack of discipline are free, the gymnasiarch shall have the authority to fine them. [...]
> Those not allowed to use the gymnasium. Stripping in order to use the gymnasium is not allowed to the following people: slaves or freedmen and their sons; men who have not been to the wrestling school; men who have prostituted themselves or who have practiced a trade in the marketplace; men in a state of drunkenness or madness. If the gymnasiarch knowingly allows any of those specified above to anoint himself or gives his permission despite accusations and proof against that person, the gymnasiarch shall pay a fine of 1000 drachmas.

- What types of people does the gymnasiarch have the right to whip and what not?

- What do you think about the existence of boys' attendants who are free?

- What categories of people are prohibited from exercising in the gymnasium?

- Do you think there is a single rationale for excluding these diverse categories of people?

- What can we learn about the free/slave distinction from the presence of slaves, freedmen, and their sons within the wider group of the excluded?

6.10 *IG* V.1 1390: Inscribed Religious Regulations in Greek, Andania, Messenia (First Century CE)

Greek inscription with the regulations of a local mystery cult.

Literature: Gawlinski 2011.

> **15–19**: Concerning clothing: Those being initiated into the Mysteries shall be barefoot and wear white clothing. Women shall not wear transparent clothes, nor have on their robes borders wider than half a finger. Women not holding office shall wear a linen tunic and a robe worth no more than 100 drachmas; girls shall wear an Egyptian or linen garment and a robe worth no

more than one mina; slave women shall wear an Egyptian or linen garment and a robe worth no more than 50 drachmas.

39–41: Concerning disorderly behavior: When the sacrifices and the Mysteries take place, everyone shall remain silent and attend to the orders being given. Anyone who disobeys or conducts oneself improperly toward the divine shall be whipped by the *hieroi* (i.e. sacred men) and excluded from the Mysteries.

75–8: Concerning offences: Anyone caught having stolen or committed any other offence in the days when the sacrifices and the Mysteries take place shall be taken to the *hieroi*. If he is a free man and is convicted, he shall pay double the amount; if he is a slave, he shall be whipped and pay double the amount of what he stole or, for other offences, a fine of 20 drachmas. If he does not pay immediately, the slave's master shall hand over the slave to the wronged person, so that the slave can work off his debt. If the master does not do so, he shall be liable to twice the amount.

80–4: That there be a refuge for slaves: The sanctuary shall be a refuge for slaves, the exact place pointed out by the *hieroi*. No one shall receive the runaways or give them food or offer them work. Anyone who acts against the aforementioned prescriptions shall be liable toward the slave's master for double the value of the slave's body and a fine of 500 drachmas. The priest shall judge the cases of running away, specifically of slaves coming from our city. Slaves whom the priest convicts, he shall hand over to their masters. If the priest does not hand them over, the master shall be permitted to depart taking his slave with him.

106–9: Concerning anointing and bathing. The *agoranomos*[95] shall make sure that those offering bathing services in the sanctuary may not charge the bathers more than two copper coins (*chalkoi*). [...] And no slave shall anoint himself.

- What distinctions between free and slave does this regulation maintain?
- Are there things prohibited to slaves?
- Is there differential treatment of slaves and freemen for the same issue?
- Are there issues on which no difference is entertained?
- How is physical punishment applied to offenders? Does it apply only to slaves?
- What rules does the regulation introduce regarding asylum? Cf. 6.17.

6.11 Seneca, *On Mercy*, 1.24: Latin Moral Philosophy (First Century CE)

Literature: George 2002.

Once a proposal was made in the Senate that slaves be distinguished from the free by their dress. It then became apparent what a dangerous threat we would face if our slaves began to realize how few we were.

---

[95] Magistrate in charge of the market.

- What was the Senate proposal? What does this proposal reveal about Roman mentality?

- Why was the plan abandoned?

- What does the abandonment of the plan imply about the number of slaves in Rome?

- Can we use this as evidence that Roman masters feared their slaves?

6.12 *UPZ* I, 121: Papyrus with Announcement in Greek, Memphis, Egypt (First Half of Second Century BCE)

Literature: Scholl 1990: no. 81; Fuhrmann 2012: 21–43.

Year 25, on the 16th day of the month Epeiph.

A slave of Aristogenes, son of Chrysippos, ambassador of Alabanda,[96] has escaped in Alexandria. His name is Hermon, but he is also called Neilos. He is of Syrian origin, from Bambyke, 18 years old, of middle height, beardless, with fine legs; he has a dimple on the chin, a mole to the left side of his nose, a scar above the upper lip on the left side. He has a tattoo depicting two foreign letters on his right wrist. He has taken with him three ochtadrachms of coined gold, 10 pearls, and one iron ring, on which an oil-flask and a strigil are represented. He is wearing a cloak and a loincloth. Whoever brings him back shall receive three talents of copper. If he points to a shrine, he will receive two talents; if to the house of a noteworthy man who can be taken to court, five talents. Whoever wishes can give information on the slave to the men at the office of the *stratêgos*.

There is also a slave who ran away together with Hermon. He is Bion, slave of Kallikrates, one of the chief attendants in the court. Bion is of short stature, wide-shouldered, stout-legged, bright-eyed. He departed with an outer garment, a child's garment and a woman's dress, worth six talents, and five (?) of copper. Whoever brings him back will receive the same reward as for the afore-mentioned slave. One should pass information on this man, too, to the men at the office of the *stratêgos*.

- Who are the fugitives? How are they described?

- What can we learn about Hermon's identity?

- Who are their masters? Is this significant for their attempt to recapture them?

- Why is the reward greater if the slaves are discovered in the house of an important man?

- How do their masters attempt to retrieve them? What is the role of the state in this (compare with 1.18)?

---

[96] A city in Karia.

6.13   Strabo, *Geography*, 12.3.40: Greek Geography (First Century BCE/First Century CE)

In the Roman world, the *publicani* (in Strabo's Greek *dêmosiônai*) were individuals or companies who purchased public contracts and reimbursed themselves with any profit they made.

Literature: Millar 1984; Groen-Vallinga and Tacoma 2015.

> In Pompeiopolis,[97] the realgar[98] mine is not very far from Pimolisa, a royal fortress now destroyed, after which the land on both sides of the river is called Pimolisene. The mound of the realgar mine is hollow from mining, as the workers have reached under its bottom level through long tunnels. The mine was run by *publicani*, who used as miners slaves put on the market after committing a criminal act. Not only is this work tough, but also they say that the air in the mines is deadly and hard to endure because of the heavy odors of the lumps, and hence the workers face an early death. And it is quite common that a mine is deserted as unprofitable, since 200 or more men have to work there, continuously wasted by disease and death.

- Who worked the realgar mines at Pompeiopolis? Why?
- How profitable were these mines?
- What can we learn about slave punishment from this source?

INTERVENING IN THE MASTER–SLAVE RELATIONSHIP

6.14   Scriptores Historiae Augustae, *Hadrian*, 18.7–11: Latin Biography (Possibly Fourth Century CE)

Hadrian was emperor between 117–138 CE. See also 6.6 and 6.15.

Literature: Knoch 2017: 111–18.

> Hadrian forbade masters to kill their slaves and ordered that masters be condemned in court if they deserve it. He forbade male or female slaves to be sold to procurers or to gladiator school managers unless a reason be furnished. He ordered that those who had wasted their property and were under their own authority be flogged in the amphitheatre and then be released. He did away with estate prisons (*ergastula*) for both free and slave. He prescribed separate baths according to one's sex. He ruled that if a master be murdered

---

[97] A city in Paphlagonia on the southern Black Sea coast.
[98] Realgar is a toxic mineral used in antiquity as a pigment and in leather manufacturing.

in his house, not all slaves should undergo investigation but only those who were near enough to be able to have knowledge of the murder.

- What change did Hadrian bring regarding the killing of slaves? Why?
- Under what conditions could slaves be sold as prostitutes and gladiators? Why?
- Why did Hadrian prohibit estate prisons?
- What can we learn about slave punishment from this passage?
- Can you find links between these various rules regarding slaves? How would you describe the tenor of Hadrian's laws?
- What difference did state intervention make on how slavery operated?

6.15   *Digest*, 1.12.1.8: Collection of Latin Juristic Texts (Sixth Century CE)

On the Digest, see 1.2. Ulpian is here commenting on a letter by the emperor Septimius Severus to Lucius Fabius Cilo, when the latter was urban prefect (204 CE).

Literature: McGinn 1990; Knoch 2017: 111–18.

Ulpian, *On the Duties of the Urban Prefect*: The statement that the prefect should hear cases of slaves making complaints against their masters should be understood thus: not as cases of slaves accusing their masters – for this is in no way permitted to a slave, unless in specified cases – but as cases of slaves if they express their complaints with respect and propriety, if they demonstrate to the prefect the brutality, harshness, starvation, through which they are being oppressed, or the obscene acts to which they have been or are being compelled. Also, the following duty was given to the urban prefect by the divine Severus: namely to protect slaves from being prostituted by their masters.

- What complaints can slaves bring in front of the prefect, and what complaints are disallowed?
- What do you think is the reason for this distinction?
- How can the prefect distinguish between reasonable punishment and savagery toward slaves?
- Why is forced prostitution included in this list of permissible slave complaints (cf. 6.14)? What implications does this have about the sexual honor of slaves?

6.16   Cicero, *Against Verres II*, 5.7: Latin Law-Court Speech (First Century BCE)

Sicily saw two major slave revolts at the end of the second century BCE: the so-called First Sicilian Slave War in 135–2 BCE and the Second in 104–100 BCE, ended by

Manius Aquillius. The episode with Lucius Domitius Ahenobarbus is thought to have taken place only a few years after that, very early in the first century BCE.

Literature: Shaw 2001: 1–27.

> Ever since Manius Aquillius departed from Sicily, the resolutions and edicts of all praetors have been to the effect that no slave should bear arms. What I am going to say is an old story and probably known to all of you on account of its harshness. When Lucius Domitius was praetor of Sicily and an enormous boar was brought to him, he marveled at it and asked who had killed it. When he heard that some shepherd had done it, he summoned the shepherd before him. The shepherd came fast and eagerly to the praetor, expecting praise and a reward. Domitius asked him how he had slain such a large beast. He responded, "with a hunting spear." Immediately afterward, by order of the praetor, the shepherd was taken for crucifixion. This perhaps seems harsh, and I say nothing either way. But this I understand: Domitius preferred to appear cruel but observant of the regulations rather than appearing lax by overlooking them.

- How do you explain the decree of Manius Aquillius against slaves' bearing arms in Sicily? Cf. 9.25a.

- Do you think that the shepherd's master might have agreed with the praetor's decision? What does this imply about possible divergences between the free–slave and the master–slave dialectics?

6.17 Diodorus, *Library*, 11.89.6–8: Greek Historiography (First Century BCE)

Diodorus describes the shrine of two local gods of Sicily, the Divine Palikoi, and its solemnity (the area includes lakes emitting sulphuric vapors). Cf. also 8.20.

Literature: Derlien 2003: 98–100; Ismard 2019: 191–222.

> This sacred land has for some years now been respected as a place of sanctuary. As a result, much assistance is given to unfortunate slaves who have fallen into the hands of callous masters. For if a slave finds refuge in this shrine, his master does not have the power to take him away by force. Instead, he can remain there unharmed, until his master convinces him to go with him, under specified conditions of humane treatment and after offering pledges, sanctified by oath, to fulfil what has been agreed. No cases of masters who violated the pledges they had given to their slaves have been recorded. For the awe these gods inspire makes those who have taken an oath keep faith with their slaves.

- How did slaves attempt to deal with masters' mistreatment?

- How did religious asylum modify the master–slave relationship? Cf. 1.23, 6.10, 9.18.

UNDERMINING THE FREE–SLAVE DISTINCTION

6.18   Ps.-Xenophon, *Constitution of the Athenians*, 1.10:[99] Greek Political Treatise (Probably Fifth Century BCE)

The writer responds to an argument against the Athenian political system.

Literature: Cataldi 2000; Vlassopoulos 2007.

> "But again, slaves and metics enjoy extreme licence in Athens, and it is not possible to strike them, nor will a slave make way for you." I will explain why this is the local practice. If it were legal that the slave or the metic or the freedman could be beaten by a free man, then very often one would strike Athenians, having mistaken them for slaves. For the people here do not wear better clothes than the slaves or the metics, and they are not at all better in appearance.

- Why was it inadvisable to strike people who do not show deference in Athens, according to the author?
- Why was it difficult to tell apart slaves from free people at Athens? Would that apply to all free people?
- What assumption about the appearance of slaves in other cities lies behind this passage?
- Could you think of a different rationale for the alleged avoidance of striking other people's slaves in Athens?

6.19   Demosthenes, *Against Meidias*, 45–48: Greek Law-Court Speech, Athens (Mid-Fourth Century BCE)

Literature: Fisher 1995; Canevaro 2018.

> The lawgiver has given to anyone who wishes the right to bring a public action for outrage (*hybris*) and made the penalty, in its entirety, payable to the city. In other words, he considered one who sets out to commit outrage to be wronging the city, not merely the victim. [...] In fact, the lawgiver went to such extremes, that he also gave people the right to bring a public action even if outrage is committed against a slave. For he thought that he should not examine the identity of the sufferer but the character of the act. And since he found the act unacceptable, he did not allow that it should be committed against either a slave or anyone else. For there is nothing, Athenians, nothing more intolerable than outrage – nothing that deserves your anger more. Take and read for me the actual law on outrage; for there is nothing like hearing the law itself. [...] You hear, Athenians, the humane character of the law. It states that not even slaves deserve to suffer outrage.

---

[99] Greek text: Marr and Rhodes 2008.

- How does the Athenian law on outrage treat free and slave persons, according to Demosthenes?

- How does Demosthenes explain the law's even-handedness regarding free and slave persons? Are his explanations plausible? Can you think of other explanations?

- On what circumstances (if any) do you imagine an Athenian bringing a public suit against someone committing outrage against a slave?

6.20 Aristophanes, *Frogs*, 948–52: Greek Comedy (405 BCE)

Prominent Athenian tragic dramatists Euripides and Aeschylus quarrel in the underworld over the value of their plays.

Literature: Demont 2007.

> **Euripides:** Moreover, from the first lines, I would not leave anyone idle, but my wives had speaking parts, and the slaves no less than their masters, and the maidens and the old women.
> **Aeschylus:** Well then – didn't you deserve death for this audacity?
> **Euripides:** No, by Apollo. Because this was a democratic act.

- What is Euripides' argument about the virtues of his plays? How do slaves figure in it?

- Why does Aeschylus disagree? How does Euripides defend himself?

- Can we take this argument seriously, or is it just comic exaggeration?

6.21 Polybius, *History*, 38.15.1–6: Greek Historiography (Second Century BCE)

The events narrated in this passage took place during the Achaean War between Rome and the Achaean League in 146 BCE.

Literature: Welwei 1977: 62–8; Texier 1979.

> Polybius says that when Kritolaos, the general of the Achaeans, died, the law stipulated that when something happened to the general in office, his predecessor would take over until the regular meeting of the Achaean Confederacy took place; so, it fell upon Diaios to be nominated and to preside over the common affairs. Therefore, after sending troops to Megara and going to Argos in person, he declared to every city that they should manumit about 12,000 home-born and home-bred slaves of military age, provide them with weapons, and send them to Corinth. But he arranged each city's contribu-

tion in a random and unequal way, exactly as was his usual practice in other issues too. Those cities lacking the appointed number of home-bred slaves were to fill up their assigned share through their other slaves.

- Why does Diaios specify that only home-born slaves should be manumitted and armed?
- Is the number of 12,000 home-born slaves of military age a large one or not? What does it imply about the importance of natural reproduction?
- Does the passage imply that there was a major fault line between purchased and home-born slaves? Cf. 6.6.

6.22   Benefactions

Literature: Bradley 1979.

6.22.a   *I.Priene* 64.253–9: Greek Honorific Inscription, Priene, Ionia (Second Century BCE)

The Council and the People of Priene honor their benefactor Moschion, son of Kydimos.
   When he received the crown of Zeus Olympios and the office of *stephanê-phoros*[100] and adorned all the public sanctuaries with garlands and honored the gods' altars with incense, he invited through public announcement the sons of those fallen in battle, and all the citizens and the *paroikoi*[101] and the foreigners and the freedmen and the slaves, to a treat of sweets and sweet wine.

6.22.b   *IG* IV 597: Greek Honorific Inscription, Argos, Peloponnese (First–Third Century CE)

The tribe of the Pamphyloi (honor) Onesiphoros, son of Onesiphoros, who acted as *agônothetês* at the Heraia and the Nemea in a solemn, just and generous manner. At each contest, he offered mass meals to all the free men for two days; he twice gave four denarii to every citizen and two denarii to all other free men; he also arranged that anointing oil be used at liberty from morning to sunset by every free and slave man at every gymnasium and bath, at his own expense.

---

[100]The *stephanêphoros* (literally, "crown bearer") was the holder of the highest office in Priene and in other Asia Minor cities.
[101]Resident foreigners, comparable with the Athenian metics.

- What benefactions are recorded in these inscriptions?

- Are slaves and freedmen included in them? In what ways? Cf. 6.9.

- Do these benefactions draw a distinction between slave and free, or do they efface this distinction?

- What conclusions, if any, can we draw from these documents as regards the social position of slaves?

6.23 Dionysius of Halicarnassus, *Roman Antiquities*, 4.22.3–23.7: Greek Historiography (First Century BCE)

The subject of this passage, the Roman king Servius Tullius, is conventionally dated to 578–35 BCE. See also 10.12, 12.32.c.

Literature: Mouritsen 2011: 10–35; Husby 2017.

This king took great care to enlarge the citizen body, as he had realized something that all the kings before him had missed. They had increased the city's population by receiving foreigners and giving them equal rights to citizenship, whatever their origin or circumstances. Tullius, however, allowed that manumitted slaves too should have equal rights to citizenship if they did not wish to leave for their own cities. Specifically, he ordered that they, too, have their properties valued together with all the other free persons and placed them in the four urban tribes in which the body of freedmen continues to be registered even down to our own times, however large it might be. And he allowed them to share in all powers available to the other plebeians.

However, as the patricians were aggrieved and vexed at this, he called the people to assembly and said that he marveled at those who were indignant at his decision because, he said, first, they thought that what made the free and the slave differ was nature and not fortune; also, because they did not test those worthy of fine things by their character and manners but by their circumstances, although they could see how uncertain and quick-changing good fortune is and that no one can easily say, not even those most blessed, for how long it will remain with one. Then he asked them to consider how many cities, both Greek and barbarian ones, had changed from slavery to freedom and from freedom to slavery. He also called it great stupidity if they did give worthy slaves a share in freedom but begrudged them citizenship. He also advised them not to set their slaves free if they considered them wicked; however, if they considered them good, they should not stand by and see them live as aliens. He also said that they would be acting in an absurd and ignorant way if they allowed all the foreigners to partake of citizenship, without distinguishing them by their circumstances or busying themselves with whether some had become free from slave, but considered those that had been their own slaves unworthy of this favor. He also said that although they thought of themselves as more sensible than the rest, they were unable to see what was simplest and lying at their feet, obvious even to the most common person: namely, that, on the one hand, masters would take great care not to free people casually, so as not to grant the greatest human good at random, and, on the other hand, slaves would be even more eager to be good toward their masters, if they learnt that, if judged worthy of freedom, they would immediately become citizens of a prosperous and great city, and that both these goods would be granted to them by their masters.

Finally, he introduced the benefit argument; he reminded those who already knew, and explained to those who did not, that a city which desires power and demands great things of itself most of all needs a large population, so that it might be able to use its own troops in all wars and not exhaust itself and its resources by hiring foreign armies. This was why, he said, earlier kings had given equal rights to citizenship to all foreigners. And if in addition they enacted this law, he said, many more young people would be raised to those who would be set free, and the city would never lack its own troops but always have armed forces, even if it should be compelled to raise war against the whole world. And besides this public advantage, the wealthiest Romans would gain much private benefit, too, if they allowed freedmen equal rights to citizenship: they would receive the freedmen's gratitude in assemblies, in voting and on any other political occasion in which they might need their support; also, they would leave those born to their freedmen as clients to their own descendants. Such were his arguments, and the patricians agreed to have this practice introduced to the city. It has continuously been observed in the city as one of its sacred and unalterable customs down to our own times.

- How does Servius Tullius account for manumission and enfranchisement from the point of view of the master–slave dialectic?

- How does he account for manumission and enfranchisement from the point of view of the free–slave dialectic? Cf. 6.24.

6.24 Appian, *Civil Wars*, 1.11.100: Greek Historiography (Second Century CE)

After the proscriptions of 82 BCE, the Roman general and statesman Sulla, now appointed dictator, reformed some Roman institutions. Sulla's family name (*nomen*) was Cornelius.

Literature: Santangelo 2007: 78–99.

To the Senate itself, which had suffered severe losses in manpower because of the civil discords and wars, Sulla enrolled about 300 more men, from the best members of the equestrian order. He assigned to the tribes the task to vote for each of them. To the plebeians he enrolled the youngest and strongest of the slaves of the proscribed men – more than 10,000. He manumitted them, declared them Roman citizens, and called them Cornelii, after himself, so that he could have at his disposal 10,000 plebeians, ready to follow his commands.

- What was the profile of the slaves freed and enfranchised by Sulla? Who had their masters been?

- What was the political importance of their enfranchisement? Cf. 6.23.

- What conclusions can we draw from this passage about the sort of circumstances permitting such a strong undermining of the free–slave distinction?

6.25   Appian, *Civil Wars*, 4.10.81: Greek Historiography (Second Century CE)

In 42 BCE, the Roman general and politician Marcus Junius Brutus took the city of Xanthos, in Lykia, in Asia Minor. He then proceeded to conquer the nearby city of Patara. Gaius Cassius Longinus, a political ally and relative of Brutus, had defeated the Rhodians a little before Brutus' attack on Patara.

> Brutus then left Xanthos and went down to Patara, a city which was something like a seaport of the Xanthians. He surrounded Patara with his army and ordered the city to obey him in everything, or else it would receive the sad treatment of the Xanthians. And some Xanthians were taken to Patara, lamenting their own lot and urging the people to take better decisions. But the people of Patara made no response to the Xanthians, and so Brutus gave them the rest of the day to deliberate and withdrew. At dawn, however, he advanced his troops. The people of Patara cried out from their walls that they would obey his wishes, and they opened the gates. He entered the city, did not kill or expel anyone, but collected all the city's silver and gold and gave out orders that each citizen of Patara should also contribute his own silver and gold, on the same penalties, and rewards for informers, as those proclaimed by Cassius when on Rhodes. The people of Patara were in the process of making their contributions, when a slave informed that his master had hidden some gold and showed it to the centurion who had been sent for it. As they were all being taken away, the master remained silent, but his mother, who followed, cried out that it was she who had concealed the gold, in an attempt to save her son. No one asked the slave any questions, but he disputed her, claiming that she was lying and that it was his master who had concealed the gold. Brutus approved of the young man's silence and his mother's suffering and let them both go free unharmed, taking their gold with them, but he had the slave hanged for having acted against his masters beyond the requirements of Brutus' order.

- What action does the slave take?

- Is he rewarded for his action?

- Why does Brutus act as he does toward the slave? What did Brutus consider to be wrong in the slave's action?

- What contradictions within the free–slave relationship, and between the free–slave and the master–slave relationships are evident in this passage?

SLAVES AND FREEDPERSONS OF RULERS

Greek and Roman cities had public slaves, who exercised various important functions in positions of trust and authority: cf. 1.15, 2.7, 3.6, 7.23. In this section, we focus on the slaves and freedpersons of rulers.

6.26   Herodotus, 8.104–6: Greek Historiography (Fifth Century BCE)

The following event took place during the Persian expedition against Greece of 480–79 BCE.

Literature: Llewellyn-Jones 2002.

Xerxes sent along with his sons Hermotimos as guardian. Hermotimos was a native of Pedasa and was considered the first among the eunuchs at the court of the king. He of all men within my knowledge exacted the greatest vengeance for a wrong he had suffered. Once, when captured by enemies and put on sale, he was bought by Panionios, a man from Chios, who had built up his property through the most impious activities. He used to buy boys who had beauty and then castrate them and sell them to Sardeis and Ephesos for a high price. For eunuchs are valued more than non-castrated men among barbarian peoples because of their complete trustworthiness. Among the many boys castrated by Panionios – for this is how he was making his living – was Hermotimos, too. And then – for you see, his fate was not all bad – he arrives from Sardeis and is given to the king along with other gifts. After some time, he received honors greater than any other eunuch at Xerxes' court.

When the king, still in Sardeis, was preparing to lead the Persian army against Athens, Hermotimos went for some business down to a part of Mysia which is under the control of the Chians. It is called Atarneus. There he finds Panionios. When he realized who he was, he started to speak to him for a long time and in a friendly manner. First, he listed the many good things he enjoyed because of Panionios; then he gave promises for many good things that he would do in return, if Panionios were to take his household and move there. Panionios accepted the offer gladly and took his wife and children there. When he had thus trapped him, together with all his family, Hermotimos said to him: "You, worst of all men, who acquired your property through deeds most impious, what harm had I, or anyone of my family, done to you or to any of yours, in respect of which you turned me from a man to a nothing? Were you of the impression that what you contrived back then would escape the gods' notice? It is they who have applied their just law and led you into my hands – for you have committed impious crimes. So, you shall have no complaints of the punishment you will receive by me." After Hermotimos had thus rebuked him, his sons were brought to Panionios, and he was forced to cut off the genitalia of his own sons, who were four. He did this under compulsion. And when he finished, his sons were forced to cut off his. This is how Hermotimos, and Revenge, surrounded and caught Panionios.

- How did Hermotimos end up as a slave in the Persian court? Cf. 9.13.

- How are Panionios' activities portrayed? Why? Cf. 8.17.

- How did Hermotimos fare as a slave eunuch in the Persian court?

- Do you think that the story concerning Hermotimos' gratitude, with which he ensnared Panionios, has an element of truth, or not?

6.27 Roman Imperial Slaves and Freedmen

Roman emperors employed their slaves and freedmen (the so-called *familia Caesaris*) not only as their personal servants but also to fill in important positions in the imperial bureaucracy across the empire. Imperial slaves were usually born in the imperial household; more rarely, they were inherited by the emperor from relatives or bought in the market. Imperial slaves filled lower positions in the hierarchy and, after being manumitted, became eligible for higher posts. For imperial slaves, see also 7.25, 9.12, 11.22, and 12.14. For imperial freedmen, see also 4.27, 10.21, 10.26, and 12.31.

Literature: Weaver 1972; Flexsenhar 2019.

—— 6.27.a *CIL* VI, 9089: Statue Base with Latin Inscription, ——
Rome (Second Century CE)

This marble triple statue (Fig. 11) was probably depicting different aspects of the deity Diana.

Literature: Weaver 1972: 58–72.

> Aelius Barbarus, freedman of the emperors, manager (*vilicus*) of this place, set this up as a gift for Diana.

- Who is the dedicator of this statue? What was his name? What was his position?

- What conclusions can we draw from this dedicated statue concerning the wealth and power of imperial freedmen?

——— 6.27.b *FD* III 4.445: Greek Honorific Inscription, ———
Delphi, Phokis (Second Century CE)

As a procurator of Boiotia, which was one of the regions of the Roman province of Achaia, Myron would have been responsible for the region's imperial finances.

Figure 11 Marble triple statue of Diana, second century CE, Rome. Source: British Museum; https://www.britishmuseum.org/collection/image/561456001.

Literature: Weaver 1972: 267–81.

> With good fortune.
>   The citizens of Delphi gave to Publius Aelius Myron, freedman of Augustus[102] and procurator of Boiotia, citizenship, membership in the Council and all the other honors given to fine and good men for their nobility. In the archonship of Aphasios, son of Kallikrates, in the month of Apellaios.

- Who is the honoree? How is he described?

- What honors are bestowed on him?

- Why did the Delphians honor this imperial freedman?

---

[102] Emperor Hadrian.

——— 6.27.c *I.Magnesia* 113, 7–24: Greek Honorific Decree, ———
Magnesia on the Maeander, Karia (ca. 100 CE)

Literature: Nutton 1977; Kudlien 1986: 129.

Because Tiberius Claudius Tyrannos, freedman of the emperor and citizen of our city, a man who has earned the approval of the divine judgement of the emperors both for his ability in the art of medicine and for his excellence of character, returned to his homeland and has led his life here in accordance to the dignity that characterizes him in all aspects of life, having behaved with humane generosity toward all the citizens, so that no one has been burdened by him beyond what his greatness deserves, for these reasons the Council and the People have judged it proper to honor the man, in expression of their approbation. It is the decision of the Council and the People that Tiberius Claudius Tyrannos, freedman of the emperor, should be honored and that he shall enjoy approbation among the people. Also, that he should be granted exemption from all taxes for the surgeries (*ergastêria*) he has established in the territory of the village Kadyie.

- What is the status of Tyrannos and what is his profession?
- Why is he honored by the Magnesians?
- What forms of social advancement were open for an imperial freedman?

7

Enslaved Persons and Their Communities

Slavery is an imposed identity, and ancient slave systems usually operated as if enslaved persons had only one identity that mattered, that of being slaves. But enslaved persons possessed multiple identities that were partly related to their roles as slaves and partly independent from slavery.[103] Enslaved persons could, of course, internalize their classification as slaves and act on the basis of this identity (7.1), but they could also maintain ethnic and religious identities from their previous lives as free persons (7.2, 7.5, 7.7). Enslaved persons could often think of themselves as free people in captivity (7.4, 7.6). Furthermore, it is important to think about people born as slaves; did they maintain the ethnic or religious identities of their ancestors, or did they forge new identities as native, but slave, inhabitants of their societies (7.3)?

Enslaved persons constructed a variety of communities on the basis of their diverse identities. The most elementary was that of slave families. Slave families could be an important means of slave control: they produced the new generation of slaves; slaves with families would be less inclined to flee; while the threat of family separation was a potent weapon in the hands of the masters (7.8). Slave families were often formed by slaves belonging to the same household; as a result, communities of slaves who belonged to the same master could stress their link to their particular master (7.11, 7.13, 7.17). But at the same time, slave families allowed slaves to find love and emotional support, to construct wider kinship networks on which they could depend and to live meaningful lives (7.9, 7.12, 7.15). Slave families could be based on pre-existing affiliations (7.16) and could also maintain the gender and age hierarchies of free families despite their fragility (7.10). It is important to remember that in some ancient societies slave families

---

[103] Vlassopoulos 2021a: 92–112.

Greek and Roman Slaveries, First Edition. Eftychia Bathrellou and Kostas Vlassopoulos.
© 2022 John Wiley & Sons, Inc. Published 2022 by John Wiley & Sons, Inc.

did not include solely slaves or former slaves but could also be based on mixed marriages (7.14).

Enslaved people also constructed or participated in communities based on work (7.19–20, 7.25), ethnicity (7.31, 7.33), and cult (7.21–4). While some of these communities were slave only (7.23–4), others were mixed associations that also included free persons (7.19). It is particularly notable that slaves could take significant roles as members of such communities (7.26–7), but equally important are the ways in which slaves tried to use membership in such communities to enhance their condition (7.18, 7.32) or to maintain pre-existing identities (7.30–1).

Like all human communities, the communities of enslaved persons manifested both solidarities and conflicts. Slave communities could have their own internal hierarchies and balances (7.42–3), which created conflicts (7.34), while some slaves could try to take advantage of their fellow-slaves (7.36–7). Slave communities could try to sort out their problems and discipline other slaves (7.35), but when they failed, the consequences could be dismal for everyone involved (7.38). Slave communities offered slaves major elements of communal life (7.40–1), which were often crucial as a source of solidarity and support (7.39, 7.44).[104]

ENSLAVED PERSONS AND THEIR MULTIPLE IDENTITIES

7.1   Theodoret, *Letters*, 70: Greek Epistolography (Mid-Fifth Century CE)

Theodoret, bishop of Kyrrhos in northern Syria, writes to the bishop of Aigai in Kilikia on behalf of a Roman noblewoman from North Africa who had ended up in Kyrrhos after the Vandals took Carthage in 439 CE.

Literature: Harper 2011: 273–9; cf. Thalmann 1996; Huemoeller 2021.

The story of the most noble Maria is fitting for a tragic play. She is the daughter of the most magnificent Eudaimon, as she herself claims and as has been attested by several others. At the disaster that has overtaken Libya, she fell from her ancestral freedom, and her lot changed to slavery. Some merchants bought her from the barbarians and sold her to some people living in our region. Along with her, a girl was also sold, who had long been a slave at Maria's house. So, both the slave and the mistress had to pull the bitter yoke of slavery together. But the slave did not wish to disregard their difference, nor did she forget that she used to belong to Maria. Instead, she preserved her goodwill in this calamity, and after serving their common masters, she would turn to the service of her reputed fellow-slave, washing her feet, making her bed, and similarly taking care of everything else. This was discovered by their owners. And thus, Maria's freedom and her slave's good character became the talk of the town. When the most faithful soldiers stationed in

[104] Vlassopoulos 2021a: 134–46.

our region found out about this – I was away at the time – they paid the price to those who had bought her and snatched her from the clutches of slavery. After my return, I was informed about both the dramatic misfortune and the soldiers' praiseworthy initiative. I prayed for blessings for them and gave the most noble maiden to one of our most pious deacons, ordering sufficient provisions to be supplied to her. Ten months passed, and she found out that her father was still alive and held office in the west; naturally, she set her heart on returning to him. Some had mentioned that many traders from the west were calling at the festival which is now being held in your region. So, the maiden requested to depart with a letter from me. This is why I have written this letter, appealing to your fear of God, so that you might look after this noble offspring and charge a man adorned with piety to negotiate with ship owners, captains, and merchants and give her to the charge of faithful men, able to restore her to her father. Especially since their reward will be abundant if they take the girl to her father against all human expectation.

- How did Maria and her slave end up being enslaved?

- How does Theodoret describe the relationship between Maria and her servant while both were slaves?

- Do you believe Theodoret's story? If so, what does this imply about how slaves saw themselves?

- Does Theodoret say what happened to Maria's slave? Why?

- How does Theodoret explain why Maria finally managed to regain her freedom and status?

7.2   *IG* II² 10051: Greek Funerary Verse Inscription, Laureion, Attica (Fourth Century BCE)

The inscription was found in Laureion, the area of the Athenian silver mines, where thousands of slaves lived and worked. (See also 2.1, 4.10, 8.27.) The epitaph is in elegiac meter, and its vocabulary and style are reminiscent of Homeric poetry.

Literature: Lauffer 1956: passim; Bäbler 1998: 94–7; Hunt 2015: 136–9; Vlassopoulos 2015: 126.

Atotas, miner.
   Great-hearted Atotas, a Paphlagonian from the Black Sea, put his body to rest from toils, far away from his land. No one could rival him in his craft. "I am from the stem of Pylaimenes,[105] who died subdued by the hand of Achilles."

---

[105] Pylaimenes is a mythical figure principally known from Homer's *Iliad*. In *Iliad* 5.576–9, he is presented as an ally of the Trojans and "leader of the great-hearted Paphlagonian shieldmen", who was killed by Menelaos.

- Who is Atotas? What do we learn about his profession and ethnicity from this inscription?
- Is Atotas a slave? Can we tell?
- What role does myth play in this inscription (see n. 105)? Is the mythic version presented here the same as that of the *Iliad*? If not, what are the effects of the divergence?
- Who might have set up this epitaph? Do we hear Atotas' voice here? If not, whose voice is this?
- What can we learn from this inscription about slave identity and community?

7.3 Plato, *Meno*, 82a–b: Greek Philosophical Dialogue (Fourth Century BCE)

Menon has asked Socrates to prove his claim that there is no learning but only recollection.

Literature: Vlassopoulos 2015: 108–9.

> **Socrates:** Well, it is not easy, but I want to give it a try for your sake. Call me one of your many attendants here, whomever you want, so that I can demonstrate on him.
> **Menon:** Of course. – You, come here.
> **Socrates:** Is he Greek? Does he speak Greek?
> **Menon:** Absolutely. He is home-born.

- What language does this slave speak? Why?
- What implications does this passage have for the identity of second-generation slaves?

7.4 Cicero, *In Support of Cluentius*, 21: Latin Law-Court Speech (69 BCE)

The cities of Larinum and Asculum were among Rome's Italian allies (*socii*). The Social War between Rome and her Italian former subjects and allies, here and elsewhere referred to as the "Italian War," took place between 91 and 88 BCE.

Literature: Robinson 2005.

> There was a woman from Larinum called Dinaea, the mother-in-law of Oppianicus. She had three sons, Marcus Aurius, Numerius Aurius, and Gnaeus Magius, and one daughter, Magia, who was married to Oppianicus. When he was a young lad, Marcus Aurius was captured at Asculum during the Italian War. He fell into the hands of the senator Quintus Sergius – the one who was

convicted of murder – and was kept in confinement (*ergastulum*) at Sergius' estate. However, Numerius Aurius, his brother, died and left their brother Gnaeus Magius as his heir. Later, Magia, Oppianicus' wife, died, too. Last, the single remaining son of Dinaea, Gnaeus Magius, died. He appointed as his heir that young Oppianicus, his sister's son, and ordered that the inheritance be shared with his mother Dinaea. In the meantime, a trustworthy and precise informer came to Dinaea. He announced that her son, Marcus Aurius, was alive and lived in slavery in the Ager Gallicus.[106]

- How did Marcus Aurius end up as a slave? What was his likely social status before enslavement?

- Would Aurius have identified himself primarily as a slave? In what other ways might he have identified himself while in captivity? Cf. 7.1.

7.5 Livy, *History*, 32.26.4–18: Latin Historiography (Late First Century BCE/Early First Century CE)

Livy discusses an event in 198 BCE, in the aftermath of the Roman victory against Carthage in the Second Carthaginian War (218–201 BCE), here referred to as the "African War." The cities mentioned in the passage were in a radius of about 60 miles from Rome.

Literature: Bradley 1989: 41–2; Golden 2013: 71–3.

If Gaul was unexpectedly quiet that year, what was almost a slave uprising broke out around Rome. Carthaginian hostages were being kept under guard at Setia. Because they were sons of prominent men, there was a large host of slaves with them. The number of the latter was growing, since, after the recent African War, captives of African origin were purchased from the booty as slaves by the people of Setia themselves. *** After they had formed a conspiracy, they sent some of their number first to the territory of Setia, then around Norba and Cerceii to incite other slaves. When all had been sufficiently prepared, they had decided to attack the people of Setia, when they would be intent on watching the games, which would fairly soon take place in the town. Setia was captured in the bloodshed of the sudden uprising. The slaves *** to occupy Norba and Cerceii.

News of this horrible incident was brought to Rome, to the praetor Lucius Cornelius Lentulus.[107] Two slaves reached him before dawn and revealed everything in an orderly manner: what had happened and what was likely to happen. The praetor ordered that they be kept under guard in his house. Then he summoned the Senate and informed them of the news brought by the informants. He received orders to set off to investigate and suppress that conspiracy. He advanced accompanied by five legates, and he compelled

---

[106] A territory by the Adriatic coast of Italy, not far from Asculum.

[107] It is generally agreed by scholars that Livy's Lentulus was a mistake for Merula and that the latter was the praetor in Rome at the time.

any men he saw in the countryside, after having them take the oath of allegiance, to take up arms and follow him. With this hastily recruited force of about 2000 armed men, he arrived at Setia, while no one knew where he was going. There, he swiftly arrested the leaders of the conspiracy, and the slaves fled the city. Men were sent out in the countryside, to hunt down ***. This was the splendid work of two slaves, the informers, and of one free man. The Senators commanded that he receive 100,000 *asses* and the slaves 25,000 each and their freedom. Their price was paid back to their masters from the treasury.

Not very long afterward, it became known that some slaves remaining from the same conspiracy were about to occupy Praeneste. The praetor Lucius Cornelius set off and exacted punishment from about 500 men, who were involved in the crime. The state was in fear that the Carthaginian hostages and captives were behind this. For this reason, night watches were instituted in the streets of Rome, the junior magistrates patrolling them. Also, the triad of officials responsible for prisons and executions were ordered to guard the Prison of the Quarries with more vigilance. Also, the praetor sent letters around to the Latin communities, advising that the hostages should be kept in private houses and not be given access to public spaces, while the captives should be bound with chains weighing at least 10 pounds and detained nowhere else but under guard in the public prison.

- Who were the people involved in this revolt? How were they related?
- Was this a revolt of Carthaginian captives, hostages, and slaves or a revolt of slaves who happened to be Carthaginian?
- Can we conclude anything about the relationships between ethnic and slave identity from this text?
- What can we learn about slave revolts from this text? Compare with 9.25, 11.13, 11.15.

7.6 Achilles Tatius, *Leukippe and Kleitophon*, 6.20–2: Greek Novel (Second Century CE)

The female protagonist Leukippe, the daughter of a noble family of Byzantion, has been captured and sold as a slave to the estate of Thersandros and Melite, a wealthy Ephesian couple.

Literature: Harper 2017; Billault 2019; Hilton 2019.

Initially, Thersandros, hoping that he would be successful in the love-affair, was wholly Leukippe's slave. But when he failed to get what he had hoped for, he let his anger take the reins. He slapped Leukippe's face and said, "Wretched slave, you are literally sick with love! I heard everything you said. Aren't you pleased that I deign to speak to you? Don't you see it as great fortune if your master covers you in kisses, but, instead, you affect to be shocked and assume the ways of someone gone mad? I believe that you are actually a whore. After all, it is an adulterer that you are in love with. But, since you don't want to have me as lover, you will have me as master." And Leukippe responded, "If you want to treat me as a tyrant would, I in turn will be your subject; but you shall not use force on me." And turning to Sosthenes, she said to him, "Be my witness and tell him how I react to blows. Because you wronged me even more than him." And Sosthenes, put to shame by having been proven guilty, said, "Master, you should card the body of this woman with whips and throw her to a million tortures, so that she might learn not to show contempt to her master." "Go on, do what Sosthenes tells you," Leukippe said. "He gives you good advice. Set up the tortures. Let him bring the torture wheel; here are my arms – stretch them out. Let him bring whips, too; here is my back – beat it. Let him bring fire; here is my body – burn it. Let him bring an iron blade; here is my throat – cut it. Behold, everyone, a new type of contest. One woman contends with all manners of torture and is victorious in all. […] Arm yourself then. Take up your whips against me, the torture wheel, the fire, the iron blade. Have Sosthenes, too, your councillor, fight by your side. Naked, alone, a woman, I have one weapon: my freedom. But freedom cannot be beaten up by blows, nor cut up with iron blades, nor burnt in fire. I will never surrender it. Even if you try to burn it up, you will find that fire is not hot enough."

- How does Thersandros reproach Leukippe?

- What forms of violence are mentioned in this passage?

- Should we consider this passage as a good reflection of how masters habitually violated sexually their slaves?

- On what does Leukippe's belief that she will not be violated rest?

- What do you think of her argument? Can we see this as an expression of a wider ideology linking freedom and sexual honor?

- Does Leukippe think of herself as a slave? If not, how does she think of herself? What implications does this have concerning the identities of enslaved persons?

7.7 Jerome, *Life of Malchus*, 6:[108] Latin Biographical Narrative (Fourth Century CE)

In this work, the Church Father Jerome describes how he met an elderly ascetic called Malchus close to Syrian Antioch. Malchus told him how he had been captured by the Saracens (8.4) and of his life in slavery and his subsequent flight and liberation (9.22). The following section comes from Malchus' first-person narrative.

---

[108] Latin text: Gray 2015.

Literature: Lenski 2011a; Gray 2015: 198–246.

Oh! How nothing is ever safe with the devil! O how intricate and unspeakable are his snares! Thus, even when I was in hiding, his envy found me! My master, seeing that his flock was increasing and discovering no deception in my stance – for I knew that the Apostle had instructed that masters be served faithfully, like God –,[109] wished to reward me, so that I would become even more faithful toward him. So, he gave me that woman fellow slave who had once been captured together with me. And when I refused and said that I was a Christian and was not allowed to take as wife a woman whose husband was still alive – for her husband, who had been captured along with us, had been taken away by another master – my master, unrelenting, turned furious, drew his sword, and started to attack me. And if I hadn't been quick enough to seize the woman by the arm, he would have shed my blood on the spot. Deep night had already come, darker than usual and all too soon for me. I take my new wife into a shabby cave. With sadness leading our "nuptial" procession, we felt unacknowledged loathing for each other. At that moment I truly felt my captivity. I threw myself on the ground and began to lament for the monk I was losing, with the following words: "Is it for this that I, wretched man, was preserved? Is it to this that my crimes have led me, that with my hair already greying I should become a husband, while before I was a virgin? What good does it do me to have shown contempt for my parents, my homeland, my paternal property in the name of the Lord, if I do the thing which I tried to avoid through my contempt? Unless I am undergoing all this because I have longed for my homeland... What are we to do, my soul? Are we to perish or win? Shall we wait for the hand of the Lord or shall I stab myself with my own blade? Turn the sword against yourself! Your death, my soul, should be feared more than that of the body. The preservation of chastity also has its martyrdom. Let the witness of Christ lie unburied in the desert. I myself shall be both persecutor and martyr." [...]

The woman intervenes and, on her instigation, she and Malchus decide to live in chastity but pretend to be a couple.

Many days passed in such "matrimony." Our "wedding" made us more dear to our masters. There was no suspicion of flight. Sometimes I was away even for a whole month, a faithful shepherd of the flock in my solitude.

- What work did Malchus do as a slave?
- Why did his master offer to give him a wife? What does this tell us about the creation of slave families?
- In what ways did Malchus' Christian identity affect his life in slavery? Compare with 2.25.
- How did Malchus' various identities fit together?

---

[109] Paul, *Eph.* 6:5–9, *Col.* 3:22–25, and [Paul], *Titus* 2:9–10; cf. 11.18.

THE SLAVE FAMILY AND THE MASTER'S HOUSEHOLD

7.8   Aesop, *Fables*, 218 Hausrath – Hunger (302 Chambry): Greek Fable Attributed to Aesop

Literature: Bradley 1984: 47–80.

> The pigeon and the crow.
> A pigeon kept in a dovecote was boasting about her many offspring. A crow heard her and said to her: "Stop giving yourself airs. The more offspring you have, the more slaves you will be gathering together." The fable shows that the most unfortunate slaves are those who give birth to children in slavery.

- What is the crow's argument?
- Why is the condition of the pigeon presented as slavery?
- What do you think of the crow's argument?
- Did bringing slave children into the world have no advantage for slaves?

7.9   *TAM* V.1 442: Greek Dedicatory Inscription, Kollyda, Lydia (First–Third Century CE)

Apart from the name of the mistress, all other names are Greek.

Literature: Chaniotis 2009; Vlassopoulos 2018a.

> Eutychos, slave *pragmateutês*[110] of Julia Tabille, together with his wife Epigone, (offer this) to Men Axiettenos as fulfilment of a vow on behalf of their son Niketas, because, when ill, he was saved by the god.

- Who are the people who erected this inscription?
- What is the occasion for the dedication?
- How does this passage relate to 7.8?
- What can we learn about enslaved persons and their families from this dedication?

---

[110] *Pragmateutês*, the Greek equivalent of the Latin term *actor*, was a business agent and financial administrator.

7.10 John Chrysostom, *Homilies on Paul's Epistle to the Ephesians*, 22.2 (*PG* 62.158): Christian Sermon in Greek (Fourth Century CE)

After a verse-by-verse analysis, here Chrysostom reflects on the whole of *Eph.* 5:22–6:9. Cf. 3.33.

Literature: Harper 2011: 33–4, 261–73.

> Every man's household is a city, and every man is the chief magistrate of his own household. That this is the case with the households of the wealthy is easy to see: there are farms here and overseers and magistrates upon magistrates. But I say that the household of the poor is a city, too. For here, too, there are magistracies: for example, the husband rules over his wife, the wife rules over the slaves, the male slaves rule over their own wives, while men and women rule over their children.

- How does Chrysostom use the model of the polis to conceptualize the household?
- What distinction does he make between rich and poor households?
- Does the hierarchical model apply to slave families as well?
- Are there ways in which hierarchy in slave families is unlike hierarchy in free families?
- To what extent do you think that Chrysostom's analysis helps us to understand slave families?

7.11 *TAM* II 466: Greek Funerary Inscription, Patara, Lykia (Date Unknown)

Literature: Zoumbaki 2005.

> To Kalokairos, a fine man, a hero.[111] His fellow slaves: Elpidephoros, Heraklides, Zosimos, Nauklerikos, Marion, Kerdon, Eugamos, Metabolikos, in memory, (honoring) a fine and [distinguished?] man, who loved his master.

- Who is honored here? What terms are used to describe him?
- Who are those who honor him? How do they describe themselves?
- Is the master's name mentioned in this inscription?
- Does this slave community present itself in a different manner than those in 12.33–4?

---

[111] The Greek word *hêrôs* (hero) is commonly used for the dead person on Hellenistic and Roman gravestones.

7.12   *TAM III 769*: Sarcophagus with Greek Inscription, Termessos, Pisidia (after 250 CE)

The slaves recorded here have geographic (Syros = Syrian; Pamphylia) and local names (Trokondas), as well as names describing characteristics (Agoraste = bought; Kalokairos = fair season). The mistress and her father bear typical combinations of Roman (Aurelius-a) and Greek (Perikleia, Perikles, Hermaios) names. The inscription uses an abbreviation typical of this place and time to present genealogies: a letter of the alphabet after personal name to indicate that the father (B), or both the father and the grandfather (C), had the same name.

Literature: Martin 2003.

> Syros C (the third, i.e. son of Syros, grandson of Syros), slave of the heirs of the late Aurelia Perikleia, daughter of Aurelius Perikles Hermaios Keuas, with the permission of his masters, (made) this sarcophagus for himself, his wife Pamphylia, his daughter Agoraste and his daughter's husband Kalokairos, and for his already interred cousin Trokondas. No one else shall place another corpse in it, because one who dares to do so shall be liable to the charge of violation of the grave and to curses for which he will have the deceased to reckon with.

- Who is the creator of this inscription? How does he represent himself?
- How do you imagine readers of this inscription reacting to the genealogy "Syros, son of Syros, grandson of Syros"?
- What links of kinship are visible in this inscription?
- Compare the names of the slaves and the masters: are there any differences? What inferences can we draw?

7.13   *RIB 445*: Altar with Latin Inscription, Chester, Britannia (Second Century CE)

Literature: Flory 1978; Birley 1980: 145–50.

> To Fortuna Redux, Aesculapius and Salus,[112] the freedmen and slaves (*familia*) of Titus Pomponius Mamilianus Rufus Antistianus Funisulanus Vettonianus, son of Titus, of the Galerian tribe, legate of the emperor,[113] gave and dedicated this.

---

[112] Fortuna Redux, literally Fortune the Home-bringer, and Salus, literally Well-being/Safety, were Roman deities.

[113] A senator of praetorian rank, appointed by the emperor as head of a legion.

- Who are the dedicators of this monument? How are they related? What does the presence of both slaves and freedmen imply?
- Who is their master?
- To which deities is this dedicated? Why?
- What implications does this monument have for master–slave relationships and for slave communities?

7.14   *IC* IV 72 iii.52–iv.23: Inscribed Laws in Greek, Gortyn, Crete (Fifth Century BCE)

On the terms *woikeus-woikea* and *dōlos*, often used to denote slaves in the laws of Gortyn, see 2.6.

Literature: D. M. Lewis 2013, 2018: 147–65; Gagarin and Perlman 2016: 357–61; Vlassopoulos 2018b: 48–9.

> If a slave woman (*woikea*) gives birth to a child while separated, she shall bring the child to the master of the man who had married her, in the presence of two witnesses. If he does not accept it, the child shall be in the hands of the master of the slave woman. But if she gets married again to the same man before the end of the year, the child shall be in the hands of the master of the male slave (*woikeus*). [...] If a woman, while separated, exposes her child before bringing it to someone, as has been written, she will have to pay, if convicted, 50 staters if the child is free and 25 staters if the child is a slave (*dōlos*). And if her husband has no house to which she can bring the child or if she cannot meet with him, she shall not be liable if she exposes the child. If a slave woman (*woikea*) becomes pregnant and gives birth out of marriage, the child shall be in the hands of the master of her father. But if her father is not alive, the child shall be in the hands of the masters of her brothers.

- Does this law recognize the right of slaves to marry?
- What links of kinship among slaves are recognized in the law?
- How did Cretan slave owners benefit from such recognition?
- How could Cretan slaves have benefited from it?
- Is it common for ancient law codes to recognize slave kinship? Cf. 1.11–2.

7.15   *Life of Aesop*, Vita G, 29–30:[114] Greek Fictional Biography (First or Second Century CE)

Aesop's new master, the Samian philosopher Xanthos, brings Aesop to his home for the first time.

---

[114] Greek text: Ferrari 1997.

Literature: Hopkins 1993.

When they arrived at the house, Xanthos said to Aesop, "Aesop, as my wife is very particular with beauty, wait in front of the gate until I announce you to her, so that she may not see your ugliness all of a sudden and then demand her dowry back and leave me." Aesop said, "If it is your wife who is the boss, go and do it quickly." Xanthos went into the house and said, "Lady, you will no longer have cause to whine and say, 'It is my slave girls who serve you!' Look! I, too, have bought a slave – a male one." Xanthos' wife said, "Thank you, lady Aphrodite. Great are you, and the dreams you send are true. You see, when I fell asleep, I saw a dream in which you had bought a very beautiful slave and gave him to me as a gift." Xanthos said, "Wait a moment, lady, and you will see a beauty you have never seen before. Honestly! You will see an Apollo, or an Endymion or a Ganymede!".

The slave girls were delighted, and one of them said, "It is for me that the master bought a husband." Another: "No! For me! I saw it in my dream." Another said the following to them: "It is the most... persuasive of us who will get him." "So, are *you* the most persuasive?" "Well, are *you*?" And they start to quarrel. Xanthos' wife says, "That chap whom you praised – where is he?" Xanthos: "By the door, lady. For it is a principle of good education not to enter another's house without invitation. He followed me to the gate and is waiting there to be summoned." Xanthos' wife says, "One of you! Let the newly bought slave in!" One of the girls, keen on marriage, said to herself while the others were quarreling, "I will go out and secure him for myself before the others." She goes outside and says, "Where is the newly bought slave?" Aesop turned and said to her, "Here, girly!" She said, "Are *you* the newly bought one?" Aesop said, "I am." The girl said, "Where is your tail?" Aesop looked at the girl and, realizing that she mocked him as a dog-faced baboon, said to her, "I do not have my tail behind, as you think, but at the front." The slave girl said, "Wait there! Don't come in, for they will all flee, as soon as they see this monstrosity!" She went inside. When she saw that her companions were still quarreling, she said, "Why don't I incite them further?! Hey, girls! Why are you having a fight on that man's behalf, by the Muses who protect you? Look at his beauty first." One of them goes outside and says, "Where is my lord? The purchased one? Where is my beautiful boy?" Aesop said, "Here I am." The girl says, "May Aphrodite strike your ugly face. Was it on *your* account that I was quarreling, you scum? Damn you. Go inside and don't you dare touch me. Stay away from me!"

- What is the wife's complaint to Xanthos? What does this tell us about households, gender, and slavery?

- Why do the slave girls fight with each other? What does this tell us about slaves' hopes and desires? What obstacles did they face in fulfilling them?

- What can this passage tell us about sexual relations and families among slaves?

7.16 *SGDI* 2183, 3–8: Greek Manumission Inscription, Delphi, Phokis (Second Century BCE)

Literature: Vlassopoulos 2010, 2015; Lewis 2017.

> [...] On the following terms did Praxias son of Eudokos, a Delphian, sell to Apollo Pythios a male body named Chresimos, in origin from Syrian Beirut, for the price of five minai of silver, together with his wife Zois, in origin from Syria, for the price of four and a half minai. [...]

- Who are the two slaves manumitted here? How are they described?

- What is their ethnic identity?

- How likely do you think it is that these Syrian slaves bore the Greek names Chresimos (literally "useful") and Zois (literally "life") before being acquired by a Greek household?

- Can the fact that this slave couple have similar ethnic origins be suggestive of slave strategies when forming families?

7.17 Columbaria

Columbaria were funerary monuments for the slaves and freedpersons of the great aristocratic families of Rome. They emerged in the Augustan period and lasted till the end of the first century CE. The remains of most dead were held in urns, placed in burial niches in the walls (Fig. 12). Columbaria were usually run by associations of slaves and freedpersons with their own officials. Cf. 1.17, 4.9, 10.16.

Literature: Caldelli and Ricci 1999; Hasegawa 2005; Galvao-Sobrinho 2012; Penner 2012; Mouritsen 2013; Borbonus 2014.

——————   7.17.a *An. Ep.* (1996), No. 253: Latin Funerary   ——————
Inscription, Rome (Augustan Period)

Marcella the younger, presented here as wife of Paullus (*scil.* Paullus Aemilius Lepidus), was a daughter of Octavia, Augustus' sister. Messalla and Regillus were probably her two sons: the latter from her marriage with Paullus, the former from her earlier marriage with M. Valerius Messala Appianus.

> Of the freedmen, freedwomen, and slaves (*familia*) of Marcella, wife of Paullus, Messala and Regillus, who contributed to this monument. Their names are inscribed inside.

- What community does this monument serve? What are its connecting links?
- What similarities and differences does this monument have with monuments such as 1.16, 2.10, 7.25, 8.1, 10.31, 12.25, and 12.33?

Tumlnello. Roma

581 — COLOMBARIO DEI FAMIGLIARI DI AUGUSTO A. D. 20, NELLA VIGNA CODINI SULLA VIA APPIA

Figure 12 Columbarium 2 at Vigna Codini, before 20 CE, Rome: image provided under CC BY licence from Wikimedia Commons.

──────────   7.17.b   *CIL* VI, 4012–13a: Latin Funerary   ──────────
Inscriptions, Rome (First Century CE)

These inscriptions come from the columbarium for the slaves and freedpersons of Livia, Augustus' wife; the columbarium, no longer extant, originally housed the remains of thousands of people in its niches and was used until the time of Nero.

Literature: Hasegawa 2005: 30–51; Borbonus 2014: 130–3.

4012: Tyrannus, slave born in the household (*verna*), three times elected councilman (*decurio*) and tribune (*tribunus*) of Augusta, gave the niche for his fellow slave Philadelphus, baker, formerly owned by Potitius.

4013a: Tyrannus, slave born in the household (*verna*), bookkeeper (*tabularius*), attendant (*apparitor*), exempt from everything related to the sacred rites. He gave to Tiberius Claudius Veteranus, freedman of the emperor, a whole columbarium. He also interred Ianthus, freedman of the emperor, his own brother.

- Who was Tyrannus? How is he described? What positions did he hold? What does this imply about slave communities?
- Which individuals were buried in the niches provided by Tyrannus?
- What is the impression given by the funerary niches in Figure 12? What does it tell us about equality and hierarchy within these slave communities?

COMMUNITIES OF WORK, CULT, AND ETHNICITY

7.18 Thucydides, 3.73: Greek Historiography (End of Fifth Century BCE)

In 427 BCE, the democrats and the oligarchs on the Ionian island of Corcyra are involved in a civil war.

Literature: Paradiso 2008; Vlassopoulos 2011a.

The following day there were a few skirmishes, and both parties sent missions to the countryside, asking the slaves to join them and promising them their freedom. Most slaves allied themselves with the democrats. Eight hundred mercenaries came from the mainland to aid the oligarchs.

- What do democrats and oligarchs do to win the civil war?
- What do the slaves decide?
- How exactly do you envisage the process through which the democrats and the oligarchs courted the slaves?
- How exactly do you envisage the process through which the majority of the slaves reached the decision to support the democrats?
- What can we learn about slave communities from this passage?

7.19 *IG II²* 2934: Greek Inscribed Dedicatory Relief, Athens (Fourth Century BCE)

The dedication is inscribed on a relief depicting Nymphs – goddesses connected with water and springs. With the exceptions of Manes and Midas (on which see 8.21), all names are Greek. Leuke and Myrrhine are female names.

Literature: Vlassopoulos 2010, 2011b.

> The washers dedicated this to the Nymphs and all the gods after a vow: Zoagoras, son of Zokypros; Zokypros, son of Zoagoras; Thallos; Leuke; Sokrates, son of Polykrates; Apollophanes, son of Euporion; Sosistratos; Manes; Myrrhine; Sosias; Sosigenes; Midas.

- Who made this dedication? What common links did they have?
- What can we establish about the status and gender of the people involved?
- Notice the names of the individuals: are any patterns visible?
- What implications does this evidence have for community formation?
- To what deity is this inscription dedicated? Is it significant?

7.20   *IG* I^3, 476.242–48: Inscribed Records in Greek, Athens (Fifth Century BCE)

This passage is part of an inscription recording the expenses incurred by the Athenians for building the Erechtheion in the Acropolis. Here, wages given to laborers for adding flutes to columns are being recorded. In this inscription citizens are recorded with just their name, while free foreigners (metics) are recorded along with their place of residence.

Literature: Randall 1953; Vlassopoulos 2007, 2011b; Epstein 2008.

Onesimos, (slave) of Nikostratos	18 drachmas and 3.5 obols;
Eudoxos, resident at Alopeke	18 drachmas;
Kleon	18 drachmas and 2 obols;
Simon, resident at Agryle	18 drachmas and 1.5 obols;
Antidotos, (slave) of Glaukos	18 drachmas and 1.5 obols;
Eudikos	18 drachmas and 1.5 obols.

- What is the status of the individuals represented in this inscription?
- Are the masters of the slaves working alongside them or not? If not, why? What implications does this have concerning the working conditions of slaves?
- How much are these people paid? Are there any pay differentials on the basis of status? If not, why?
- What social interactions can you envisage this mixed group involved in? Can you imagine them interacting at lunch break or having drinks after work?

7.21   *ID 2531*: Greek Curse Inscription, Delos, Cyclades (Second/First Century BCE)

Literature: Bömer 1990: 93; Maillot forthcoming.

> Theogenes [...] raises his hands to the Sun and the Pure Goddess (*Hagnê Thea*) against an impious woman. She swore that she would not deprive him of anything nor wrong him, and, if she received a deposit, that she would not keep it for herself. I, having faith in the Pure Goddess, did believe in her oath and did not do anything wrong against her. She, however, received a deposit for freedom but deprived me of it. May she not escape the power of the Goddess. And I demand and request that all the worshippers (*therapeutai*) curse her at the right time.

- Who is Theogenes? Can we establish his status?
- Why is Theogenes calling on divine help?
- Who was the "impious woman"? What was her relationship to Theogenes?
- Who might the "worshippers" be? How might they be related to Theogenes?
- Can we learn anything about slave communities from this inscription?

7.22   *I.Lindos* 630: Greek Honorific Inscription, Lindos, Rhodes, Dodecanese (ca. 50 BCE)

The text is inscribed on a marble altar, between the representations of two wreaths. Soteriastai, literally "persons who offer cult to Soter," was a name used for members of cultic associations honoring a god with the epithet "Soter" (literally "Saviour"), usually Zeus. Lysistratos, the man who presumably founded this particular association, is otherwise unknown. On *engeneis* at Rhodes, see also 2.2.

Literature: http://ancientassociations.ku.dk/assoc/77.

> Athanodoros, a slave born in Rhodes (*engenês*), has been honored by the Soteriastai around Lysistratos with a golden and an olive wreath.
>   Good man, farewell!

- Who is honored here? How is he described?
- Who honors him? What do you think is their connection to the honoree?
- Can we learn anything about slave communities from this inscription?

7.23   *IG* XII.1 31: Greek Dedicatory Inscription, Rhodes, Dodecanese (First Century CE)

Literature: Zoumbaki 2005; Boyxen 2018: 228–32.

[By decision of] the city's public slaves' [association of devotees of Zeus Atab-yri]os: Eulimenos, public secretary, who has served as priest of Zeus Atabyri-os, dedicated these bulls to Zeus A[tabyrios] as a token of [than]ks, [on behalf of] our Rhodian masters.

- What body decided to make this dedication? What is its character, and what is the status of its members?
- What is the status of the person who actually made the dedication? How is he presented?
- What is the purpose of this dedication?
- What picture of the relationships between slaves and citizens on the island of Rhodes does this inscription offer? How does this picture relate to the island's economy and political history?

7.24   *SEG* XXXVIII 546: Greek Funerary Inscription, Byllis, Illyria (Third Century CE)

Epitaph inscribed on the right half of a stele; on the left half, there is a relief depicting a standing man, with the Greek word for "destiny" (*moira*) written near his head. The "Lecheateans," who describe themselves as a cult association (*thiasos*), might have been connected to Leches, a son of the god Poseidon, or to Poseidon himself.

Literature: Zoumbaki 2005.

Farewell, Epigonos, of 45 years of age. The association (*thiasos*) of the Lech-eateans which consists of slaves.

- Who was the deceased?
- What can we learn about slave communities from this inscription and the monument bearing it?

7.25   *I.Ephesos* 2200A: Latin Funerary Inscription, Ephesos, Ionia (Second/Third Century CE)

For *collegia*, voluntary associations, see 12.33.

Literature: Weaver 1972: 118; Flexsenhar 2019: 86–7.

> To the divine spirits:
>
> For Acilia Lamyra, his beloved wife, Apollonius, home-born slave (*verna*) of our Augustus and treasurer (*arcarius*) of the province of Asia, erected this monument, together with a sarcophagus – also for himself and his people. These are being taken care of by the *collegia* of the freedmen and slaves of our lord Augustus which are written below: the great *collegium*, that of the bookkeepers (*tabullarii*) of Minerva, those of the registrars (*commentarienses*), foremen (*decurii*) and recordkeepers (*tabellarii*) of Faustina. This monument shall not pass to the heir.

- Who erected this monument, and what was his status?
- Who is appointed responsible for the monument's maintenance? What do these people share and what is their status?
- What conclusions can we draw from this about community formation?

7.26 *CIL* I², 2685: Latin Dedicatory Inscription, Minturnae, Italy (First Half of First Century BCE)

In Latin inscriptions of this time the names of male patrons of freed persons are explicitly mentioned, while female patrons are only indicated by a generic sign standing for "freed(wo)man of a woman." The following inscription is one of many inscribed stelae dedicated by local cultic associations at Minturnae; these associations were led by boards of twelve officials who bore the titles *magistri* (fem. *magistrae*) or *ministri* (fem. *ministrae*).

Literature: Flower 2017: 226–33.

> In the year that [...] were members of the Board of two.
>
> The following female officials (*magistrae*) present this to Venus as a gift:
>
> Tertia Domatia, daughter of S[purius]
> Alfia Flora, freedwoman of a woman
> Cahia Astaphium, freedwoman of a woman
> Dosithea, slave of Calidus Numerius
> Stolia, slave of Minidus Lucius
> Allenia Salvia, freedwoman of [...]
> Co[...] Creusa, freedwoman of Marcus
>
> *The beginnings of four more names follow, before the stone breaks.*

- What is the legal status of the individuals mentioned in this inscription?
- Do enslaved and freed women have the same masters and patrons?

- What was the role undertaken by these enslaved and freed women?

- By what processes do you envisage these women appointed to their position? Cf. 7.27.

- How do you think these appointments might have mattered for these women?

7.27   *CIL* VI, 30982: Altar with Latin Inscription, Rome (Late First Century BCE/Early First Century CE)

This association of carpenters had senior officials with the title of "leaders" (*magistri*) and junior officials titled "attendants" (*ministri*); the masters of these slaves appear in another inscription as *magistri* of this association (*An.Ep.* 1941, no. 71). For images and sketches of this altar, see http://www.edr-edr.it/edr_programmi/res_complex_comune.php?do=book&id_nr=edr075876

Literature: Pearse 1975; Madigan 2013: 10–16; https://gdrg.ugent.be/guilddocuments/2979.

> Attendants (*ministri*) during the second five-year period (*lustrum*):
>
> [...], slave of Gaius Julius Milo
> [...], slave of Marcus Julius Amphio
> Erilis, slave of Marcus Antonius Andro (or Andronicus)
> Utilis, slave of Gaius Fictorius Flaccus
> Menophilus, slave of Gaius Tacitus Rufus
> Marcilus, slave of Numerius [...] Stabilio

- What is this monument? What is depicted on it?

- Who are the dedicators? What is their status? In what capacity do they make the dedication?

- What can we learn about the participation of slaves in professional communities from this source?

7.28   *CIL* XIII, 507: Latin Dedicatory Inscription, Lactora, Gaul (176 CE)

Literature: Salerno 2016–7.

> To the Mother of the gods, Julia Valentina and Hygia, slave of Silana, offered a taurobolium.[115] On the 15th day before the Calends of November, in the consulship of Pollio and Aper, and the priesthood of Zminthius son of Proculianus.

---

[115] A religious rite involving the sacrifice of a bull.

- Are the two women who made this dedication of the same status?

- Are they related in any way? What do you imagine might have brought them together?

7.29   *I.Oropos* 329: Greek Inscription Recording Manumission, Oropos, Boiotia (Third Century BCE)

Marble stele dedicated to the gods Amphiaraos and Hygieia, recording a manumission; broken at the top. At Amphiaraos' sanctuary at Oropos, worshippers practiced incubation for healing and divination purposes.

Literature: Lewis 1957; Noy, Panayotov and Bloedhorn 2004: 177–80.

> [... under the following terms:] Moschos shall [remain] with Phr[ynidas for one ye]ar and be free, not belonging to any[one in any] way. If something happens[116] to Phrynidas before this time passes, Moschos shall go away free wherever he himself might wish. With good fortune. Witnesses: Athenodoros, son of Mnasikon, Oropian; Biottos, son of Eudikos, Athenian; Charinos, son of Anticharmos, Athenian; Athenades, son of Epigonos, Oropian; Hippon, son of Aischylos, Oropian. Moschos, son of Moschion,[117] a Judaean, (set this up) after seeing a dream, at the command of god Amphiaraos and Hygieia, according to which Amphiaraos and Hygieia ordered him to inscribe a stele and set it up by the altar.

- What can we learn about Moschos' ethnic and cultural identity from this inscription? What relationships of his are mentioned?

- Is there a contradiction between Moschos' Judaean identity and his participation in the practice of incubation in a pagan temple?

- Can this inscription tell us anything about the link between slavery and ethnic and religious identity?

7.30   *SGDI* 1722, 1–4: Greek Manumission Inscription, Delphi, Phokis (Second Century BCE)

Literature: Noy, Panayotov and Bloedhorn 2004: 171–3.

> In the archonship of Archon, son of Kallias, in the month of Endyspoitropios, Atisidas, son of Orthaios, sold to Apollo Pythios three female bodies, whose names are Antigona, Judaean in origin, and her daughters Theodora and Dorothea, for the price of seven minai of silver. And he has received the full price. [...]

---

[116] A euphemistic reference to death.
[117] The names Moschos and Moschion are Greek.

- Which slaves are manumitted in this inscription? What are their relationships?
- What can we establish about the ethnic identity and religion of these three slaves?
- What are the names of these three slaves? Is there anything interesting about their names, which are Greek and, in the daughters' case, mean "god's gift"? Could they be related to their Judaean identities?
- Can you imagine how the two girls were given the names they have?
- Can this inscription be used as evidence of slave agency? How?

7.31 Philo, *Embassy to Gaius*, 155–7: Greek Treatise (First Century CE)

In this treatise, Philo argues that the character and actions of the emperor Caligula were behind the violence against the Alexandrian Jews in 38 CE. At this point, Philo argues that the relationship between the Jews and Augustus was one of mutual respect. Cf. Tacitus, *Annals*, 2.85.

Literature: Noy 2000: 255–67.

How was it then that Augustus acknowledged the great section of Rome on the other side of the Tiber, which he knew was occupied and inhabited by Jews? The majority were Romans who had been manumitted. That is, they had been taken to Italy as captives and were manumitted by those who had bought them, without being forced to falsify their ancestral customs. So, he also knew that they organized prayers and held gatherings for this purpose, especially on the holy seventh day, when they publicly receive training in their ancestral philosophy. He also knew that they collected money for sacred purposes from first-fruits and sent it to Jerusalem with those who would offer sacrifices. Nonetheless, he did not expel them from Rome, nor did he deprive them of their Roman citizenship because they also showed respect for their Jewish one; nor did he interfere with their prayers or prevented them from gathering in order to be instructed in the laws; nor did he oppose their collection of first-fruits. Instead, he showed so much respect for our customs, that he, well-nigh together with his whole household, adorned our temple with extravagant dedications and also commanded that sacrifices of whole-burnt unblemished offerings be offered from his own expenses every day, perpetually, as first-offering to the most-high god. These are offered until today, and will be offered forever, as a declaration of truly imperial conduct.

- What are the origins of the Jewish community at Rome, according to Philo?
- What happened to the Jewish slaves after they were manumitted?
- How did the former Jewish slaves manage to maintain their religious identity and community to such an impressive extent?
- Were all members of the Jewish community at Rome former slaves? What motives might have brought free Jews to Rome?

- Should we imagine a similar kind of community made of freedpersons and free immigrants for other ethnic communities of the Roman Empire? Or was there something peculiar about the Jewish community?

- To what extent did the peculiar Roman enfranchisement of freedpersons account for the vitality of this Jewish community?

7.32   [Paul], *First Letter to Timothy*, 6:1–2: Greek Biblical Text (First Century CE)

This letter is attributed to the apostle Paul; most historians believe that it was written pseudonymously decades later, along with the other two so-called Pastoral Epistles (Second Letter to Timothy, Letter to Titus).

Literature: Glancy 2002a: 145–8.

> All who are under the yoke of slavery should regard their own masters as worthy of every honor, lest the name of God and our teaching be slandered. Those who have believing masters should not be disrespectful toward them because they are brothers; instead, they should be better slaves, because those receiving their good service are believers and dear to them.

- What advice does the author give to Christian slaves?
- Why should Christian slaves obey their masters according to the author? How should Christian slaves behave towards their Christian masters?
- What danger could a community including both slaves and masters create, according to the author?
- What can we learn about communities involving slaves from this passage?

7.33   Synesius, *On Kingship*, 20: Greek Deliberative Oratory (Around 400 CE)

In this oration, Synesius offers advice to the emperor Arcadius. He advocates the curbing of the power of foreigners, most probably Goths, referring to them contemptuously as Scythians. He particularly warns against the en masse drafting of the "Scythians" into the Roman army and their holding of military commands and other important offices. The so-called Third Servile War occurred around 70 BCE.

Literature: Lenski 2008, 2011b.

> Among the many things that I marvel at is especially our absurd conduct. For every household which prospers even a little owns a slave from Scythia; in each one, the waiter, the cook, the water bearer is a Scythian; of our attendants, those who carry folding chairs on their shoulders so that their owners

can have a seat when in the street are all Scythians. –This race has long been shown to be most useful and suitable to be slaves to the Romans. – The fact then that these blond men, who arrange their hair in the fashion of the men of Euboia, are in private life the slaves of those of whom they are magistrates in public life is unusual and could be the most paradoxical element of the spectacle. I wouldn't know what the so-called riddle is, if not this.

In Gaul, Crixus and Spartacus, who used to bear weapons in dishonor, in order to be the scapegoats of the Roman people in the arena, ran away resenting Roman laws. So, they conspired and organized the so-called Servile War, which turned out to be one of the most grievous for the Romans at the time. Against them, the Romans had to deploy consuls and generals and Pompey's good fortune, for the city had come close to be ravaged off the earth. And yet, those who revolted together with Spartacus and Crixus were not of the same race as they, nor of the same race as one another; their common fortune, however, having obtained a cause, made them of the same mind. For, I believe, all slaves by nature become an enemy if they can expect to overcome their masters. Is it the same in our case, too? Are we nourishing the seeds of absurd things on an altogether greater scale? For in our case those that could initiate a revolt are not just two dishonored men but armies which are huge, murderous, and of the same race as our slaves. By bad fortune, they have intruded in the Roman Empire and provide generals of great reputation among themselves and among us because of our own cowardice. You should know that, when they wish it, they will employ our slaves, too, along with the soldiers they already have – soldiers most reckless and audacious, who shall take their fill of independence through committing the unholiest deeds.

- How does the slave revolt led by Spartacus and Crixus compare with Synesius' feared revolt of his contemporary Scythian slaves?
- What will incite the Scythian slaves to revolt, according to Synesius? What is the role of ethnicity in this? Cf. 11.14.a–c.

SOLIDARITIES AND CONFLICTS

7.34 Aesop, *Fables*, 261 Hausrath – Hunger (355 Chambry): Greek Fable Attributed to Aesop

Someone bought a parrot and let it loose in his house to live. The parrot took advantage of the gentle treatment; with a leap, he sat on the hearth and from there croaked as he pleased. A cat saw him and asked him who he was and where he had come from. He said, "The master just bought me." "Impudent creature," the cat said, "are you crying so loud, although new? The masters do not allow this even to me, who am home-born. If I ever do it, they get mad at me and send me away." He responded, "Keep away from me, missy! The masters aren't displeased with my voice as they are with yours." This story is apt for a censorious man, one always attempting to throw accusations at others.

- How does slavery inform the way that the story is narrated?
- What is the status of the parrot and the cat in the master's household?
- What is the cat's complaint?
- What can we learn from this passage about relationships among slaves?

7.35 Alciphron, *Letters*, 2.23:[118] Greek Literary Epistolography (Second/Third Century CE)

Literature: Biraud and Zucker 2018.

Lenaios to Korydon: I had just cleared the threshing floor and was putting aside the winnowing fan, when the master came. He stood by, watched, and praised my industriousness. Then, out of I don't know where, the Korykian demon appeared to me,[119] most wicked Strombichos. When he saw me following the master, he took the coat I had left aside while working, put it under his arm, and went off with it, so that I might incur both harm and the laughter of my fellow slaves.

- Why does Strombichos play a prank on Lenaios?
- Does Lenaios care for the opinion of his fellow slaves?
- In what ways do the strategies Lenaios and Strombichos adopt toward their master and other slaves differ?

7.36 *An.Ep.* (2010), 108: Latin Curse Tablet, Saguntum, Spain (Middle of First to Middle of Second Century CE)

Literature: Tomlin 2010; Alvar Nuño 2016.

Felicio, slave of Aurelianus, asks and entrusts the money that Heracla, my fellow slave, received from me, so that he might suffer an attack upon his bosom, his eye and his strength, whoever they are [...?]. I entrust this money to the honor (?) of the priest.

---

[118] Greek text: Schepers 1905.
[119] The inhabitants of Korykos, an important harbor in Kilikia, in south-eastern Asia Minor, were proverbial informers.

- Who is the curser? How does he describe himself?
- Who is the target of the curse? Can you imagine why?
- What does this text suggest about relationships among slaves (compare with 7.37)?

7.37   *An.Ep.* (2008), 792: Latin Curse Tablet, Leicester, Britannia (Middle of Second–Middle of Third Century CE)

Female names are underlined.

Literature: Tomlin 2008.

> I give the one who committed the wrong from the slave quarters to the god Maglus.[120] I give him who committed the theft from the slave quarters, the one who stole the cloak of Servandus.
>
> | | |
> |---|---|
> | Silvester Rigomandus | Iuventius |
> | Senilis Venustinus | Alocus |
> | Vorvena | Cennosus |
> | Calaminus | Germanus |
> | Felicianus | Senedo |
> | Rufedo | Cunovendus |
> | Vendicina | Regalis |
> | Ingenuinus | Nigella |
>
> I give in order that the god might take away the person who stole the cloak of Servandus before the ninth day.

- Who made this curse and whom did he consider suspects for the theft of his cloak? Why?
- What aspects of slave community does this curse tablet illustrate?

7.38   *Acts of Andrew*, 17–8, 20–22:[121] Apocryphal Christian Text in Greek (Probably Second/Third Century CE)

Maximilla, the wife of Aegeates, proconsul of the city of Patras in the Peloponnese, has been converted to Christianity by the apostle Andrew, along with Stratokles, her brother-in-law, and Iphidama, her female slave. With Andrew's encouragement, she decides to abstain from sexual activity and contrives a way to achieve this.

---

[120] A god of Celtic origin (to judge by his name), otherwise unattested.
[121] Greek text: Prieur 1989.

Literature: Glancy 2002a: 21–4; Cobb 2017.

Maximilla then came up with the following idea. She had a young slave girl who was very beautiful and excessively unrestrained by nature. Her name was Euklia. Maximilla summoned her and told her what the girl too desired and found pleasure in: "You can rely on my generosity for anything you might need, if you consider making a pact with me and observing what I assign you to do." So, she said to Euklia what she wanted and secured her confidence. And since she wanted to spend the rest of her life in chastity, she found relief in the following, which lasted for quite some time. As it is a habit of women to adorn themselves adopting the Opponent's ways, it is in such a manner that Maximilla adorned Euklia and instructed her to lie with Aegeates, as if she were Maximilla herself. And he, treating Euklia as if his own wife, let her go out, to her own bedroom, every time she left his bed, since Maximilla also used to do that. So, Maximilla, refreshed and rejoicing in the Lord, did not part from Andrew, and she did that undetected for a long time.

Eight months later, however, Euklia demanded from her mistress to set her free; Maximilla gave her what she asked on the same day. After a few days, she also asked for a substantial sum of money; Maximilla gave it to her immediately. Then she asked for some of her jewels; Maximilla had no objections. Put simply, although on each occasion Maximilla would give her clothes, linen, headbands, this was not enough for her; boasting, puffed up, she revealed the affair to her fellow slaves. They, however, became indignant at her bragging. At the beginning they tried to silence her with their railing. But she would laugh and show them the gifts she had received from their mistress. Her fellow slaves recognized these and did not know what to do. Euklia, wanting to give further proof for her claims, made two of her fellow slaves stand by the head of her master while he was drunk, so that they would be convinced that she really did lie with him as though she were Maximilla herself. Weighed down by deep sleep, he got awoken by her, and Euklia and her fellow slaves who were watching the incident heard him saying, "My lady Maximilla, why so late?" She kept silent. Those who had stood to witness quietly left the bedroom.

Maximilla, however, thinking that Euklia kept silent and was faithful to her because of the gifts she had received from her, used to find refreshment by Andrew's side at night, together with Stratokles and all the other brothers. [...] The household slaves, however, when they found out about the affair and how Maximilla would daily go to Andrew with Stratokles and what time she would return to her own bedroom, caught her as if she were some stranger. And precisely as she was entering the proconsul's residence, striving not to be seen, they forcibly uncovered her head and stood looking at their mistress. Some of them wanted to make the affair known and inform Aegeates; others tried to stop them, pretending they felt affection for their mistress. So, they tried to silence those with them and beat them as if the latter were madmen, pushing them away. As they were thus fighting against each other, Maximilla jumped into her bedroom, praying to the Lord to turn all evil away from her. After one hour, those fighting against their fellow slaves about her rushed into her room. They spoke to her in flattery, expecting to get something out of her, as they were slaves of Aegeates. The blessed Maximilla did not refuse to give them what they demanded. She summoned Iphidama and told her, "Let us give those men what they deserve." Thus, she ordered that one thousand denarii be given to those feigning love for her, commanding them not to reveal the affair to anyone. They swore, more than once, to keep silent about what they had seen.

But instigated by their father the devil, they immediately rushed to their master, with the money in hand. And they told him the whole story: how their own fellow slave revealed to them Maximilla's ruse, as she no longer wanted to share a bed with Aegeates, having rejected sex with him as a terrible and shameful act. The proconsul investigated and confirmed everything: how Euklia lied with him as his own wife, how she told everything to her fellow slaves. He interrogated her too and discovered all her motives; under torture, she revealed everything that she had received from her mistress in order to keep silent. Aegeates, indignant at Euklia for her boasts to her fellow slaves and for her words, which defamed the mistress – he wanted to keep the whole thing quiet, affectionate as he was toward his wife – cut off Euklia's tongue, mutilated her, and ordered that she be thrown out. After a few days without any food, Euklia was eaten up by dogs. And his other slaves, those who had told him what I mentioned, three in number, he crucified.

- Why does Maximilla think she can count on Euklia?
- How does Euklia exploit her position?
- Why does Euklia reveal her mistress's secret to her fellow slaves? How do they react toward her?
- What is the slaves' ruse against Maximilla?
- How do Aegeates' slaves hope to benefit from the situation?
- What can we learn about slave communities from this source?

7.39   *CEL* I, 3: Latin Letter on Papyrus, Busiris, Egypt (Second Half of First Century BCE)

Egypt was conquered by Rome in 30 BCE, but there was a Roman presence there before that. All names mentioned are Greek.

Literature: Bieżuńska-Małowist 1974: 99.

External side of the letter: To Menander [...], slave of Diogenes.
Internal side: Phileros says hello to all his fellow slaves. If you are doing well, well done. Know that until now Trochilus has been doing enough. As for the rest, I ask from you, my fellow slaves, to defend me while I am absent. As for the rest, everything in the house is fine. Farewell.

- Who is the author and his addressees? What is their status?

- What is the subject of the letter? What is Phileros asking from his fellow-slaves?

- What are the implications of a letter exchanged among slaves written in Latin in a Greek-speaking area?

- What can we learn about slave communities from this source?

7.40   *Tab. Vind.* 301: Diptych Writing Tablet Inscribed in Latin, Vindolanda, Britannia (First/Second Century CE)

The tablet comes from a Roman fort. The Saturnalia were a festival of particular significance for slaves; the word denoting the item connected to the Saturnalia has not been understood securely by scholars, and we mark it with a question mark.

Literature: Bradley 1979; Bowman and Thomas 1994: 276–8; Zelnick-Abramovitz 2012.

> Severus to his Candidus, greetings.
>   I ask you, brother, to settle the (?) of the Saturnalia for four or six *asses*; and radishes, for no less than half a *denarius*.
>   Farewell, brother.
> *At the back*: To Candidus, slave of Genialis, from Severus, *cornicularius*.[122]

- Who are the correspondents? Can we establish their status?

- What is the letter about? How does it illuminate slave life?

7.41   *I.Rhegion* 58: Terracotta Tile with Graffiti in Greek, Rhegium, Italy (Late First Century BCE/Early First Century CE)

Tile inscribed before firing (Frontcover image); used to repair the roof of an older tomb. The layout of the graffiti resembles to an extent that of a funerary inscription.

Literature: Lattanzi, Lazzarini and Mosino 1989; Buonocore 1991; Caruso 2018; cf. Aubert 1994: 226–7.

> a. *Main graffito (written centre, in large letters)*:
>   Clemens, slave of Alfius Primio.
> b. *Below a, in smaller letters*:
>   Inscribed by Anthos of Rhegium; made by the potter Hermeros:

---

[122] A military title for an assistant to an army officer.

> "Phalakros, greetings! Soterichos, you faggot and useless kiln worker! Primogenes, you worthless purchase!"[123]
> (This is) a tell-tale tile.[124]
>
> c. *To the right of a, written in a 90 degrees angle, in small letters*:
>
> To the ruffian (?) Primogenes, the worthless purchase. For he is the son of an alley cat (?).
> *Further below*: Primo(genes?).

- What kind of text is this? Why was it inscribed?

- Which people are mentioned? Can we establish their status?

- Can we learn anything about this workshop community from this tile?

7.42 *Digest*, 1.18.21: Collection of Latin Juristic Texts (Sixth Century CE)

On the Digest, see 1.2.

Literature: Buckland 1908: 33–6; Giannella 2014: 124–38; Perry 2015.

> Julius Paulus, *On the Duties of Assessors*: When the governor (*praeses*) is conducting an investigation into the case of the corruption of a male slave or the illicit sexual penetration of a servant girl or that of a male slave, if it is alleged that the slave who suffered corruption is the agent (*actor rerum*) of a person or some other slave who is of such kind that the issue extends not only to harming the essential quality of that slave but to destroying the whole household (*domus*), the governor must take an extremely severe stance.

- What offences against slaves did the governor investigate?

- What factors aggravated the offence and should be taken into particular account?

- Why was it important that the corrupted slave was an agent?

- What consequences do you imagine that the corruption of a slave would have on the rest of the slaves in the same household?

- What does this source imply about the significance of slave community?

---

[123] It is unclear whether the message in the quotation marks addresses various persons (named or nicknamed Phalakros, Soterichos, and so on) or its addressee is only Clemens (see a), against whom a series of insults is directed. Apart from being attested as proper names, *phalakros* can mean "baldy," and *primogenês* can mean "first-born".

[124] The word translated here as "tell-tale" (*aisôpitana*) is not attested elsewhere and literally means "from the land of Aesop." The phrase to which it belongs has alternatively been understood (by Aubert 1994: 226–7) to belong to the list of insults and mean "Aisopitana, female potter," whereby "Aisopitana" could be the name or nickname of a female potter or another insult against Clemens (something like "you fabulist woman potter!").

7.43 *CIL* IX, 3028: Latin Funerary Inscription, Teate Marrucinorum, Italy (Second Century CE)

Literature: Aubert 1994: 159–62; Carlsen 1995: 70–80.

> To Hippocrates, manager (*vilicus*) of Plautus.
>   The rural slaves (*familia rustica*), over whom he ruled with moderation.

- Who is commemorated in this epitaph? What is his status?
- Who are the commemorators?
- How do they praise Hippocrates? What does this imply about the relationships among a slave *familia*?

7.44 *CIL* VI, 22355A: Latin Funerary Inscription, Rome (First Century CE)

Literature: Bodel 2017; MacLean 2018: 136–43.

> Aulus Memmius Urbanus to his fellow freedman and dearest comrade Aulus Memmius Clarus. Between you and me, my most venerable fellow freedman, no quarrel ever took place that I'm aware of. And through this epitaph, I call the gods above and those below to be my witnesses that on the same day you and I met on the slave trader's platform, in the same house we became free, and no one ever separated us, except this, the day of your death.

- Which persons are involved in this inscription? What do their names tell us about their lives and statuses?
- What is the relationship between these two persons?
- In what circumstances did they first meet?
- What does this monument tell us about slave agency?

8

Slavery and the Wider World

The link between slavery and the wider world is based on a crucial distinction between slaving zones and no-slaving zones.[125] The slaving zone of a particular society is the areas from which it derived its slaves through practices such as violent capture (8.2) or trade (8.5). Slaving zones could focus on outsiders (8.4), or they could also include members of the same ethnic or religious community (8.3). In the course of antiquity, imperial conquest and the expansion of commercial networks (8.6–8) created slaving zones that covered the Mediterranean, the Black Sea, temperate Europe, and the Near East (8.1).

No-slaving zones are areas whose inhabitants were not subject to enslavement as a result of warfare or other practices. Many ancient communities took measures to ensure that their members could not be enslaved within their community (8.10); they thus drew a communal moral circle, caring for those within it but considering those outside as fair game (8.11, 8.15). In other cases, we find calls to expand the moral circle to include people who belonged to the same ethnic or cultural group (8.12). Political communities could take practical measures to ensure the ransoming of enslaved members of the community (8.13), but empires and monotheistic religions were crucial in expanding no-slaving zones in antiquity (8.17). Empires could choose to protect their subjects from enslavement under certain circumstances (8.14); that said, imperial no-slaving zones were often imperfect because revolts, civil wars, and banditry could lead to the enslavement of imperial subjects within the empire (8.9, 8.16).

As a result, geopolitics had a crucial impact on the history of ancient slave systems. Geopolitical conjunctures could stabilize slave systems (8.18) or expand

---

[125] Fynn-Paul 2009; Fynn-Paul and Pargas 2018; Vlassopoulos 2021a: 83–91.

Greek and Roman Slaveries, First Edition. Eftychia Bathrellou and Kostas Vlassopoulos.
© 2022 John Wiley & Sons, Inc. Published 2022 by John Wiley & Sons, Inc.

slave making on a massive scale (8.19) while offering opportunities that slaves could attempt to seize (8.20). Various practices tried to maintain the alterity of enslaved outsiders (8.21–2), but slaves could also stress their alterity for their own reasons (8.23), while there were also cases in which slave alterity was positively valued (8.24). Enslavement and captivity had huge consequences, both for the lives of the individuals caught in these processes (8.25), as well as for societies and cultures as a whole. Enslaved persons were major vectors of cultural and technological transmission between their original homelands and the societies where they ended up as slaves; they could transmit their languages (8.29) or their cultural practices (8.28), create new cults (8.27), or play a part in transmitting cults from their homeland (8.30). In the opposite direction, enslaved persons who managed to return to their original homelands could also transfer valuable knowledge (8.26).

SLAVING ZONES

8.1 *EAD XXX 418*: Greek Funerary Inscription, Delos, Cyclades (Second Century BCE)

For Delos and slavery, see 2.14–5, 8.19. With few exceptions, notably, the Arabic name Zaidos and the Thracian name Bithys, the names of most of the deceased men and women addressed in the inscription are Greek (Map 1).

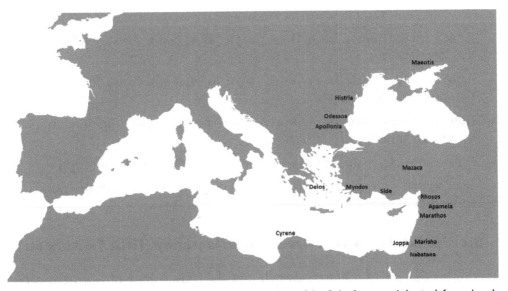

Map 1: Map of the places of origin of slaves mentioned in 8.1. Source: Adapted from Lewis 2017, 2018: 277–82.

Literature: Lewis 2017, 2018: 277–82.

Isidoros of Maeotis,
Damas of Maeotis,
Isidoros of Apameia,
Bithys of Histria,
Kalliope of Odessos,
Homonoia,
Hermolaos of Rhosos,
Antipatros of Mazaka,
Asklepiades of Side,
Apollonides of Marisha,
Nikephoros of Joppa,
Menelaos of Marathos,
Poses of Marathos,
Herakleides of Maeotis,
Nikias of Maeotis,
Ammonia of Cyrene,
and her daughter Apollonia,
Nikeratos of Apameia,
Laodike of Apameia,
Damon of Myndos,
Zaidos of Nabataea,
Damas of Histria –
you, the good men and women (*chrêstoi*) of Protarchos,
farewell.

- Which are the homelands of these people? How many areas are represented in this inscription?

- Apart from specifying their place of origin, in what other ways does this inscription describe the deceased?

- How could we explain the appearance of so many people from different places on a single funerary inscription?

- What can we learn about the geography of slavery from this inscription?

- How should we explain the coexistence of Greek names with the non-Greek ethnicities of most of these slaves?

8.2 Herodotus, 4.183: Greek Historiography (Fifth Century BCE)

Having spoken about the nomads living in the coastal zone of Northern Africa, Herodotus moves on to consider the interior. Augila is the complex of oases known today as Awjila (in modern Libya).

Literature: Liverani 2000; Fentress 2011; Bradley 2012: 164–80.

> After some 10 days' journey away from Augila, there is yet another hill of salt, which has water and many fruit-bearing palm trees, as at the other places. There live men who are called Garamantes – a great nation. They sow in earth which they place upon the salt. [...] These Garamantes hunt down the Ethiopian Troglodytai, chasing them with four-horse carriages. The Ethiopian Troglodytai are the fastest on foot of all the people about whom accounts have been brought to us. They live on snakes, lizards, and reptiles of this sort. Their language is not thought to be similar to any other; it sounds like the squeaking of bats.

- Who are the Garamantes? What is their relationship to the Troglodytai?
- Is this story evidence of the slave trade?

8.3   Xenophon, *Anabasis*, 7.3–4: Greek Historical Narrative (First Half of Fourth Century BCE)

Around 400 BCE, the mercenary army of the Ten Thousand enters the service of the Thracian prince Seuthes, who is hoping to use them in order to terrorize neighboring communities into accepting his authority.

Literature: Lewis 2018: 282–6.

> 7.3.35: When he came outside, Seuthes addressed the generals themselves and said to them, "Generals, our enemies are not yet aware of our alliance. So, if we attack them before they manage to put up their guard and prepare their defence in order to avoid capture, we would most certainly capture both people and property."
> 7.3.48–4.1–2: The outcome of these attacks was a crowd of about 1000 enslaved people, 2000 cattle, and 10,000 other livestock gathered together. Then they (i.e. the Ten Thousand and Seuthes' forces) camped on the spot. The following day, Seuthes had the villages burnt down completely, sparing not a single house, in order to instill to the rest of his enemies fear for what might happen if they did not comply. Then he prepared to go back again. He sent off Herakleides to Perinthos[126] to sell the booty, so that he could get money to pay the soldiers. Seuthes himself, along with the Greeks, made camp on the plain of the Thynians.

- What was the purpose of this campaign?
- How many captives does the attack against Seuthes' enemies produce? How are they disposed of?
- How did Greek adventurers and Greek colonies such as Perinthos link Thracian communities and Greek slaveholding societies?

---

[126] A Greek colony on the northern coast of the Sea of Marmara.

8.4   Jerome, *Life of Malchus*, 4.1–5.3:[127] Latin Biographical Narrative (Fourth Century CE)

The speaker (see also 7.7) leaves his monastery in Syrian Beroia to return to his mother in Syrian Edessa, where he was planning to receive and use the inheritance he had refused when he left home and became a monk. "Saracens" and "Ishmaelites" were names commonly employed by the Romans for Arab nomads in the Syrian desert.

Literature: Lenski 2011a; Gray 2015: 165–98.

> On the route from Beroia to Edessa, close to the public road, there is un-inhabited and uncultivated land where the Saracens, with their abodes continuously shifting, roam about. Fear of them makes travelers gather together in large numbers in that area, hoping to ward off the impending danger through mutual support. In my company there were men and women, old, young, and children, altogether about 70. And look! All of a sudden, riders on horses and camels, Ishmaelites, make their assault, their long hair decorated with headbands, their bodies half naked, their cloaks and wide boots dragged behind. Quivers were hanging from their shoulders. They brandished unstrung bows and carried long spears. For they had not come for battle but for plunder. We were snatched, scattered, dragged in different directions. At this time, I, who was going to return as a property owner by inheritance after a long absence, but repenting too late of my plan, enter by lot into the servitude of the same master together with another captive, a woman. We were led off, or rather, carried high on camels, through the vast desert, always in fear of falling. We were hanging from rather than sitting on the animals. Our food was half-raw meat; our drink was camel's milk. At last, after we crossed a large river, we arrived at the inner desert. Ordered to venerate the mistress and her children according to the custom of those people, we bend our necks. Here, as if confined in a prison, I learn to walk about in a different manner, that is, naked. Indeed, the extreme climate does not permit one to cover anything else apart from one's modesty. Sheep are brought to me to tend, and, in comparing my woes, I at least enjoy the solace of seeing my masters and fellow slaves very rarely.

- How do the Saracens acquire their slaves? What conditions favored their raiding?
- How was the speaker employed by his master? Was he the only slave of this master?
- How important was slavery for the Saracens and in what ways?

8.5   Diodorus, *Library*, 5.26.3: Greek Historiography (First Century BCE)

Large numbers of wine amphoras from the Italian peninsula, dated to the late Republican period, have been found in southern Gaul. Scholars have been debating how to interpret this phenomenon by linking it to passages like this one.

---

[127] Latin text: Gray 2015.

Literature: Laubenheimer 2013; Tchernia 2016: 286–92.

> The Gauls are exceedingly inebrious and fill themselves up with the wine the traders import, drinking it unmixed. Because of their craving for it, they guzzle their drink, and once drunk, they fall into a stupor or into a manic state. Thus, many Italian merchants, motivated by their habitual greediness, see the Gauls' propensity for wine as a godsend. They transport the wine through the navigable rivers by boats and through the plains on carriages and receive for it incredible prices. For a jar of wine, they receive a slave, getting a servant in return for a drink.

- How did Italian merchants conduct trade in Gaul?
- How profitable was this trade?
- How does Diodorus explain the low price for slaves?
- How could Gauls afford to sell slaves so cheaply? Where do you think the slaves came from?
- Do you believe Diodorus' story? Is there other evidence to support his account?

8.6 Polybius, *History*, 30.15: Greek Historiography (Second Century BCE)

The Roman general and statesman Aemilius Paulus defeated the Macedonians and their king Perseus at 168 BCE.

Literature: Volkmann 1961: 139–42.

> Polybius says that after his destruction of Perseus and the Macedonians Paulus took 70 cities of Epeiros, most of which belonged to the Molossians. He thus enslaved 150,000 men.

- What consequences would Roman imperialism have on local communities like those of Epeiros?
- What do you think would be the consequences of so many people entering the slave market at once? Cf. 5.14.

8.7 The Reliefs of Trajan's Column: Rome (Early Second Century CE)

The column celebrates the victory of emperor Trajan in the Dacian Wars (101–6 CE). While the Romans were heavily influenced by Greek art and iconography, the depiction of captivity, which figures prominently in Roman art, is effectively absent from Greek iconography (Fig. 13).

Literature: de Souza 2011.

- How is captivity represented in these images? Can we learn anything about the reality of captivity from them?

Figure 13: a) Relief from Trajan's column, early second century CE, Rome: image from C. Cichorius, *Die Reliefs der Traianssäule: Erster Tafelband: Die Reliefs des Ersten Dakischen Krieges, Tafeln 1–57*, Plate XXXIII, Berlin, 1896. b) Relief from Trajan's column, early second century CE, Rome: image from C. Cichorius, *Die Reliefs der Traianssäule: Zweiter Tafelband: Die Reliefs des Zweiten Dakischen Krieges, Tafeln 58–113*, Plate CVII, Berlin, 1900

- What was the purpose of these images? Why is captivity depicted?
- Why is captivity not celebrated in classical and Hellenistic Greek art? Compare with the ideology evident in 8.12.

8.8 Symmachus, *Letters*, 2.78: Latin Epistolography (393–4 CE)

Symmachus (see 4.18.d) writes to a friend stationed on the Rhine frontier.

Literature: Cecconi 2002: 393–400; Lenski 2008.

> Symmachus to his brother Flavianus. Some people find pleasure in gain and profit. What pleases me is expenditure on fulfilling my vows. Accordingly, eager for the citizens' gratitude, I strive to add a new form of grandeur to the expenses of my son's quaestorian games: namely to bestow five slaves on each of the chariot stables of the Eternal City. And since procuring slaves is easy at the frontier and their price tends to be reasonable there, I beseech you most earnestly to give orders that, with the help of able men, 20 young slaves suitable for the aforementioned duty may be furnished. To this purpose, I have sent you *** *solidi*. After evaluation of the men, selection should be made not according to their beauty but according to their age and good health. Farewell.

- What was Symmachus' request?
- Why was buying slaves in the frontier cheap?
- What does this imply about the Roman slave supply?
- What criteria does Symmachus want to use for the selection of slaves? What can we learn about Roman slavery from this?

8.9 Josephus, *The Jewish War*, 6.414–20: Greek Historiography (First Century CE)

The Jewish revolt against Rome erupted in 66 CE; in 70 CE, the Romans finally succeeded in capturing Jerusalem after a long siege.

Literature: Bradley 2004.

> Since the Roman soldiers had started to feel exhaustion from killing and the number of those who were still alive appeared to be very large, Caesar gave orders that they should kill only the armed men who showed resistance; the rest of the people should be taken captive. Along with the men specified by Caesar's orders, the soldiers went on killing the old and the sick. Those in good condition, who could be of use to them, they drove to the temple and shut them within the walls of the women's court. Caesar appointed as guard one of his freedmen; he also appointed Fronto, one of his friends, to decide the fate of each captive. Those whom other captives denounced as rebellious and predatory, he killed. Of young men, he selected the tallest and most

handsome ones and reserved them for the triumph. Of the rest, he put into bonds those above 17 years old and sent them for hard labor to Egypt. And Titus[128] sent a great number of men as a gift to the provinces, to be killed in the arenas, fighting against other men or against wild beasts. Those under 17 years old were sold away. Now, in the course of the days that Fronto made his decisions, about 11,000 people died of starvation. Some of them would not receive food because of the guards' hatred against them; others would refuse to eat the food that was given them. And as the captives were so many, there was a shortage even in bread. The total number of people captive throughout the whole duration of this war was 97,000. Those who died during the course of the entire siege were 110,000.

- How did the Romans distinguish between different groups of captives?
- What was the fate of the different groups of captives?
- Which factors decided the fate of captives?
- How should we envisage the relationship between captivity and slavery?
- Was Judaea part of the Roman Empire? Was the Roman Empire a perfect no-slaving zone for its inhabitants?

NO-SLAVING ZONES

8.10 *Leviticus*, 25:39–46: Biblical Text in Greek – Septuagint[129] (Original Hebrew Probably Between 538–332 BCE)

God addresses Moses at the Mount Sinai.

Literature: van Seters 2007; Lewis 2018: 202–11.

If any of your brothers who lives by you is brought low and sells himself to you, he shall not work for you as your slave. He shall be to you like a hired hand or an alien resident, and he shall work at your place until the year of redemption. Then, upon redemption, he and his children are to go away to their own clan and depart to their ancestral possessions. Since those whom I took out of the land of Egypt are my slaves, it is forbidden that they be sold as slaves. You shall not overwork your brother to exhaustion but fear your lord god. Your male and female slaves shall be sourced from the neighboring nations; it is from them that you shall acquire male and female slaves. You shall also acquire your slaves from the sons of the alien residents in your land and from those of their relatives that are born here. They will become your property. And you shall distribute and bequeath them to your children after you, and they can belong to you forever. But no one shall overwork his brother, one of the sons of Israel, to exhaustion.

---

[128] Son of emperor Vespasian and future emperor.
[129] Greek text: Rahlfs and Hanhart 2006.

- How should Jews treat Jewish debtors?

- What is the justification given for this treatment?

- From which sources should Jews acquire their slaves? Why?

- How do the attitudes in this passage compare with 8.11?

8.11 Xenophon, *Memorabilia*, 4.2.13–5: Greek Collection of Socratic Conversations (First Half of Fourth Century BCE)

Literature: Garlan 1987.

Socrates: Shall we write the letter "J" here and the letter "I" there and then put under "J" what seems to us to be a deed of justice, and under "I" what seems to be a deed of injustice?
Euthydemos: If you think this too is necessary, do so.

Socrates jotted down the letters as he had proposed, and said:

S: Now, does lying occur among men?
E: Yes, it does.
S: Where then shall we put it?
E: Clearly under Injustice.
S: Well, does deceit occur too?
E: Very much so.
S: Where shall we put this then?
E: This too should clearly go under Injustice.
S: And what about ill-doing?
E: This too.
S: And what about enslaving?
E: This too.
S: None of these, then, shall we put under Justice, Euthydemos?
E: That'd be terrible.
S: But what if an elected general enslaves an enemy city which is unjust; will we say that he is committing injustice?
E: Of course, not.
S: Shall we not say that he does justice?
E: Very much so.
S: And what if he deceives them while at war with them?
E: This, too, would be just.
S: And if he steals and plunders their property; won't his actions be just?
E: Very much so. But earlier I took it that you were asking these questions in relation only to one's friends.
S: So, those things that we put under Injustice, should they also be put under Justice?

- Why does Euthydemos originally define enslavement as injustice?
- What distinction allows the speakers to redefine enslavement as just?

- What does this passage tell us about the members of the "moral circle" of the members of Greek cities? Did they deem all human beings worthy of the same moral treatment as their fellow citizens?

8.12   Plato, *Republic*, 5.469b–c: Greek Philosophical Dialogue (Fourth Century BCE)

Greek poleis were constantly fighting wars against one another, which often led to the enslavement of the defeated. Despite the lack of political unity, a sense of common ethnic and cultural identity was often asserted with varying effects. The interlocutors in this dialogue discuss the creation of a new community with an ideal constitution.

Literature: Garlan 1987; Rosivach 1999.

Socrates: How should our soldiers behave toward the enemies?
Glaukon: In what respect?
S: First, in regards to enslavement, does it seem right for Greeks to enslave Greek cities? Or is it rather, to the extent possible, that they should not allow other cities to do so but accustom them to spare the Greek race, guarding against enslavement by the barbarians?
G: Sparing them is altogether the better course.
S: So, they should not own Greek slaves either, and they should advise the other Greeks not to?
G: By all means; in that way, they would be more likely to turn against the barbarians and abstain from attacking one another.

- How do the speakers suggest that Greek cities should treat one another? What consequences would such a view have on enslavement?
- Did Greeks stop enslaving one another? Cf. 3.31.
- What practices regarding Greek captives and slaves might such views facilitate? Cf. 8.13.

8.13   *I.Miletos* 13, 140A: Greek Treaty Inscription, Miletos, Ionia (After 260 BCE)

Treaty between Miletos, in Asia Minor, and Cretan Knossos, along with many other Cretan cities, who were famous for engaging in piratical activities across the Aegean.

Literature: Gabrielsen 2003.

[...] Men of Knossos shall not buy men of Miletos, or vice versa, when it is known that the person on sale is free. Whoever does proceed with the purchase, although he knows that the person on sale is free, shall lose the money he deposited, and the person shall be free. Whoever does make such a purchase ignorant of the fact that the person on sale is free shall return the person and receive back the money he paid for his purchase. If someone buys a person who is a slave, he shall receive back the money he paid for his purchase and return the slave. If the buyer in question does not return the person he bought, he should be taken to the *kosmoi*, if in Knossos, and to the *prytaneis*, if in Miletos.[130] [...] The above terms also apply to the people of Tylisos, Rhaukos, Chersonesos, Milatos, Eltynia, Herakleion, Priansos, Apollonia, Petra, Itanos, Praisos, Istron, Olous, Dreros, Lato, Eleutherna, Axos, Kydonia, and Phalasarna.[131]

- What is agreed? Why?
- Why was it considered important that even slaves should be returned?
- Why did Miletos sign treaties with so many Cretan communities?

8.14 *SB* V, 8008, 33–61: Papyrus with Royal Ordinance in Greek, Egypt (Third Century BCE)

Royal ordinance (*prostagma*) about the registration of livestock and slaves in Syria and Phoenicia for taxation purposes.

Literature: Bieżuńska-Małowist 1974: 10–39; Scholl 1990: no. 3.

[...] By order of the king: if anyone in Syria and Phoenicia has purchased a free native person or has carried away and held such a person or acquired such a person in some other way [...] person [...shall declare this person] to the *oikonomos* in charge in each *hyparcheia*[132] within 20 days after the day of the publication of the ordinance. Anyone who does not register or present the person shall be deprived of this person and shall deposit 6000 drachmas for every person to the royal treasury, and the king shall give a verdict on his case. Any informer will be given [...] drachmas for every person. Those who demonstrate that they purchased the registered and presented persons while the latter were slaves shall be given these persons back. Of the persons sold in the royal public auctions, if anyone claims he or she is free, their purchasers shall have their possessions guaranteed. Those who are military settlers or in military expedition in Syria and Phoenicia and co-habit with native women whom they have taken up need not register them. And in the future, no one shall be permitted to purchase or accept as security free native persons, under any pretext, with the exception of those given away by the administrator of the revenues in Syria and Phoenicia for execution of a debt, in relation to

---

[130] *Kosmoi* and *prytaneis* were boards of magistrates in each city, respectively.
[131] Cretan cities.
[132] *Oikonomoi* were financial officers in areas outside Egypt controlled by the Ptolemies. These possessions were divided in the so-called *hyparcheiai*, for administrative purposes.

whom execution of their debt may take place even through their persons, as it is set out in the law of farming contracts. Otherwise, both the purchasers and those who offer free native persons as security will be liable to the same penalties. [...]

- What are the consequences of this ordinance for free native persons in Syria and Phoenicia?

- Does this ordinance protect such persons from every kind of enslavement?

- Why do you think the Ptolemies tried to control the enslavement of free native populations?

8.15 Dio Chrysostom, *Oration 15*, 13–17:[133] Greek Epideictic Oratory (First/Second Century CE)

This oration purports to report a dispute over freedom and slavery. At this point, one participant argues against the assumption that every person who is someone's slave is really and truly a slave.

Literature: Rosivach 1999; Panzeri 2011; Roy 2012.

But do you think that all who are held as slaves <are slaves?> Aren't there many to whom this happens unjustly, while they are free? Some have already gone before the court and proved that they were free; others tolerate it to the end because they have no clear proof of their freedom or because their so-called masters are <nice> to them. [...] Weren't many of the Athenians captured in Sicily held as slaves in Sicily and in the Peloponnese, although they were free? In many other battles, too, aren't captives held in slavery? – others for a determinate amount of time, until they find those who will ransom them, others forever? In those times, even the son of Kallias[134] was apparently held as slave in Thrace for a long time, after the battle over Akanthos, in which the Athenians were defeated. [...] And innumerable others have suffered this fate. I insist that even many of those held as slaves here in our time are free men. For if an Athenian is captured at war and taken to the Persians or is taken to Thrace or Sicily and is sold there, we shan't say that he is a slave, since he is free; but if a Thracian or a Persian is brought here, one not only born to free parents but also the son of a tyrant or a king, we shall not concede that he is a free man. Aren't you aware of the law of Athens, as well as of many other communities, that does not allow a man who was born a slave to have a share in citizenship? But in the case of the son of Kallias [...], after he arrived back from Thrace, where he had lived for many years and been whipped many times, no one would have thought right that

---

[133] Greek text: von Arnim 1893–96.
[134] Kallias was a prominent Athenian, of aristocratic lineage and extremely wealthy, who lived in the second half of the fifth and the first half of the fourth century BCE.

he should lose his Athenian citizenship. So, there are occasions when the law too denies that those who were unjustly held as slaves have become slaves.

- Why are many slaves not really slaves, according to the speaker?
- Would Athenians consider fellow citizens enslaved abroad as real slaves? Why?
- According to the speaker, would Athenians consider a noble foreigner enslaved at Athens as a real slave? Why?
- What does this differential attitude tell us about Greek conceptions of slavery and enslavement?

8.16 Augustine, *New Letters*, 10.2–8: Latin Epistolography (Early Fifth Century CE)

Augustine, bishop of the coastal city of Hippo in Numidia in North Africa, sent the following memorandum to Alypius, bishop of Numidian Thagaste, when the latter was in Italy and about to meet the emperor.

Literature: Lepelley 1981; Rouge 1983; Szidat 1985; Harper 2011: 92–5.

[...] There are so many of those commonly called slave dealers (*mangones*) in Africa that they empty it of a great part of its human population, transferring their trade, almost all of whom are free people, to provinces across the sea. Only few are found to have been sold by their parents. Anyway, they are not sold according to what Roman law permits, namely for a 25-year period of labor, but the dealers buy them as slaves and sell them off across the sea as slaves.[135] It is extremely rare that the dealers buy true slaves from their masters. Besides, from this multitude of merchants a great number of corrupters and plunderers has sprung forth; they have grown so insolent, that they are said to invade far-away places, where few men live, and to abduct violently people whom they then sell to those merchants. And they do this in packs and with great clamor, with the frightening appearance of soldiers or barbarians.

I omit that rumor most recently announced to us, namely that in some village, the men were murdered, and the women and children were snatched away to be sold through aggressions of the aforementioned type. But the place where this occurred, if it really occurred, was not mentioned. However, once when I was among people freed by such wretched captivity through the efforts of our church, I myself asked a girl in what way she had been sold to the slave dealers. She said that she had been kidnapped from the house of her parents. Then I asked her whether she was alone in the house when these men found her. She replied that it had happened in the presence of her parents and brothers. A brother of hers was also there with us – he had come to fetch her – and, as she was little, he revealed to us how it had happened. He said that such raiders had made their attacks in the night; for then their

---

[135] For the Roman laws on the sale of free children, see Harper 2011: 391–423.

victims concealed themselves from them in whatever way they could, rather than dared to resist them, thinking that they were barbarians. However, if there weren't any merchants, such things would not be taking place.

I don't believe that this evil devastating Africa is completely unheard of where you are. It was incomparably less serious some time ago, when the emperor Honorius sent a law to the prefect Hadrian putting a check upon trading activities of this type. He decreed that businessmen of such infamy be punished with leaden whips, outlawed, and sent into perpetual exile. There are no provisions in this law for those who sell free people after first they lure and abduct them, which is what these people almost always do; there are only general provisions for all those who transport groups of slaves (*familiae*) to be sold to provinces across the sea. It orders that these slaves become property of the imperial treasury, which in no way would be said for free people. I have appended this law to this memorandum, although it can perhaps be found more easily at Rome. It is a useful law and could remedy this plague. However, we have started to apply it only as much as it is necessary so that people might become free but not in order to punish those merchants because of whom so many and grave crimes are being perpetrated. With this law, we deter those we can, but we do not punish them. In fact, we even fear lest others might use this law and drag to their deserved punishment those abominable and deplorable men seized by us.

I am therefore writing this to your Blessedness, so that, if possible, it be decided by our most pious and Christian emperors that, in cases when people are liberated from these men through the actions of the Church, the perpetrators might not face the danger of death which is prescribed by this law, especially the beating with leaden whips, a punishment which easily leads to death. At the same time, it is probably necessary that this law be made known to the public, so that a check be put upon these men. Otherwise, if we stop trying out of fear of these things, free people will lamentably be taken into perpetual slavery. If *we* do nothing for those people, will there be many among those with some authority on the coast who, out of their Christian or human sense of pity, would rather not receive money for such cruel crossings but instead remove those wretched people from the ships or not allow them to go on board?

It is the duty of whichever authority or office is responsible for the enforcement of this law, or of any other passed on this issue, to ensure it be put into effect. Otherwise, Africa will be emptied of its inhabitants to a great extent. And a great multitude of people of both sexes, in packs and bands, like a constantly flowing river, will lose their personal freedom to something worse than captivity in the hands of barbarians. For many have been ransomed away from the barbarians, but those who are transported to provinces across the sea cannot be assisted with ransom. Also, there is resistance against the barbarians, with the Roman army fighting effectively and successfully, so that Roman citizens might not be held in captivity by the barbarians. But who can resist these businessmen, who trade not in animals but in human beings, not in barbarians but in Roman citizens of the provinces? Dispersed as they are, they take people from everywhere and anywhere, either after abducting them by force or deceiving them with guile, into the hands of those who promise them their value. Who can, then, resist these people for the sake of Roman freedom? I don't mean our freedom as a community but the freedom of each one of us.

It is utterly impossible to say satisfactorily how many have fallen into this vile trade, astonishingly blinded by greed and infected in I don't know what way by this plague. Who would believe that we found a woman – and indeed here, among ourselves, at Hippo – who used to lure the women of Gibbada on the pretext of buying wood and then locked them up, beat them, and sold them? Who would believe that one of the tenants (*colonus*) of our church, a perfectly satisfactory man, has sold his wife and the mother of his children, not because he was offended by some fault of hers but only because he was spurred by the fever of this plague? A young man of about 20 years old, accountant and prudent secretary of our monastery, was lured and sold away; only with difficulty did the church manage to liberate him.

I would in no way be able to list all crimes of this sort of which I have experience, even if I wanted to. Hear only one example, from which you might get a full picture of what is being perpetrated in the whole of Africa and along all its coasts. About four months before I wrote this, a crowd was brought here by Galatian merchants – it is they alone, or at least for the most part, who eagerly apply themselves to such trade – in order to be transported away from the coast of Hippo. They had been collected from different places but mostly from Numidia. A faithful man happened to be there, who knew of our custom to show mercy in such cases. He informed the church. Immediately, about 120 people were freed by us – although I myself was not there – others from the boat which they had had to board, others from the place where they had been put to hide. Of these there were barely five or six who had been sold by their parents. As far as the rest were concerned, however, almost no one who heard the various ways through which they had fallen into the hands of the Galatians, via men who had lured and abducted them, could control his or her tears.

It is now up to your holy Prudence to consider the extent and intensity of the transport of wretched souls raging in other coastal places if the greed and cruelty of the Galatians prove so burning and audacious at Hippo Regius. For here, with the mercy of God, the church's diligence remains alert in such issues and with its help wretched human beings are freed from captivity; also, the businessmen of this trade are punished – far less severely than what this law prescribes but by the loss of their profits. In the name of Christian love, I beseech your Love to take action so that I might not have written this in vain. For the Galatians are not short of patrons. Through them they demand from us those whom the Lord freed through his church – even when they have been returned to those looking for them, who came to us bringing letters from their bishops. They have also started to cause trouble to those faithful children of ours to whom we entrusted the freed people to stay with – for the church is not able to feed all those it frees. They do this even as I am dictating this, despite the fact that letters from an authority which they could be afraid of have arrived. Nor have they in any way abandoned their demands.

- What does Augustine present as peculiar about the practices of the slave traders?

- How was it possible for free people to be enslaved in a Roman province?

- How common do you think these practices were? Is this evidence of Late Roman crisis?

- Was violent capture the only means through which free people were enslaved? What other cases does the memorandum reveal?

- What procedures for reclaiming the freedom of captives are illustrated?

- What can we learn about the geography of the slave trade from this memorandum? What do you think of the scale illustrated here?

8.17 Procopius, *On Wars*, 8.3.12–21: Greek Historiography (Sixth Century CE)

Literature: Hopkins 1978: 172–96; Guyot 1980; Ringrose 2003.

Beyond the Apsilioi and at the other end of the crescent,[136] the Abasgoi live along the coast, reaching until the mountains of Caucasus. [...] The Abasgoi have suffered most terribly at the hands of their rulers because of their rulers' enormous greed. For any native boys of fine countenance and beautiful body the two kings happened to see, they ruthlessly dragged away from their parents, turned them to eunuchs, and sold them at a high price into Roman territory, to whoever wished to buy them. The kings used to have the boys' fathers killed immediately afterward, so that none of them might ever try to exact vengeance from the king for the wrong done to the boys; also, so that there would be no one among their subjects distrusting them. Thus, the beautiful appearance of their boys led them to destruction. And the poor parents were being destroyed from the misfortune of having sons of such deadly beauty. It is for this reason that most eunuchs among the Romans, including at the emperor's court, happened to be Abasgoi by birth. However, during the reign of the present emperor Justinian, the Abasgoi have changed into a less savage way of life in all respects. They chose to convert to Christianity, and the emperor Justinian sent to them one of the eunuchs of the palace called Euphratas, an Abasgos by birth, in order to announce to the kings Justinian's explicit prohibition against any mutilation of male genitalia in the future – no knife were to force nature anymore. The Abasgoi rejoiced in this announcement, and encouraged by the decree of the Roman emperor, they too tried to put an end to this practice with all their strength. For each one of them had lived in fear of ever begetting a handsome son. It was in that period that the emperor Justinian built a church in honor of the Theotokos among the Abasgoi, which he supplied with priests. He thus achieved that the Abasgoi be instructed in all Christian observances, and as a result, the Abasgoi dethroned their two kings and appeared to be living in freedom.

- How did the Romans acquire their eunuchs?

- How were these eunuchs employed?

- If Roman emperors (including Justinian) were happy to employ eunuchs, why did Justinian try to stop the Abasgoi from creating eunuchs? Did his policy have any consequences that benefitted him?

- What effects did religion have on no-slaving zones?

---

[136] That is, on the eastern Black Sea coast.

GEOPOLITICS AND SLAVERY

8.18 Aristotle, *Politics*, 1269a34–b12: Greek Philosophical Treatise (Fourth Century BCE)

At this point in book two of his *Politics*, Aristotle proceeds to discuss some problems of the Spartan constitution. For Sparta's helots, the dependent people of Crete and the *penestai* of Thessaly, cf. 1.3.

Literature: Luraghi 2009.

It is a given that the city which is to be governed well needs to have leisure from activities aiming to secure the essentials of life. But it is not easy to grasp in what way this can be achieved. The *penestai* of Thessaly attacked the Thessalians many times, and so did the helots to the Laconians – in fact, it is as if they constantly lie in wait for Spartan misfortunes. But nothing of the sort has yet happened to the Cretans. The reason probably lies in the fact that neighboring Cretan cities, although at war with each other, are no ally to the rebels; it is not to their interest, since they, too, possess dependent people (*perioikoi*). But all Sparta's neighbors were hostile to it: the Argives and the Messenians and the Arcadians. And initially, the *penestai*, too, revolted from the Thessalians, because the Thessalians were still at war with their neighbors, the Achaeans, the Perrhaebians and the Magnetians. Moreover, it seems that, even if there was no other difficulty, managing such people is a troublesome task, that is in what way one should treat them. For when they are not controlled tightly, they behave insolently and demand to be treated equally to those in authority (*kyrioi*); and when they live a hard life, they plot against those in authority and hate them. It is then clear that those who have such problems with their helots cannot find the best way to secure leisure.

- Why did Cretan cities not suffer from servile revolts, according to Aristotle?
- What factors potentially affecting slave actions against their masters are identified in the passage?

8.19 Strabo, *Geography*, 14.5.2: Greek Geography (End of First Century BCE/Early First Century CE)

Diodotos Tryphon, a rebel against the Seleucid kings who eventually became a Seleucid king, was particularly active from the mid 140s until his death in 138 BCE. The Romans sacked Carthage and Corinth in 146 BCE.

Literature: Avidov 1997; Rauh 1997; Gabrielsen 2003; Lewis 2019; Mavrojannis 2019.

The responsibility for the fact that the Kilikians started to put together gangs of pirates lies with Tryphon and the worthlessness of the succession of kings who at the time ruled over both Syria and Kilikia. For to his rebellion, other rebellions, too, were added, and as brothers were in conflict with one another, they handed the land to its attackers. Moreover, the exportation of slaves became extremely profitable and thus a great motive for criminal action. Not only could people be captured easily, but also the trading center was not that far away – a large and very wealthy center, Delos, which had the capacity to receive and send off tens of thousands of slaves in one day. Hence, the following proverb: "Merchant, sail in; unload; everything has been sold off." The reason behind this was that after the destruction of Carthage and Corinth, the Romans became rich and started to use many slaves. On the face of such ease, the pirates flourished to massive numbers, acting as both kidnappers and slave traders. Both the kings of Cyprus and those of Egypt assisted in these acts, as they were enemies of the Syrians. Nor were the Rhodians their friends, and hence they did not try to assist them at all. Moreover, the pirates passed themselves off as slave traders, and their criminal action was thus impossible to check.

- How does Strabo explain the beginning of large-scale Kilikian piracy?
- In what ways was piracy affected by international politics?
- What is the link between piracy and the slave trade, according to Strabo?

8.20 Diodorus, *Library*, Book 36, Testimonium, Part II, 1.1–3 Goukowsky (= 36.3.1–3 Walton): Greek Historiography (First Century BCE)

Literature: Cf. Morton 2012: 163–72.

During Marius' campaign against the Cimbri,[137] the Senate authorized Marius to seek the alliance of the nations from beyond the sea. Marius, then, sent a request for aid to Nikomedes, king of Bithynia. His response was that most Bithynians had been seized by the collectors of the Roman public revenues (i.e. the *publicani*) and were slaves in the Roman provinces. The Senate then passed a decree that none of Rome's free allies should be a slave in the provinces and that the governors should take care that they be set free. At that time, Licinius Nerva was the governor of Sicily, and in accordance with the Senate's decree, he manumitted many slaves after first holding hearings. The result was that more than 800 people gained freedom within a few days. Everyone on the island who was a slave was buoyed up with hopes of freedom. However, the notables got together and kept urging the governor to give up this enterprise. And he, either convinced by money or having become a slave to favors done to him, gave up his keenness for these hearings and started to rebuke those coming to him in order to gain their freedom and to order them to turn back to their particular owners. The slaves, instead, turned to

[137] A Germanic people who repeatedly attempted to migrate to the Italian peninsula in the last decade of the second century BCE. After they annihilated a Roman army in 105 BCE, Roman general and statesman Gaius Marius undertook to organize Roman defense against them. He finally defeated them in 101 BCE.

one another, and after leaving Syracuse and finding refuge at the sanctuary of the Palikoi,[138] started to talk to one another in favor of an uprising.

- What caused widespread enslavement among Roman allies in the eastern Mediterranean?

- Why did the Roman Senate decide to intervene?

- How did the Senate's decree affect the Sicilian slave owners, and how did it affect the slaves in Sicily? Were only the slaves who had previously been free allies affected? If not, why?

- What can we learn about the impact of local and international politics on the lives of slaves from this passage?

DELIMITING SLAVE ALTERITY

8.21   Strabo, *Geography*, 7.3.12: Greek Geography (Late First Century BCE/Early First Century CE)

Literature: Vlassopoulos 2010; Lewis 2017; Harrison 2019.

A different division of the land also took place in the past and still remains valid, for some of the people are called Dacians, while some are called Getae. They call Getae those living eastwards, toward the Black Sea; they call Dacians those living at the other end, toward Germania and the sources of the Ister. I think that in the past, these used to be called Daoi, and it was because of this that Getas and Daos became the prevailing slave names among the people of Attica. This derivation is more probable than that from the Scythian people called "Daai" as the latter live far away, near Hyrkania, and it is not probable that slaves were taken to Attica from there. For slaves would be given names on the basis of the places they were taken from. Either they would give them the name of their nation – for example, Lydos or Syros – or they would call them by names prevalent there – for example, they would call a Phrygian slave Manes or Midas, while a Paphlagonian slave would be called Tibios.

- Which methods of marking slave alterity does Strabo discuss here?

8.22   Digest, 21.1.31.21: Collection of Latin Juristic Texts (Sixth Century CE)

On the Digest, see 1.2.

---

[138] Cf. 6.17.

Literature: Bradley 1991.

> Ulpian, *On the Edict of the Curule Aedile*, Book 1: Those who sell slaves must proclaim the slaves' ethnic origin at the sale. For in many cases, a slave's ethnic origin can either attract or deter a buyer. Therefore, it is in our interest to know a slave's ethnic origin. For it is assumed that some slaves are good because they are of a nation of good reputation, while some are considered bad because they are of a nation of a rather bad reputation. If, then, no proclamation of a slave's nation be made, an action will be granted to the buyer and to all interested parties, through which the buyer may return the slave.

- Why are sellers of slaves obliged to declare their slaves' origins? Cf. 9.11.

- What features would make a nation a valuable source for slaves? And what features would work in the opposite direction?

- What implications does this attitude have for slave identity? Compare with 2.18.

8.23   Menander, *The Shield*, 185–211:[139] Greek Comedy (Late Fourth/Early Third Century BCE)

Smikrines, an old man from Athens, tries to secure the help of the slave Daos, so that he might marry his young niece, who has just become a heiress. The niece, however, has been betrothed by Smikrines' brother to another, younger, man, and the rest of the family, including Daos, would prefer her to marry him, instead of Smikrines.

Literature: Sherk 1970; Jacques 1996.

> **Smikrines:** I will marry this maiden. In fact, I think the law too more or less states this, Daos. So, you, too, should have been considering how these things could be arranged correctly. You are not a stranger.
>
> **Daos:** Smikrines, I think that the dictum "know thyself" has been thought through with great care. Let me abide by this and refer to me matters appropriate to a good slave, demanding an account of these. [...] But as for inheritance, Smikrines, or, by Zeus, heiress, marriage, family, and degree of kinship, don't involve Daos in such things anymore. You yourselves should deal with issues concerning free men – those of you to whom this will apply.
>
> **Smikrines:** In gods' name, do you think that I am acting unfeelingly?
>
> **Daos:** I'm from Phrygia. Many of the things you consider fine seem to me terrible and vice versa. Don't take any notice of me. You understand things better than I do – naturally.
>
> **Smikrines:** Now you almost seem to be saying something like "don't bother me" or something of that kind. I understand.

---

[139] Greek text: Ireland 2010.

- With what argument does Smikrines try to persuade Daos to help him?

- What is Daos' argument for refusing to get involved?

- Is it the slave or the master who chooses to emphasize slave alterity? Why?

- Can we learn anything from this comic scene about the ethnic identities of slaves?

8.24 Pausanias, *Periegesis*, 7.5.6–8:[140] Greek Travel Writing (Second Century CE)

Pausanias tells a story on the origins of Herakles' cult image at Erythrai in Asia Minor. The image came from the Phoenician Tyre on a raft. The raft came to a stop at the cape called Mesate, midway between the harbor of Erythrai and the island of Chios.

When the raft stopped off the cape, both the Erythraeans and the Chians labored hard in order to make the image land each on their own shores. Finally, a man from Erythrai, who lived off the sea and the catching of fish but had lost his eyesight due to an illness – his name was Phormion – this fisherman saw in a dream vision that the wives of the Erythraeans should cut their hair, which the men would then weave into a rope and thus pull the raft to themselves. However, the citizen women did not at all wish to follow the instructions of the dream. But the women of Thracian origin, both those who were slaves at Erythrai and the free women who made their living there, offered to have their hair cut. And this is how the Erythraeans pulled the raft. Thracian women are hence the only women allowed to enter the temple of Herakles, and the locals still keep the rope weaved from the hair to my own day. The same people say that the fisherman recovered his eyesight and was able to see for the rest of his life.

- How did the people of Erythrai manage to secure the image?

- What was the status of the Thracian women who helped the Erythraeans?

- What link between slave identity and ethnicity is visible in this passage?

THE CONSEQUENCES OF CAPTIVITY

8.25 Xenophon, *Anabasis*, 4.8.4–7: Greek Historical Narrative (First Half of Fourth Century BCE)

The mercenary army of the Ten Thousand (see 8.3) has its way blocked by an unknown people.

Literature: Ma 2004: 330–3; Hunt 2015: 128–31.

Just then one of the light troops came to Xenophon. He said he had been a slave in Athens, and he understood the language of the enemy. "I think,"

---

[140] Greek text: Jones 1933.

he said, "that this is my homeland and, if there is no problem, I would like to speak with these men." "There is no problem," Xenophon said. "You can speak with them; first, find out who they are." When he asked them, they responded they were Makronians.[141] "Well then, ask them," said Xenophon, "why they are arrayed against us and want to be our enemies." They responded, "Because you too are coming against our land." The generals directed the man to say that they did not want to harm them but had fought the king, and "we are now returning to Greece and wish to reach the sea." The Makronians were asking if the Greeks would give them pledges of this. They responded that they wanted both to give and to receive pledges. And so, the Makronians gave to the Greeks a barbarian lance, while the Greeks gave them a Greek one. For they said these were the pledges. And both sides called upon the gods to be their witness.

- What is the life story of the Makronian soldier?
- How is it possible that he understood the Makronian language but was not sure of his origins?
- What can we learn about ancient connectivity from this slave's story?

8.26   Charon of Lampsakos, *BNJ* 262 F 1: Greek Historiography (Fifth Century BCE)

The Bisaltai[142] made a military expedition to Kardia[143] and won. The leader of the Bisaltai was Naris. When a boy, this Naris had been sold to Kardia, bought by a Kardian master and become a barber. The Kardians had an oracle to the effect that the Bisaltai would attack them, and often they would sit at the barbershop and talk about this. So, Naris ran away from Kardia to his homeland, got appointed leader by the Bisaltai, and prepared the Bisaltai to attack the Kardians. Now, all the Kardians had trained their horses to dance at dinner parties to the music of the aulos.[144] So they would stand on their hind legs and dance with their front legs, <as if gesturing>, being thoroughly familiar with the aulos pieces. Naris knew this, and so he bought from Kardia a girl who played the aulos. She arrived at the Bisaltai and trained many to play the aulos. Taking those along, Naris advanced with the army against Kardia. When the battle was underway, he ordered them to play the aulos pieces familiar to the Kardian horses. When the horses heard the aulos, they stood on their hide legs and turned to dancing. The strength of the Kardians was in the cavalry, and they were thus defeated.

---

[141] A people living around Trabzon on the south coast of the Black Sea.
[142] A Thracian tribe.
[143] A Greek colony in the Thracian Chersonese.
[144] A wind instrument.

- What was the origin of Naris?
- What did he do as a slave? How did he find about the Kardian oracle?
- How did he try to teach the Bisaltai to use the aulos?
- What can we learn about the traffic of slaves between Kardia and the Bisaltai from this passage? How did slavery link communities?
- Can we learn anything about the attachment of slaves to their ethnic origins from this story?

8.27 *IG* II² 1366: Inscribed Cult Regulations in Greek, Laureion, Attica (First Century CE)

This inscription was found at Laureion, the area of Athens' silver mines, where thousands of slaves worked (see also 2.1, 4.10, 7.2). It records the foundation of a sanctuary in honor of Men Tyrannos, an Anatolian deity, and relevant regulations.

Literature: https://ancientassociations.ku.dk/assoc/307.

Xanthos of Lykia, slave of Gaius Orbius, founded a sanctuary of [Men] Tyrannos, after the god had chosen him, for good fortune. And [no one] shall enter when impure. One shall be purified after contact with garlic, [pigs] and women. Men may enter when they have washed from head to foot on the same day; women may enter when they have washed from head to foot for seven days after menstruation, including on the same day. Also, for 10 days after contact with a corpse, and for 40 days after the loss of a fetus. No one shall offer sacrifice without the founder of the sanctuary. If one does so by force, the sacrifice shall be unacceptable to the god. One shall offer to the god what is due: namely, right leg, skin, head, feet, breast, olive oil for the altar, lamp, kindling, and libation. And may the god be merciful to those serving him with simplicity of soul. If what is human fate befalls the founder or he falls ill or departs somewhere, no man shall have authority (in the sanctuary) except for the one to whom the founder himself might hand it over. And if one concerns oneself overzealously or interferes with the god's property and affairs, one shall have to account for an offence to Men Tyrannos, for which he shall not be able to atone. One who sacrifices on the seventh day shall do all that is due toward the god. He shall take away a leg and a shoulder from the sacrificial animal he might bring; the rest shall be cut up at the sanctuary. One who offers a sacrifice to the god from the new month to the 15th day or one who fills a sacrificial table for the god shall take away half of it. Those who wish may gather and form a contribution society (*eranos*) for Men Tyrannos, for good fortune; similarly, the contributors (*eranistai*) shall provide the god with what is due, namely right leg, skin, a kotyle of olive oil, a chous of wine, a choinix of cake, three other cakes, two choinix measures of small cake, and music. If the contributors recline at the sanctuary, they should also bring a garland and a woollen fillet. And may the god be merciful to those who approach with simplicity.

- Who is the founder of this sanctuary, and how does he present himself?

- What can we learn from the founder's self-presentation, his founding of the sanctuary, and the precise regulations he drafted regarding slave agency and slave authority?

- What god is the sanctuary dedicated to, and what is the sanctuary's location? Can these facts show us anything regarding ways slaves adopted to keep or build their own identities?

8.28   Slaves, Freedmen, and Intercultural Transmission

Cf. 12.31.

Literature: Treggiari 1969: 110–42; Rawson 1985; Moatti 2015: 47–50; Hunt 2018: 92–8.

———   8.28.a   Jerome, *Chronicle*, on 188 BCE: Latin Chronicle   ———
(Fourth Century CE)

Lucius Livius, better known as Livius Andronicus, lived in the third century BCE and was thought to be the first to write Latin poetry using Greek models.

> Lucius Livius, considered a distinguished writer of tragedies, was offered his freedom by Livius Salinator, whose children he taught, by merit of his intelligence.

———   8.28.b   Suetonius, *Life of Terence*, 1: Latin Biography   ———
(Early Second Century CE)

Terence, an extremely influential poet of *fabulae palliatae* (i.e. Latin adaptations of Greek comedies), produced his plays in Rome in the 160s BCE. Carthage was completely destroyed by the Romans in 146 BCE.

> Publius Terentius Afer was born in Carthage. At Rome he was a slave of the senator Terentius Lucanus. Because of his intelligence and beauty, his master not only offered him an expensive education but also soon manumitted him. Some reckon that he had been a captive. Fenestella showed that he could in no way have been one, since his birth and death fell between the end of the Second Punic War and the beginning of the Third. Nor would it have been possible that he came into the hands of a Roman master if he had been captured by the Numidians or the Gaetuli,[145] for there was no trade between the Italian and the African peoples before the destruction of Carthage.

---

[145]Peoples of North Africa.

———————   8.28.c   Suda, τ 588: Greek Encyclopedia   ———————
(Tenth Century CE)

Timagenes was a first-century-BCE orator and historian. His work has not survived.

> Timagenes: son of a royal banker, Alexandrian, orator. As some claim, he was an Egyptian. In the time of Pompey the Great, he was taken captive to Rome by Gabinius and was redeemed by Faustus, Sulla's son. He worked as a sophist at Rome at the time of the same Pompey and afterward at the time of Caesar Augustus and later in the same time as Caecilius. He lost his position at the school because of his frank speech and then lived in the land called Ager Tusculanus. He died in Albanum. Needing to vomit after dinner, he choked on his vomit. He wrote many books.

———————   8.28.d   Suda, α 1129: Greek Encyclopedia   ———————
(Tenth Century CE)

Alexander Polyhistor was a first-century-BCE Greek ethnographer and philosopher, renowned for his vast erudition.

> Alexander of Miletos: He was also called Polyhistor and Cornelius, because, after his capture, he was sold to Cornelius Lentulus and worked for him as a tutor. Later, he was manumitted. He lived at Rome at the time of Sulla and later. He died in Laurentum, in a fire which destroyed his house. When his wife Helene learnt this, she hanged herself. He was a grammarian, one of the students of Crates. He was the author of a great number of works. He also wrote a work titled *On Rome* in five books.

———————   8.28.e   Suda, τ 1185: Greek Encyclopedia   ———————
(Tenth Century CE)

Tyrannion the Younger was an eminent grammarian of the first century BCE.

> Tyrannion the Younger: Phoenician, son of Artemidoros, student of Tyrannion the Elder. This is why he was named Tyrannion, whereas previously he was called Diokles. He, too, was captured during the war between Antony and Caesar. He was purchased by one Dymas, who was a freedman of Caesar. Later, he was given as a gift to Terentia, Cicero's wife. She manumitted him and he then worked as a sophist at Rome. He wrote about 68 books, some of which are the following. [...]

- How did these people become slaves? Where did they come from?

- How were they employed as slaves?

- How did they manage to win their freedom?

- To what extent did their life before slavery determine their lives as slaves and beyond? What can we learn from this concerning the multiple identities of enslaved persons?

- What was their impact on Roman culture? Why did they have such an impact? Cf. 12.16.

8.29 Paulinus of Pella, *Thanksgiving (Eucharisticon)*, 73–80: Latin Autobiographical Poetry (Fifth Century CE)

While knowledge of Greek was essential for elite education in the early imperial period, by late antiquity it had become relatively rare in the western Mediterranean. Paulinus came from a senatorial family of southwestern Gaul but was born in Pella in Macedonia, during the praetorian prefecture of his father; Paulinus was active in politics and literature.

Literature: Laes and Vuolanto 2017.

> I was forced to read and learn the doctrines of Socrates, the war fictions of Homer and Odysseus' wanderings. From the very first, I was also commanded to transverse the works of Virgil, when I had barely learnt the Latin tongue, accustomed as I was to converse with our Greek slaves, to whom I had been attached through a long time of play and schooling. So, I confess, it was hard work for me, a boy, to appreciate the style of works written in an unknown language.

- How did Paulinus acquire the ability to speak Greek?

- What scenarios can you imagine to explain how this elite family in Gaul had Greek slaves?

- Does this passage illustrate a link between slavery and cultural transmission?

8.30 Philostorgius, *Church History*, 2.5 (as Epitomized by the Patriarch Photios): Greek Ecclesiastical History (Fifth Century CE)

For the Goths, see 11.14. After a Gothic civil war in the 340s CE, Ulfilas led a group of Goths in the Roman territory, became the first Gothic bishop, invented a script for translating the Bible into Gothic, and played a crucial role in the Christianization of the Goths.

Literature: Lenski 1995, 2008.

> According to Philostorgius, in those years, a great number of the Scythians living north of the Danube – those previously called Getai while now are called Goths – crossed to the land of the Romans. They had been driven out of their ancestral abodes because of their faith. This nation had been Christianized, says Philostorgius, in the following manner. When Valerian and Gallienus were emperors,[146] a large part of the Scythians living north of the Danube crossed into Roman territory. They raided much of Europe and then crossed over to Asia and invaded Galatia and Cappadocia. They took many captives, among whom several members of the clergy, and returned to their own land laden with booty. This pious assemblage of captives intermingled with the barbarians and converted many to the faith; they made them adopt the Christian beliefs instead of pagan ones. Ulfilas' ancestors had come precisely from these captives. They were of Cappadocian origin, from a village called Sadagolthina, near the city of Parnassos. This Ulfilas then was the leader of this exit of the Christian Goths toward the Roman empire, having been ordained as their first bishop.

- What were the origins of Ulfilas' family?
- What role did captivity and enslavement play in the Christianization of the Goths? Cf. 2.25.

---

[146] In the 250s CE.

9

Experiencing and Resisting Enslavement

The experience of enslavement affected a significant percentage of the population of ancient societies. There were multiple avenues of enslavement; not only did they shape how slave systems operated and developed over time, but they also impinged on enslaved people in quite different ways. While some forms of enslavement were effectively universal, others were peculiar to particular societies or came to be restricted or eliminated. Violence was undoubtedly the most significant form of enslavement, which could potentially affect anyone in ancient societies. While captivity in war was common (9.2, 9.4), we also need to take into account the violent enslavement conducted by individuals for a variety of reasons (9.1, 9.3). Various other crises or forms of human misery could lead to enslavement. Poverty and famine could force people to sell themselves or their children (9.5–7) or become debt bondsmen (9.11). In other cases, widespread ancient practices, such as the exposure of unwanted children, became a ready source of slaves (9.9–10). Finally, the slave trade was a ubiquitous feature of ancient slave systems and a traumatic experience in the lives of many slaves (9.12–3, 9.20).

The experiences of enslavement were accompanied by the experiences of resistance. We have examined in Chapters 6 and 7 the experiences of resistance that were inherent in the master–slave relationship and in relationships between free and slave, respectively. In this chapter, we focus on how slaves tried to escape the experience of enslavement; the various forms of escape involved considerable dangers and were often lethal. But they made a huge difference in the lives of those slaves who attempted them and often also of those who did not, while they could have important consequences for ancient societies and their history. A major route was that of passing: trying to pass as free people and enjoy the privileges of free status or even citizenship while escaping the indignities of being classified as slaves and treated accordingly (9.14–7). Flight was a common phenomenon that ancient

Greek and Roman Slaveries, First Edition. Eftychia Bathrellou and Kostas Vlassopoulos.
© 2022 John Wiley & Sons, Inc. Published 2022 by John Wiley & Sons, Inc.

societies tried to prevent in various ways (9.18, 9.21). Flight required slaves to show enormous cunning and preparation (9.22); it often required the support of networks and communities because fugitives would commonly need to pass as free people in the communities they sought refuge (9.14, 9.23). Alternatively, fugitives could attempt to create maroon communities, which existed alongside their enslavers in various mixtures of conflict and accommodation (9.24).

The last, and relatively rare, resort was that of revolt. We use as a case study one of the most important revolts involving slaves in global history, which occurred in Sicily between 135 and 2 BCE. As with all cases of slave resistance, a revolt is an intensification of hopes and grievances (9.25.b), as well as a culmination of diverse tensions and contradictions within slave systems (9.25.a, 9.25.g) and the various forms in which slaves exercised their agency. Revolts thus offer remarkable glimpses of the multiple identities of enslaved persons (9.25.b, 9.25.e), the nature of their communities and leaders (9.25.b), and their hopes and aims (9.25.e–f).

ENSLAVEMENT BY FORCE

9.1   *IGDO* 23: Letter on Lead Lamella in Greek, Olbia, Black Sea (*ca.* 500 BCE)

This is the earliest surviving Greek letter. Achillodoros, Protagoras, and Anaxagoras are Greek names.

Literature: Bravo 1980; Eidinow and Taylor 2010; Parmenter 2020.

At the back of the lamella:
Achillodoros' piece of lead, to his son and to Anaxagoras.

On the interior side:
Protagoras, your father is sending you this message. He is being wronged by Matasys. Matasys is trying to enslave him and has deprived him of his cargo. Go to Anaxagoras and tell him what has happened. For Matasys claims that your father is a slave of Anaxagoras and says, "Anaxagoras is in hold of my things: my slaves, male and female, and my houses." But your father cries out loud and says that there is nothing between Matasys and himself and that he is free and that there is nothing between Matasys and himself. If there is an issue between Matasys and Anaxagoras, they themselves know it between themselves. Do tell these things to Anaxagoras and to the wife. And your father is sending you another message: take your mother and your brothers, who are among the Arbinatai,[147] to the city. And the dockyard warden himself shall go to Anaxagoras and then immediately down.

- What is the conflict between Matasys and Anaxagoras? Does it involve slaves?

- Why does Achillodoros face the threat of enslavement? How does he try to protect himself?

---

[147] A non-Greek people on the Black Sea coast.

9.2   Ps.-Demosthenes, *Against Nikostratos*, 6–8, 10–11: Greek Law-Court Speech, Athens (Mid-Fourth Century BCE)

Literature: Garlan 1987; Gabrielsen 2003; Roy 2012; Sosin 2017.

While I was away, three slaves ran away from Nikostratos, from his farm: two were of those I had given to him, one was of those he himself had purchased. While after them, he was captured by a trireme, taken to Aegina,[148] and sold there. When I completed my voyage as trierarch, Deinon came to me – the brother of Nikostratos here – and told me of this man's misfortune and that he himself had not gone to his help, although Nikostratos had been sending him messages, for lack of funds for the journey. He also said to me he had information that his brother was in a terrible state. When I heard this, I grieved at his misfortune and immediately sent to his help Deinon, his brother, after giving him 300 drachmas for the journey. When Nikostratos here returned home, he came to me. At first he embraced me and praised me for supplying his brother with funds for the journey. He lamented his own misfortune and, while accusing his family, begged me to help him, as in the past, too, I had acted as a true friend to him. In tears and saying that he had been ransomed for 26 minas, he kept asking me to make some contribution toward the ransom money. Hearing this, I felt pity for him. Seeing that he was in a bad state and was showing to me the wounds from the bonds on his calves – the scars are still visible, but if you ask him to show you, he will refuse – I responded that I had been a true friend to him in the past and now, too, in this misfortune, I would help him. I said I released him of the debt of the 300 drachmas, i.e. the money I had given to his brother for his journey when he went to fetch him, and would contribute 1000 drachmas to the collection for the ransom money. [...] A few days later, he came to me in tears, saying that the foreigners, who had put up the ransom money, were demanding back the remaining sum. [...] "Please," he said, "be the one who gives me the remaining money, before the end of thirty days. Otherwise, the 1000 drachmas I have already paid to them will be lost, and I myself will be liable to seizure. [...] As you know," he said, "the laws dictate that a man ransomed from the enemy shall belong to the person who redeemed him, if he fails to pay back to him the ransom money." [...]

- What happened to Nikostratos when he went away in pursuit of the runaway slaves?

- How did he manage to regain his freedom?

- What could have happened to Nikostratos if he had not had wealthy friends?

- What does this story reveal about the danger of enslavement?

---

[148] See 12.4.

9.3 *Dodone* 123: Lead Tablet with Oracular Question in Greek, Dodona, Epeiros (Fourth Century BCE)

Literature: Eidinow 2012; Desbiens 2017: 37–40.

> God. Good fortune.
>   Didn't Archonidas and Archebios, the son of Archonidas, and Sosandros, who was at the time a slave of Archonidas or of his wife, enslave the female attendant (*aozos*[149]) of Aristokles?

- What people are mentioned on this oracular tablet? What are their relationships?
- What was Sosandros' status at the time the inscription was written? What was his status in the past?
- Do we know the precise status of Aristokles' attendant when enslaved by Archonidas?
- How and why could the attendant's enslavement have taken place?
- What can we learn from the life stories of Sosandros and the anonymous female attendant of Aristokles about status in the ancient world?

9.4 *SEG* XXXIX 1711: Greek Funerary Inscription, Egypt (First Century CE?)

Apart from meaning "sibling," the words "brother" and "sister" could also denote one's partner or spouse in Egypt.

Literature: van Minnen 2000; Łajtar 2010.

> Valeria, also called Thermouthis, about forty-(?) years of age.
>   She died, being the sister of Publius Valerius, a soldier, having received his benefaction, together with my daughters Kleopatra and Euphrosyne. I was taken captive when I was four years old, remaining enslaved for 38 years. My brother Publius bought and ransomed me, together with my children. He put on my head the garland of the free while I was still alive, and I saw my children become free. I am thankful to him. [...] After my death, he did all that was due. Good health to all, my friends and neighbors! And everyone reading this should tell his soul that death is inevitable. And you, brother, don't deprive yourself of anything.

- Who is the deceased? What is her ethnic origin, and what do we learn about her life story?

---

[149] *Aozos* is a very rare word, derived from a word meaning "offshoot" and probably denoting an attendant or servant.

- Who set up this inscription? What is his ethnic origin, and what is his relationship with the deceased?

- Was her freedom important to Thermouthis? How can we tell? Is it her voice that we hear here?

SELF-SALE

Literature: Ramin and Veyne 1981; Silver 2011.

9.5 Diodorus, *Library*, 26.20: Greek Historiography (First Century BCE)

> Diodorus says that the Syracusans, in want of food because of their destitution after the city's fall,[150] would declare themselves slaves, so that they would be sold off and receive food by their buyers. Thus, on top of their other losses, fortune imposed upon the defeated Syracusans such a great calamity that they voluntarily chose slavery instead of the freedom offered to them.

- What circumstances made the Syracusans sell themselves? What did they try to achieve by doing so?

- How common were such circumstances in ancient societies?

- What factors could have stopped such practices in ancient societies? Cf. 8.10–4.

9.6 Basil of Caesarea, *Sermon On "I Will Destroy My Storehouses"* (Luke 12:18), 4: Christian Sermon in Greek (Fourth Century CE)

In this sermon, Basil addresses the greedy wealthy.

Literature: Vuolanto 2003; Harper 2011: 391–423.

> The look of your gold pleases you exceedingly, but to the loud moan of the needy behind you, you pay no heed. How can I put before your eyes the sufferings of the poor? The poor man examines what he has inside and sees that he has no gold, nor will he ever acquire any. His furniture and clothes, such as are the possessions of the destitute, are not worth more than a few obols in total. What then? In the end, he raises his eyes to his children, so that he might take them to the market and thus find a deterrent to death. Consider here the battle between the compulsion of hunger and fatherly disposition. The former threatens with the most pitiful death; nature pulls the other direction, urging the father to die together with his children. Many times he rushes forward;

---

[150] Syracuse fell to the Romans in 212 BCE.

many times he checks himself; in the end, he submits, forced by unyielding and inexorable necessity. What are the deliberations of this father? "Which of them shall I sell first? Whose looks will the grain seller like? Shall I go to my firstborn? But I respect his privileges as the eldest. To the youngest then? But I pity his young age, which is unable to perceive our misfortunes. This one has taken much after his parents. That one is good at learning. Alas – there is no way out! How should I behave? Which of them shall I strike upon? The soul of which beast shall I adopt? How shall I forget my nature? But if I keep all of them, I will see all of them wasted by suffering. If I give up one of them, with what eyes shall I look at the others? I will have already made them suspect me and mistrust me. How will I manage the house when I have deprived myself of my children? How shall I come to the table when this is what has put food on it?" So, he goes on to sell his most beloved child, his face filled with tears. But *you* are not moved by his suffering; you pay no heed to nature.

- What is the father's dilemma? How does he try to sort it out?
- What circumstances could bring people to such a dilemma? Cf. 9.7.
- Does Basil portray the selling of free children as legal? Cf. 8.16.
- What was Basil's rhetorical aim? To what extent could that affect the reliability of this passage?

9.7 Selling Children in Various Ancient Societies

Literature: Alexianu 2011.

—————— 9.7.a   Herodotus, 5.6: Greek Historiography   ——————
(Fifth Century BCE)

The other Thracians have the following custom: they sell their children, to be taken to other lands.

—————— 9.7.b   Suda, α 1384: Greek Encyclopedia   ——————
(Tenth Century CE)

Halônêton: bought in exchange for salt. Equivalent to "barbarian." Cf. the saying "a slave bought in exchange for salt." It denotes worthlessness because the merchants would take salt inland and get slaves in exchange. And "a man bought in exchange for salt": similar to "a barbarian." For the Thracians would sell slaves for salt.

———— 9.7.c   Philostratus, *Life of Apollonius*, 8.7.554–75:   ————
Greek Biography (First Half of Third Century CE)

In this part of the speech he reportedly wrote to defend himself to the Emperor Domitian, Apollonius of Tyana, a Pythagorean philosopher and sage of the first century CE, counters the charge that he had sacrificed a young boy from Arcadia for the purposes of divination. The accuser has failed to give details of the identity of the boy, which suggests, so Apollonius tries to show, that the accusation was false.

> Therefore, he accuses me on behalf of a slave boy. For, by gods, shouldn't we rank as slave one who himself has no name, nor do his parents, and who has no city or estate? No name has been supplied for any of this. So, who was the slave's seller? Who bought him from the Arcadians? If their nation is suitable for divinatory sacrifices, then it stands to reason that the boy was bought for a lot of money and that someone sailed to the Peloponnese to bring the Arcadian boy to us here over the sea. Slaves from the Black Sea, or from Lydia or from the Phrygians, one could have bought here, too; one can hit upon herds of such people roaming about here. For these nations, together with many other barbarian ones, have always been subjugated to others and no longer consider it shameful to be slaves. In fact, it is a local custom of the Phrygians to sell their own and not to give a thought to those enslaved. But the Greeks remain lovers of freedom, and no Greek man will sell a slave outside the borders. This is why no enslavers or slave dealers approach them – least of all in Arcadia, where not only are the people prone to live in freedom more than all other Greeks but also are in need of great numbers of slaves.

- What is the native custom in the barbarian countries mentioned in the three passages?
- Do Greeks have the same customs, according to the last passage?
- Do you think that Apollonius' distinction is based on reality or ideology? If on reality, how could we explain this difference?

9.8 *P.Oxy.* XLVI, 3312: Papyrus with Private Letter in Greek, Oxyrhynchos, Egypt (Second Century CE)

This private letter records in passing information about an unusual case of becoming an imperial freedman. On imperial slaves and freedmen, see 6.27.

Literature: Horsley 1983: 7–9; Weaver 2004; Silver 2011.

> [...] his children – may the evil eye never touch them – and your sister Isidora, and Athenais. And send to me definite information about how many months pregnant Dionysiarion is. Gaia sends you her greetings, and so do her children and her husband. You should also know that Herminos went off

to Rome and became a freedman of Caesar in order to get official posts. Send my greetings to all your people one by one; all my people send you theirs. I wish you farewell.

- What information concerning Herminos is relayed in this letter?
- What is a "freedman of Caesar"? Cf. 6.27, 10.21–2.
- What motives did Herminos have to desire such a status?
- Through what process do you envisage Herminos becoming an imperial freedman? Cf. 10.25.

EXPOSURE

Exposure of babies was legal in most ancient societies, and exposed children could be adopted by those who found them, or they could be raised as slaves. But there were important differences between ancient societies regarding how common this practice was, whether the parents or masters of exposed babies had the right to recover them at any time, and whether exposed free children raised as slaves could regain their free status later if they could prove their origins.

Literature: Patterson 1985; Harris 1994, 1999; Ricl 2009; Evans-Grubbs 2010.

9.9 Aelian, *Various History*, 2.7:[151] Miscellaneous Collection of Anecdotes and Historical Facts in Greek (Second/Third Century CE)

The following law is in force in Thebes and is right and extremely humane. No Theban man is allowed to expose a child or cast it out in the wilderness, condemning it to death. If the child's father is in extreme poverty, he must take the child, whether boy or girl, to the authorities as soon as it is born, in its swaddling clothes. After receiving the baby, the authorities sell it to the person who has paid the lowest price. An agreement and contract is made on the terms that the person in question will raise the baby and, when it grows up, will keep it as his slave, thus receiving the child's services as his recompence for having raised it.

- What conditions made people not wish to raise their babies?
- What was the future of these babies in Thebes?
- How common was such a law, judging from the rhetoric of the passage?

---

[151] Greek text: Dilts 1974.

9.10 *C.Pap.Gr.* 1.14,1–30 (= *P.Rein.* 2.103): Papyrus with Wet-Nurse Contract in Greek, Oxyrhynchos, Egypt (First Century CE)

Literature: Backhuys 2017: 229–31.

The 12th year of Tiberius Caesar Augustus, 26th day of Pachon, in the city of the Oxyrhynchians, in the Thebaid.

Taseus, daughter of Peteeus, a Persian woman, with her guardian and guarantor for the fulfilment of everything in this document, namely her husband Petseiris, son of Horos, a Persian of the Epigone, both from Tanais in the Middle Toparchy, enter into an agreement with Paapis, son of Phnas (?), that, already since the 17th day of the current month Pachon, she has received from him in the street a female child whom he took from a dung heap to raise as a slave and to whom he gave the name Thermoutharion, so that she might [rear] it and breastfeed it with her own milk and also be the child's nurse for two years starting from the same 17th day of Pachon.

In return of the stated obligations, Paapis is to provide 60 silver drachmas per year for food, clothing, and the other expenses for the child. Taseus and her husband and guarantor Petseiris acknowledge that they have since this moment received full payment of the 60 drachmas for the first year from Paapis from his hand from his house. At the end of the first year, Paapis shall pay to her the 60 silver drachmas for the second year in one single payment. During these two years, Paapis shall provide her with two kotylai of olive oil per month. It is therefore incumbent that Taseus provide every protection and care to the child, as this contract imposes upon her. She is not allowed to have intercourse with a man, so as not to harm her milk, nor to become pregnant, nor to breastfeed another child in parallel, nor [...]. She should return the child to Paapis in a safe and good condition, as this contract imposes upon her. If the child meets with some fatality, which is obvious that it was a fatality, Taseus shall not be considered responsible. If Paapis chooses to hand over to her another child, she is to nourish it for the remaining time according to the aforementioned terms, but if Taseus does not wish to do so, she is to give back to Paapis whatever is shown she owes to him for the time she did not act as nurse. And if she violates the contract and does not act according to the terms written down, she is to pay to Paapis what she has received or she shall also owe to him another 50%, and she shall give 200 drachmas more as compensation for damages and as penalty and the same amount to the public treasury. And Paapis shall have the right to exact his money from the aforementioned people and from whomever he might choose and from all their belongings. [...]

- Whose baby does Paapis hand to Taseus to nurse? Why does he undertake the expense?

- What might Paapis do if the child dies accidentally before the completion of the two years? What does the possibility that he might give to Taseus another child to nurse show about raising exposed children in Egypt?

- How common do you think was exposure of babies in the ancient world, and how often did exposed babies become slaves?

DEBT BONDAGE AND ENSLAVEMENT FOR DEBT

See also 2.20, 8.10, 8.14, 11.5, 11.8, and 12.18.

9.11   Quintilian, *Minor Declamations*, 311: Latin Fictitious Law-Court Speech to Be Used as Rhetorical Model (Probably First Century CE)

The speech is purportedly delivered by the heirs of a wealthy man who had freed all his slaves in his will. They argue against the claim of a freeborn man, who had been assigned ("addicted") to his creditor to work off his debt and therefore lived and worked in the house of the deceased, that he, too, should be freed according to the will, although he had not yet paid off the debt.

Literature: Kleijwegt 2013.

We realize that what we should fear most in this case is the favor commonly felt for all who assert their claims to freedom. Against this, we realize we must not only argue as having the safeguarding of the law as our priority but also say that what we contend is no less in the interest of the man whom we seem to be opposing – if, of course, he fulfils his obligation. For the question today is whether he is a slave. We make no complaint of the generosity, befitting a free man, of the person who made us his heirs. He manumitted slaves. Does anyone find any fault with that? Is it with reluctance or sadness that we see their becoming part of the citizen body? To our minds, being a debtor and being a freeborn man (*ingenuus*) are distinct categories.

   It does not escape us that it looks as if the dispute is proceeding in a contrary manner. For if one of us called this man a slave, he would actually have many things to say for himself, things which would show him a free man. For what does the law say? "A person addicted for debt should be in servitude (*servire*) until he pays off his debt," I think; not "he should be a slave." This is very important. For we rightly speak of those who fall into the hands of pirates or are captured by the enemy as being in servitude. What nature gave to the freeborn cannot be snatched away by any injury of Fortune.[152] Although I expect that there is not one among you who does not see this clearly, I wish to demonstrate it through some obvious arguments. First of all, this man has a name, is in the census, is in a tribe; none of these things, I think, can be found in a slave. "But his current condition intervenes, and he has to be in servitude until he pays off his debt." It is precisely this that does not apply to a slave: namely to have it in his own power to define when he can stop being in servitude. Imagine, judges. If he becomes free – either after offering the money he owes or by your pronouncement on the basis of the will – will he then be a freedman (*libertinus*)? I think not. But if we accept that a man who passes from slavery to freedom is in no other position than in that of a freedman, while this man, when released from this coerced condition of his,

---

[152] Although part of the transmitted Latin text, the last two sentences might not have been part of the original.

will be as freeborn (*ingenuus*) as he had been, then clearly he is not a slave today. There are many other things you may look at if you wish. A slave is either home-born or left by inheritance or purchased. Under which of these categories of slaves do you place this man? He does not say that he is home-born or left by inheritance or purchased. So, his condition depends entirely on a loan. What follows? That he is not a <slave>.

So much for the actual wording of the will. Now I would like to scrutinize also the intention of the deceased. Nothing should weight more for us; nothing should be more sacred to our minds. So, is it credible that this is what he meant, namely that he wanted even the man addicted for debt to be free? Why he manumitted his slaves is clear. He was pleased with their services; he wanted to show gratitude for their dutifulness (*obsequium*). One of them had treated him when ill, another had followed him when abroad, another had supervised his domestic affairs when he was very occupied, another had practiced this very thing: loaning money. He wished those whom he had loved and by whom he himself had been loved to be free. But what did he owe this man except anger?

"But it seems harsh and inhumane that this man alone should be in the bonds of servitude." First of all, if there is harshness, it is in the law which commands that those addicted for debt be in servitude until they pay it off. Do you then require that we say something in defense of this law? It is not for an average person, like me, nor is it part of my duty, to try to defend a law instituted by our far-sighted and wise ancestors. Nonetheless, if you wish to look into it, what could be more equitable? In what other way could your patrimonies be guarded and your fortunes sustained? Or shall one accept money from you, squander it in all kinds of vices, and then not be obliged by some coercive means to pay it back? Do such bonds seem harsh to someone? Does the condition of servitude seem harsh? He should return what he received. In this law, it is not servitude what is being determined but something eminently just: a motive for returning money.

- Why do the speakers try to distinguish between slaves and debt bondsmen?
- What arguments do they use to make the distinction?
- How do they justify the justice of manumitting the slaves but keeping the addicted debtor in bondage?
- What differences were there between debt bondsmen and slaves?
- Is debt bondage a situation in which law might differ substantially from actual practice? What factors might create a huge cleavage between law and practice? Cf. 2.20, 8.10, 8.14.

TRADE

Literature: Straus 2004b.

9.12 *An.Ep.* (2003), No. 1016 (Latin Text after Camodeca 2006): Deed of Slave Sale, London, Britannia (Late First/Early Second Century CE)

All individuals mentioned in this document have Latin names. Mancipation (*mancipatio*) was a process of archaic origin for buying certain kinds of goods, including slaves: the buyer received the slave in the presence of the seller, witnesses, and a man holding the scales, which notionally weighed out the slave's price.

Literature: Tomlin 2003; Camodeca 2006; Korporowicz 2011; Czajkowski and Eckhardt 2018.

> Vegetus, assistant slave (*vicarius*) of Montanus, the latter being slave of the emperor and formerly slave of Jucundus,[153] bought and received by mancipation from Albicianus [...] for 600 denarii a girl called Fortunata (or of whatever other name she is known), a Diablinte[154] by origin. It is warranted that the girl in question is transferred in good health and that she is not a fugitive nor of the type who tends to wander off (*erro*). But if anyone should have laid claim to the girl in question or any share in her, with the consequence that Vegetus, assistant slave of Montanus, slave of the Emperor Caesar, or he to whom this issue is relevant, be not allowed to have her and possess her [...].[155]

- What is the identity of the buyer?
- What is the name and origin of the sold slave, and how is she described? What other features of her are mentioned and why?
- Are there other slaves mentioned in this document? Cf. 12.14.
- What can we learn about slavery from the identities of the various slaves mentioned?

9.13 *P.Cair.Zen.* 1.59076 (Excerpted): Papyrus with Letter in Greek, Egypt (257 BCE)

Literature: Scholl 1990: no. 48.

> Toubias to Apollonios. Greetings.
> [...] I have sent over Aeneas to you bringing one eunuch and four slave boys [...] and of noble origins. Two of them are uncircumcised. Below we

---

[153] The name of the former owner was often indicated for slaves who then became members of the *familia Caesaris*.
[154] A Celtic tribe in northern Gaul.
[155] The rest has not survived.

have appended descriptions of the boys, so that you can recognize them. Farewell. Year 29, 10th day of the month Xandikos.

Aimos. About 10 years old. Dark-haired, curly-haired, black-eyed, strong jaws and moles on his right cheek, uncircumcised.

Atikos. About 8 years old. Honey-colored skin, curly-haired, very mildly flat-nosed, black-eyed, scar under his right eye, uncircumcised.

Audomos. About 10 years old. Black-eyed, curly-haired, snub-nosed, his mouth protruded, scar near his right eyebrow, circumcised.

Okaimos. About 7 years old. Round-faced, snub-nosed, blue-eyed, reddish hair, straight-haired, scar on his forehead, above the right eyebrow, circumcised.

- How might Toubias have acquired the eunuch and the four boys he sends to Apollonios? Cf. 6.26.

- What characteristics of the slaves does he list? Why? Which are singled out as more important? Why?

- What can we surmise of how the eunuch and the boys experienced enslavement, castration, and transportation in a foreign country? Cf. 8.17.

PASSING

9.14   Lysias, *Against Pankleon*, 1–15 (Selections): Greek Law-Court Speech, Athens (Late Fifth/Early Fourth Century BCE)

After the destruction of the city of Plataea by the Thebans in 427 BCE, the Athenians offered Athenian citizenship to any Plataean who would register for it. Accordingly, lawsuits against Plataeans in Athens were brought not before the polemarch, the magistrate responsible for metics, but before the same magistrates who received lawsuits against Athenian citizens.

Literature: Vlassopoulos 2009.

Men of the jury, I would not have the ability to speak at length on this matter, nor do I think it necessary. But I will try to prove to you that it was following the correct procedure that I brought the lawsuit against this Pankleon here, since he is not a Plataean. As Pankleon had been repeatedly wronging me for a long time, I went to the fuller's where he worked and gave him a summons to appear before the polemarch, thinking that he was a metic. When he said that he was a Plataean, I asked him to which deme he belonged, after one of those present advised me to give him an additional summons to appear before whatever tribe he claimed to belong to. [...]

First, I asked Euthykritos, whom I knew as the oldest of the Plataeans and thought would be the best informed, whether he knew one Pankleon, Plataean, son of Hipparmodoros. Since he responded that he knew Hipparmodoros but of no son of his – neither Pankleon nor any other – I then went on to ask all those I knew to be Plataeans. [...] All said they did not know him, except for one who said that he did not know of any citizen of that name, but that there was a slave called Pankleon who had run away from his own household. And he mentioned the age of this man here and the craft he practices. [...] Well, not many days later I saw Pankleon here being led away as slave (*agomenon*) by Nikomedes, who had testified he was his master. I approached, wishing to learn what would be done about him. Then, after they stopped fighting, some of those with Pankleon said that he had a brother who would remove him back into freedom (*aphairesis eis eleutherian*). On this basis, they pledged that they would bring the brother to the marketplace and went away. The following day, in view of this special plea and the court case itself, I thought that I should take some witnesses and appear there, so that I might know the man who would remove Pankleon back into freedom and hear what he would say in order to do so.

Now, neither a brother nor anyone else came to fulfil the pledges; a woman came claiming that he was her slave, disputing the claim of Nikomedes and saying she would not allow him to lead Pankleon away as slave. Now, I would have to speak at great length to report all that was said at this point. Those with Pankleon and Pankleon himself reached such a level of violence, that, although both Nikomedes and the woman wanted to let him go if anyone came to remove him back into freedom or lead him away claiming him as his slave, they did neither of the two but carried him off and went away. [...] It is easy, then, to realize that not even Pankleon considers himself a Plataean – nor even a free man. For when a man has chosen to be carried off violently and thus render those close to him liable for the violence rather than to have himself removed back into freedom and exact punishment from those leading him away to slavery, it is not difficult to recognize that he knew very well that he was a slave and feared to appoint sureties and stand trial for his person.

Now, I think that you perceive pretty clearly from this that he is far from being a Plataean. But you will easily find out from what he did that not even Pankleon himself, who best knows his own situation, believed that you would think he was a Plataean. In the pre-trial oath for the suit that Aristodikos here brought against him, when he disputed that he should be tried before the polemarch, it was declared on testimony that he was not a Plataean. Pankleon then formally declared he would prosecute the witness; however, he did not pursue the matter further and so allowed Aristodikos to win the trial against him. And when he failed to pay his debt on the appointed day, he paid the penalty on whatever terms he could persuade Aristodikos to accept. [...] Now, before he made this agreement with Aristodikos, he left Athens out of fear of him and moved to Thebes. And yet I believe you know that if he was a Plataean, it would be expected that he might move anywhere rather than to Thebes.

- What status does the speaker attribute to Pankleon initially?

- What status does Pankleon claim?

- How does the speaker try to find out Pankleon's true status?

- Which persons claim Pankleon as a slave? Is there anything strange about this?

- How does Pankleon manage to escape being enslaved? Who supports him? What can we learn from this about the role of slave networks?

- Do you think Pankleon is metic, slave, or citizen?

- What can we learn about claims to status in Athens from this story?

9.15 *IG* XII.5 1004.1–9: Greek Honorific Inscription, Ios, Southern-Central Aegean (Fourth Century BCE)

Literature: Vlassopoulos 2007.

> Archagathos proposed; the presidents Sokrates, Aischron, Stesitimos, Posideios put to the vote: because Zenon, the man left behind by the *nêsiarchos*[156] Bakchon, when approached by the ambassadors sent to him by the People on the issue of the slaves who had run away from Ios on the undecked ships, called the trierarchs back, conducted an investigation and recovered the slaves and did so in a manner in every way indicative of his love of honor, the Council and the People decided that Zenon be praised for his excellence and his goodwill toward the People of Ios and that he be a *proxenos*[157] and benefactor of the People of Ios – both he himself and his descendants – along with the existing ones.

- Why is Zenon honored?

- How did these slaves try to escape slavery?

9.16 Pliny the Younger, *Letters*, 10.74: Latin Epistolography (Early Second Century CE)

Pliny writes to the Emperor Trajan. Decibalus was king of Dacia, defeated by the Romans when Trajan was emperor, in 102 CE, but continuing aggravation against them until his death at 106. His sending presents to Pacorus, the king of Parthia, is perhaps suggestive of his effort to enlist Parthian support in his war against the Romans.

---

[156] A principal official of the League of the Islanders in the southern Aegean, established in the late fourth century BCE.

[157] *Proxenoi* looked after the interests of another city in their own community.

Literature: Bradley 1994: 23–4.

> Appuleius, my lord, a soldier at the garrison at Nikomedeia, wrote to me that a certain man named Callidromus, while detained by the bakers Maximus and Dionysius, to whom he had hired out his labor, had run away and sought refuge at your statue. He was taken to the magistrates and declared that at some point he had been a slave of Laberius Maximus[158] and that, after being captured by Susagus in Moesia, had been sent as a gift by Decibalus to Pacorus, king of Parthia. He had stayed at the latter's service for many years and then fled and finally arrived at Nikomedeia. He was then led to me and, when he recounted the same things, I thought that he should be sent off to you. This I did with some delay, as I have been trying to find a jewel bearing the likeness of Pacorus together with his regalia, that he repeatedly declared as having been stolen from him. I wanted to send it to you, if I had been able to discover it, together with the small lump of ore I did send, which he insisted he had brought with him from a Parthian mine. I have stamped it with my ring, the sign on which is a four-horse chariot.

- What was Callidromus' story?
- What was he doing at Nikomedeia?
- Why did he decide to reveal his true identity at this precise moment?
- Why were all these details of interest to Pliny? Why did he report them to Trajan? If Callidromus is lying, might he have a motive for telling such a story?
- To what extent is this story useful for recovering slave experiences?

9.17   Code of Justinian, 10.33.2: Collection of Imperial Laws and Rescripts in Latin (Sixth Century CE)

Imperial rescript by the emperors Diocletian and Maximian in response to a female petitioner, dated to around 300 CE.

Literature: Evans-Grubbs 2013: 69–70.

> If the provincial governor learns that he who is serving as aedile[159] is your slave and perceives that the slave had aspired to become aedile knowing his status, the governor shall inflict an appropriate punishment, because the honor of the council was violated by a servile stain. If, however, because his mother was considered free by the public opinion, he, having been born to a *decurio*,[160] proceeded to attain this honor by mistake, the governor will subject him to your ownership.

---

[158] A Roman senator and general, favored by Trajan.
[159] One of the chief magistrates of Roman cities.
[160] *Decuriones* were men who were members of city councils.

- What possibilities does the law envisage for a slave in the role of aedile?

- In the scenario of a slave who knew his status and yet became aedile, what conclusions should we draw about slave passing?

- In the scenario of a slave mother who was considered free, what should we conclude about slave passing?

FLIGHT

Cf. 1.18, 6.12.

Literature: Bellen 1971; Fuhrmann 2012: 21–43.

9.18 *Digest*, 21.1.17, Prologue–12: Collection of Latin Juristic Texts (Sixth Century CE)

The men whose opinions are reported by Ulpian in the following excerpts were Roman jurists of the first century BCE and the first century CE.

Ulpian, *On the Edict of the Curule Aedile*, Book 1: Ofilius defines a fugitive as follows: "A fugitive is one who remained away from his master's house for the purpose of flight, so that he might hide himself from his master." [...] It is also mentioned in the work of Vivianus that a fugitive is to be understood from his attitude of mind rather and not merely from the fact of flight. For one who runs away from the enemy, or from a robber, or a fire or the collapse of a building, although it is true that he has fled, is nonetheless no fugitive. Nor is one who has run away from the instructor to whom he had been brought for training if he fled because he was treated inordinately badly. Vivianus says the same also holds for cases whereby a slave runs away from one to whom he had been lent, if he fled for the same reason. He also says the same for cases whereby the slave runs away because he has been treated brutally. This applies if the slave fled such people and then returned to his master, but if he did not return to his master, then, Vivianus says, this slave is to be considered undoubtedly a fugitive.

The same Vivianus says, "When Proculus was asked about a slave who had concealed himself in the house, in the hope of finding an occasion for flight, he said that, although he who remained in the house could not be considered as being in flight, he was nonetheless a fugitive. If, however, he had concealed himself for the time that his master's anger was seething, he was not a fugitive. Neither would be one who, upon observing his master wishing to whip him, took himself to a friend, to ask him to plead on his behalf. Nor is a fugitive one who has left in order to throw himself from a height; rather, he wanted to kill himself. On the other hand, one who ascends to a high point of the house in order to throw himself down could be called a fugitive. For," Vivianus said, "what is often stated, especially by ignorant people, namely that one who stays away for the night without the consent of his master is a fugitive, is not true. This should, instead, be assessed by his attitude of mind." Upon considering whether a slave boy who leaves his instructor and returns back to his mother is a fugitive, the same Vivianus says, "If the boy fled in order to hide himself and not return to his master, then he is a fugitive. If, however, he acted thus, so that he might achieve forgiveness for some error more easily with the support of his mother, then he is not a fugitive." [...]

In Labeo and Caelius, the question is posed whether one who flees to a place of asylum or betakes himself to a place where men declaring themselves for sale tend to go is a fugitive. I think that one who does what is considered permissible to do publicly is not a fugitive. Nor do I consider as a fugitive one who flees to the statue of the emperor; for he does not act so with the intention of running away. Nor do I consider a fugitive one who flees to a place of asylum or another similar place, because he does not act so with the intention of running away. If, however, he first fled and afterwards sought refuge, then he has not ceased being a fugitive.

- What forms of slave flight does the text discuss?
- Which forms of flight are not considered as evidence that the slaves are fugitives? Why?
- What does the legal treatment of flight tell us about how Romans envisaged slave agency?
- What can we learn about the master–slave dialectic from the various cases of slave flight?
- What can we learn concerning the free–slave dialectic from the various cases of slave flight?
- What can we learn about slave communities from the various cases of slave flight?
- What were the consequences of being labeled a fugitive? Cf. 9.19–20.

9.19 Phaedrus, *Fables*, Perroti's Appendix 20:[161] Latin Verse Fable (First Century CE)

Literature: Vlassopoulos 2018a.

Aesop and the Runaway slave, or "don't add bad to evil."

A slave running away from his cruel master happened to meet Aesop, who was known to him as a neighbor. "Why are you upset?" "I'll tell you frankly, father – for you deserve to be called father – since my complaints can safely be entrusted to you. Beatings, I get more than I can take; food, I get less than I need. Time and again, I'm sent off to the farm, with no provisions for the road. The master dines in the house: I am on my feet all night long. The master has been invited out: I lie in some by-lane until dawn. I have earned my freedom, yet my hair is gray, and I am still a slave. If I knew that any of this was of my own fault, I would endure it with a patient heart. But I am

[161] Latin text: Perry 1965.

constantly hungry, and I suffer miserably at the hands of my brutal master. It is for these reasons, and for others that would take long to relate, that I have decided to go away, wherever my feet take me." "Well, listen," said Aesop. "Now, as you say, you have done nothing wrong, and yet you suffer terribly. What if you do wrong? What do you think will happen to you then?" Hearing such advice, the slave was deterred from running away.

- Why is this slave considering flight?
- Which of his expectations are disappointed? What does this tell us about slaves' views of slavery?
- On what grounds does Aesop advise against flight?
- To what extent do you think this is a useful illustration of the motives both for fleeing and for staying put?

9.20   *Philogelos*, 122:[162] Greek Collection of Jokes (Late Antiquity)

Literature: Harper 2011: 248.

A man from Abdera[163] was trying to sell a pan which was missing its ear-shaped handles. When asked why he had made away with the handles, he responded, "So that it might not hear that it is on sale and run away."

- On what analogy with real life is this joke based?
- Why would slaves flee if they heard they would be sold? What did they fear?
- What consequences could sale have on slave lives? Compare with 1.25.

9.21   *CIL* XV, 7193: Tag for Collar with Latin Inscription, Rome (Second Half of Fourth Century CE) (Fig. 14)

Literature: Thurmond 1994: 481; Hillner 2001; Trimble 2016.

Hold me, so as I might not flee, and return me to my master Viventius in the estate of Callistus.

- What was the purpose of this tag and the collar to which it would have been rivetted?
- How exactly would it perform its function?

---

[162] Greek text: Thierfelder 1968.
[163] People from Abdera were considered proverbial idiots.

Figure 14 Bronze tag for collar with Latin inscription, second half of fourth century CE, Rome: British Museum, inv. no. 1975,0902.6.

9.22 Jerome, *Life of Malchus*, 7.3–9.3:[164] Latin Biographical Narrative (Fourth Century CE)

Observing the activities of ants makes the narrator, now a slave living together with a woman fellow-slave, long for his earlier life as a monk. For this text, see also 7.7, 8.4.

Literature: Lenski 2011a; Gray 2015: 265–74.

[…] I started to be weary of captivity and to long for the cells of the monastery. I also desired to imitate those ants, in whose life work is undertaken for the good of all and, since nothing belongs to anyone, everything belongs to all. I return to my place. The woman meets me. My face betrayed the sadness of my soul. She asks why I am dispirited. She hears my reasons. I urge flight. This isn't refused. I ask for silence. She grants her promise. Whispering constantly, we fluctuate between hope and fear. In my flock, there were two he-goats of remarkable size. I kill them and make skin-bags, while with their meat, I prepare our food for the journey. When it started to get dark and our masters thought that we were lying in our private space, we set out on our journey, carrying the skin-bags and the pieces of meat. And when

---

[164] Latin text: Gray 2015.

we had reached the river – it was 10 miles away – we inflated the skin-bags, climbed upon them, and entrusted ourselves to the waters, paddling a little with our feet under water. Our intention was that, the river carrying us downstream and depositing us on the other bank, further away from where we had embarked, our followers should lose our traces. But meanwhile the meat got wet, some of it fell into the river, so we could hardly hope for more than three days' rations. We drank as much as we could, preparing for the thirst that was to come. We ran, constantly looking behind our back, and moving mostly through the night, because of the ambushes of the Saracens, who wandered far and wide, and because of the extreme heat of the sun. Wretched me! I feel fear even when I mention this, and, although safe now, I shudder from head to foot. Two days later, we indistinctly saw far away two men on camels approaching rapidly. Immediately, the mind foreboding doom thought that the master was planning our death, and saw the sun darkening. And while we were in fear and realizing that we had been betrayed by our footprints in the sand, a cave appeared to our right, which extended far below the earth. [...]

The narrator and the woman hide inside the cave.

What do you think was our state of mind, how great our terror, when in front of the cave, not far from us, there stood our master and a fellow slave? They had already reached our hiding place, guided by our footprints.

- Why did the narrator decide to flee?

- How did the two slaves prepare their flight? What was their plan for escape?

- Who were their pursuers? What does this tell us about the complexity of slavery?

9.23 Ps.-Lucian, *The Ass*, 34–5: Greek Novel (Second Century CE?)

Lucius, the narrator and protagonist of this novel, is a man transformed into an ass. At this point in the story, Lucius-ass belongs to the household of two newlyweds. They live in the town, while the ass lives on their farm, which is run and lived in by their slaves. It has just been decided that he should be neutered the following day. Cf. also 5.10.

Literature: Paschalis 2019.

It was the dead of night, and a messenger from town came to the house in the farm. He said that, as the newlywed maiden [...] and her bridegroom were both walking on the seashore late in the evening, the sea suddenly rose, snatched them out of sight, and this became the end of their calamity – an end in death. As the house had been left bereft of its young masters, those on the farm decided not to remain in slavery anymore; they plundered all that was inside, ran away, and tried to take themselves to safety. The horse keeper took me in his charge, seized also all he could, and tied them on myself, on the horses and on other beasts. I was vexed at having to carry a true donkey's load, but I gladly accepted this obstruction to my castration. We traveled through the night on an exhausting journey, and after three more days, we arrived at Beroia: a large and populous city in Macedonia. It was there that those in charge of us decided to settle us and themselves. And then we beasts were put up for sale, and a loud-voiced herald standing in the middle of the marketplace started to proclaim us for sale.

- Why do the slaves decide to flee?
- Why is there nobody to stop the slaves? What does this tell us about surveillance and management of large estates?
- Why do the slaves aim for a large and populous city?

9.24 Nymphodorus of Syracuse, *Circumnavigation of Asia, BNJ 572 F 4*: Greek Ethnography (End of Third Century BCE)

Literature: Fuks 1984: 260–9; Cartledge 1985; Forsdyke 2012: 37–89.

The slaves of the Chians often run away from them. They rush to the mountains and ransack the country houses of the Chians in large groups. For the island's landscape is rough and thickly wooded. The Chians themselves tell the story of a slave who, a little before our time, ran away to live in the mountains and, being a brave man and successful at war, led the runaways as a king might have led an army. Many times did the Chians send an expedition against him, but they were unable to achieve anything. When Drimakos – this was the name of the runaway – saw them perishing in vain, he said to them the following words: "What the slaves are doing to you, Chian masters, will never stop. How could it stop, when it occurs in accordance with an oracle given by god? However, if you make a treaty with me and leave us in peace, I will be the origin of many benefits for you." The Chians made a treaty and a truce with him for some time, and he made his own measures and weights and his own seal. He showed them to the Chians and explained why he had done so: "Whatever I might take from you I will take using these measures and weights; when I take what I need, I will seal up your storehouses with this seal and leave. Any slaves that might run away from you I will keep with me if, when I enquire the reason of their flight, I form the opinion that they flew because they had suffered something irreparable. But if they produce no justification, I will send them away to their masters." The other slaves, seeing that the Chians were content with this development, started to run away much less, fearing Drimakos' judgement. The runaways that were already with him feared him much more than their own masters and did all he required of them, obeying him as they would a general. You see, he punished those who were undisciplined and allowed no one to plunder a farm or commit any other wrong whatever without his consent. At festivals, he marched out and took from the farms wine and fine animals for sacrifice – unless the masters themselves offered them to him. And anyone he perceived plotting against him or setting a trap for him, he punished.

Later – for the city had proclaimed a great reward to the man who would capture Drimakos or bring his head in – this Drimakos, when he became older, summoned the boy he was a lover of to some place and said to him, "Of all people, it is you I have loved most, and you are my boy and my son and everything else. I have lived a long life, but you are young and in your prime. So, what is my point? You must become a gentleman. So, since the city of the Chians offers a great reward to the one who might kill me and promises his freedom, you must take my head, take it to Chios, receive the money from the city, and prosper with god's blessing." The youth protested, but Drimakos convinced him to do it. So, he took Drimakos' head, received from the Chians the proclaimed reward, buried the runaway's body, and left for his own land. The Chians started once more to be wronged and plundered by their slaves, and this reminded them of the dead man's reasonableness; so, they founded a hero shrine for him in the countryside and called it "of the kindly hero." And even today the runaways offer to him the first fruits of their plunder. They also say that he appears in the dream of many Chians and warns them of their slaves' plans against them. Those to whom he appears go to the place where his shrine is and offer a sacrifice to him.

- Why is slave flight a serious prospect at Chios? Cf. 1.5.
- How did the fugitives survive?
- What were the mutual advantages for Drimakos and the Chians in the agreement they reached?
- What can we learn about relationships between slaves and how slaves viewed slavery on the basis of this passage?
- Are there novelistic elements in this story? Do they undermine its historicity?
- Are you surprised by the role of Drimakos on Chios after his death?

REVOLT

See also 7.5.

9.25   The First Slave Revolt in Sicily (135–2 BCE)

Literature: Vogt 1974: 39–92; Bradley 1989; Shaw 2001; Urbainczyk 2008; Morton 2012, 2013, 2014.

———————   9.25.a   Diodorus, *Library*, Book 34, fr. 2 Goukowsky   ———————
(= 34/35.2.27–31 Walton): Greek Historiography
(First Century BCE)

Diodorus says that all those who owned a lot of land bought up entire slave pens for agricultural labor. [...] As a result, the whole of Sicily was flooded with so many slaves that anyone hearing of this excess found it incredible. *** For, in fact, the Sicilians who owned great fortunes were competing with the Italians in arrogance, greediness, and wickedness. Specifically, the Italians who owned great numbers of slaves had driven their herdsmen to routine unprincipled behavior, so much so that they did not provide food for them but allowed them to steal. And because such power was given to people who, because of their physical strength, were able to achieve whatever they decided to do, people who, moreover, had opportunities, since they had freedom of movement and time in their hands and who were forced by lack of food to attempt reckless deeds, lawlessness increased fast. First, they would murder travelers journeying on their own or with one other person at deserted spots. Then they would get together in groups and violently raid the farms of the less powerful during the night; they plundered their property and killed those who resisted them.

Their daring kept increasing, and it was impossible to travel in Sicily during the night, nor could those who used to live in the countryside safely stay there, but everything was filled with violence, robbery, and murder of every kind. Since the herdsmen had lived in the open and had acquired military equipment, it was not surprising that they were all being filled up with courage and boldness. They carried with them clubs, spears, and strong shepherds' crooks; they covered their bodies with wolf-skins and wild boar-skins; so, their appearance inspired fear and was not very different from that of warriors. Packs of strong dogs followed each one of them. The dogs and the amount of food, milk, and meat they had at their disposal made their bodies and souls grow wild. So, the whole countryside seemed as if it was full of scattered armies – as if the boldness of the slaves had been armed by their masters' guardianship. The governors were making attempts to suppress the madness of the slaves, but as they did not dare to punish them, because of the power and authority of the slaves' masters, they were compelled to watch with folded arms the ravaging of the province. Since most owners were Romans of the equestrian rank and could decide the cases of province governors when the latter were facing prosecution, they inspired fear to those in office.

- To what factors does Diodorus attribute the slaves' lawless behavior? Cf. 5.31.
- What circumstances does Diodorus identify as inducing to the slave revolt? Cf. 11.12.

——— 9.25.b Diodorus, *Library*, Book 34, Testimonium, 2 ———
Goukowsky (= 34/35.2.4 Walton): Greek Historiography
(First Century BCE)

Literature: Morton 2013.

> Harassed by hardships and often unjustifiably humiliated through beatings, the slaves could no longer bear this situation. They therefore got together whenever they found opportunity and talked to one another about an uprising, until they put their plan into action.
>
> Antigenes of Enna had a slave of Syrian origin, from Apameia.[165] The fellow had the ways of a magician and wonder-worker. He used to pretend that he could foretell the future through divine orders he received in his sleep. As he was quite good at this, he used to deceive many. He went on from there and did not restrict himself to oneiromancy but pretended he had visions of gods while awake and heard from them what was going to happen. He invented many things, some of which would by chance turn out to be true. As no one scrutinized the prophecies which did not come true while attention was given to those fulfilled, his reputation grew. In the end, using some device or other, he would go into something like a state of divine possession, let fire and flames come out of his mouth, and then prophesy what was going to happen. He used to make holes on the two edges of a nutshell, or something of that kind, and put fire inside, together with a substance capable of feeding the fire. Then he put it in his mouth and with his breath produced sometimes sparks, other times flame.
>
> This man used to say before the uprising that the Syrian goddess made appearances to him and told him that he would become king. And this he would relate not only to other people but also to his very owner. The thing was turning to a joke, and Antigenes, enchanted by the marvel-mongering, used to take Eunous to dinners – Eunous was the wonder-worker's name – and ask him about his kingdom and how he would treat each of those present. And the fellow used to tell everything without wavering, including that he would treat the slave owners with moderation, and in general talked wonders of every kind. The guests would laugh, and some of them would lift from the table and give him big portions of food, adding that, when he became king, he should remember the favor they were doing him. Nonetheless, wonder-working resulted in real kingship in the end, and he reciprocated in earnest the favors done to him for a laugh by those welcoming him at the dinners.

- How does Diodorus present the would-be leader of the slave revolt?

- What elements in this description explain why Eunous would become a leader of the slaves?

- Why does Diodorus present Eunous in such a manner? How credible do you find this depiction?

---

[165] Cf. 8.1.

—————— 9.25.c Diodorus, *Library*, Book 34, fr. 8 ——————
Goukowsky (=34/35.2.24b Walton): Greek Historiography
(First Century BCE)

Diodorus says that the slaves conspired with one another considering an uprising and the murder of their masters. They went to Eunous, who lived nearby, and put questions to him about whether the gods approved of their decision. As a wonder-worker in a state of divine possession, Eunous, after hearing what they had come for, made it clear that the gods allowed them to rise up, as long as they attempted their attack immediately, without any delay. For, he continued, fate had decreed Enna as their homeland, since it was the citadel of the whole island. At hearing such words and understanding that the divine was supporting them in their decision, they set up their souls to be ready for the uprising, so that there would be no delay in what they had decided to do. Immediately, they started to free those who had been bound and of the others they took on their side those living nearby. So, about 400 assembled at a farm near Enna. At night they made an agreement among themselves and exchanged assurances and oaths over sacrifices. Then they armed themselves as much as circumstances allowed them. Nonetheless, all of them took up the most powerful weapon for the destruction of their arrogant masters: their anger. Eunous was their leader. And urging each other, they attacked the city in the middle of the night and went on to kill its citizens.

- How does Eunous convince slaves of divine approval for their revolt?

- How does Diodorus portray the role of religion in the slave decision to revolt? How reliable do you find his narrative?

- What can we learn about the organization of a slave revolt from this passage?

—————— 9.25.d Diodorus, *Library*, Book 34, Testimonium, ——————
5 Goukowsky (=34/35.2.15–6 Walton): Greek Historiography
(First Century BCE)

Eunous then was given authority among the rebels over everything. He called an assembly and killed all the citizens of Enna that had been captured, except for those whose craft was to make weapons; those he chained and submitted to hard labor. [...] Eunous placed a crown upon his head and arranged himself as king in all aspects; his wife, a Syrian of the same city as himself, he appointed queen; those he thought as superior in sagacity he made members of his council; among those, there was one called Achaios, an Achaean in origin, a man superior both in physical strength and in wisdom. In three days, he armed more than 6000 men in any way he could and brought together others, too, who used axes, mattocks, slings, sickles, sticks burned at one end, even cooking spits. With them, he would attack and raid the whole of the countryside. And as an infinite number of slaves continued to join him, he found the courage to fight even against the Roman governors. Many times he overpowered them in battle with the number of his men, having already more than 10,000 soldiers.

- What was the political organization adopted by the rebels? How can their choice be explained?
- What can we learn concerning the identities of enslaved persons from this passage?

——— 9.25.e Diodorus, *Library*, Book 34, fr. 13 Goukowsky ———
(=34/35.2.24 Walton): Greek Historiography
(First Century BCE)

Diodorus says that Eunous, the king of the rebels, called himself Antiochos and named the rebels Syrians.

- What factors explain the choice of names for the king and his subjects? Cf. 8.19.

——————— 9.25.f Bronze Coin of King Antiochos ———————
(135–2 BCE)

Demeter, depicted in Figure 15, was the chief deity of Sicily, whose enormous grain production was considered the gift of the goddess.

Literature: Manganaro 1982; Morton 2012: 12–46.
Obverse: veiled head of Demeter.
Reverse: ear of barley; legend "(coin of) King Antiochos."

Figure 15 Bronze coin of King Antiochos. Source: British Museum: 1868,0730.156; Asset number: 316587001; https://www.britishmuseum.org/collection/image/316587001.

- Why do you imagine the rebels needed to mint coins?

- What does this tell us about their aims?

- What does the iconography of the coin tell us about the aims of the revolt?

———   9.25.g   Diodorus, *Library*, Book 34, fr. 20 Goukowsky   ———
(=34/35.2.48 Walton): Greek Historiography
(First Century BCE)

Diodorus says that, although many and great evils fell upon the Sicilians, the mass of the common people not only did not have any sympathy but, on the contrary, rejoiced in envious resentment, because of their uneven fortune and anomalous life. While before they had felt sorrow, their resentment now turned to joy, as it observed that the brilliant fortune of the wealthy had fallen and taken the form which it used to despise. What was worst of all: although the rebels showed sensible foresight for the future and would not set fire to the farms nor would they ravage the property and crops stored there but kept away from those doing agricultural work, the common people, because of their envious resentment, raided the countryside using the runaways as a pretext, and not only did they loot the properties but also set fire to the farms.

- Were all free Sicilians negatively affected by the slave revolt?

- What did the poor Sicilians do during the slaves' revolt? Did they join forces with the rebels against the Sicilian wealthy? If not, why?

10

After Slavery
Manumission, Freedmen, and Freedwomen

This chapter explores the processes through which slaves gained their freedom and the constraints, opportunities, and challenges that freedpersons faced. There were various paths to manumission: slaves could take advantage of their personal relations with their masters through loyal service (10.5, 10.10) or as a consequence of sexual relations and unions (10.3–4). Slaves worked hard to create the savings needed to buy their freedom (10.9); they could also join together to collect resources and negotiate a collective manumission (10.6) or use their family links (10.2) or social networks to secure the necessary funds (10.7–8). Achieving freedom often brought slaves in front of terrible dilemmas (10.1).

Manumission posed serious problems for slaveholding societies; the interests of masters could clash with communal priorities and the hopes of freedpersons, generating major debates (10.12–3). Manumission did not necessarily bring independence; ancient societies had various forms of conditional freedom because freedpersons often continued to serve their masters or depend on them (10.14–7). The desire for freedom could sometimes bring unexpected problems (10.18). At the same time, though, manumission could bring to some freedpersons, particularly those belonging to powerful masters, opportunities that were unavailable for most free people (10.19–22).

Freedpersons had to negotiate their new status, which involved both continuities and discontinuities from their life in slavery. They could stress their links to their patrons (10.30) or emphasize their skills, moral virtues, and successes (10.24–5, 10.27–8); their solidarity (10.32); or their links to their homelands (10.26). Advertising their families was a potent means of declaring that they had escaped the existential threat of social death (10.29, 10.31).

Greek and Roman Slaveries, First Edition. Eftychia Bathrellou and Kostas Vlassopoulos.
© 2022 John Wiley & Sons, Inc. Published 2022 by John Wiley & Sons, Inc.

AVENUES TO FREEDOM

10.1 *FD* III 6.38, 3–13: Greek Manumission Inscription, Delphi, Phokis (First Century CE)

Literature: Zelnick-Abramovitz 2005: 229–30.

Eu[poria] sold to Apollo Pythios two bodies, whose names were Epiphanea and Epaphro, for the price of six minas of silver; I have received the full price. And I have appointed Dorotheos, son of Kritolaos, and Kleandros, son of Philon, as warrantors according to the laws of the city, on the following terms: Epiphanea and Epaphro are to remain (*paramenein*[166]) with Euporia during her whole lifetime giving no reason for reproach, doing everything they are ordered to do. But if they don't do so, Euporia shall have the authority to punish them in any manner she wishes. After my own death, Epaphro shall give to my grandson Glaukias, son of Lyson, three two-year-old infants. If she does not have the infants, she shall give him 200 denarii. And after five years, Epiphanea shall give to my son Sostratos a three-year-old child, and after three years, she shall also give to my grandson Glaukias a three-year-old child. And Epaphro and Epiphanea shall be free.

- What would Epaphro and Epiphanea need to do to gain their release from slavery? What would Euporia and her relatives gain from this?
- What dilemmas did these slaves face in trying to gain their freedom?
- Does the option available to Epaphro and Epiphanea mean that manumission was more accessible to women than to men? Or does it mean that female slaves were more exploitable?

10.2 *SGDI* 1708, 3–28: Greek Manumission Inscription, Delphi, Phokis (Second Century BCE)

Literature: Tucker 1982: 229–30.

[...] On the following conditions did Timo, wife of Eudikos, with the approval of her son Ladikos, sell a female body, a girl, whose name is Meda, for the price of two minai of silver, just as Meda entrusted the purchase money to the god, so that she be free and not liable to seizure by anyone for her entire lifetime, doing whatever she might wish. [...]
   Specifically: Meda shall provide food to Sosibios, her own father, and to her mother Soso and maintain them with dignity when she becomes of age, if Sosibios and Soso need food or dignified care, whether they might be slaves or have become free. If, however, Meda does not provide food or dignified care to Sosibios and Soso while they are in need, Sosibios and Soso shall have

---

[166] Cf. 10.14.

the power to punish Meda in any manner they wish; also, another person, whomever Sosibios and Soso might appoint, shall have the power to punish her on behalf of Sosibios and Soso. If anyone seizes Meda in order to enslave her, the seller Timo and the warrantor Dromokleidas shall secure the purchase money for the god. If they do not do so, the seller and the warrantor shall pay to Meda and to Sosibios and to Soso four minai of silver, according to the law. [...]

- Who is the manumitted slave?

- Who are her parents? What is their status?

- What is the age of the manumitted slave? Could the slave really have amassed the money to pay for her freedom?

- What are the obligations of the manumitted slave toward her parents?

- What can we learn about slave kinship and the process of manumission from this inscription? Cf. 10.1.

- What measures are taken so that Meda's current mistress might protect her from future enslavement? What might these measures suggest about the relationship between Meda's mistress and Meda and her parents?

10.3   *SEG XXVI 691, 7–13*: Inscribed List Recording Manumissions in Greek, Phthiotic Thebes, Thessaly (First–Third Century CE)

Literature: Zelnick-Abramovitz 2005: 167–9.

In the generalship of Andrianos, on the fourth day of the month of Poseidon: Zosimos, son of Zosimos, [freed] Zosimos and Leon, his children, and they [can call themselves] my children.

In the generalship of Nikostratos, the same Zosimos freed Didyme, his wife, together with his daughter born to her, the girl Antioche, and they shall not belong to anyone, nor be subject to the laws pertaining to manumitted slaves.

- What relationships between the master and his various slaves does the text reveal?

- Are there any links between the names of the master and his slaves?

- What will be the status of the slaves after manumission?

- What does this inscription reveal about the dialectical relationship between masters and slaves?

10.4 *FD* III 3.333, 1–6: Greek Manumission Inscription, Delphi, Phokis (First Century BCE)

Literature: Zelnick-Abramovitz 2005: 167–9, 260, 2019.

In the archonship of Diokles, son of Philistion, in the month of Eilaios, making the following thoughts and considerations, Kleomantis, son of Dinon, released Eisias, his female slave raised by him (*threpta*), from her obligation to remain with him. And I have received the money recorded in the announcement of her obligation to remain (*paramonê*). Also, (I released) Nikostratos, my son born to her during her period of remaining, whom I renamed Kleomantis upon adoption, so that they shall be free most truly and fully, belonging to no one in any way. And if the fate of mankind befalls Kleomantis, all that is left behind by him shall belong to Sosyla[167] to use. And if something happens[168] to Sosyla, everything shall belong to Eisias and Kleomantis, and nothing should belong to anyone else in any way. And Eisias shall perform all the rites related to burial, just as the rest of mankind.

- What is the relationship between Kleomantis, Eisias, and Nikostratos?
- Who will inherit Kleomantis' property? Why?
- Can we decide whether Eisias has used her sex as a strategy to gain freedom? What other scenarios can you imagine?

10.5 *SEG* XXVI 644: Inscribed List in Greek, Azoros, Thessaly (Late First Century BCE)

Inscription recording payments to the city by freed slaves.

On the 14th year of Augustus, when Apollodoros was general, on the 10th day of the intercalary month, Aristoteles, son of Demochares, and Adea, daughter of Philotas, his wife, and Demochares, son of Aristoteles, their son, citizens of Larissa, set free gratuitously Zosime, their female slave, who had been pleasing to them, and she shall not fall under the remit of the laws of freedmen, nor of anyone else in any way. She gave to the city the 22½ denarii that were due.

- What strategy did Zosime use to gain her freedom? How does it differ from the strategies presented in 10.1–4 and 10.6–10?

---

[167] A female name.
[168] A euphemistic reference to death; cf. 6.40, 7.29.

10.6 *Arch.Eph.* (1917), 10, No. 305.1–22 (p. 12): Inscribed List in Greek, Chyretiai, Thessaly (First Century CE)

All names mentioned are Greek, with the exception of the Latin names Cassius, Primus, and Maro. Female names are italicized.

Literature: Vlassopoulos 2019.

> When treasurer of the city was Arhybbas, son of Polyxenos, by blood son of Euethidas, in the year when Eubiotos was general, in the month of Agagylios. The freedmen and freedwomen of Lykos and *Platea*: Epaphras, Aischylos, Kerdon, Epigonos, Anteros, Eutychos, Ision, Karpos, Libanos, Sosipatros, Epaktos, Dionysios, Cassius, Eirenaios, Koi[.]s, Astikos Primus, Neon, Ploutarchos, Maro, *Rhome, Syntyche, Georgia, Elpis, Eupraxis, Tychike, Erotis, Artemisia, Artemo* – they each gave to the city the 22½ denarii that were due. [...]

- How many slaves did these masters manumit? What does that imply about their household?

- Under what conditions do you envisage the simultaneous manumission of so many slaves?

- Can we use this inscription to understand the negotiations involved in the process of manumission?

10.7 *SGDI* 1791, 1–4 and 8–11: Greek Manumission Inscription, Delphi, Phokis (Second Century BCE)

Literature: Zelnick-Abramowitz 2005: 220–1.

> In the archonship of Laias, in the month of Daidaphorios, on the following conditions did Amyntas, son of Sosias, of Delphi, sell to Apollo Pythios a male body whose name is Glaukias, whom he had bought as a child from Chairis and Eukarpidas, of Lebadea, for the price of 5 minai of silver. [...] Glaukias shall repay the *eranos*-loan[169] collected by Athambos and Euagoras by paying in two halves, at a four-month interval, 5 staters and 10 obols, to the name of Amyntas, until he has paid the whole amount of the *eranos*-loan. If he does not repay the money, the purchase shall be invalid. [...]

- How did Glaukias fund his manumission?

- Who might Athambos, Euagoras, and Amyntas have been?

---

[169] In *eranos*-loans, the money was collected through contributions by several people. Cf. 2.1, 9.2.

10.8 Ignatius, *Letters*, 7.4: Greek Epistolography (Late First/Early Second Century CE)

Ignatius, bishop of Antioch, instructs Polykarpos, bishop of Smyrna.

Literature: Harrill 1993; Glancy 2018; Shaner 2018: 87–109.

> Widows should not be neglected; after their guardian, you should be the one who looks after them. Nothing should be done without your say; nor should you do anything without God – which you do not. Show steadiness. Gatherings should be called more often; seek after everyone by name. Don't behave arrogantly toward slaves, whether male or female; nor should they puff themselves up; rather, they should show more zeal as slaves for the glory of God, so that God may grant them a better freedom. They shouldn't desire to get manumitted from the common funds, so that they might not be found slaves to desire.

- What advice does Ignatius give concerning the treatment of slaves?

- To whom does Ignatius intend his advice about how to treat slaves? What does that imply about the membership of Christian communities? Cf. the audience of 11.16.

- What advice does he give to Christian slaves? Cf. 11.18.

- How could Christian slaves try to achieve their manumission, according to Ignatius? What is Ignatius' advice in this respect?

10.9 *CIL* II²/7, 432: Latin Funerary Inscription, Cordoba, Spain (Early First Century CE)

Roman masters could set aside various resources and entrust their slaves to use them for various purposes (*peculium*); these resources could also include other slaves (cf. 12.14). Upon manumission, it was decided whether freedpersons would keep (part of) their *peculium* or not.

Literature: Roth 2005, 2010b; Incelli 2016.

> [...] Calpurnius Urbanus, freedman of [...] Calpurnius Salvianus, manumitted by will. He did not receive any other benefit (?) apart from the [...] price of the freedom [...] of his female slave (*famula*). They lie here.

- How was Urbanus liberated?

- What other benefit did Urbanus receive?

- Why do you think Urbanus *owned* his female slave, and why would he be interested in securing her freedom? Cf. 10.25.

- Why would he need his master's benevolence to free his own slave?

- What can we learn about slave strategies for forming and preserving families from this case?

10.10   Gaius, *Institutes*, 1.18–9:[170] Latin Juristic Treatise (Second Century CE)

Literature: Gardner 1989; Wacke 2001; Mouritsen 2011: 80–92; Huemoeller 2020.

> The *lex Aelia Sentia*[171] introduced a requirement concerning the age of slaves. Specifically, this law did not intend that slaves younger than 30 years of age become Roman citizens upon manumission unless they had been freed by *vindicta*[172] and the reason of their manumission had been proved as just before a council. A just reason for manumission is, for example, if someone manumits before a council a son, or daughter, or brother, or sister, or a child he has brought up, or the slave who looked after him as a child (*paedagogus*), or a slave in order to use him as his agent (*procurator*), or a slave woman for the sake of marriage.

- Why did the law introduce this particular age limit?

- What were the exceptions to the age limit? What kinds of relationships between masters and slaves do they presuppose?

- Did other ancient societies allow marriage between masters and slaves or former slaves? Cf. 3.19, 11.1.

10.11   *CIL* III, 1854: Latin Funerary Verse Inscription, Narona, Dalmatia (First Half of First Century CE)

Literature: Mihăilescu-Bîrliba 2006: no. 279.

> [...] Fortunata, freedwoman of Gaius, 18 years of age, lies here. If dutifulness makes it beneficial to anyone to have shown modesty and respect in life, I beseech you, Spirits of the Dead, may the earth rest lightly upon me. Freedom was once promised to me but was forestalled and subsumed to fate under the judgement of Dis.[173] You who have Fortune standing by your side, live happy! My hope was crushed by fate in Illyria.

---

[170] Latin text: de Zulueta 1946.

[171] Passed in 4 CE. Cf. 4.4.b, 10.13.

[172] Manumission by *vindicta* consisted of a public declaration by the master that he wished to free his slave. The declaration was done before a magistrate and was followed by the symbolic gesture of placing a rod on the head of the slave. During the imperial period, access to a magistrate for performing this ritual would have been difficult for many areas in the Empire. Cf. the last paragraph of 10.13.

[173] Ruler of the Underworld.

- Was Fortunata manumitted?

- What conditions were required for her manumission? Cf. 10.10.

MANUMISSION: PROBLEMS AND CHALLENGES

10.12 Dionysius of Halicarnassus, *Roman Antiquities*, 4.24: Greek Historiography (First Century BCE)

Dionysius here makes a digression from his narrative of events of the sixth century BCE to reflect on the enfranchisement of manumitted slaves, attributed to the Roman king Servius Tullius (conventionally dated 578–35 BCE). Cf. 6.23.

Literature: Mouritsen 2011: 10–35; Vermote 2016.

Now that I've reached this part of my narrative, I think it is necessary to give an account of the contemporary Roman practices regarding slaves, so that no one might accuse the king who first undertook to confer citizenship to those who had been slaves, or the men who accepted this law, of throwing away fine things indiscriminately. The Romans acquired their slaves by the most just means: that is, they either bought from the public treasury war captives sold at auction; or the general granted permission that war captives might be kept by their captors together with the other spoils; or they bought the slaves from others who had acquired them by these same means. So, neither Tullius, who established the practice, nor those who accepted and preserved it thought that they were doing anything shameful or harmful to the common good, if those who had been deprived of their freedom and homeland at war and had proven good to their enslavers, or to those who bought them off their enslavers, should be given both those things by their masters. And the majority were granted their freedom as a gift, because of their noble nature. This was the dominant way of release from one's masters; a few paid ransom money, raised from dutiful and just work.

In our times, however, things are different. Circumstances have reached such deep confusion, and the fine things of the Roman city have become so dishonored and defiled, that some make money from robbery, or housebreaking, or prostitution or any other wicked source, purchase their freedom with this money, and straightaway are Roman citizens. And those who have been confidants and accomplishes of their masters in poisonings and murders and in wrongs against the gods or the common good receive by their masters this favor in return. Others are given their freedom so that they might confer to their manumittors the wheat given to them by the public treasury on a monthly basis or any other humane benefit given by those in power to the citizens who are in want. Others are given their freedom because of their masters' hollowness and vain thirst for popularity. I myself know of some who have allowed that all their slaves become free after their death, so that they might be called "righteous" when dead and many might follow their bier bearing the liberty cap on their heads.[174] In these processions, as was possible to hear from those who knew, some of those who took part had just come out of prison – wrong-doers who had committed crimes deserving a thousand deaths.

- What are the just ways of acquiring slaves according to Dionysius?
- In what ways did Roman slaves of old acquire their freedom, according to the author?
- How do Roman slaves in recent times become free, according to the author?
- Why are masters who manumit slaves considered to be good and popular? Cf. 3.1.
- What conception of slavery underlies this description? Is slavery assimilated to a reciprocal benefaction?
- Is this a conception which solely serves to justify manumission? How does it fit with other conceptions of slavery? Cf. 1.27–30.

10.13 Tacitus, *Annals*, 13.26–7:[175] Latin Historiography (Early Second Century CE)

Tacitus here reports two debates that took place in the reign of Nero (54–68 CE): the first took place in the Senate, the second, which followed that in the Senate, in the emperor's council. After the reforms of Augustus, the two types of manumission mentioned in the passage created two different kinds of freedpersons. Formal manumission required the conditions set out in 3.1, 4.4.b, 10.10 and 10.12 and gave the ex-slave not only freedom but also Roman citizenship; informal manumission resulted in the ex-slave's gaining the status of a Junian Latin. This status subjected ex-slaves to a series of restrictions, legal disabilities, and obligations vis-à-vis their patrons. It was in the patron's power to "repeat" the manumission of a Junian Latin in a formal manner (*iteratio*), which resulted in the freedperson's becoming a Roman citizen.

Literature: Roth 2010b; Mouritsen 2011: 51–65.

During the same period, a debate took place in the Senate about the wrongdoings of freedmen. The demand was expressed that the patron be given the right to revoke the liberty of those freedmen who ill deserved it. There was no lack of those supporting the proposal. The consuls, however, did not dare to initiate the motion without the knowledge of the emperor,

---

[174] On freedmen's "liberty cap," see 11.16.
[175]Latin text: Heubner 1994.

yet they recorded in writing the consensus of the Senate. †The emperor
<hesitated> to make a decision on his own, as his council was composed
of few men, who, in addition, held different views. Some complained that
disrespect, consolidated by freedom, had erupted to such an extent that
freedmen would employ force or act on an equal footing with their patrons, would make resolutions and, even, raise their hands to beat them –
impudently, even offering proposals for their own punishment!†[176] For
what else was allowed to an aggrieved patron, other than to relegate the
freedman beyond the hundredth milestone, to the coast of Campania? All
other legal actions were indiscriminate and available to patrons and freedmen equally. Some weapon should be given to the patron, which could
not be spurned. It would not be too grave a thing that freedmen kept their
freedom by the same means they had acquired it: namely by respectful
allegiance (*obsequium*). But those who manifestly commit crimes should
deservedly be dragged back to slavery, so that those whom benefaction did
not reform might be coerced through fear.

It was argued against the above thesis that the errors of a few should prove
ruinous to themselves but not diminish the rights of all. For the body of
freedmen was widely extended. From them, for the most part, came the
tribes, the decuriae, the assistants of magistrates and priests, and also the
cohorts conscripted in the city. Moreover, the freedmen is where many of the
equestrians and many of the senators derive their origins from. If the freedmen were set apart, the scarcity of the truly freeborn (*ingenui*) would become
obvious. It was not without a purpose that our ancestors, when they divided
the orders of rank, made freedom the common property of all. Moreover,
two types of manumission were established, so that there be room for regret
or for a new benefaction. Those not manumitted by their patron through
manumission by the rod (*vindicta*) are constrained as if by the shackles of
slavery. Each should examine the merits of a case and concede slowly that
which, once given, should not be taken away. This last opinion prevailed,
and Caesar wrote to the Senate to weigh the cases of freedmen individually,
every time they were accused by their patrons, but there should be no collective diminution of rights.

- Given the actions of the consuls and the emperor, how serious was the topic of
  freedpersons? Why?

- What actions of freedpersons does the passage note?

- According to the prevailing view in the emperor's council, how could Roman
  masters avoid having ungrateful freedpersons?

- Did all Roman freedpersons acquire Roman citizenship?

- What can we learn about Roman views of slavery and manumission from this
  passage?

---

[176] We cannot be certain that this was the precise original content of the passage between the two
cruces (†).

CONDITIONAL FREEDOM

10.14   The *Paramonê*

Many Greek manumission inscriptions specify that slaves will have to remain (*paramenein*) with and work for their former masters for a certain period of time, often until their masters' deaths. Scholars debate whether people in *paramonê* should be considered slaves, free or in a semi-free status. See also 10.1, 10.4.

Literature: Zelnick-Abramovitz 2005: 222–48, 2019; Sosin 2015; Vlassopoulos 2019.

———   10.14.a   *IG* IX.1 194, 6–23: Greek Manumission Inscription,   ———
Tithorea, Phokis (Second Century CE)

[...] Onasiphoron, daughter of Herakleidas, a Tithorean[177] woman, sold to the god Sarapis two female bodies, whose names are Nikasion and Storge, for the price of 3000 denarii. She has received the full price for their freedom on the following terms: she shall not enslave Nikasion or Storge, nor take them away nor use them as security. If she does, she shall pay to the god Sarapis 4000 denarii. [...] Nikasion and Storge shall remain (*paramenein*) with Onasiphoron as slaves throughout the latter's entire lifetime, but in relation to other people, they shall be free.

- What will be the status of Nikasion and Storge in regard to their mistress during the period of *paramonê*?

- What will be their status in relation to other people during the same time?

- What does this imply about the significance of the master–slave and the free–slave dialectics?

———   10.14.b   *SGDI* 2156, 2–5 and 12–19: Greek Manumission   ———
Inscription, Delphi, Phokis (First Century CE)

[...] Philon, son of Straton, sold to Apollo Pythios for the purpose of freedom bodies (*sômata*) whose names are Stephanos, Eukleidas, Ktema, Moschion,[178] for the price of three minai of silver for each, and he has received

---

[177]From Tithorea, a city in central Greece.
[178]Ktema and Moschion are female names.

the full price. [...] Stephanos, Eukleidas, Ktema, and Moschion shall remain (*paramenein*) with Philon and Euameris, Philon's wife, throughout the entire lifetime of Philon and Euameris, serving them and doing all they can and are ordered to do by Philon and Euameris. If they do not remain or obey, Philon and Euameris shall have power to punish those who do not obey and to whip, put in fetters, and let out for hire the labor of the one who does not remain with them. [...]

- Under what conditions are the four slaves manumitted?
- How will any dispute between the masters and their former slaves be settled? Cf. 10.14.c.
- Are these four freedmen and freedwomen really free?

―――― 10.14.c. *SGDI* 1696, 1–5 and 8–13: Greek Manumission ――――
Inscription, Delphi, Phokis (Second Century BCE)

In the archonship of Eucharis, in the month Dai[daphori]os, on the following terms did Lirion, with the approval of her husband Theugenes, sell to Apollo Pythios a male body whose name is Manes, Paphlagonian in origin, for the price of three minai of silver. And she has received the full price, as Manes entrusted the purchase money to the god, on condition that he be free for his whole lifetime, doing whatever he might wish. [...] Manes shall remain (*paramenein*) by Lirion for three years, doing all that he is ordered to do as far as is possible without giving reason for reproach. If, however, Manes does not remain by Lirion without giving reason for reproach, as has been recorded, Manes and Lirion shall be brought in front of three men and judged on the issue she accuses him of. And whatever they might decide shall be binding. The three-year period starts in the year after Eucharis' archonship. If human fate befalls Manes and he leaves some possession behind, this shall belong to Lirion, and Manes shall have no power to give his possessions to anyone.

- Under what conditions is Manes freed?
- How will any disputes between Manes and his master be settled? Cf. 10.14.b.
- Who will inherit Manes' property?

10.15 *Digest*, 47.10.7.2: Collection of Latin Juristic Texts (Sixth Century CE)

On the Digest, see 1.2.

Literature: Gardner 1993: 45–8.

> Ulpian, *On the Edict*, Book 57: Besides, it is relevant that the insult (*iniuria*) someone suffered be specified, so that we might know from the nature of the insult whether the action for insult (*iudicium iniuriarum*) should be granted to a freedman against his patron. For we should remember that an action for insult against one's patron is not granted to a freedman in all cases, but occasionally, if the insult he suffered is aggravated (*atrox*), for example, if he is treated like a slave. Otherwise, we shall grant to the patron the right to coerce his freedman lightly, and the praetor will not tolerate the freedman's complaint of an insult he suffered unless the praetor is moved by the aggravation present in the act. For the praetor should not tolerate the slave of a master, now free, complaining that the master reproached him or beat him lightly or corrected him. But if the master did this with whips or rods or if he inflicted a quite serious wound, then it will be most fair that the praetor should support the freedman.

- Which acts are Roman patrons allowed to inflict on their freedpersons? Why?
- Which acts are prohibited to Roman patrons? Why?
- What does this passage tell us about the similarities and differences between Roman slaves and freedpersons? Cf. 3.12.

10.16   *CIL* VI, 6301: Latin Funerary Inscription, Rome (First Half of First Century CE)

For the funerary monument including this inscription, see 1.17 and 4.9.

Literature: Hasegawa 2005: 33–4.

> Titus Statilius Spinther, freedman of Taurus, in charge of the litter-bearers. Titus Statilius Crescens made (the monument).

- What was the legal and work status of Spinther?
- For whom did Spinther probably work after his manumission? What might have been the implications of this for Spinther's autonomy after manumission?

10.17   *I.Leukopetra 52*, 1–18: Greek Consecration Inscription, Leukopetra, Macedonia (Third Century CE)

Literature: Harper 2011: 369–78; Caneva and Delli Pizzi 2015; Zanovello 2018.

I, Aureliane Kosmia, holding the "right of three children,"[179] offer to the Autochthonous Mother of the Gods a slave named Menoitas, born to me from my female slave Euphrosyne, whom I have assigned to the goddess since he was an infant. For this reason, I did not sell him, nor did I offer him as a gift, nor did I pledge him as security. And no one else shall have power over the aforementioned slave apart from the goddess alone. And he shall serve the goddess on the customary days.

- Is Menoitas manumitted?
- What will be his obligations after the consecration? How onerous do they seem to be?
- Were consecrated slaves closer to freedpersons, people in *paramonê* or slaves of human masters?

10.18   Epictetus, *Discourses*, 4.1 (*On Freedom*), Chapters 33–7: Philosophical Lectures in Greek (Late First/Early Second Century CE)

Epictetus was an important Stoic philosopher and former slave.

Literature: Herschbell 1995.

The slave wishes to be let free immediately. Why? Because he desires to give money to the collectors of the 5% tax,[180] do you think? No. But because he imagines that the obstacles and difficulties he has had so far are due to his lack of freedom. "If I'm let free," he says, "at once everything will be smooth-running, I won't need to heed anyone, I will speak to everyone as an equal, as one of them, I will walk wherever I feel like, I will come and go as I please." Next, he's made free and, at once, not having anywhere to eat, he seeks whom he might flatter, at whose house he might have dinner. Next, two possibilities: either he earns his living by his body and experiences the most frightful sufferings; if he gets some shelter, he's actually fallen into a slavery much harsher than his earlier one; or he gets prosperous but, inexperienced as he is in fine things, finds himself in love with some young thing and, not getting what he wants, bursts into tears and desires his slavery. "What harm did it do me? Another clothed me; another gave me shoes; another fed me, another looked after me when I was ill. A bit of service was all I offered him. But now, wretched me! How do I suffer! – a slave to many, instead of one."

- What advantages of freedom does this imaginary slave assume?
- In what ways are his assumptions disappointed, according to Epictetus?

---

[179] See 1.18.
[180] The Roman manumission tax.

- How reliable is this passage for understanding the experience of freedpersons?

- Does this text tell us more about Epictetus' experiences as a freedman or his Stoic philosophy? Or both?

OPPORTUNITIES

See also 3.25, 12.15, 12.29–31.

10.19   Cicero, *Against Verres II*, 1.123–4: Latin Law-Court Speech (First Century BCE)

Cicero here tries to demonstrate Verres' arrogance when he was urban praetor in Rome.

Literature: López Barja de Quiroga 2010; Mouritsen 2011: 248–78.

Publius Trebonius appointed as his heirs many good and honorable men; one of those was a freedman of his. Publius had a brother, Aulus Trebonius, who had been declared an outlaw. He wanted to make provision for him and wrote in his will that his heirs should take an oath to make sure that no less than half of the share of each would come to Aulus Trebonius, that outlawed man. The freedman takes the oath. The other heirs go to Verres and point out that they should not take that oath, as they would be acting against the *lex Cornelia*,[181] which forbade to assist an outlawed man. They gain permission not to take the oath; he gives them possession of their whole share. I do not find fault with this. It was certainly unfair that an outlawed man, when in need, be given something of his brother's possessions. The freedman believed that, unless he took the oath according to the will of his patron, he would be committing a villainy. Verres refused that the freedman be given possession of his inheritance, so that he might not be able to assist his outlawed patron and so that he be punished for having acted according to the will of his other patron.

You give possession to the one who did not take the oath: I agree. It is within the rights of the praetor. You deprive of it the one who took the oath: with what precedent? He is helping an outlawed man: there is a law, there is a penalty. How does this apply to the person determining what is right? Do you find him at fault because he helped the patron who was then in dire straits or because he respected the will of his other patron, the dead one, from whom he had received the greatest benefaction? Which of the two do you find reprehensible? And this was that great man's response, uttered from his magistrate's seat: "A freedman be heir to such a wealthy Roman of the equestrian rank! God forbid!" Oh, how humble this rank is, since he got up from that seat alive!

---

[181] A law passed by Sulla regarding the treatment of the "proscribed," Roman citizens declared outlaws (82–1 BCE).

- What can we learn about the relationship between Publius Trebonius and his freedman from this text?

- What opportunities did rich and powerful former masters open for their freed-persons? Cf. 5.30.

10.20   *CIL* XI, 5400: Latin Inscription, Assisi, Italy (First–Third Century CE)

Literature: Kleijwegt 2006c; Laird 2015: 215–22.

Publius Decimius Eros Merula, freedman of Publius, clinical doctor, surgeon, eye specialist, priest of Augustus (*sevir*).[182]
He gave 50,000 sesterces for his freedom;
he gave 2000 sesterces to the community (*res publica*) for becoming a *sevir*;
he gave 30,000 sesterces to the temple of Hercules for statues to be set up;
he gave 37,000 sesterces to the public treasury for the paving of streets;
the day before he died he left an estate of 14,000 (?[183]) sesterces.

- What kind of inscription is this, and who might have set it up?

- How is the deceased presented in this inscription?

- What aspects and events of his life are recorded?

- What do these choices suggest for the ways a freedman could earn a good standing in his community?

10.21   Pliny the Younger, *Panegyric of Trajan*, 88.1–3: Latin Panegyric (100 CE)

Literature: Mouritsen 2011: 66–119.

Most emperors, while being the citizens' masters, were also their freedmen's slaves. They were governed by their freedmen's council, their freedmen's com-mands. Their freedmen were their ears, their freedmen were their mouths; it was via them, or, rather, of them, that praetorships, consulships and priest-hoods were petitioned. You, on the other hand, hold your freedmen in great esteem, but as befits freedmen, and you believe that it abundantly suffices if they are appreciated for their ability and sound character. For you know very

---

[182] In the early imperial period, many Roman cities had positions like the *seviri* and other titles including the name of Augustus (*Augustales*); the holders of these titles and positions, who were usually, but not exclusively, freedmen, received honors for their various public benefactions and expenses.

[183] This number cannot be discerned clearly on the stone. For this reading, see *Supplementa Italica* 23, 2007, 283–4.

well that great freedmen are the principal indication of an emperor who is not great. In the first place, you do not employ any freedman unless he was selected and appraised by you or your father or one of the better emperors. Moreover, you daily train them in such a way that they measure themselves not against your position but their own and that they be all the more worthy of our honor because we are not obliged to bestow it to them.

- In what ways did many emperors use their freedmen? How does Pliny view these uses?
- How does Trajan use his freedmen?
- How does the relationship between the emperor and his freedmen reflect the emperor's character, according to Pliny?

10.22   Seneca, *Letters*, 47.9: Latin Moral Philosophy in Epistolary Form (First Century ce)

Gaius Julius Callistus, a freedman of the emperor Caligula, became extremely powerful under the emperors Caligula and Claudius. Seneca speaks about an earlier master of Callistus, who had sold him at the marketplace, presumably before he entered the imperial household. For this text, cf. 4.8, 5.12, and 11.16.

Literature: Weaver 1972; Duncan-Jones 2016: 142–53.

But how many masters does a master have among his slaves! I have seen the master of Callistus standing before Callistus' door and, while others were admitted, he who had fastened on him his sale ticket and exhibited him for sale among worthless slaves, was refused entry. The slave assigned to the first … division at the market, with whom the crier tries his voice, repaid the favor done to him by the master! It was now Callistus' turn to reject him and judge him unworthy of his house! The master sold Callistus; but what price did Callistus have the master pay!

- How did Callistus treat his former master?
- To what did Callistus owe his power over his former master?

DEFINING A NEW STATUS?

10.23   *Rhetorical Expressions* (Λέξεις ῥητορικαί), Lexica Bekkeriana V, p. 242, 3–6: Greek Lexicon (Tenth Century ce)

Participation in festival processions was an important means of emphasizing the communitarian aspect of ancient cities and showcasing their hierarchies.

Literature: Wijma 2014: 37–64.

> "Bearing oak through the marketplace": the bearing of an oak branch through the marketplace in the festival of the Panathenaea by each of the participating manumitted slaves and other barbarians.

- How did freedmen participate in the Panathenaea?
- What does this imply about their new status within the city?

10.24 *An.Ep.* (1980) No. 503: Latin Funerary Inscription, Brescia, Italy (Late Second/Early Third Century ᴄᴇ)

Literature: Kleijwegt 2006c.

> Marcus Hostilius Dicaeus.[184]
>   I came to this city when I was 14 years of age. The home into which I came – neither home nor master did I change, except for this, the eternal one. I lived for 70 years. No one summoned me to court or before a judge. You who are standing and reading this, tell us: if this is not the best, what is better? Clodia Paullina Optuma gave this site.

- What is the status of Marcus Hostilius Dicaeus upon his death? How can we tell?
- What is he proud about?
- How do his moral virtues relate to slavery?
- Is Dicaeus ashamed of his life in slavery?
- What can we learn from this source about conceptions of slavery by Roman slaves and freedpersons? Cf. 10.25.

10.25 Petronius, *Satyrica*, 57: Latin Novel (First Century ᴄᴇ)

In this excerpt from the novel (cf. 4.33), a fellow freedman of Trimalchio criticizes another guest at Trimalchio's banquet for deriding Trimalchio's lack of sophistication.

Literature: Boyce 1991; Kleijwegt 2006c; Andreau 2009.

> He is laughing. What has he got to laugh about? Did his father buy him with good money when he was born? You are a Roman knight; well, I am the son

---

[184] *Dicaeus* is a Greek cognomen meaning "just".

of a king. "Why then did you use to be a slave?" Because I myself gave my-self up to slavery and preferred to be a Roman citizen, rather than a tribute-paying man from the provinces (*tributarius*). And now I hope I live in a way that no one can make fun of me. I am a man among men. I walk about with my head uncovered. I owe not a single copper coin to anybody. I've never had to arrange for delayed payments. No one has ever told me at the forum "pay back what you owe me." I have bought some pieces of land; I've put a little something in my strongbox. I keep 20 ewes and a dog. I redeemed the woman with whom I share my bed (*contubernalis*), so that no one can wipe his hands on her bosom. I paid 1000 denarii for freedom. I was made a priest of Augustus for free.[185] I hope to die in such a manner, that I have nothing to blush about in the grave.

Are you so hard at work, that you can't look behind you? You see the lice on others but not the bugs on yourself. You are the only one to whom we freedmen seem laughable. Here is your teacher, a man older than you; he likes us. You are a milksop, you can't even prattle, a clay pot, a wet "whip," more sluggish, not better. You are more prosperous: so, have two lunches and two dinners! I prefer my trustworthiness to treasure chests. To top it all, who had to ask me twice to pay up? I was a slave for 40 years, yet nobody knows whether I am slave or free. I was a long-haired boy when I arrived at this place. At that point the town hall had not yet been built. I tried hard to keep my master satisfied – a great, distinguished man, whose fingernail was worth more than your whole body. And there would be in the house people who would try to trip me up, here and there, yet I slipped away, thanks to the genius of my master. These are real victories. For to be born free is as easy as saying, "Come here!"

- How did the speaker become a slave? How credible do you find this?

- What makes the speaker proud? What sort of achievements or features does he mention?

- Is he proud of his former master? Is he proud of his life as a slave? Why?

- Do you find his pride surprising?

- What does the speaker resent in the attitude of his adversary?

- Is there anything peculiarly Roman in the arguments and identities of this freedman?

- How does this text compare with inscriptions by Roman freedpersons? Cf. 10.24 and 10.31.

- What kind of text is this? Can we use it to reconstruct the ideology of Roman freedpersons?

---

[185] Cf. 10.20.

10.26 Freedpersons and Their Homelands

Literature: Reynolds 1982: 156–64; Weaver 2004; Osgood 2006: 274–6.

— 　10.26.a　*I.Aph.* 1.2: Greek Dedicatory Inscription, Aphrodisias,　—
　　　　　Karia (Late First Century BCE/Early First Century CE)

> Gaius Julius Zoilos, priest of the goddess Aphrodite.
>   Being savior and benefactor of his homeland, he (offered) the temple to
> Aphrodite.

— 　10.26.b　*I.Aph.* 8.1.i: Greek Dedicatory Inscription, Aphrodisias,　—
　　　　　Karia (Late First Century BCE/Early First Century CE)

> Gaius Julius Zoilos, freedman of the divine Julius' son Caesar,[186] having held
> the office of *stephanêphoros*[187] for 10 times in a row, (offered) the *logêion* and
> the *proskênion*,[188] together with all their decorations, [to Aphrodite and to]
> the people.

- Where was Zoilos from? What was his status?
- What was his relationship to Aphrodisias?
- What roles did he hold in Aphrodisias?
- What kind of inscriptions are these? What do they record? What does this reveal about Zoilos' wealth and prestige?
- What can we learn about the opportunities available to imperial freedmen from these documents?

— 　10.26.c　Reliefs from Zoilos' Funerary Monument, Aphrodisias,　—
　　　　　Karia (Late First Century BCE/Early First Century CE)

The figures in the reliefs (Fig. 16) bear identifying inscriptions in Greek. In the first three-figure scene on the right, Zoilos, in the middle, wearing traveler's clothes, is crowned by the *Dêmos* (people) and the Polis (city). In the three-figure scene on

---

[186]Augustus.
[187]Title of the chief magistrate of Aphrodisias.
[188]Parts of the stage building of a theater.

Figure 16 Reliefs from the funerary monument of Zoilos, late first century BCE/early first century CE, Aphrodisias: image by the authors.

the left Zoilos, in the middle, wearing the Roman toga, is offered a shield by Bravery, while crowned by Honor.

- Why is Zoilos represented with travelers' clothes in the first scene? What does this imply about his relationship with Aphrodisias?
- Why is Zoilos represented with the Roman toga, the quintessential representation of the Roman citizen, in the second scene?
- What do these scenes imply about Zoilos' life and identities before, during, and after slavery?

10.27 *CIL* VI, 11595: Funerary Relief with Latin Inscription, Rome (30 BCE–30 CE)

To the left and right of the central panel of this funerary relief (Fig. 17) are depicted grain measures (*modii*).

Literature: George 2006; Lovén 2012.

> *Under the central relief*: Lucius Ampudius Philomusus, freedman of Lucius and a woman.
> *Left, inside the representation of a grain measure*: Lucius Ampudius Philomusus, freedman of Lucius and a woman, corn merchant (?).

- Who is mentioned in the inscription? How is he described?
- Which people are depicted in the relief? Who are they? How might they be related to Philomusus?

Figure 17   Funerary relief of Ampudius Philomusus, 30 BCE–30 CE, Rome: British Museum, inv. no. 1920,0220.1.

- What can we learn about their profession from the text and the iconography?

10.28   *CIL* XIV, 2721–2: Funerary Relief with Latin Inscription, Tusculum, Lazio (Late First Century BCE/Early First Century CE) (Fig. 18)

Literature: George 2006; Daoust 2019.

Under the figure on the left: Publius Licinius Philonicus, freedman of Publius. *Under the figure on the right*: Publius Licinius Demetrius, freedman of Publius, for his patron.

- Which people are depicted in this relief (see Fig. 18)? How are they described? What is the relationship between them?

- What is depicted on the pediment and right relief? How do these items relate to the lives of the deceased?

- What is depicted on the left relief? How do these items relate to the lives of the deceased?

Figure 18 Funerary relief of Philonicus and Demetrius, late first century BCE/early first century CE, Tusculum: British Museum, inv. no. 1954,1214.1.

10.29   *CIL* V, 723: Latin Funerary Inscription, Turin, Italy (31–70 CE)

Literature: Holleran 2013.

> Cornelia Venusta, freedwoman of Lucius, nail maker, made this when alive for herself and for Publius Aebutius, son of Marcus, of the Stellatina tribe, nail maker, priest of Augustus (*Augustalis*),[189] her husband, and for Crescens, freedwoman, and for Muro, her favorite slave girl.

- Which people will be buried in this grave? What are their statuses and their relationships?
- What can we learn about the communities of freedpeople from this text?

10.30   Families and Freedpeople

Literature: Zanker 1975: 296–8.

---

[189] See n. 182.

10.30.a *CIL* VI, 2170: Funerary Relief with Latin Inscription, Rome (50 BCE–30 CE) (Fig. 19)

Figure 19 Funerary relief of Antistius Sarculo and Antistia Plutia, late first century BCE/early first century CE, Rome: British Museum, inv. no. 1858,0819.2.

Text running across the left two-thirds of the space: Lucius Antistius Sarculo, son of Gnaeus, of the Horatia tribe, Salian priest of the Alban association, as well as Master of the Salian priests.[190]

Text running under the portrait on the right: Antistia Plutia, freedwoman of Lucius.

Text inscribed at the bottom, running across the whole monument: Rufus, freedman, and Anthus, freedman, had these portraits made for their patron and patroness, because they deserved it.

10.30.b *CIL* VI, 2171: Latin Funerary Inscription, Rome (Second Half of First Century BCE)

Lucius Antestius Sarculo, son of Gnaeus, of the Horatia tribe, Salian priest of the Alban association.

Antestia Plutia, freedwoman of Lucius

---

[190]The Salii were associations of priests of the god Mars. The Alban association was based in the Alban hills, just outside Rome.

Fufia, daughter of Publius, Tertia, her sister
Lucius Antestius Quinctio, freedman of Lucius
Lucius Antistius Rufus, freedman of Lucius
Lucius Antistius Thamyrus, freedman of Lucius and of a woman
Lucius Antistius Anthus, freedman of Lucius and of a woman
Lucius Antistius Eros the Cappadocian, freedman of Lucius

- Who is Antistius Sarculo? How is he described?
- Who is Antistia Plutia? How is she described in texts a and b?
- What is the relationship between Sarculo and Plutia?
- Which persons have erected monument a? What is their relationship to Sarculo and Plutia? Why have they erected this monument?
- Who is buried in the funerary monument mentioned in inscription b?
- What can this source tell us about the relationship between masters and slaves and freedpersons and patrons?

10.31   *CIL* VI, 9499: Funerary Relief with Latin Metrical Inscription, Rome (75–50 BCE)

The two people depicted in Figure 20 have Greek cognomina. Hermia is a Greek name derived from the god Hermes, while the name Philemation or Philematium derives from a Greek noun meaning "little kiss."

Figure 20   Funerary relief of Aurelius Hermia and Aurelia Philematium, 75–50 BCE, Rome: British Museum, inv. no. 1867,0508.55.

Literature: Koortbojian 2006; Massaro 2007.

> *Left column*: Lucius Aurelius Hermia, freedman of Lucius. Butcher, from the Viminal hill.
>   She whom fate made go before me, chaste of body, my only wife, who lovingly presided over my soul, lived faithful to a faithful husband, with equal devotion. Not because of any self-interest did she walk away from her duty.
>
> Aurelia, freedwoman of Lucius
>
> *Right column*: Aurelia Philemation, freedwoman of Lucius
>   When alive, I was named Aurelia Philematium. I was chaste, modest, not in contact with the crowd, faithful to my husband. My husband was a fellow freedman, whom, alas, I have lost. In fact, in reality he was much more: he was a parent to me. When I was seven years old, he took me in his lap; at 40, I came into the power of death. Thanks to my incessant dutiful care, he flourished in the eyes of all [...].

- What is the legal status of the two deceased persons? How are they related?
- How does Hermia describe his relationship to his wife?
- How does Philemation describe her relationship to her husband?
- How are Hermia and Philemation depicted in the relief?
- What values do the inscription and the reliefs reflect? Are these values peculiar to freedpeople or not?

10.32   *CIL* VI, 18524: Funerary Relief with Latin Inscription, Rome (Late First Century BCE/Early First Century CE)

The iconographic motif of two figures clasping their right hands depicted in Figure 21 is normally used in representations of married couples.

Literature: Stupperich 1983; Brooten 1996: 59–60.

> Fonteia Eleusis, freedwoman of a woman †.........† Fonteia Helena, freedwoman of a woman.[191]

- Who are the people depicted in this relief?
- How are they depicted? Can we draw any conclusions from this?
- What relationship between them can we establish?
- What are the implications of two freedwomen buried together? What does this tell us about the communities of freedwomen?

---

[191] The exact interpretation of the text between the names of the two women is disputed.

Figure 21 Funerary relief of Fonteia Eleusis and Fonteia Helena, late first century BCE/early first century CE, Rome: British Museum, inv. no. 1973,0109.1.

11

Slavery and Historical Change

Did ancient slavery change over time; if so, in what ways? Which agents, factors, and processes effected change? The traditional narrative distinguishes between societies with slaves and slave societies. Societies with slaves had few slaves, who, moreover, did not play a dominant economic role; slave societies had large numbers of slaves, who were the major source of elite income. In this narrative, early Greek and Roman societies were societies with slaves. Athens was transformed into a slave society with the reforms of Solon; this meant that Athenian citizens were no longer available for exploitation by the elite, who had to import slaves on a massive scale as a response. In Rome during the second century BCE, the profits of imperial expansion allowed the elite to substitute the peasantry with masses of agricultural slaves. Finally, during late antiquity, the depression of the status of free peasants and the establishment of slaves as farm tenants transformed ancient societies again into societies with slaves.[192]

This chapter includes sources that can help us to debate the validity of the distinction between societies with slaves and slave societies and its associated narrative.[193] Is slavery in the Homeric world and early Rome different from that of later periods? If so, in what ways (11.1–5)? Does the evidence from archaic Greece (11.6–8) and republican Rome (11.9–10) support the traditional narrative of a transition from societies with slaves into slave societies, or do we need to seek alternative narratives? At the same time, the chapter breaks new ground by exploring alternative factors and processes of historical change. Slave agency played a crucial role in the course of ancient history, in large-scale warfare (11.11), processes of ethnogenesis (11.12–3), and intercultural conflicts (11.14–5). We also explore the role of ideology in historical change, including philosophical currents

---

[192] Hopkins 1978; Finley 1980; Bradley and Cartledge 2011.
[193] Lenski and Cameron 2018; Lewis 2018; Vlassopoulos 2021a.

Greek and Roman Slaveries, First Edition. Eftychia Bathrellou and Kostas Vlassopoulos.
© 2022 John Wiley & Sons, Inc. Published 2022 by John Wiley & Sons, Inc.

such as Stoicism (11.16) and monotheistic religions such as Judaism (11.17) and Christianity (11.18–21). The state was an equally important factor of historical change, and we use as an example the impact of changing Roman state policies on mixed marriages (11.22). Finally, we explore the validity of the traditional narrative that posits a transition from ancient slave societies into medieval societies with slaves, using examples from Byzantium (11.23, 11.25), Spain (11.24), and Italy (11.26).

EARLY SLAVERY?

Literature: Rihll 1996; Ndoye 2010; Harris 2012; van Wees 2013; Lewis 2018: 107–24.

11.1 Homer, *Odyssey*, 14.199–213: Greek Epic Poetry (Probably Eighth Century BCE)

On Ithaca, Odysseus, still in disguise and not yet wishing to reveal his true identity, tells his slave Eumaios a false story about his origins.

> From broad Crete I claim my origin to be; I am the son of a wealthy man. Many other sons were raised in his halls, legitimate ones, born to his married wife. But I was born to a bought mother, a concubine. And yet, Kastor son of Hylax honored me equally with his legitimate sons. Of that man I claim my origin to be, who was honored like a god by the people in those times among the Cretans, for his prosperity, his wealth, and his renowned sons. But the fates of death took him away to the house of Hades. His high-minded sons divided his property and cast lots for it. To me, however, they gave extremely little and allotted a dwelling. But I brought home a wife who came from men with many possessions because of my valor; for I was no weakling, nor one who fled from battle.

- How does the speaker present himself in this passage?
- Was the son of a slave woman recognized as a free person in Homeric Crete?
- How did his status differ from that of legitimate free children?
- What can we learn about the master–slave relationship from this passage?
- Did the status of children by slaves change in the classical period? Cf. 12.22.
- If so, how can we explain this change?

11.2 Homer, *Odyssey*, 14.449–52: Greek Epic Poetry (Probably Eighth Century BCE)

The scene takes place in the hut of the swineherd Eumaios, one of Odysseus' most loyal slaves.

> And bread was served to them by Mesaulios, whom the swineherd himself alone had acquired after his master had gone away, independently from his mistress and the old Laertes.[194] He had bought him from some Taphians with his own goods.

- Who are Mesaulios and Eumaios? How do they relate to each other?
- Is it surprising that a slave could own another slave?
- What does this fact imply about slaves and slavery in Homeric society?
- Was such a thing possible in later times? Cf. 12.14–5.

11.3   Homer, *Odyssey*, 11.488–91: Greek Epic Poetry (Probably Eighth Century BCE)

The dead Achilles speaks to Odysseus in the underworld.

> Don't try to speak soothingly to me about death, renowned Odysseus. I'd rather be on earth and work for someone else as hired laborer – for a landless man, who does not have much to live on – than to be king of all the perished dead.

- Which status does Achilles describe as preferable to being king among the dead?
- Does this mean that being a slave in Homeric society was not the lowest status imaginable?
- Are there other reasons for which Achilles imagines being a hired laborer and not a slave as the worst fate that could happen to him while alive?
- Can we use this passage to depict a process in which the status of slaves deteriorated from Homeric into classical times?

11.4   Slavery, Freedom, and Manumission

——— 11.4.a   Homer, *Odyssey*, 21.209–16: Greek Epic Poetry ——— (Probably Eighth Century BCE)

Odysseus reveals his true identity to his slaves Eumaios and Philoitios.

> I know that you alone of my slaves have been hoping for my arrival. Of the others, I didn't hear anyone praying that I might return and come back

---

[194] Odysseus' father.

home. To you two, then, I will tell the truth, just as it is going to happen. If god might subdue the noble suitors for my sake, I will bring to you wives and bestow on you possessions and houses, built near my own. And in future you will be companions and brothers of Telemachos[195] in my eyes.

- What does Odysseus promise as a reward?
- Would a slave in the classical period get the same rewards as the Homeric slaves?
- Is there anything unexpectedly missing from Odysseus' promise?
- How should we interpret this omission?

—— 11.4.b Plutarch, *Greek Questions*, 294c–d: Greek Antiquarian ——
Treatise (Late First/Second Century CE)

Question: Who are the Koliadai of Ithaca, and what is the "phagilos"?

Answer: After Odysseus killed the suitors, the relatives of the dead revolted. Both parties called upon Neoptolemos to arbitrate. He deemed right that Odysseus migrated and left Kephallenia, Zakynthos, and Ithaca on account of the blood he had shed and that the companions and family of the suitors bring every year a recompense to Odysseus for the wrongs committed in his house. So, Odysseus moved to Italy. [...] Telemachos freed those around Eumaios and mixed them with the citizens. So, the clan (*genos*) of the Koliadai descends from Eumaios and that of the Boukolidai descends from Philoitios.

- How does Plutarch describe the rewards of Eumaios and Philoitios?
- Are you surprised that two *genê* of Ithaca describe themselves as descendants of slaves? If not, why?
- In what ways does Plutarch's description of rewards differ from that offered by Odysseus in Homer?
- How should we explain this difference?
- Is it likely that the mythical version presented by Plutarch originated in the same period as the Homeric one, or does Plutarch's version reflect Roman influence? Cf. 6.23, 10.12.
- Can we learn anything about the history of slavery from this passage?

---

[195] Odysseus' son.

11.5   Dionysius of Halicarnassus, *Roman Archaeology*, 2.27: Greek Historiography (First Century ʙᴄᴇ)

The right of the Roman *paterfamilias* to sell his son is already attested in the laws of the Twelve Tables from the fifth century ʙᴄᴇ. By the imperial period, the procedure of selling the son three times had come to be used to emancipate a son from the *patria potestas*.

Literature: López Barja de Quiroga 2006; Kleijwegt 2013.

> The Roman lawgiver did not stop even at this point but gave the father the power to sell his son, without paying attention to whether this permission might be perceived as rough and harsher than natural affection would entail. And he also legislated something that those raised in the loose manners of the Greeks would consider as cruel and tyrannical – he allowed the father to make money by selling his son up to three times, giving the father a greater power over his son than masters have over their slaves. For among the slaves, if one is sold and later gains his freedom, he is his own master for ever after, but a son who was sold by his father, if he gained his freedom, would come again under his power, and if he was for the second time sold and freed, he would still be the slave of his father, as before; only after the third sale was he released from the father.

- What power did Roman fathers have over their sons?
- In what circumstances would a father use this power? Cf. 9.5–7.
- How was this power used in later periods of Roman history? What does this tell us about the history of slavery?

FROM SOCIETIES WITH SLAVES TO SLAVE SOCIETIES?

11.6   Athenaeus, *The Learned Banqueters*, 6.265b–c: Greek Antiquarian Treatise (End of Second Century ᴄᴇ)

One of the participants in the fictional banquet conversations narrated in Athenaeus' work talks about slaves. For slaves on Chios, cf. 1.5 and 9.24.

Literature: Vidal-Naquet 1986; Paradiso 1991; Descat 2006; Occhipinti 2015.

> The first Greeks I know to have used purchased slaves were the Chians, as is recorded by Theopompus in book 17 of his *Histories*.[196] "The Chians were the first Greeks, after the Thessalians and the Lacedaemonians, to use slaves.

---

[196] Theopompus of Chios was a fourth-century ʙᴄᴇ historian.

However, they acquired them in a different way. [...] Specifically, the Lacedaemonians and the Thessalians will be shown to have constructed their slave class from the Greeks who had earlier inhabited the land that they have now got, that is, from the Achaeans and from the Perrhaebians and Magnesians respectively. The Lacedaemonians called the enslaved population helots, while the Thessalians called them *penestai*. But the slaves of the Chians are not Greeks and are acquired through payment of a price." In my opinion, this is why the divine became indignant at the Chians, and years later they were dragged to war because of their slaves. [...] I also think that none of you is ignorant of what the fine Herodotus wrote about Panionios of Chios[197] and the just deserts he suffered for having castrated free boys and sold them off. Also, both Nicolaus the Peripatetic philosopher and Posidonius the Stoic say in their respective *Histories* that the Chians were enslaved by Mithridates of Cappadocia and were submitted in chains to their own slaves, so that they might be taken away to Kolchis to settle there. So genuine was the wrath of the divine against them for being the first ones to use purchased slaves, when most people attended to their needs themselves.

- What original feat is credited to the Chians?

- How would Theopompus know? Where was he from?

- How credible is this attribution? Compare this with passage 1.5.

- How did the gods react to this innovation, according to the passage?

- What evidence does Athenaeus cite to document divine reaction?

- What is the justification for this divine disapprobation?

- Does this passage contend that slavery has a history (cf. 11.7 and 11.9)?

11.7   Athenaeus, *The Learned Banqueters*, 6.264c–d (= *BNJ 566 F 11a*): Greek Antiquarian Treatise (End of Second Century CE)

On the context of this excerpt in Athenaeus' work, see 11.6. The Lokrians and Phokians were communities of central Greece, which were considered relatively underdeveloped, compared with other areas of the Greek world.

Literature: Lewis forthcoming.

In the ninth book of his *Histories*, Timaeus of Tauromenium[198] wrote: "In the past, it was not an ancestral custom of the Greeks to be served by purchased people (*argyrônêtoi*)." He continues: "They used to accuse Aristotle for having wholly misunderstood the customs of the Lokrians. For neither among the Lokrians nor among the Phokians was it customary to possess slaves, whether

---

[197] See 6.26.
[198] A Greek historian of ca. 350–260 BCE.

female or male, except in recent times. The first person to have two slave girls attend to her was the wife of Philomelos,[199] the sacker of Delphi. At about the same time, Mnason, the companion of Aristotle, acquired 1000 slaves and was accused by the Phokians for having deprived so many citizens of their living. For it was the custom that in domestic tasks, the young would serve the old."

- Did slavery exist in the early Greek world, according to this passage?
- What evidence is used to support this view?
- Does the evidence from Homer (11.1–4) support this view? Cf. also 3.29–30.
- Is this passage useful for writing the history of Greek slavery, or is it more illuminating for the history of Greek thought about slavery?

11.8 Aristotle, *Constitution of the Athenians*, 2, 4–6: Greek Philosophical Treatise (Fourth Century BCE)

The treatise places the following reforms after the Kylonian affair (second half of seventh century BCE). On Solon, see 6.5.

Literature: Mactoux 1988; Rihll 1996; Harris 2002; Ito 2004; Canevaro forthcoming.

After these events, it so happened that for a long time, there was civil strife between the notables and the many. For the Athenian constitution was oligarchic in all other ways and, crucially, in that the poor, along with their wives and children, were slaves to the rich. The poor were called "dependents" (*pelatai*) and "six-parters" (*hektêmoroi*), as they worked the farms of the wealthy for the rent of one sixth. The whole land was in few hands, and, if the poor did not pay their rents, they themselves along with their children were liable to be seized. And in all cases, loans were received on the security of one's person until the time of Solon. He was the first to become "leader of the people" (*prostatês*). For the many, the most grievous and bitterest of the things related to the constitution was their slavery; that said, they were also discontented with the other things too; for, to speak loosely, they had no share in anything. [...] As was said above, loans were received on the security of one's person, and the land was in few hands. And while such was the organization of the constitution, with the many being slaves to the few, the people rose against the notables. As the strife was severe, and they had been opposing each other for a long time, they chose Solon as mediator and magistrate by common consent and committed the constitution to him. [...] When Solon took over responsibility of the situation, he liberated the people once and for all, since he put an end to loans on the security of one's person. And he set laws and cancelled debts, both private and public. They call these cancellations "the shaking-off of burdens" (*seisachtheia*), as they shook off the burden weighing on them.

---

[199] Philomelos of Phokis was active in the middle of the fourth century BCE.

- What was the land distribution in Athens, according to Aristotle? What was the cause of enslavement for debt before Solon?

- What reforms did Solon make?

- Did Solon redistribute the land? If not, how did the landless peasants solve their problems after Solon's reform?

- Did Solon's reform create a slave society for the first time in Athenian history?

- If not, what exactly was the significance of his laws for the history of Athenian slavery?

11.9   Pliny the Elder, *Natural History*, 33.26–7:[200] Latin Encyclopedic Work (First Century CE)

Literature: Bradley 1985; Cheesman 2009.

> What life did the men of old lead! What innocence was there when nothing was locked with seals! Nowadays, even food and drink are protected from theft via signet rings. This is the achievement of our legions of slaves! An unfamiliar crowd inside the house and, already, we need to have someone announcing names even in the case of our slaves! Things were different with the older generations. One slave, "the boy Marcus" (*Marcipor*), or "the boy Lucius" (*Lucipor*), of the same clan as his master, used to eat all his meals together with the master. There was no need to keep watch over the members of the household in the house. Nowadays, delicacies are provided in order to be snatched away and, with them, those who will snatch them away. Not even sealing the keys themselves is adequate protection!

- How does Pliny describe the difference between past and present?

- What is the reason that surveillance of slaves was less necessary in the past?

- To what extent can we take this comment as evidence for a changing history of Roman slavery?

11.10   Appian, *Civil Wars*, 1.1.7: Greek Historiography (Second Century CE)

By the early third century BCE, the Romans had effectively conquered most of the Italian peninsula. Appian here discusses the consequences of the Roman conquest during the second century BCE.

Literature: Hopkins 1978: 1–98; Oakley 1993; Jongman 2003; Launaro 2011; Shaw 2014.

---

[200] Latin text: Rackham et al. 1938–63.

The Romans gradually subdued Italy by war. They would occupy a part of the land and found cities or enlist their own citizens in already existing cities, giving them land lots. These communities they regarded as garrisons. Of the land they each time conquered by war, they would immediately distribute or sell or rent out among the settlers that which was already cultivated. But the land which was at the time uncultivated because of the war, of which there was very much, they did not then have the time to distribute, and so they proclaimed it available to anyone wishing to cultivate it, for a toll of its yearly crops: one tenth of the sown crops, one fifth of the produce of fruit trees. They also specified a toll for those keeping grazing livestock, according to the size of the animals. They took these actions to assist the increase of the Italian population, which they considered as extremely hard-working and enduring, in order to have allies who were their kin.

The outcome, however, was the exact opposite. For the wealthy took over the greatest part of the undistributed land and, growing in confidence that, as time passed, no one would take it away from them, they started to acquire, sometimes by purchase, sometimes by force, any fields that adjoined their own or any small plots of land belonging to poor people. The result was that, instead of small farms, they came to farm vast plains, which they worked using agricultural laborers and shepherds whom they had purchased. They did this to avoid having their free workers taken away from agricultural work for military expeditions. Moreover, the possession of slaves brought them much gain through the great number of children of their slaves; they increased undisturbed, since they did not have to participate in war. The result was that the powerful became extremely wealthy, the number of slaves increased throughout the land, whereas the Italians suffered from population diminution and shortage of manpower.

- How did the Roman conquest affect Italian communities?
- How did wealthy Romans benefit from the Roman conquest?
- What consequences did the conquest have for the free poor, according to the passage?
- What was the role of slavery in these developments?
- Should we see these developments as heralding the transition from societies with slaves into slave societies in Italy? Cf. 11.8.

SLAVE AGENCY, EVENTS, AND CHANGE

11.11   Slave Agency and the Peloponnesian War

See also 1.4–5, 1.26, and 7.18.

Literature: Hunt 1998; Vlassopoulos forthcoming.

——————   **11.11.a   Thucydides, 5.14.3: Greek Historiography**   ——————
                            (Late Fifth Century BCE)

In 425 BCE, the Athenians successfully occupied the island of Sphakteria and fortified other locations in the Spartan territory; the Spartans originally aimed to
subdue the Athenians by invading the Athenian territory and destroying the
crops. The passage describes the Spartan mentality in the eve of the peace treaty
of 421 BCE, known also as the Peace of Nikias (see 1.4).

> The Lacedaemonians were more inclined to contemplate peace [...] as the
> war was not turning out as they had expected. They had been of the opinion
> that they would crush the Athenian power within a few years if they ravaged
> their land. Instead, the Sphakteria disaster had befallen them – the great-
> est misfortune Sparta had ever suffered. Their land was continuously raided
> from Pylos and Kythera. The helots were deserting, and the Lacedaemonians
> lived in constant fear that even those who remained might use the present
> situation and revolt, trusting on those abroad, as they had done in the past.

- How did the Athenian actions enable helot agency?

- What did helots do and what did the Spartans fear they might do? Cf. 11.11.b.

- To what extent did helot agency affect the signing of the Peace of Nikias?

——————   **11.11.b   Thucydides, 4.80.2–5: Greek Historiography**   ——————
                            (Late Fifth Century BCE)

In 424 BCE, the Spartans decided to send an expeditionary force to Thrace under
the general Brasidas to incite the Athenian subjects in the area into revolt. The
expedition proved successful and forced the Athenians to agree to the Peace of
Nikias in 421 BCE. The passage explores one of the factors that weighed in the
Spartan decision making.

Literature: Jordan 1990; Harvey 2004; Paradiso 2004.

> Moreover, the Lacedaemonians were willing to send out of the way on a pre-
> text some of the helots, lest they might exploit the current situation – Pylos
> was in the hands of the Athenians – and revolt. For the Lacedaemonians
> had even done the following out of fear of the number and unpredictability
> of the helots. – In fact, the Lacedaemonian stance towards the helots had
> always revolved mostly around the issue of security. – They proclaimed that
> any helots claiming to have shown excellence at war and thus benefitting
> the Spartans could undergo a trial, so that the Spartans could manumit the
> selected. This was a test, as, in their opinion, those who were foremost in
> claiming they should get manumitted would be men of mettle, all the more
> apt to attack them. They selected about 2000 helots. The latter crowned

themselves with garlands and went from shrine to shrine as men who had already been freed. But soon afterward, the Lacedaemonians did away with them, and no one heard how each of them died. So, on this occasion, too, the Lacedaemonians happily sent 700 helots to Brasidas to serve as hoplites; Brasidas hired the rest of the men he needed from the Peloponnese.

- How serious did the Spartans take the helot threat, according to the passage?
- What had the Spartans proclaimed in the earlier incident, and what does the Spartan promise tell us about the role of the helots in the war?
- How credible is Thucydides' account of that incident?
- What does the decision to send the helots with Brasidas tell us about Spartan–helot relations?
- Is Spartan policy toward the helots consistent or not?
- To what extent did helot action affect the outcome of the war between 431 and 421 BCE?
- What should we conclude about slave agency from the various ways in which helots acted during the Peloponnesian War?

——— 11.11.c Thucydides, 7.27.3–5: Greek Historiography ———
(Late Fifth Century BCE)

In 412 BCE, the Spartans succeeded in fortifying Dekeleia in the Athenian territory.

Literature: Hanson 1992.

Dekeleia, which had been fortified that summer by the whole of the Spartan army, [...] was the cause of much damage for the Athenians. First of all, it made things deteriorate through both destruction of property and loss of human life. Beforehand, the Lacedaemonian attacks used to be brief and were not preventing the Athenians from benefitting from the land for the rest of the time. That summer, however, the occupation was constant. In fact, sometimes even additional troops would attack them or, other times, the regular guards would rampage through the country, plundering, to cover their needs. Finally, Agis, the Spartan king, was there in person, conducting military operations with great zeal. So, the damage to the Athenians was great. They had been deprived from the use of all their land, while more than 20,000 slaves had deserted, many of whom artisans; they had also lost all their livestock, including their draft animals.

- How did the Spartan occupation affect the Athenian slaves?
- What can we learn about the size of the Athenian slave population from this passage? Cf. 12.4–5.
- How did slave agency affect the Athenian conduct of the war?

——————   11.11.d   Aristophanes, *Frogs*, 31–4: Greek Comedy   ——————
                            (Late Fifth Century BCE)

In 406 BCE, when the Spartans blockaded the Athenian fleet in Lesbos, the Athenians manumitted and enfranchised thousands of slaves to man a new fleet. This fleet defeated the Spartans at Arginousai. In this comic scene, the god Dionysus converses with Xanthias, his slave. Cf. 11.11.e.

Literature: Hunt 2001.

> **Dionysus:** Well, since you claim you get no benefit from riding the donkey, pick it up and take your turn carrying it.
> **Xanthias:** How unfortunate I am! Why wasn't I at that sea-battle? Then I would be telling you to go to hell.

——————   11.11.e   Scholia to Aristophanes' *Frogs*, 33: Greek   ——————
                            Exegetical Commentary

For the context, see 11.11.d.

> "Why wasn't I at that sea battle?": This is chronologically apt, since in the previous year, in the archonship of Antigenes, the Athenians, who had been defeated in other, earlier, sea battles, were victorious in a sea battle near Arginousai. Their slaves fought together with them, and they manumitted them. So, it is because of this that he says, playfully, that, "If I had participated in the sea battle, I would have been set free".

- How did the Athenians try to sort out their manpower shortage?
- How did slave agency affect the development of the war?
- What should we conclude about slave agency from the various ways in which Athenian slaves acted during the Peloponnesian War?

11.12   The Ethnogenesis of the Brettians

Cf. the reference to the *peridinoi* in 5.6.

Literature: Shaw 1984; Lombardo 1987; Mele 1994.

——————   11.12.a   Diodorus, *Library*, 16.15: Greek Historiography   ——————
                            (First Century BCE)

Diodorus places the following events in the middle of the fourth century BCE.

[...] At that time in Italy, a large number of people gathered around Lucania. They were a mixture from every region but mostly runaway slaves. At first, they lived as marauders. Because their everyday life consisted in living in the open and making raids, they acquired experience and training in warfare. As a result, they were superior to the native people in battle and achieved an increase in power which was quite considerable. First, they took by siege the city of Terina and plundered it completely. Then after subduing Hipponion, Thurii, and many other cities, they set up a common state. They were called Brettians because the majority were slaves. For, runaways were called "brettii" in the local language. This is then how the Brettian population was formed in Italy.

- What was the role of slaves in the ethnogenesis of the Brettians?

- Which particular group of slaves was important? Why?

- Were the Brettians a slave-only group? Can we learn anything about slave agency from their case?

———   11.12.b   Strabo, *Geography*, 6.1.4: Greek Geography   ———
(End of First Century BCE/Early First Century CE)

It was the Lucanians who gave its name to that nation. For they call those who defect "Brettians." According to the Lucanians, the Brettians used to work for them as shepherds, but later, when control was relaxed, started to behave like free men and defected from them. This took place when Dion raised an expedition against Dionysios and stirred everyone against everyone else.[201]

- Who were the Brettians, according to Strabo? What assumptions about the status of shepherds does the passage make? Cf. 2.3.a, 9.25a.

- In what ways does the account of Strabo differ from that of Diodorus?

- Can we see common elements of slave agency in these two accounts?

11.13   Slave Rebellion and the Ethnogenesis of the Limigantes

The Sarmatians were an Indo-Iranian people, who, in the course of the first century CE, became dominant along the Danube bend, often fighting with the Romans. Through raiding and warfare, they acquired a large number of slaves. The events narrated below took place around 334 CE, when the Sarmatians were attacked by their Gothic neighbors (referred to in this passage as Scythians, the standard term for all Black Sea nomads; for Goths, see 11.14).

Literature: Lenski 2018: 29–30.

---

[201]The conflict between Dion and the tyrant of Syracuse Dionysios took place in the 350s BCE.

——— 11.13.a Eusebius, *Life of Constantine*, 4.6.1–2: Greek ———
Biography (Fourth Century CE)

> It was God himself who drove the Sarmatians at Constantine's feet, and it is more or less in the following manner that He subdued men who exulted in their barbarian spirit. When the Scythians rose against them, the Sarmatian masters gave weapons to their slaves, to build up defense against the enemy. As the slaves took control, they raised their weapons against their masters and drove everyone from their native land. They found no other haven from perdition than Constantine. And he, apt at offering salvation, admitted them all to the land of the Romans. He selected for his own armies those capable for this, while to the rest he allotted pieces of land to cultivate and make their living from it. As a result, the Sarmatians acknowledge that their misfortune turned out for the good, as they now enjoy Roman freedom, instead of living in barbarian savagery.

——— 11.13.b Ammianus Marcellinus, *History*, 19.11.1: Latin ———
Historiography (Fourth Century CE)

The events in this passage took place in the 350s CE. The defeated Sarmatians who crossed into the Roman territory were called Agaragantes, and their former slaves were now called the Limigantes.

> In the midst of these uncertain circumstances, the emperor Constantius, who was still resting for the winter at Sirmium, was aroused by frightening and grave messages, which pointed to what he was mostly in fear of. The news was that the Sarmatian Limigantes – who, as we pointed out earlier, had driven their masters away from their ancestral abodes – having gradually moved away from the places which had been assigned to them the previous year so that they might not attempt any wrongdoing, as they are not trustworthy, had occupied the regions bordering upon the frontiers and were ranging freely, as was their native custom. They would cause extreme disturbance unless they were driven away.

- Why did the Sarmatians arm their slaves?
- How did their slaves take advantage of the situation?
- What does slave success imply about their numbers?
- What consequences on ethnic formation did the success of the Sarmatian slaves lead to?

11.14   The Goths and the Fall of Rome

In 376 CE, the nomadic Huns invaded the areas around the Black Sea that were ruled by the Goths. In desperation, the Goths requested permission to relocate south of the Danube, within Roman imperial territory. The permission was granted, but because of the horrific circumstances created by the Roman authorities, as described in the following passages, the Goths rose in revolt and in 378 CE defeated in battle and killed the Roman emperor Valens. The Gothic groups maintained an independent role in the Balkans for decades, until turning west, besieging Rome several times and famously sacking it in 410 CE, ultimately creating an independent kingdom in southern France and Spain and playing a key role in the collapse of the Roman Empire in the West.

Literature: Vuolanto 2003: 170–9; Lenski 2008.

11.14.a   Ammianus Marcellinus, *History*, 31.4.9–11:
Latin Historiography (Fourth Century CE)

> At the head of the Roman army, there were Lupicinus and Maximus. The one was commander (*comes*) in Thrace, the other a pernicious general. They outdid each other in temerity. Their insidious greed was the cause of all our evils. We shall omit the other crimes they – or others acting with their consent – committed for the worst motives against the foreigners as they arrived, who until then they were not to blame. We shall speak only about one act of which even judges prejudiced in their favor would find no excuse to absolve them. An unheard of and sorrowful act. After the barbarians crossed the river, they were plagued by lack of food. The two despicable commanders put in motion a shameful trade: they exchanged any dogs their insatiable greed could gather from far and wide for one slave each. Even sons of foreign chieftains were included among those exchanged.

- What was the consequence of the greed of the Roman commanders?
- How useful is this passage for understanding the ancient slave trade? Cf. 8.5, 8.16, and 9.5.

11.14.b   Ammianus Marcellinus, *History*, 31.6.5: Latin
Historiography (Fourth Century CE)

> The Goths approved their king's counsel [...] and, dispersed throughout Thrace, advanced with great caution. Meanwhile, those who had surrendered themselves to them and those they had captured showed to them the

> rich areas, particularly those in which it was said that sufficient food supplies might be found. Their innate confidence was increased immensely by the helpful fact that great numbers of their own people were flocking to them every day: those who had been sold into slavery by merchants and many others, whom, when they first crossed, nearly dead of hunger, they had exchanged for a drink of feeble wine or some horrid bits of bread.

- How did the experience of enslavement affect the actions of the Goths?

- How did slave agency affect the conflict between Romans and Goths?

—— 11.14.c Zosimus, *New History*, 5.42.3: Greek Historiography ——
(Fifth Century CE)

In 408 CE, Alaric, king of the Visigoths, besieged Rome.

> And almost all the slaves who lived throughout Rome would every day, so to speak, leave the city and join the barbarians, and so there was a multitude of about 40,000 people gathered together.

- What did slaves do during the siege of Rome? Cf. 11.11.

- How important was slave agency during the whole conflict between Romans and Goths?

- How significant were moments of crisis for the exercise of slave agency?

11.15 Procopius, *On Wars*, 1.20.1–8: Greek Historiography (Sixth Century CE)

Procopius narrates conflicts between Ethiopia and the Homeritai in modern Yemen, which took place between 525–570 CE.

Literature: Bowersock 2012: 1–27.

> At the time of this war, Hellestheaios, the king of the Ethiopians, who was a Christian and greatly devout to this faith, realized that among the Homeritai of the mainland across,[202] there were both many Jews and a large number of people adhering to that old faith which is today called "Hellenic,"[203] and that they plotted against the Christians of that land in no small way. So, he gathered a fleet and an army and made an expedition against them. After

---

[202] The Arabian peninsula.
[203] Meaning "pagan".

defeating them in battle, he killed many Homeritai and their king and appointed another king, who was a Christian. That king was one of the Homeritai by birth, and his name was Esimiphaios. After prescribing that Esimiphaios pay an annual tax to the Ethiopians, Hellestheaios returned home.

Many slaves among Hellestheaios' Ethiopian army, together with men who were prone to committing villainies, did not at all want to follow their king, so they deserted him and stayed put, out of desire for the land of the Homeritai, which is exceedingly rich. Soon after, this rabble, together with some other men, revolted against the king Esimiphaios, imprisoned him in one of that land's fortresses, and appointed a new king for the Homeritai. His name was Abramos. This Abramos was a Christian and slave of a Roman citizen who lived in the Ethiopian city of Adulis[204] and was engaged in the sea trade. [...]

There follow further failed Ethiopian expeditions to subdue Abramos.

The king of Ethiopians got frightened, and from that moment on, he made no further expeditions against Abramos. When Hellestheaios died, Abramos agreed to continue paying tribute to the Ethiopian king who succeeded Hellestheaios, and he thus strengthened his rule. But these things happened later.

- What was the composition of the Ethiopian army? What can we learn about slaving strategies from this?
- What motivated the slave rebels?
- Who became their leader?
- What was the role of slave agency in the events narrated here?
- Did these events constitute a slave revolt?

IDEOLOGY AND HISTORICAL CHANGE

11.16 Seneca, *Letters*, 47.1, 10–12, 17–19: Latin Moral Philosophy in Epistolary Form (First Century CE)

On this letter, see also 4.8, 5.12, and 10.22.

Literature: Manning 1989; Garnsey 1996: 128–52; Bradley 2008.

I was happy to hear from those who have come from you that you live with your slaves on familiar terms. This is becoming to your intelligence and education. "They are slaves." No! They are human beings. "They are slaves." No! They are housemates. "They are slaves." No! They are lowborn friends. "They are slaves." No! They are fellow slaves, if you think that fortune has the same power over both free and slave. [...]

---

[204] An emporium on the western coast of the Red Sea (in modern Eritrea).

You need to keep in mind that he whom you call your slave has sprung from the same roots, delights in the same sky, breaths as you do, lives as you do, dies as you do. It is as possible for you to see a freeborn man (*ingenuus*) in him as it is for him to see a slave in you. At the time of the Varian disaster,[205] many men born to most noble families, who were beginning their senatorial career via the army, were crushed by fortune. Fortune turned some of them into shepherds, others to guardians of cottages. So, dare now condemn the man to whose fortune you might have to descend while you are condemning him! I wouldn't now want to involve myself in a long argument and discuss how we treat slaves: we are excessively arrogant, cruel, and abusive to them. But the heart of my advice is the following: live with your inferior in the same way as you would like your superior to live with you. And every time you think of how much power you have over your slave, think of how much power your master has over you. "But I don't have any master," you will say. You are still young. Perhaps you will have one in the future. Don't you know at what age Hecuba became a slave? Or Croesus? Or Darius' mother, or Plato, or Diogenes? [...]

"He is a slave!" Yes, but perhaps he is free in his spirit. "He is a slave!" But will this harm him? Show me who is not a slave: one is a slave to lust; another to avarice; another to ambition; all are slaves to hope; all are slaves to fear. I will give you an ex-consul who is a slave to a little old lady; a wealthy man who is a slave to a little slave girl; I will show you the most noble of youths being slaves to pantomime artists. There is no slavery more shameful than the slavery to which we submit ourselves willingly. So, you shouldn't let those squeamish people deter you from showing yourself cheerful toward your slaves, as a superior, but not with arrogance. They should respect you, rather than fear you. Some might claim that I am now calling for slaves to wear the liberty cap[206] and masters to be cast down from their high position because I said, "It's preferable that slaves should respect rather than fear their masters." "What does he precisely mean?" they say. "Should they respect their masters as clients, as morning callers?" Those who say such things have forgotten that what is sufficient for a god cannot be insufficient for a master. He who is respected is also loved. Love cannot be mixed with fear. So, I judge it most right if you don't want to be feared by your slaves and you admonish them with words; the whip can correct only speechless animals.

- What attitudes to slaves does Seneca criticize? On what grounds? Cf. 1.30.

- What modalities of slavery are visible in this passage? Cf. 1.27–9.

- Was Seneca and Stoic philosophy in favor of abolishing slavery?

- If not, could Stoic ideas still have an impact on the history of slavery? If so, how?

---

[205] A reference to a devastating Roman defeat by Germanic tribes in 9 CE.

[206] Bearing the "liberty cap" (*pilleus*) was part of the ritual of manumission. Cf. 10.12.

11.17   Philo, *Every Good Man Is Free*, 75–9: Greek Philosophical Treatise (First Century CE)

In this treatise, Philo argues that it is the wise, good men who are free, independent of whether they are formally owned by a master – an idea advanced by the Stoics, but for Philo (see sections 56–57), inspired or preceded by Jewish thought. At this point, Philo gives historical examples of wise, good, and therefore truly free men. The Essenes, a Jewish religious group, are his first extensive example.

Literature: Garnsey 1996: 157–72; Neutel 2015: 144–83; Ramelli 2016: 82–96.

Palestinian Syria, too, is fertile ground for nobleness. A great part of it is inhabited by the very populous nation of the Jews. Among these, there are some called Essenes, more than 4000 in number. In my opinion, they are named after an inexact form of the Greek word for piety, because they have become particularly devout in their worship of god: not by sacrificing animals but by demanding from themselves to make their thoughts befitting to what is holy. First of all, these men live in villages. They have turned themselves away from cities, because of the habitual lawlessness of those living there; for they realize that souls can be damaged incurably by those among whom one lives, as if struck by a disease caused by infectious air. Some of them work the land, others pursue a craft – one of those contributing to peace – and so they benefit themselves and those close to them. They do not hoard silver or gold, nor do they acquire big portions of land out of desire for the proceeds, but they try to furnish themselves with as much as is needed for life's essentials. For they have, almost uniquely, become money-less and property-less not because of lack of good fortune but by deliberate action and consider themselves exceedingly wealthy, as they judge that to need little and be content with it is abundance – which it is. Among them you will find no maker of arrows, or javelins, swords, helmets, breastplates, or shields, nor, in general, any weapon maker, or engine maker or anyone making anything related to warfare. Nor, in fact, will you find anyone pursuing activities related to peace but conducive to vice. For example, they know nothing of commerce or retail or ship owning, thus expelling anything that might lead to greed. And there are no slaves among them, but they are all free, serving one another. They particularly condemn masters, not only as unjust men, who destroy equality, but also as impious men, who undo the law of nature: nature gave birth and raised, like a mother, everyone equal to everybody else and thus created legitimate brothers – not in words only but in reality; this kinship, however, has been shaken by devious greed, which grew and created estrangement instead of kinship and enmity instead of love.

- What was the Essene attitude to wealth?
- What was the Essene attitude to slavery? How did they justify their stance?
- Did the Essenes try to change the world around them, or did they create their own world?

11.18 *1 Peter*, 2:18–23: Greek Biblical Text (First Century CE)

The author here expands on his earlier instruction that Christians submit themselves "for the Lord's sake to every human authority" (2:13).

Literature: Garnsey 1996: 173–88; Glancy 2002a: 148–51; Vlassopoulos 2021b.

> Slaves should submit to their masters in profound fear – not only to masters who are good and fair but also to masters who are harsh. For this is gratifying: namely, that one who suffers unjustly endures the pain because of his consciousness of god. For what glory is there if you endure a beating when you are in error? But if you endure sufferings when you are doing good, this is gratifying in the eyes of god. For to this you have been called, because Christ, too, suffered on your behalf, leaving behind a model for you, so that you might follow his footsteps. He who "committed no sin and no deceit was found in his mouth" (Isaiah 53:9). He who, when reviled, did not revile back; when suffering, did not use threats, but gave himself to the one who judges justly. [...]

- To whom is this advice offered? What does it imply about the composition of Christian communities? Cf. 7.32, 10.8.
- What are Christian slaves advised to do? On what grounds?
- Could the justification of suffering offer slaves a means of making sense of their terrible conditions?
- What can we learn about Christian attitudes to slavery from this passage?
- Is this the only Christian attitude to relations between masters and slaves? Cf. 3.13.

11.19 Synodal Letter of the Council of Gangra, Canon 3: Church Regulations in Greek (ca. 340 CE)

This Church synod condemned an ascetic group called the Eustathians and their various practices.

Literature: de Churruca 1982; Grieser 2001; McKeown 2012; Vlassopoulos 2021b.

> If one, on the pretext of piety, incites a slave to despise his master and leave his service,[207] instead of serving his master in good will and with every honor, let him be excommunicated.

- How did the Eustathians instruct slaves to deal with their masters? Why?
- Does this imply that the Eustathians were against slavery? Cf. 11.17.

---

[207] The Greek word for leaving (*anachôrein*) is also used to refer to "leaving" the secular world (cf. anchoritism).

- How did Church authorities deal with Eustathian practices? Why?
- In what ways did Christian ideas affect slavery in this case?

11.20 Chrysippus of Jerusalem, *Enkomion of St. Theodore*, pp. 73–4 Sigalas (*BHG* 1765c): Saint's Life in Greek (Fifth Century CE)

Literature: Harper 2011: 256–61.

> As though he has taken over Zachariah the god-bearer's sickle against thieves[208] and been entrusted to use it against run-away slaves, too, Theodore puts a check on the wicked actions of thieves and binds together the feet of run-away slaves everywhere. And to whichever church dedicated to Theodore one might run to, whether one wishes that his stolen goods be revealed or asks for his slaves' escape to be stopped, then it suffices that one takes a small wax seal and keeps it safe in his home. With this seal, one can capture those who robbed him or those who ran away.

- Why would Christians appeal to St. Theodore for help?
- What does this imply about the Church's attitude to masters and slaves?
- How does this compare with 11.19?

11.21 Basil of Caesarea, *Homilies on Fasting*, 1.7 (*PG* 31.176): Christian Sermon in Greek (Fourth Century CE)

In this exhortation to fasting, Basil presents the effects of fasting on the running of the household. In large Greek and Roman households, cooks specialized in the slaughtering and preparation of meat.

Literature: Bradley 1979; Klein 2000; Vlassopoulos 2021b.

> The cook's knife has stopped; the table is content to bear only foods that grow of themselves. The Sabbath was given to the Jews, so that "your beast of burden and your slave can rest" (*Exod.* 23:12), it says. Let fasting become a rest from their continuous toils for the slaves serving you all year long. Give a rest to your cook, a break to your waiter; let the hand of the cupbearer pause; let also him who bakes your dainties stop at last. And let your house be still for once from the myriads of noises, the smoke, the odor of roasting meat, and from those running up and down, serving the belly as if it were an inexorable mistress.

- Who is addressed in this passage? What are they advised to do?
- What consequences for the lives of slaves would this advice have? Cf. 3.13.

---

[208] A reference to the Septuagint translation of *Zech.* 5:1–4.

THE STATE AND HISTORICAL CHANGE

11.22   The Roman State and Mixed Marriages

In 52 CE, the Roman Senate passed a decree proposed by emperor Claudius (*senatus consultum Claudianum* [SCC]) concerning unions between free women and slaves belonging to other people. It is thought that the main purpose of SCC was to maintain control over imperial slaves and freedmen, who often married freeborn women. SCC was later modified by Hadrian (117–38), Constantine (306–37), and other emperors, before being abolished by Justinian (527–65).

Literature: Harper 2010b.

———————   11.22.a   Gaius, *Institutes*, 1.82–4 and 160:[209] Latin   ———————
Juristic Text (Second Century CE)

82–4: [...] According to the law of nations,[210] the child born to a slave woman and a free man is a slave, while that of a free woman and a slave man is born a free person. However, we should note whether another law or an enactment that has the force of law changes in any case this rule of the law of nations. For, under the SCC, a woman who is a Roman citizen and has had sexual intercourse (*coiit*) with the slave of someone else with the permission of his master remains free, according to the agreement, while the child born to her is a slave. For what was agreed between her and the master of the slave she had intercourse with is declared valid by the decree of the Senate. Subsequently, however, the divine Hadrian, moved by the inequity of this situation and its legal unseemliness, restored the rule of the law of nations, so that when the woman herself remains free, the child she gives birth will be free.

160: The greatest loss of status (*diminutio kapitis maxima*) occurs when someone loses simultaneously both his or her citizenship and his or her freedom. [...] For example: the women who, under the SCC, become slaves of the masters of the men with whom they have had sexual intercourse, if the masters had not given their consent when requested.

- What was the status of children of mixed unions according to the law of nations? Compare with 12.26.

- What happened to a free woman living with a slave according to the SCC?

- What happened to the children of a free woman and a slave according to the SCC?

- How did Hadrian's law modify the SCC? What was the logic behind the modification?

---

[209] Latin text: de Zulueta 1946.
[210] On the law of nations (*ius gentium*), see under 1.11.

——————   11.22.b   Theodosian Code, 4.12.3: Law of Emperor   ——————
Constantine in Latin (320 CE)

The same emperor (i.e. Constantine) to the people: since the ancient law coerces free-born women who have joined in cohabitation (*contubernium*) slaves belonging to the imperial treasury to a diminution of their birth rights, without offering any pardon on the basis of their ignorance or age, it is proper that the bonds of such unions be avoided. But if a freeborn woman, either in ignorance or, even, willingly forms a union with a slave of the imperial treasury, then her own status as a freeborn woman will not suffer any impairment, but her offspring, born to a father who is a slave of the imperial treasury and to a freeborn mother, will hold a middle destiny: as free children of slave men and bastard children of free women, such offspring shall be Latins. And although freed from the constraints of slavery, they will be held under a patron's privilege.

It is our will that this law be observed, and we restrict it to the slaves of the imperial treasury, and to † those with origins in † our patrimonial estates, and to our estates which are leased long term (*emphyteuticaria*), and to those who belong to the staff of our private property (*res privata*). For we detract nothing from the old law in relation to the municipalities (*res publicae*). It is our will that no slaves of any city become associated to this law, so that the cities may hold the full power of the old decree.[211]

- In what ways did Constantine modify the SCC? What remained the same?

- How does the Constantinian reform relate to the original purpose of the SCC?

——————   11.22.c   Code of Justinian, 7.24.1: Law of Emperor   ——————
Justinian in Latin (533 CE)

The emperor Justinian to Hermogenes, master of offices: since in our times we have undergone many labors on behalf of the freedom of our subjects, we believe that it is rather impious that some women be defrauded of their freedom, and what was introduced against natural freedom because of the ferocity of enemies be now imposed because of the lust of most worthless men. We therefore wish hereafter to put an end to the SCC and to all its provisions about notices and decisions of legal actions. Our purpose is that no woman designated free might be led to slavery contrary to the freedom she has as her birthright, either because she was deceived or because she was overpowered by an unfortunate passion or in some other way. Also, that the worst disgrace

---

[211] The transmitted Latin text of this paragraph is problematic, and we cannot be certain about the exact original wording. We based our translation on the Latin text printed in Harper 2010b: 623, but our understanding of it differs from his to an extent.

might not come upon the bright reputation of her relatives, so that she who perchance has relatives of distinguished rank might not end up the property of another person and perchance fear a master inferior to her relatives.

- How did Justinian justify the abolition of the SCC?
- How did the SCC fit in with the Roman ideology concerning the inalienability of freedom?

ANCIENT TO MEDIEVAL: FROM SLAVE SOCIETIES BACK TO SOCIETIES WITH SLAVES?

11.23   Agathias, *Histories*, 2.7.1–5: Greek Historiography (Sixth Century CE)

The episode narrated in this passage took place when a force of Franks and Alemanni faced the army of the Eastern Roman Empire led by the general Narses in Casilinum in Campania in 554 CE.

Literature: Lenski 2016: 287–90.

Such was more or less the Franks' eagerness to attack, and they had already taken their weapons in hand. Narses, too, ordered the Romans to take up their arms and started to lead them out of the camp, until they reached the point in the area separating them from the enemy where they should form up for battle. But when the army had begun its march and the general was already on his horse, he receives a message that one of the Heruls,[212] not one of the insignificant many, but a particularly noble and prominent one, had killed one of his own slaves in the most pitiable manner for some minor offence. Immediately, Narses reined in his horse and ordered the murderer to be brought to the middle, as it would be impious to go to battle without first cleansing and consecrating the pollution. The barbarian, when asked, admitted what he had done and did not disown it. Not only that, but he insisted that it was within the rights of owners to punish their own slaves as they liked and that both these and the others would be met with similar treatment if they didn't show sense. Since he seemed not to have regretted his outrageous conduct but was bold, arrogant even, and apparently truly murderous, Narses commanded his bodyguards to kill the man. A sword pierced his belly, and he died. The Heruls, however, since they were barbarians, were grieved and angry and were contemplating abstaining from the battle. Narses, having thus in a way expelled the pollution of the impure murder and given little heed to the Heruls, set off for the front of his army, announcing to all, in loud voice, that he who wished to share in the victory should follow him.

---

[212] A Germanic tribe, at the time in the service of the Eastern Roman Empire.

- Why does Narses halt his march to the battlefield?

- How does the Herul justify his act? How does the justification compare with classical attitudes to slavery?

- Why did Narses kill the Herul?

- Is Narses' attitude evidence of a radical change in terms of treating slaves? If so, how would you explain this change?

- Is it possible that Narses' execution of the Herul has little to do with slavery and more to do with other issues?

11.24   The Donation and Will of Vincent of Huesca, Spain, Written in Latin (Second Half of Sixth Century CE)[213]

Vincent, a clergyman of the Holy Church of Huesca, made a donation to the monastery of Asán (551 CE) and, subsequently, bequeathed by will to the Church of Huesca (576 CE) what he inherited from his parents. In addition, the will includes a number of manumissions and donations. While the text distinguishes between the statuses of being freeborn, free, or a Roman citizen as the outcomes of manumission, it is debatable whether these terms are used interchangeably or with different meanings in mind.

Literature: Roth 2016.

Donation, Folio 1, column 1, ll. 33–38:
Therefore, by the text of this donation I transfer to you, most blessed father, and to this holy congregation, to which the Lord considered right to call me, these places, with their buildings, fields, vineyards, olive trees, gardens, meadows, pastures, waters and water-courses, entrances, accesses, tenants (*coloni*), or slaves (*servi*), together with all their rights; in fact, with their *peculium*[214] (*scil*. I also transfer) the flocks of ewes, cows, and mares, which are under my ownership (*dominium*).

Will, Folio 2, ll. 1–17:
[…] we made a charter of free birth (*cartula ingenuitatis*). Confirming this now, we donate to him in the place Plasencia four *centuae* of vineyards and two unattached slaves (*mancipia vagantia*) as chattel.

To Dominus, with whom we had the same wet nurse, we donate 20 *modii* of arable land at the estate (*domus*) at Ceresa, together with a laborer, who will be obliged to cultivate the land for him in the name of the Lord.

I decree that Elicianis be free-born (*ingenuus*). We give him six *centuae* of land at the estate at Ceresa.

However, regarding that debt which accumulated because of the negligence of some […], through my actions before my ordination, you are to make it good, Holy Church of Huesca, so that you should take over the farm (*casa*)

---

[213] Latin text: Fortacín Piedrafita 1983.
[214] See 4.37.

at Calasanz for yourself and possess it forever, with the help of the Lord; and peacefully, as is proper, you should define its bounds together with our son Gerontius.

I want to give the young boy who is called Dalmatianus to Severus the doctor.

We decree that Campinus, with his wife and children, be free (*liberi*), whatever pertains to the *peculium* having been granted.

We decree that Eugenius, with his children, be Roman citizens, whatever pertains to the *peculium* having been released.

We decree that Monnellus be free-born (*ingenuus*); we grant him the *colonica*[215] which he holds in the site of Gestaín.

And we decree that Mattheus be free-born; we give to him ten *centuae* of land in the place Alueza.

And as we earlier released him in the presence of our sons, I decree that Eucerius be free (*liber*).

We decree that Marturius and Ilipidius be free. [...]

- How many slaves are manumitted in this document? How many other slaves are mentioned?

- What is the status of Dalmatianus? How many other people with unclear status are mentioned?

- What is included in the *peculium* of these slaves? How does this relate to the *peculium* of slaves in earlier periods? Cf. 4.37–8, 5.14, 10.9.

- How do you imagine the lives of these agricultural slaves? To what extent can we see similarities and differences from agricultural slaves in earlier periods? Cf. 1.7, 9.23, 12.18–9.

11.25   Eustathius, *Practice (Peira)*, 30.75: Greek Legal Textbook (ca. 1000 CE)

This legal textbook contains court rulings of Eustathius, a holder of a high imperial office (*magistros*) and senior judge in Constantinople around 1000 CE. The following court ruling comes from the textbook's section on testimony.

Literature: Köpstein 1993.

A bishop died and a neighboring *spatharokandidatos*[216] came and, together with two of the bishop's slaves, searched for gold. He discovered a small sack. Later, when asked, he produced it not filled to capacity, while the slaves insisted that the sack had been full of gold. The case was brought before the *magistros* who happened to be the judge, and he judged the issue after first

---

[215] It is unclear whether this relates to a specific form of land exploitation or a specific kind of landholding.

[216] A title held by mid-ranking court dignitaries in the Eastern Roman Empire.

speaking to the *spatharokandidatos* in the following way: "Why did you enter alone with the slaves and searched for gold?" He responded: "What I found I have brought forward." As the slaves objected that gold had been stolen from the sack, the *magistros* ruled that the slaves should take an oath. The *spatharokandidatos* countered that slaves are not permitted by law to take an oath, and "I am not going to be found guilty." The *magistros* said: "You took these men as witnesses, and you made a search for gold with them and trusting in them you took the money. Therefore, since they are the same men whom you took as accomplishes and witnesses and partners, you should now accept their oath that you had taken more gold and not just this. For if you had not intended wrongdoing and theft, you would not have entered another man's house with slaves, nor would you have examined his things." He passed judgement, the slaves took an oath, and the *spatharokandidatos* was found guilty and gave back the rest of the money.

- What is the cause of this dispute?
- On what grounds does the *spatharokandidatos* deny the ability of slaves to act as witnesses?
- On what grounds does the judge justify his decision?
- Is this decision evidence that attitudes to slavery had radically changed by around 1000 CE? Or does it tell us more about changing attitudes to law?

11.26 *Laws of Liutprand,* 140: Lombard Legal Code in Latin (734 CE)

The Lombards, who ruled most of Italy between 568 and 774 CE, recognized a range of statuses for manumitted slaves, from completely free (*fulcfree*) to semi-free (*aldii*).

Literature: Rio 2017: 232; Vlassopoulos 2021b.

If a free man who owns a married couple of either slaves or people of a semi-free status (*aldii*) and, instigated by the Enemy of the human race, has had sexual intercourse with the same female slave who has his male slave as her husband or with the *aldia* who is the partner of his *aldius*, he has committed adultery. Hence, we decree the following: this man should lose his male slave or his *aldius*, with whose wife he committed adultery, and, similarly, the woman herself, too. And they may go away wherever they want as free people (*fulcfree*) and be released from bonds according to the law of the folk, as if they had been released formally, through public procedure. For it is not pleasing to God that any man should have sexual intercourse with the wife of another.

- What is the penalty if a master has sex with a married female slave or an *aldia*?

- What justification is given for this regulation?

- To what extent is slave marriage legally recognized?

- Is this a radically different conception of slave marriage than that found in ancient societies?

- Did Christianity change the sexual exploitation of slaves? Did Christianity change slavery? Cf. 11.18–21.

12

Comparing Ancient Slaveries

In this chapter, we explore some of the similarities and differences between ancient slaving systems. We start with three multilingual inscriptions, in which parallel texts in different languages show interesting variations. Do these variations reflect different linguistic choices and epigraphic traditions, or do they result from differences between ancient slave systems (12.1–3)? Continuing the debate on the distinction between slave societies and societies with slaves (Chapter 11), we assess the significance of slavery and the numbers of slaves in classical Athens (12.4–5), in Asia Minor (12.6) and Jewish (12.7) communities during the Achaemenid period, in Hellenistic Anatolia (12.10), Roman Pergamon (12.8), and late-antique Thera (12.9). We then examine major differences in the scale of slaveholdings between various periods and societies (12.11–5) and the historical significance of these differences, in particular the consequences of slaves or former slaves being large-scale slaveholders (12.14–5). There were also important differences in terms of what slaving strategies were prioritized in the various ancient societies and the consequences of these diverse choices for the structures of those societies and the conditions of their slaves (12.16–21).

Relations between masters and slaves (12.22–5) and free and slave (12.26–8) show also significant variations between the various ancient slave systems, whether one looks at relations within households (12.22–3), mixed marriages (12.26–7), or attitudes to homoerotic relations (12.28). We then turn to manumission practices and the status and opportunities of freedpersons, which differ substantially among ancient societies (12.29–31). We conclude with a comparative examination of slave communities: in what way did different societies and their characteristics shape the particular form taken by their slave communities (12.32–4)? The comparative study of ancient slaving systems is crucial for understanding the history of slavery in antiquity.

Greek and Roman Slaveries, First Edition. Eftychia Bathrellou and Kostas Vlassopoulos.
© 2022 John Wiley & Sons, Inc. Published 2022 by John Wiley & Sons, Inc.

12.1 *Ima.Ita.*, Terventum 25: Inscribed Roof Tile, Pietrabbondante, Samnium (ca. 100 BCE)

This text is a bilingual inscription, in Oscan and Latin, scratched on a roof tile between four footprints, stamped before the tile was put to dry. It is a matter of debate whether *detfri* in the Oscan text is a person's name or a term denoting profession or status; similarly, it is not certain whether *amica* in the Latin text is a woman's name or the Latin word for female friend.[217]

Literature: Aubert 1994: 224–6; Wallace-Hadrill 2008: 90–1.

> **Oscan:** The *detfri* of H(eren)n(us) Sattius (or: Detfri, of H(eren)n(us) Sattius) stamped (it) with her (or: his) sole.
> **Latin:** Herennus' female friend (or: Amica, (slave) of Herennus) stamped (it) when we were putting the tile alongside the others.

- What is the purpose of this text? Would anybody ever see it?
- How do these two individuals present themselves?
- Who is the link between these two people? How should we interpret this link? Why do they mention this link in this kind of inscription?
- Can we learn anything about Roman and Italic slavery from this inscription?

12.2 *SEG* XXIII 514: Bilingual Dedicatory Inscription, Delos, Cyclades (Second Century BCE)

The names in the Greek part of the inscription are hellenized versions of the Roman names in the Latin part. Mercurius was the Roman equivalent of the god Hermes; Maia was Hermes' mother. *Magistri*, a Latin word, refers to leading cult personnel (see also 7.26); *hermaistai*, a Greek word, means people worshipping the god Hermes.

Literature: Hasenohr 2003, 2007, 2017; Schumacher 2006: 13–16.

Latin:	Greek:
Quintus Novellius, son of Marcus	Kointos No[vellios of Maarkos]
Lucius Mamilius, son of Lucius	Leukios Mamil[ios of Leukios]
Lucius Capinius, son of Lucius	Leukios Kapinios [of Leukios]
Quintus Maecius, freedman of Quintus	Kointos Maikios of Ko[intos]
Tiberius Staius, freedman of Minatus	Teberios Staios [of Minatos]
Lucius Vicirius, freedman of Lucius,	Leukios Ouikerios [of Leukios],
magis[*tri*, to Mercurius and]	*hermaistai*, dedicated this,
Maia.	and also the railing.

---

[217] For our understanding of the Oscan text, we rely on *Ima. Ita.*

- How is legal status indicated in the Latin part of the inscription?
- Is legal status indicated in the Greek part?
- How do you explain this discrepancy?
- Does the difference reflect real differences between Greek and Roman slavery? Or is the difference the result of different epigraphic traditions? Cf. 12.3.

12.3 *SEG* L 1030: Trilingual Dedicatory Inscription on a Bronze Column Base, Sardinia (First Century BCE)

The island of Sardinia was long under the Carthaginians, before passing in 238 BCE into Roman rule.

Literature: Culasso Gastaldi 2000; Pennacchietti 2002.

Latin: Cleon, slave of the partnership (*socii*) of the salt workers, offered this gift, willingly and deservedly, to Aesculapius Merre, who deserves it.

Greek: Kleon, who is in charge of the saltworks, set up this altar as dedication to Asklepios Merres, according to a command.

Punic: To lord Eschmun-Merre. Bronze altar, weighing 100 libres, dedicated by Cleon, the one of the partnership at the saltworks. He heard his voice, and he cured him. In the year of the suffetes Himilkot and Abdeshmun, sons (?) of HMLK.[218]

- Why did Cleon express his dedication in three different languages?
- How is Cleon presented in the Latin inscription? What is his status?
- How is Cleon presented in the Greek inscription? Is his status manifest? What about the Punic inscription?
- How do you explain this difference between the Greek, Punic, and Latin inscription?
- Does the difference reflect real differences between Punic, Greek, and Roman slavery? Or is the difference the result of different epigraphic traditions?

THE SIGNIFICANCE OF SLAVERY IN VARIOUS ANCIENT SLAVE SYSTEMS

12.4 Athenaeus, *The Learned Banqueters*, 6.272a–d: Greek Antiquarian Treatise (End of Second Century CE)

Aegina is a small island in the Saronic Gulf. It is impossible that it could physically hold half a million inhabitants.

---

[218] For our understanding of the Punic text, we rely on the works cited under "Literature".

Literature: Garlan 1988: 55–60.

> Timaeus of Tauromenium[219] [...] said that Corinth reached such prosperity that it had acquired 460,000 slaves. This is why, I believe, the Pythia had named the Corinthians "ration measurers." Ctesicles, in book 3 of his *Chronicles*, says that in Athens, during the 11<7>th Olympiad, Demetrios of Phaleron conducted a census of those living in Attica,[220] and the Athenians were found to be 21,000, the metics 10,000, and the slaves 400,000. [...] Aristotle, in his *Constitution of the Aeginetans*, says that even among the Aeginetans there were 470,000 slaves.

- How many slaves were there in Athens in the census of Demetrios? What is the ratio between citizens, metics, and slaves?

- How does this number compare with the numbers reported for Corinth and Aegina?[221]

- Are these numbers credible? If not, why?

- What are the implications for Greek societies if these numbers were credible?

12.5 Hyperides, Fragment 29 Marzi:[222] Greek Law-Court Speech, Athens (330s BCE)

After the victory of Philip of Macedon over an alliance of forces of southern Greece, including Athens, at Chaironeia in 338 BCE, Athens feared a possible invasion from Philip. To increase Athens' manpower in these emergency circumstances, the orator Hyperides proposed a decree to restore to citizenship all exiles and disenfranchised, to offer citizenship to metics, and to free and give arms to slaves. The following fragmentary passage comes from a speech Hyperides delivered when he was subsequently indicted by another Athenian politician, Aristogeiton, for having proposed an illegal decree. He was acquitted.

Literature: Garlan 1988: 55–60.

> That first more than 150,000 slaves from the silver mines and the rest of the countryside, then state debtors, the disenfranchised, those voted out of citizenship and the metics....

- What was Hyperides' proposal?

- How many slaves did Hyperides think would be liberated?

---

[219] See 11.7.
[220] Late fourth century BCE.
[221] A small island in the Saronic gulf.
[222] Marzi 1977.

- Do you think the number mentioned was based on evidence or on speculation?

- How does the number compare with those mentioned in the previous passage?

- If we cannot know the absolute number of slaves in Athens, are there other ways we can try to establish their relative importance in Athenian society and economy?

12.6 Xenophon, *Anabasis*, 7.8.8–22: Greek Historical Narrative (First Half of Fourth Century BCE)

Around 400 BCE, the mercenary army of the Ten Thousand, led by Xenophon, arrives at Pergamon in northern Asia Minor.

Literature: Lewis 2018: 247–54.

Here Xenophon is offered hospitality by Hellas, wife of Gongylos of Eretria and mother of Gorgion and Gongylos. She informs him that there is in the plain one Asidates, a Persian man. And if Xenophon should go in the night with 300 men, he could capture the man himself, his wife, his children, and his possessions, which were quite a lot. [...] Accordingly, Xenophon proceeded to sacrifice. And Basias, the seer from Eleia, who was present, said that the omens were excellent and that the Persian could be easily captured.

After dinner, Xenophon set off, having taken with him the captains who were his closest friends and *** those who had always been reliable, in order to do them a good turn. But others, too, force themselves in and join him, about 600. The captains were trying to send them away, so that they wouldn't have to give them shares – as if the booty had already been taken. They arrived around midnight. The slaves who lived in the area around the tower ran away, together with most of the livestock. Xenophon's men paid no attention to them, as their aim was to capture Asidates himself and his belongings. It was, however, impossible to take the tower by attacking it directly. It was very big and tall and had many battlements; its defenders were many and good fighters. So, they attempted to dig a tunnel in order to enter. The wall was eight clay bricks thick.

The defenders manage to keep Xenophon's men away, and more forces come to Asidates' assistance.

[...] So, then it was time for Xenophon's men to see how they would get away. They took whatever cattle there had been, and livestock and slaves, placed them in the center of a square they formed, and set out driving them along. Their main concern was no longer the booty but that their departure might not become a rout if they departed having left the goods behind. If this were to happen, the enemy would become bolder, while their own soldiers more disheartened. As things stood, however, they departed like men fighting for booty. [...] Xenophon and his men were getting a very hard time from the arrows and sling-stones. Marching on a circular formation, so as to have their shields between the arrows and themselves, they barely manage to cross the river Karkasos. Nearly half of them are wounded. [...] So, they manage to return to safety, with about 200 slaves and livestock enough for sacrifices.

- What can we learn about Asidates, his wealth, and his mode of life from this passage?

- How many slaves did he own? How significant was slavery for a provincial Persian grandee?

12.7 *Esdras* B 2:64–67 (= *Ezra* 2:64–67): Biblical Text in Greek – Septuagint[223] (Original Hebrew Probably Between 538 and 332 BCE)

In 587/6 BCE, the Neobabylonian empire exiled a significant part of the Jewish population to Babylon. After the conquest of Babylon by the Persians in 539 BCE, the Jews were allowed to return to Judaea. The text describes a census of people and property of the Jews who decided to return.

Literature: Magdalene and Wunsch 2011; Wunsch 2013; Lewis 2018: 199–222.

> The whole assembly together: 42,360 people, excluding male and female slaves. The latter were 7337. Of these 200 were singers. Their horses were 736, their mules were 245, their camels were 435, and their donkeys were 6720.

- What was the number of the free Jews? What was the number of their slaves? What was the free-to-slave ratio?

- What does this imply about the significance of slavery for Jewish communities?

12.8 Galen, *The Diagnosis and Treatment of the Affections Peculiar to Each Person's Soul (De propriorum animi cuiuslibet affectuum dignotione et curatione)*, 9.12–13, p. 33,12–25 De Boer[224] (V.49–50 Kühn): Greek Medical Treatise (Late Second/Early Third Century CE)

Galen locates the cause of his addressee's grief in covetousness.

Literature: MacMullen 1987; Morley 2011: 266–74.

> If you thus look at all our fellow citizens, I said, you will find no more than 30 who are wealthier than you. Hence, you are wealthier than all the rest and, evidently, wealthier also than their slaves and, moreover, wealthier than an equal number of women. So, if our fellow citizens are about 40,000 all together and you add to them the women and the slaves, you will realize

---

[223] Greek text: Rahlfs and Hanhart 2006.
[224] *CMG* V 4,1,1.

that you are wealthier than 120,000 people and yet not satisfied with that! Instead, you wish to surpass those, too, and are eager to become the very first in wealth. However, it is much better to be first in self-sufficiency, which is in your power to achieve, for to be the first in wealth is not a work of virtue but of fortune, which can make slaves and freedmen wealthier than us, who are considered to be of noble birth.

- How does Galen calculate the population of Pergamon?
- What was the ratio between free and slave, according to Galen?
- Why does Galen make this calculation? What is his point?
- Is Galen's calculation based on evidence? Can we trust his calculation?

12.9 *SEG* LV 915: Greek Cadastral Inscription, Thera, Aegean (Fourth Century CE)

A series of inscriptions from late antiquity record cadastres of land and other taxable resources, following the fiscal reforms initiated by emperor Diocletian. The two stones of this inscription record 152 rural slaves belonging to a single slave owner, whose name has not survived. Female names are underlined; names of children younger than 14 years of age are in italics. In some cases, it appears that the slaves are arranged in family groups, with the older men or women (presumably parents) listed first followed by younger slaves, who are presumably their children.

Literature: Harper 2008.

Stone A
Column I
Slaves in the countryside
Hygeia, 50 years old
Ktesibios, 28 years old
Sambatia, 20 years old
Zosimos [...]
Oxycholios [...]
Ktesibios [...]
Aphrodisios, 25 years old
Glauke, 33 years old
Theodoulos [...]
Chione [...]
Epaphroditos [...]
E[...]na, 35 years old
Italia, 8 years old
Kimon, 5 years old
Gamike, 30 years old

Column II
Zosimos, 10 years old
[...]etos [...]
[...]eos, 8 years old
Soteira, 35 years old
Euxeinos, 15 years old
Alexandros [...]
Eutychianos [...]
Eugenios [...]
Soteira [...]
Helene, 6 years old
Eutychia, 3 years old
Philoumene [...]
Soteira [...]
Zosimos, 66 years old
Eutychia, 60 years old
Glauke, 40 years old
Kalemere, 4 years old

Column III
[...]
[...], 20 years old
[...], 3 years old
Drosine [...]
[...], 25 years old
[...]
Eutychia, 6 years old
[...], 30 years old
[...]
[...]pous, [...]
[...]
[...], about 40 years old
Stephanos [...]
Epagathe, around 40 years old
Drakontidas [...]
Epagathe, 24 years old

Column IV
Tyche, 56 years old
Theodote, 36 years old
Eutychia, 46 years old
Apellas [...]
[...]se, 7 years old
Dioskoros [...]
Aphrodemos
Glauke [...]
(fragments of 6 names)
Epikteta, 56 years old
Oxycholios, 20? years old
Epikteta, 18 years old

Column V
Dem[...]
Eutychia, 55 years old
Eugenios, 50 years old
Mousogenia, 40 years old
Eutychia [...]
Sophronios [...]
Drosine, 15 years old
Soteira, 7 years old
Eugenios, 4 years old
Zosimios, 65 years old
Zosime, 60 years old
Eum[...], 18 years old
[...]elios, 13 years old
[...]
[...], 46 years old

Stone B
Column I
Gamike, 34 years old

Zopyra, 10 years old
Sophron, 8 years old
Pardalion, 5 years old
Elpis, about 40 years old
Pannychios [...]
Eustathia, 50 years old
Zosime, 10 years old
[...], 8 years old
[...]des [...]
[...], about 40 years old
[...], 40 years old
[...]
Eutychia, 4 years old
Theodoulos [...]
Epagathe, 56 years old
Philoxenos [...]
Claudiana [...]

Column II
Epiktesis, 21 years old
Ammianus, about 40 years old
Ammias, 20 years old
Eutychos, 1 year old
Hilara [...]
Zosime, 9 years old
Eutychos, 40 years old
Theodoule, 25 years old
Lampadion (or Lampadios) [...]
Eutychos, 4 years old
Agathon, 60 years old
Tyche, 52 years old
Zosimos [...]
[...]
Epiktesis [...]
Eugenios [...]
Pra[...], 56 years old
Eu[...], 27 years old
[...], 8 years old

Column III
Aphrodisia, 4 years old
Oxycholios, 30 years old
Eusebes, 50 years old
Moscho [...]
Eusebes, 12 years old
Chara, 10 years old
Hygeia, 7 years old
Zosimos [...]
Eutychianos, about 40 years old
Eutychia, 9 years old
El[...] 51 years old

Elpidianos, 48 years old	*Dionysios, 25 years old*
[...], 22 years old	Dionysios, 5 years old
[...]	Elpis [...]
[...], about 40 years old	*Mousa, 10 years old*
[...]	Oxycholios
Drosinos [...]	Soteira
Eutychia, 30 years old	Soteira
Column IV	*(fragments of 7 more names*
[...]lymieros [...]	*follow)*

- What is the ratio between male and female slaves in this inscription? How many children are there?

- What implications about the sources of slaves, their renewal, and family structures does this have?

- What names do these slaves have? What relationships between their names can we draw? What implications does this have?

- What should we conclude from this text concerning the role of slavery in a small island like Thera?

- What implications does this text have for the importance of slavery in late antiquity?

12.10 Strabo, *Geography*, 12.2.3: Greek Geography (End of First Century BCE/Early First Century CE)

Literature: Hülsen 2008; Caneva and Delli Pizzi 2015.

In the Antitaurus mountains, there are deep and narrow valleys, in which the city of Komana has been founded, as has also the shrine in honor of the goddess Enyo, whom they call Ma. The city is of considerable size. Among its inhabitants, there is a great multitude of those possessed by the goddess and of temple slaves (*hierodouloi*). The inhabitants are Kataonians. They are classed as subjects of the king in other respects, but they chiefly obey the priest. The priest has authority over the shrine and the temple slaves, who were more than 6000 when I visited the city – men and women together. A lot of land, too, is attached to the shrine. The revenue is given to the priest, and he is thus the second in honor in Cappadocia after the king. In the majority of cases, both the kings and the priests belonged to the same families.

- How is the temple city of Komana described?

- What is the number of temple slaves at Komana?

- What role does slavery play at Komana?

THE SCALE OF SLAVEHOLDINGS

12.11 Demosthenes, *Against Meidias*, 157–8: Greek Law-Court Speech, Athens (Mid-Fourth Century BCE)

Literature: Davidson 1997: 213–49; Porter 2019.

> This is how I behaved toward you. But how did Meidias? To this day, he has never led a *symmoria*,[225] although no one deprived him of anything of his patrimony; on the contrary, he received a large property from his father. So, which are his splendid deeds? What liturgies has he performed? Which are his grand expenditures? I can't see any such thing, except if one looks at the following: he built a house at Eleusis which is so big that it shadows over all its neighboring houses; and his wife is driven to the Mysteries, and wherever else she might wish, with a pair of white horses from Sikyon; and he struts through the marketplace followed by three or four attendants, dropping words such as "drinking cups," "drinking horns," "bowls," so that the passers-by might hear.

- How does Meidias display his extravagance and luxury?
- How does slavery figure in Meidias' display of wealth and status?
- How extravagant was Meidias in comparison with 4.20 and 12.12?

12.12 Athenaeus, *The Learned Banqueters*, 6.272d–e: Greek Antiquarian Treatise (End of Second Century CE)

Here the host of the fictional banquet conversations narrated in Athenaeus' work responds to his guest Masurius, who had just spoken about the number of slaves living in some Greek cities: cf. 12.4.

Literature: López Barja de Quiroga 2020.

> To this, Larensius responded: "But every Roman – and you have an exact knowledge of these things, my good Masurius – owns immense numbers of slaves. In fact, very many own 10,000 slaves or 20,000 or even more, and they do not own them so that they generate income for them, as that Greek millionaire, Nikias,[226] did; in fact, most Romans have most of their slaves parading along with them."

---

[225] A *symmoria* was an administrative grouping of wealthy Athenians, who were liable to pay certain taxes; the leader of a *symmoria* had to advance the relevant taxes personally and subsequently collect from other *symmoria* members their share.
[226] On Nikias and his slaves, see 4.10.

- How many slaves do rich Romans own?

- How do Romans use their slaves, according to the passage? Compare with 4.20.

- What differences between Greek and Roman slaving strategies does Larensius note? How credible do you find his argument?

12.13 Libanius, *Orations*, 31.11: Greek Deliberative Oratory (Fourth Century CE)

Libanius petitions the Council of Antioch to assist financially the teachers of oratory by describing their difficult living conditions.

Literature: Liebeschuetz 1972: 45–8; Kaster 1988.

> Some of the teachers do not have their own house, not even a small one, but stay in the house of others, like cobblers. Whoever has bought a house has not yet paid off his loan, so the house owner is in lower spirits than those who have not bought a house. As far as slaves go, one teacher has three, another two, another even fewer. In the absence of more slaves, they misbehave and are insolent toward their masters, since some teachers have not often had slaves, while others have had to keep slaves in a way unworthy of themselves.

- How does Libanius try to portray the poverty of teachers?

- How is slavery used for this purpose? What kind of audience would consider such numbers of slaves as evidence of poverty?

- What does this tell us about slavery and late antique societies?

- Why did slaves misbehave? What does this tell us about master–slave relationships?

12.14 *CIL* VI, 5197: Latin Funerary Inscription, Rome (First Century CE)

Literature: Weaver 1964, 1972: 200–6; Reduzzi-Merola 1990.

> To the well-deserving Musicus Scurranus, (slave) of Tiberius Caesar Augustus, treasurer (*dispensator*) of the Gallic Treasury of the province Lugdunensis, from his underslaves (*vicarii*) who were with him at Rome when he died.
> Venustus, business agent (*negotiator*)
> Decimianus, treasurer (*sumptuarius*)
> Dicaeus, secretary (*a manu*)
> Mutatus, secretary
> Creticus, secretary
> Agathopous, doctor

> Epaphra, in charge of silver
> Primius, in charge of wardrobe
> Communis, bedchamber servant
> Pothus, attendant
> Tiasus, cook
> Facilis, attendant
> Anthus, in charge of silver
> Hedylus, bedchamber servant
> Firmus, cook
> Secunda

- What is the status of the deceased, and what is his relationship with the people who set up this inscription in his honor?
- What are the roles of these slaves? What do their roles tell us about the lifestyle of the deceased?
- Secunda is the only female mentioned. How is she described? Why?
- Would these have been the only slaves under Musicus Scurranus?
- To whom would these people belong after Scurranus' death?
- What does this inscription reveal about Roman slavery?

12.15 Pliny the Elder, *Natural History*, 33.134–5:[227] Latin Encyclopedic Work (First Century CE)

A total of 3,600 pairs of oxen could cultivate 360,000 jugera of land, which is presumably roughly the size of Isidorus' estate; a slave could cultivate between 15 and 20 jugera.

Literature: Oost 1958; Brunt 1975.

> From later years, we know of many men who were freed from slavery and were wealthier than Sulla or Crassus. Little before our own time, when Claudius was emperor, there were three at the same time: Callistus, Pallas, and Narcissus.[228] So that we might avoid talking about those (as if they were still powerful), there is Gaius Caecilius Isidorus, freedman of Gaius. In the consulship of Gaius Asinius Gallus and Gaius Marcius Censorinus,[229] on the sixth day before the Calends of February, he declared in his will that, although he had lost much at the civil war, he nevertheless left 4116 slaves, 3600 pairs of oxen, 257,000 heads of other livestock, 60 million sesterces in cash, and instructed that 1,100,000 sesterces be spent on his funeral.

---

[227] Latin text: Rackham et al. 1938–63.
[228] These were imperial freedmen.
[229] In 8 BCE.

- What kind of freedmen were Pallas or Narcissus (cf. 12.14)? How did they manage to become so rich?

- Does Isidorus belong to the same category? How do you imagine that he managed to become so wealthy?

- What are the implications for the operation of Roman slavery of a freedman owning thousands of slaves?

- How much land could Isidorus' slaves cultivate? Would all of them be employed in land cultivation?

- Could Isidorus cultivate all of his lands solely with his own slaves? If not, how did he do it? What does this imply about labor strategies in land cultivation?

SLAVING STRATEGIES

12.16 Suetonius, *On Grammarians*, 21: Latin Biography (Early Second Century CE)

Literature: Christes 1979.

Gaius Melissus, a native of Spoletium, was freeborn, but because of a disagreement between his parents, he was exposed. Thanks to the care and attentiveness of the man who reared him (*educator*), he received a superior education and was given as a gift to Maecenas[230] to work as a grammarian. As he could see that Maecenas appreciated him and treated him as a friend, although his mother tried to assert his freedom, he nonetheless remained in slavery; he valued more his current condition than his true origins. In consequence, he was soon manumitted and even ingratiated himself with Augustus. On the latter's instruction, he undertook the task to organize the library in the Portico of Octavia. In addition, as he himself writes, in his 60th year he began to compose books on *Trifles*, now titled *Jests*. He completed 150 of those and later added other books, of a different character. He even invented a new type of *fabulae togatae*, which he named *fabulae trabeatae*.[231]

- How did Melissus become a slave? Cf. 9.9–10.

- Why did he choose to remain a slave?

- What was his profession?

- Why did Romans leave such positions to slaves? What was the situation among the Greeks? Cf. 8.28.

---

[230] An extremely wealthy and powerful man, patron of many poets, including Virgil and Horace.
[231] *Fabulae togatae* were Latin theatre plays, mainly comedies, with a Roman setting; the name of *fabulae trabeatae* suggests that their protagonists were Roman equestrians.

12.17 Pliny the Elder, *Natural History*, 35.20, 77:[232] Latin Encyclopedic Work (First Century CE)

Literature: Harris 2015; Grawehr 2019.

> 77. Under Pamphilus' authority,[233] it came about, first in Sikyon, later in the whole of Greece, that freeborn boys were given lessons in drawing on wooden panels, which had been omitted previously, and thus this art was received into the first rank of the arts considered suitable for the free (*artes liberales*). It had always enjoyed the honor of being practiced by freeborn men, and soon afterwards by men of rank, while it had always been forbidden to slaves to be instructed in it. This is why there are no celebrated works of this art, nor of relief making, made by someone who has been a slave.
>
> 20. Later,[234] painting was not seen as an art suitable for men of rank, unless one wishes to mention Turpilius, a Roman citizen of the equestrian rank from Venetia, of our own generation, for his beautiful works still surviving at Verona.

- What was the status of painting and painters among late classical and Hellenistic Greeks?

- What was the status of painting and painters among Romans?

- What was the role of slavery in explaining these differences? Cf. 4.22, 12.31.

12.18 Tacitus, *Germania*, 24–5: Latin Ethnography (Early Second Century CE)

Literature: Thompson 1957; Lenski 2008; Rio 2012.

> [...] Amazingly, the German tribes play at dice when sober, classifying it among serious activities. They do so with such abandon in winning and losing that when they have lost everything, they gamble their freedom and their person in one last, extraordinary throw. The loser enters slavery voluntarily. Even if he is a younger man or a stronger man, he submits to being bound and sold. Such is their perverse stubbornness in the matter; they themselves call it a matter of trustworthiness. Slaves of this type they hand over through trade, so as to absolve themselves of the shame of their victory.
>
> The other slaves they do not employ, as is our custom, for duties within the household. Each slave has his own place, each governs his own hearth.

---

[232] Latin text: Rackham et al. 1938–63.

[233] A fourth-century-BCE painter from Amphipolis, in Macedonia, who worked mostly in Sikyon, in the northern Peloponnese.

[234] After Pacuvius, a distinguished Latin playwright and painter of the second century BCE.

The master exacts from him a certain amount of grain, or livestock or cloth, like from a tenant (*colonus*), and the slave complies to this extent. The other duties in the master's house are done by his wife and children. Rarely do they whip slaves or punish them by chaining them or with hard labor. They tend to kill slaves not in order to inflict a harsh punishment but in a fit of anger, like an enemy, but there is no punishment. Freedmen are not very superior to slaves. They rarely have power in the household and have none in the state, except among those tribes which are ruled by a king. There, they rise above the freeborn and even above the nobility. In the other communities, the weakness of freedmen is an assertion of the power of freedom.

- For what reasons do Germans become enslaved, according to Tacitus?

- How do Germans use slaves, according to the passage? Why so?

- How do German slaves, as Tacitus presents them, compare with Spartan helots? Cf. 1.3–9.

- What is the position of freedmen in Germany?

- Why are freedmen more important in tribes ruled by kings? Why does the inferiority of freedmen mark the freedom of the state?

- Is this depiction of German slavery merely a mirror image of Roman slavery? What is Tacitus' authorial agenda?

- Can we learn anything useful about Roman slavery from this passage?

12.19 Longus, *Daphnis and Chloe*, 3.30–31, 4.1, 4.5–9:[235] Greek Novel (Second/Third Century CE)

In the countryside of Mytilene, on the island of Lesbos, Lamon and Myrtale, a slave couple, found many years ago an exposed baby boy, Daphnis, while a neighboring free couple, Dryas and Nape, found an exposed baby girl, Chloe. Daphnis and Chloe have grown up together and ultimately fall in love; Daphnis has miraculously found a large amount of money, which enables him to ask Chloe's parents for her hand, offering the money as a gift, while asking them to say nothing to his parents about the money.

Literature: Bowie 2019.

When Dryas and Nape saw all this money, which they didn't expect, they immediately started to promise that they would give Chloe to him and that they would convince Lamon. Now, Nape remained there and with the help of Daphnis was driving around the oxen with the threshing boards for the threshing. Dryas stored the purse where Chloe's recognition tokens had been

---

[235] Greek text: Reeve 1982.

put and quickly went to Lamon and Myrtale, aiming to do an extraordinary thing: to ask for their son's hand in marriage! He found them measuring barley that they had just been winnowing. They were downcast, as the measured barley was nearly less than the seeds they had sown. Dryas tried to console them, pointing out that the famine had been affecting everyone everywhere. Then he started to ask for Daphnis to be married to Chloe, saying that, while other suitors were offering many gifts, he would accept nothing from Lamon and Nape but would even give them something from his own possessions. For Chloe and Daphnis had grown up together and, when herding their flocks, had bonded in a friendship which could not be broken easily. And they were now of an age that they could go to bed together. Dryas then continued saying such things, since, if he convinced them, the 3000 drachmas would become his prize. Lamon now, no longer able to use poverty as an excuse, since Dryas and his family were not looking down upon them, nor Daphnis' age, since he was already a young lad, did not tell the truth, namely that Daphnis deserved a superior match, but, after remaining silent for a while, gave the following answer.

"You are right to value neighbors over strangers and not to consider wealth superior to poverty matched with virtue. May Pan and the Nymphs love you for this. I, too, am eager for this marriage to take place. For I am almost an old man already and in need of more working hands. So, I'd be mad not to have your own household becoming related to my own – a great asset. Chloe, too, is a sought-after bride – a beautiful girl, in her prime, and good in all respects. However, since I am a slave and not at all in authority of my own affairs, I need to inform and get the consent of my master. So, let us postpone the wedding until the autumn. Those who come here from the city say that the master will come then. Daphnis and Chloe can become husband and wife then. Now, they can love each other like siblings. But, Dryas, there is one thing you should know: you are eager for a lad who is superior to us." Lamon said as much and then kissed Dryas and offered him a drink, as it was now high noon. Then he walked with him some of the way home, always treating him as a friend. [...]

A few weeks later...

One of Lamon's fellow slaves came from the city of Mytilene and announced that the master would arrive a bit before the grape harvest. He wished to check whether the attack from the sea of the men from Methymna had caused any damage to the fields. As the summer was ending and autumn was arriving, Lamon was turning his place into a site which was a pleasure to look at. He would be clearing the water springs, so that the water would be clean; removing the dung out of the courtyard, to get rid of the disturbing smell; tending the gardens, so that they would look beautiful. [...] Lamon kept urging Daphnis to fatten the goats as much as possible, saying that the master would definitely see them, since he had not visited for such a long time. Daphnis was optimistic that he would receive praise for them. He had doubled their number, not one of them had been snatched by a wolf, and they had become fatter than the sheep. And wishing to make the master look more positively towards his marriage, he offered the goats every care and attention. He would take them out to graze very early in the morning and would drive them back early in the evening. He would water them twice a day. He would look for the best pasture land. He also made sure he got new troughs, many milk pails, and bigger baskets. He tended the goats so carefully that he would even polish their horns and tend to their hair. [...]

They were thus occupied when a second messenger arrived from the city. He gave them orders to finish the grape harvest as soon as possible. He himself would stay there until the grapes had been turned into must. Then he would return to the city to fetch their master – after the end of the vine harvest, that is. This Eudromos – for that was his name – they welcomed as warmly as they could. At the same time, they would take the grapes to the presses, then they would place the must into the jars. But they left the green bunches on the vines, so that when the city visitors came they could experience the spectacle and pleasure of the grape harvest.

When Eudromos was about to return to the city, Daphnis gave him many gifts but principally produce of his flocks of goats: well-ripen cheeses, a kid born late in the year, a goat fleece, white and thick, to have for his winter errands. Eudromos was very pleased and kissed Daphnis and gave promises to put in a good word for him to the master. So, he went away, thinking of Daphnis as his friend, while Daphnis continued tending his flocks together with Chloe but in agony. She, too, was in great fear. For he was a young lad, used to looking only at goats, the mountain, farmers, and Chloe, and now he was about to meet his master, whom he knew only by name before. So, she was anxious for Daphnis and how his meeting with his master would go, and her heart was very troubled, lest their dreams about marriage would never come true. So, their kisses were continuous and their embraces so tight as if they were one body, but at the same time timid and glum, as if the master were already there, and they were in fear of him and wanting to escape his notice. On top of this, a great trouble befell them.

There was one Lampis, an arrogant cow-man. He, too, was one of the men who asked Dryas for Chloe's hand and, eager for the match, had already given many gifts. When he realized that, if his master consented, Daphnis would take Chloe as his wife, he was looking for some scheme to turn the master against them. As he knew that the master took great pleasure in the garden, he decided to make a mess of it and ruin it as much as he could. He did not dare to cut the trees, for fear that he would be caught because of the noise. So, he attacked the flowerbeds, wishing to ruin them. He waited until the night and then jumped over the wall. Some beds he dug up; others he broke up; the rest he trampled upon like a pig. Then he left, without anyone noticing him. The next day, Lamon went to the garden, wanting to channel to the flowers water from the spring. When he saw the place ruined, as if by an enemy and not by a robber, he immediately tore off his tunic and with a loud cry called upon the gods. Myrtale dropped what she was doing and ran to him, and Daphnis left his goats and hurried there. When they saw it, they started to utter loud cries, and as they cried, they wept, and their grief was a novel kind of grief: grief for flowers. They were weeping in fear of their master, but even a stranger would have wept if he had been present. The whole place had been defaced. [...] Lamon was even saying the following, in his shock: "Oh, poor rose-bed! How you have been broken down. Oh, my poor violets, so trampled! Oh, poor hyacinths and narcissi, dug up by a wicked man. Spring will come, but they will not blossom. Summer will come, but they will not flourish. Another autumn will come, but they will garland no one. And you, lord Dionysus, didn't you pity these poor flowers, beside which you used to live and which you used to look at and by which I garlanded you many times? How can I now show the garden to the master? How will he react when he sees it? He will have me hanged, me an old man, on a pine tree, like Marsyas. And probably Daphnis, too, if he thinks that his goats did this."

They were now weeping, shedding hot tears, lamenting no longer the flowers but their own lives. Chloe, too, was lamenting Daphnis, mourning over the prospect that he might be hanged. She continuously prayed that their master may not come again and her days were miserable, as if Daphnis was already being whipped in front of her eyes. Night was already falling when Eudromos told them that the elder master would arrive in three days, while his son would come ahead of him, on the following day. So, they reviewed what had happened, sharing it with Eudromos, and asked him for his opinion. As he was fond of Daphnis, he urged them to admit what had happened to the young master first. He also promised to help them – the young master held him in esteem, as they had been nursed by the same woman. And when the new day came, they did what they had decided.

- Is the master of Daphnis a resident landowner or not? How does this shape the working conditions of his slaves? What slaving strategies are evident in this passage? Cf. 9.23.

- Compare the working conditions of these slaves with those in 1.3–9 and 12.18. How should we explain any similarities or differences?

- What is the status of Chloe? How is her marriage with Daphnis portrayed? Would she have been able to marry him in all ancient societies? Cf. 12.26.

- How do the slaves try to deal with the problem of the ruined garden? What can we learn about slave communities from this?

12.20 Ps.-Aristotle, *On Marvellous Things Heard*, 837a–b: Greek Paradoxographical Collection (Hellenistic or Roman Imperial Period)

In the islands called Gymnesiai,[236] near Iberia, [...] oil is said not to come from olive trees but from the terebinth; the produce is most similar to ours and shares all its characteristics. They also say that the Iberians who inhabit these islands are such womanizers that they give to merchants four or five male slaves in exchange for a female one. And when they join the Carthaginian army, they apparently buy nothing else but women with the money paid

---

[236] The Balearic islands.

to them. It is forbidden to all on the islands to have gold or silver. There is an additional story concerning the prohibition of bringing money onto the islands. It is along the following lines: Herakles made the expedition against Iberia because of the wealth of its inhabitants.

- What is the primary slaving strategy employed by these Iberians?
- What consequences does this have for the slave system of these islands?

12.21 Attitudes to Slave Reproduction

Literature: Bradley 1984: 47–80; Klees 1998: 155–60.

12.21.a Xenophon, *Oeconomicus*, 9.5: Greek Treatise on Household Management (First Half of Fourth Century BCE)

And I showed to my wife the women's quarter, separated from the men's quarter by a bolted door, so that nothing might be taken out which should not be and that the slaves might not conceive children without our consent. For those who are good generally show more goodwill if they bear children, but those who are wicked become readier to do evil when they have a partner.

12.21.b Columella, *On Rural Affairs*, 1.8.19:[237] Latin Agricultural Treatise (First Century CE)

To women of high fertility, who should be rewarded for a certain number of offspring, we granted relief from work and, occasionally, their freedom, too, after they had reared many children. She who had three sons attained relief from work; she who had more her freedom, too. Such justice and care on the part of the head of the household (*pater familias*) will much contribute to the increase of his patrimony.

- Does Xenophon consider slave procreation desirable under all circumstances?
- What kind of slave surveillance does Xenophon advise?
- How does Columella approach slave procreation?
- What incentives does Columella give to fertile slaves?

---

[237] Latin text: Ash, Forster, and Heffer 1941–55.

- Why does parenthood make good slaves better and bad slaves worse? What can we learn about slave communities from this?

- Do Xenophon and Columella talk about the same kind of slaves? What difference might the size of slaveholdings make to attitudes to procreation?

- Do Xenophon and Columella discuss the same issue, or do they emphasize different aspects of the same issue?

- Can we use these passages as evidence for different Greek and Roman attitudes to slave procreation?

MASTERS AND SLAVES

12.22 Isaeus, *On the Estate of Philoktemon*, 19–23: Greek Law-Court Speech, Athens (First Half of Fourth Century BCE)

Athenian fathers would enroll their legitimate male children (that is, those born to them from their married wives, who, after 451 BCE, had to be Athenian citizens for the children to be eligible for citizenship) to their phratry. Thus, phratry membership was a mark of both legitimacy and Athenian citizenship. Admission to a phratry was marked by the phratry members' taking a portion of meat from the sacrifice offered by the father on the occasion; rejection of membership was demonstrated by leading the sacrificial victim away from the altar. Athenian women and men could enter into second marriage after divorce or after the death of their first spouse. All legitimate sons, of all marriages, had an equal share to their fathers' property.

Literature: Vlassopoulos 2009; Glazebrook 2014.

Euktemon had a freedwoman, men of the jury, who ran a tenement house of his in the Piraeus and kept prostitutes. As one of these she acquired one called Alke, whom, I think, many of you know. This Alke, after her purchase, worked for many years as a prostitute, but as soon as she became older, she gave it up. While she was living at the tenement house, she was with a freedman – his name was Dion – who she said was the father of these lads. And Dion brought them up as his own. Some time later, Dion, who had committed some offense and feared for his person, retired to Sikyon. Euktemon then set up this woman, Alke, to manage his tenement house at Kerameikos, the one by the gate where wine is sold. After she was established there, men of the jury, she became the cause of many evils.

Every time Euktemon came for the rent, he would stay about and spend most of his time at the tenement house. Sometimes he would abandon his wife and children and the house he lived in and even take his meals with the woman. Despite the angry protests of his wife and sons, not only did he not stop, but in the end he used to live there all the time. And he got into such a condition, either from drugs or from illness or from something else, that he was persuaded by her to enroll the oldest of her two sons to his phratry under his own name. But when his son Philoktemon refused to acquiesce and his phratry members did not admit the boy and the sacrificial victim was led away from the altar, Euktemon, extremely angry at his son and wishing to spite him, arranged to marry a sister of Demokrates of Aphidnai, so as to

produce children by her and introduce them into his family unless Philoktemon accepted to allow this man to be enrolled. His kin, knowing that, given
his age, Euktemon would not be able to father children, but children would
be produced in some other way, and even greater disputes would be caused
from this, advised Philoktemon to allow Euktemon to enroll this lad on Euktemon's terms and to give him one farm.

- Who are Alke and Dion? How are they related?
- How does Alke relate to Euktemon?
- What was Alke's strategy? Was it successful?
- How does the author portray Euktemon and the introduction of Alke's son to the phratry? Was this lawful?
- Do you trust the speaker's representation of events?
- What can we learn about master–slave and free–slave relationships in classical Athens from this passage?

12.23 Philostratus, *Lives of the Sophists*, 516–8: Greek Biography (First Half of Third Century CE)

Philostratus focuses here on Scopelianus of Klazomenai, in Asia Minor – a sophist
active in the late first and early second century CE.

The reasons why Scopelianus' father ended up treating him harshly, whereas
before he was gentle and calm toward him, are given in many versions – "it
was because of this," "it was because of that," "the reasons were more than
one" – but I will present the one which is closest to the truth. After Scopelianus' mother, the old man went about introducing to his home a woman
whom he had not exactly wedded – not according to the laws. Seeing this,
Scopelianus tried to talk some sense into him and deter him; this, however, is
displeasing to old men. On her part, the woman was putting together a story
against Scopelianus, alleging that he was in love with her but could not stand
that he had utterly failed. A slave cook of the old man, Kytheros by name,
was assisting her in her slanders, by fawning discreetly on his master, exactly
like in a play, and saying things of this sort: "Master, your son wishes you
were already dead. And he doesn't trust old age with your death, it to happen naturally and not before long, but he is plotting it himself, attempting
to hire the help of my own hands, too. He has in his possession lethal drags
for you, and he keeps ordering me to put the most powerful of these in one
of your dishes. If I do as he says, he promises me my freedom, together with
farms, houses, money, and anything I might want from your household; if
I don't, he threatens me with whipping, torture, heavy chains and grievous
pillory." With such fawning he got round his master, and so when, soon after, the master was dying and got down to writing a will, he was appointed
heir, and on top called the old man's "son," his "eyes," his "whole soul." We

should not be surprised that he managed to enchant a man who was old and, possibly, also somewhat unstable, because of his old age and the very fact he was in love – for not even young men keep their good sense when in love; rather, that he appeared to be superior even to Scopelianus' powerful skill and vigor in the law courts. He contended against him in court over the will and used Scopelianus' wealth to outmatch Scopelianus' powerful skill. By drawing from the estate and using enormous sums of money to buy every tongue and the votes of the judges, he gained victory on all fronts. Hence, Scopelianus used to say that Anaxagoras' land had become a sheep pasture, whereas his had become a slave pasture.[238] Kytheros became prominent in public life, too, but when he was turning old, he saw his property underproducing and started to be the object of substantial contempt. In fact, once he was even beaten up by a man of whom he demanded money. So, he went to Scopelianus as a suppliant and begged him to let go of his anger, forget past wrongs, and take back his father's property. But he asked him to leave him a part of the house, since that was large anyway, so that he wouldn't have to live as a slave, together with two of the coastal farms. And to this day, that part of the house in which Kytheros lived until he died is called "the house of Kytheros."

- Who is Kytheros? How does he relate to Scopelianus and his father?

- How does the story of Kytheros compare with the story of Alke? What strategies did they each follow?

- Was it legal for Kytheros to inherit the property of his master? Would that have been legally possible in classical Athens?

- What was Kytheros' position in the society of Roman Klazomenai after he inherited his former master's wealth? Was that possible in classical Athens?

- In what ways did Kytheros' former slave status affect his decisions in his old age? Would the situation be necessarily different in classical Athens?

- What similarities and differences do the stories of Alke and Kytheros show?

12.24 *CIL* XIV, 2298: Latin Funerary Verse Inscription, Ariccia, Italy (First Century CE)

Marcus Aurelius Cotta Maximus Messalinus was a Roman senator, friend of the emperors Augustus and Tiberius.

Literature: Kleijwegt 2006c; Landrea 2016.

Marcus Aurelius Zosimus, freedman of Cotta Maximus, attendant (*accensus*) of his patron.

---

[238] The philosopher Anaxagoras (fifth century BCE), who, like Scopelianus, was from Klazomenai, was notorious for not looking after his patrimony and allowing the land he inherited to become grazing land.

I was a freedman, I admit. But as reading this will show, my shadow has been ennobled by my patron Cotta. Several times did he give me funds worth the equestrian census, willingly. He ordered that my children be raised, and he provided for them. And he always entrusted his wealth to me. He himself gave dowries to my daughters like a father. And for my son Cottanus, he secured the rank of military tribune, which he worthily held in Caesar's army. What did Cotta not offer? Cotta, who now, in sorrow, offered even these verses, to be looked at on my tomb. Aurelia Saturnina, (wife?) of Zosimus.

- What do we learn about the freedman Zosimus from this inscription?
- How is the relationship between Zosimus and his patron presented in this inscription?
- Why would a master, then patron, offer so much to a slave, then freedman, of his?
- Whose voice do we hear here? Zosimus' or his patron's?
- Does this inscription create honor for Zosimus, for his patron, or for both? How?

12.25 *CIL* VI, 23770a: Latin Funerary Inscription, Rome (First Century BCE)

Literature: Laubry 2016.

Marcus Papinius Zibax, freedman of Quintus <and> Marcus, still alive, gives this site for himself, and his freedmen and his fellow freedmen and fellow freedwomen: 12 feet in breadth by 12 feet in depth.

- What was Zibax's status?
- For which groups of people is this funeral monument intended? How are these people related to Zibax?
- What can we learn about Zibax from this monument?
- Why is this kind of monument a Roman peculiarity? What can it tell us about the differences between Roman and other ancient slaveries?

FREE AND SLAVE

12.26 *IC* IV 72 vi.56–vii.10: Inscribed Laws in Greek, Gortyn, Crete (Fifth Century BCE)

Literature: D. M. Lewis 2013, 2018: 147–65; Gagarin and Perlman 2016: 386–9; Vlassopoulos 2018a: 48–9.

[If a slave man] goes to a free woman and marries her, their children shall be free. If the free woman goes to the slave man, the children shall be slaves. If both free and slave children are born to the same mother, if the mother dies and there is property, the free children shall have it. If there are no free children, the next of kin shall take up the property.

- What determines the status of a child born to a free woman and a slave man according to the laws of Gortyn? What is the possible logic of this provision?

- Were mixed marriages allowed in all ancient societies? Cf. 11.22.a, 12.22–3.

- How do you imagine the consequences of a mother having both free and slave children or of slaves having freeborn relatives?

- How do the laws of Gortyn privilege free over slave children?

12.27 *I.Bouthrôtos*: Greek Inscriptions Recording Manumissions, Bouthrotos, Epeiros (After 163 BCE)

The inscriptions of Bouthrotos often record manumissions by groups of manumittors. This could reflect multiple ownership of a slave but more probably reflects the acquiescence of spouses, children, and relatives to the manumission of slaves; thus, the groups manumitting slaves are probably kinship groups.

Literature: Cabanes 1974: 206–7; Vlassopoulos 2018b.

a. (17.31–2): Eurymmas, Tauriskos, and Aristomachos (have manumitted) Sibylla and Antigonos.
b. (25.29–31): Eurymmas, Tauriskos, Aristomachos, and Sibylla (have manumitted) Euboula.
c. (25.10–12): Aristokles, Alexandros, Andriskos, Philista, and Megallis (have manumitted) Neaira.
d. (31.89–93): Aristokles, son of Alexandros, Philoumena, Megallis, Philista, Alexandros, Andriskos, Kleopatra, and Neaira (have manumitted) Stratonika.

- Who are the manumittors in a? How do they relate to the manumittors in b?

- Who are the manumittors in c? How do they relate to the manumittors in d?

- Are there links between the manumitted slaves in a and b and the manumittors in c and d, respectively?

- In what ways could we explain the presence of Sibylla and Neaira among the manumittors?

- Were such forms of incorporating manumitted slaves possible in all ancient societies? Cf. Kleijwegt 2006b.

12.28 Plutarch, *Roman Questions*, 287f–288a (= Question 101): Greek Antiquarian Work (Late First/Early Second Century CE)

Literature: Goette 1986; Williams 1995.

> **Question:** Why do the Romans adorn their boys' necks with amulets they call *bullae*?
>
> **Answer:** Was it perhaps, as so many other things, in honor of their abducted wives[239] that they voted that the children born to their wives should have the amulets? [...] Or is it because of the following reason? As comedies testify even today, desiring and loving slave boys in their prime was not considered unseemly or disgraceful among the men of old, but they were very strict about abstaining from free boys. So would free boys wear this badge, so as there might be no confusion if they met when naked? [...]

- What was the aim served by *bullae*, according to the second explanation?
- Why were Romans fond of pederastic relations with slaves but not with free boys?
- Did Greeks share the Roman distinction between sex with free and slave boys?
- Can this difference between Greeks and Romans tell us anything interesting about the role of slavery in their respective societies?

MANUMISSION AND FREEDPERSONS

12.29 Artemidorus, *The Interpretation of Dreams*, 1.45.22–25: Greek Dream Book (Second Century CE)

Roman freedmen received the *praenomen* and family name (*nomen*) of their masters and kept their slave name as their *cognomen*. Cf. 2.8.

Literature: Klees 1990; Kleijwegt 2006b; Thonemann 2020: 191–8.

> I know of someone who, when a slave, saw in his dream that he had three penises. He became free and had three names, instead of one: in addition to his own, he also took the two names of his manumittor.

- What are the implications of Roman freedpersons receiving the family name of their former masters? Cf. 12.2.

---

[239] According to this popular myth, Romulus and his men abducted and raped Sabine women, so that the children of these unions would populate the newly founded city of Rome.

- Did something like that exist in Greek societies? Cf. 2.3.b.
- Does this difference have any implications for freedpersons in the various ancient societies?

12.30 *CIL* XI, 137: Marble Sarcophagus with Latin Funerary Inscription, Ravenna, Italy (Late First Century BCE/Early First Century CE)

The sarcophagus sports to the right of the inscription a relief representation of Fortuna holding a cornucopia.

Literature: Gnoli 2005–8.

> Gaius Julius Mygdonius, a Parthian in origin,[240] born a free man, captured when young, given away to Roman territory. When I was made a Roman citizen by a helpful fate, I set up a chest[241] for when I would become 50 years old. Ever since youth, I sought to reach my old age. Now, stone, receive me willingly; with you I shall become released from cares.

- How would this man have been "given" away to Roman territory after his capture?
- In what circumstances could he have become a Roman citizen? Cf. 10.12–3.
- How do his identities as Parthian, former slave, and Roman citizen fit together?
- What can we learn about mobility and status change from this inscription? Is there something peculiarly Roman at work here?

12.31 Pliny the Elder, *Natural History*, 35.199–201:[242] Latin Encyclopedic Work (First Century CE)

The second group of slaves mentioned, all slaves of powerful Roman generals and politicians, became powerful themselves, especially after their manumission.

Literature: Mouritsen 2011: 93–118.

> Another type of chalk-like earth is called "silversmith's," as it is suitable for silver polishing. But the most inferior type of chalk is that which it was our ancestors' custom to use for drawing the finishing line in races in the circus and for marking the feet of slaves on sale when they had been brought from overseas. Instances are Publilius of Antioch, the founder of the mimic stage;

---

[240] The Parthian Empire was the main adversary of Rome between the first century BCE and the early third century CE.

[241] The Latin word *arca*, literally chest, can refer either to a money safe or to a coffin.

[242] Latin text: Rackham et al. 1938–63.

his relative Manilius Antiochus, the founder of astronomy; and, similarly, Staberius Eros, our first grammarian. Our forefathers saw these men being brought here on the same ship.

But why would one mention these men, recommended as they are by their honored scholarly achievements? Others seen on the slave dealer's platform were Chrysogonus, slave of Sulla; Amphio, slave of Quintus Catulus; Hector, slave of Lucius Lucullus; Demetrius, slave of Pompey; Auge, slave of Demetrius – although the same Auge is also thought to have belonged to Pompey –; Hipparchus, slave of Mark Antony; Menas and Menecrates, slaves of Sextus Pompeius; and others, whom this is not the occasion to enumerate and who became rich through the blood of Roman citizens and the license caused by the proscriptions.[243] This is the mark on these herds of slaves for sale and the disgrace of our own insolent fortune! We, too, have seen these men acquiring so much power that we have seen the honor of the praetorship bestowed upon them by decree of the Senate at the command of Agrippina, the wife of the emperor Claudius.[244] We even nearly saw them sent back with the rods of office decorated in laurels to the places from which they arrived here with feet marked with chalk!

- How does Pliny react to the phenomena of social mobility for slaves and freedmen that he mentions?

- What made possible the key role of slaves and freedmen in Roman literature and culture? Did slaves and freedmen have an equivalent role in other ancient societies? Cf. 8.28, 12.16.

- What made possible the key role of slaves and freedmen of Roman emperors and grandees (cf. 6.27)? Did slaves and freedmen have an equivalent role in other ancient societies?

THE FORMATION OF SLAVE COMMUNITIES

12.32 The Compitalia

Literature: Hasenohr 2003, 2007, 2017; North 2012; Zelnick-Abramovitz 2012; Tran 2014; Fischer 2017; Flower 2017; Padilla Peralta 2017.

—— 12.32.a Athenaeus, *The Learned Banqueters*, 14.639b–d: Greek —— Antiquarian Treatise (End of Second Century CE)

"Kronia," the name of a Greek festival in honor of the god Kronos, is used here for the Roman Saturnalia. The age of Kronos was imagined as a primeval time of bliss.

---

[243] On the proscriptions, see 4.17, 5.25, 6.25.
[244] Probably an exaggerated reference to a decree bestowing such distinction upon one imperial freedman, Pallas.

When Masurius had completed his long speech, what is known as "second tables" were brought around for us. These are offered to us often – not only during the Kronia, when it is the custom among the Romans to offer a meal to their slaves, while taking upon themselves to do the services otherwise offered to them by their slaves. This is a Greek custom. In Crete, for example, at the festival of the Hermaia, something similar happens, as says Carystius in his *Historical Commentaries*. The slaves feast while the masters attend to them and serve them. So, too, in Troezen, in the month of Geraistios. A festival takes place then, which lasts many days. On one of these, the slaves play knucklebones together with the citizens, and the masters offer a feast to their slaves, as the same Carystius mentions. Berosos, in the first book of his *History of Babylon*, says that in the month of Loos, starting on the 16th, a festival takes place in Babylon which is called Sakaia and lasts five days. During this time, it is the custom that the masters be ruled by their slaves; one slave, dressed in a robe which resembles that of a king, is in control of the house; this slave is called "zoganes." Ctesias, too, in the second book of his *Persian History*, mentions this festival. The people of Kos, however, do the opposite, as is related by Macareus in the third book of his *History of Kos*. Specifically, when they perform sacrifices in honor of Hera, the slaves do not participate in the feast. This is why Phylarchus says: "†..........† free men alone perform the rites to men †...........† to whom belongs the day of freedom; no slave at all enters – not even for a moment."

- What forms of role reversal between masters and slaves are described in the passage?

- In what ways does the festival on Kos differ from the others mentioned?

- What do you think is the meaning and purpose of these festivals? Cf. 3.29, 12.32.c.

───────   12.32.b Festus, *On the Meaning of Words*, 273.7: Latin   ───────
Lexicographical Work (Second Century CE)

Balls and effigies of men and women, made of wool, were hung up at the crossroad shrines at the Compitalia, because they considered that day a feast in honor of the gods of the underworld, whom they call Lares. For these, they placed as many balls as there were slaves and as many effigies as there were free people, so that the Lares spare the living and be content with these balls and likenesses.

- How are free people represented in the rituals of the Compitalia? How are slaves represented?

- Why are both slave and free represented, and what is the meaning of the difference in their representation?

——— 12.32.c Dionysius of Halicarnassus, *Roman Archaeology,* ———
4.14.3–4: Greek Historiography (First Century BCE)

In this passage, Dionysius is commenting on the reforms of the Roman king Servius in the sixth century BCE (cf. 6.23, 10.12).

> Then, Servius commanded that shrines should be erected in all narrow lanes by the inhabitants of the neighborhood in honor of the heroes whose statues stood in front of the houses. He also made a law that a sacrifice to them should take place every year, every family offering a cake. He ordered not the free but the slaves to be the ones present at and contributing to the performance of the rites – those at the neighborhood shrines in front of the houses – together with those celebrating them, for the ministry of servants is pleasing to the heroes.[245] The Romans celebrated this festival until our own time most solemnly and sumptuously a few days after the festival of the Kronia. They called it "Compitalia" on account of the narrow lanes, for they call narrow lanes *compiti*.[246] And they preserve the ancient custom in relation to the rites, propitiating the heroes through their servants. On the days of the festival, they remove every mark of slavery from them. This humane gesture of the masters, which has an element of grandeur and solemnity, tames the wild element in the slaves, so that they might be more agreeable and grateful to their masters and less grieved by the burdens of their fortune.

- What role do slaves play in the celebration of the Compitalia? How does their role in the festival compare with their representation as described in 12.32.b?
- How does Dionysius explain this? How credible do you find his explanation?
- Is Dionysius surprised by this Roman practice? If so, why?

——— 12.32.d *ID* 1760: Greek Dedicatory Inscription, Delos, ———
Cyclades (100–98 BCE)

The international port of Delos had a strong Italian presence, including a large number of freedmen and slaves (cf. 2.14–5, 7.21, 8.1, 8.19, 12.2). The Italians formed their own associations, which took care of their cults and celebrated festivals like the Compitalia. The names of the Competaliasts (i.e. the men organizing and celebrating the Compitalia) are Greek, and the *praenomina* and *nomina* of their masters are Italic and Latin.

> Damas, (slave) of Manius Clovius
> Thraseas, (slave) of Quintus and Publius Samiarius

---
[245] i.e. the Lares Compitales.
[246] The Latin word *compitus* (or, more commonly, *compitum*) means "crossroads," not "narrow lane," as claimed by Dionysius.

Agathokles, (slave) of Lucius Paconius
Alexandros, (slave) of Lucius Babullius
Aulus Apollodoros, (freedman) of Decimus Atanius
Xenon, (slave) of Lucius and Marcus Mondicius
Stephanos, (slave) of Quintus [...]
Damonikos, (slave) of Quintus Maecius
Antiochos, (slave) of Titus Crepereius
Tryphon, (slave) of Lucius Audius.
Upon becoming Competaliasts, the aforementioned dedicated this in the
year when Theodosios was magistrate.

- How are these people described? Can we determine their status? Compare with 12.2.

- What post did these people fill (compare with 7.26–7)? How does this compare with what we know about the Compitalia?

- Judging from the names, what is the origin of these people? What are the implications of the fact that they are organizing a Roman festival in the Greek city of Delos?

——— 12.32.e Fresco from the House of Sutoria Primigenia, ———
Pompeii, Italy (First Century CE)

Figure 22 Fresco from the House of Sutoria Primigenia, Pompeii, first century CE: reproduced with permission from Flower 2017, Plate 9; su concessione del Ministero della Cultura – Parco Archeologico di Pompeii.

Apart from the crossroad cult of the Lares, there were also cults and shrines dedicated to them within Roman and Italian houses. This fresco (Fig. 22) decorated the kitchen of the house. Images of the Lares frame the scene.

Literature: Joshel and Petersen 2014: 24–86.

- Apart from the Lares, how many other figures are represented in this scene?
- Do they all have the same size? Can this help us identify the figures? Can any of them be identified as slaves? Cf. 2.10.
- In which room is this scene painted? Which household members were likely to use this room? What significance, if any, might this have?
- How does this depiction relate to the participation of slaves in the cult of Lares? Cf. 12.32.b, 12.32.c.
- What can we learn about slave communities from this scene?

12.33 *TAM* V.1 71: **Greek Funerary Inscription, Silandos, Lydia (Second Century** CE**)**

In the following Greek funerary inscription and in many other Greek inscriptions, the Latin words *collegium* (a word used to denote a magisterial or priestly or, as here, a private association of persons) and *familia* (literally "family," which is variably used in Latin for the nuclear or the extended family or a lineage, or for the whole household of a *paterfamilias*, or for his slaves only) appear in Hellenized forms. For the word "hero" in Greek funerary inscriptions, see 7.11.

Literature: Flory 1978; Zoumbaki 2005.

> The *collegium* of the *familia* of Gaius Julius Quadratus, based in Theseus' Thermai, a village in Mokaddene, honored Epitynchanon, hero, eight years old, as his father Epitynchanon and his mother Soteris had made provisions.

- What group has created this inscription? How do they define themselves?
- What is the significance of the terms *collegium* and *familia*? Why are these Latin terms used in a Greek inscription? What conclusions can we draw from this?
- Who is the deceased? How can we reconstruct his life on the basis of this inscription?
- What are the implications of the fact that this slave community uses the term "honor" for one of its members? How does this relate to Patterson's view of slaves as "socially dishonored persons"? Cf. 1.11–18.
- What can we learn about slave communities on the basis of this inscription?

12.34 *SEG* XLVI 1475: Greek Honorific Inscription, Miletos, Ionia (First–Third Century ᴄᴇ)

For the term *familia*, see under 12.33.

Literature: Flory 1978.

> Tiberius Julius Frugi Damianus, son of Titus Damianus, high priest of Asia,[247] of the tribe Cornelia; the *familia* (honors) its own master.

- Who is the honoree?
- Who have erected this honorific inscription?
- Why do the slaves use a Latin term to describe themselves?
- How does this inscription relate to 12.33?
- What conclusions about the formation of slave communities can we draw from this document?

---

[247] The term refers to the priesthood of the imperial cult of the province of Asia, a very prestigious position.

Bibliography

Acton, P. (2014) *Poiesis: Manufacturing in Classical Athens*. Oxford.

Akrigg, B. and Tordoff, R. (eds.) (2013) *Slaves and Slavery in Ancient Greek Comic Drama*. Cambridge.

Alexianu, M. (2011) "Lexicographers, paroemiographers and slaves-for-salt barter in ancient Thrace," *Phoenix*, 65, 389–94.

Alvar Nuño, A. (2016) "Le malheur de Politoria: sur la malédiction d'une esclave contre sa matrone," in Dondin-Payre and Tran (2016), 101–11.

Anastasiadis, V. I. and Doukellis, P. N. (eds.) (2005) *Esclavage antique et discriminations socioculturelles*. Bern.

Andreau, J. (2009) "Freedmen in the *Satyrica*," in J. R. Prag and I. D. Repath (eds.), *Petronius: A Handbook*, Chichester and Malden, MA, 114–24.

Andreau, J. and Descat, R. (2011) *The Slave in Greece and Rome*. Madison, WI and London.

Annequin, J. (1987) "Les esclaves rêvent aussi... Remarques sur *La clé des songes* d'Artémidore," *Dialogues d'histoire ancienne*, 13, 71–113.

Annequin, J. (2005) "L'autre corps du maître: les représentations oniriques dans l'*Onirocriticon* d'Artémidore de Daldis," in Anastasiadis and Doukellis (2005), 305–13.

Annequin, J. and Garrido-Hory, M. (eds.) (1994) *Religion et anthropologie de l'esclavage et des formes de dépendance*. Besançon.

Arnaoutoglou, I. (2007) "Fear of slaves in ancient Greek legal texts," in Serghidou (2007), 133–44.

Ash, H. B., Forster, E. S. and Heffer, E. H. (1941–55) *Columella On Agriculture*. 3 vols. Cambridge, MA.

Astin, A. E. (1978) *Cato the Censor*. Oxford.

Aubert, J.-J. (1993) "Workshop managers," in W. V. Harris (ed.), *The Inscribed Economy: Production and Distribution in the Roman Empire in the Light of instrumentum domesticum*, Ann Arbor, MI, 171–81.

Aubert, J.-J. (1994) *Business Managers in Ancient Rome: A Social and Economic Study of Institores, 200 BC-AD 250*. Leiden.

Greek and Roman Slaveries, First Edition. Eftychia Bathrellou and Kostas Vlassopoulos.
© 2022 John Wiley & Sons, Inc. Published 2022 by John Wiley & Sons, Inc.

Aubert, J.-J. (2009) "Productive investments in agriculture: *instrumentum fundi* and *peculium* in the later Roman Republic," in J. Carlsen and E. Lo Cascio (eds.), *Agricoltura e scambi nell'Italia tardo-repubblicana*, Bari, 167–85.

Avidov, A. (1997) "Were the Cilicians a nation of pirates?" *Mediterranean Historical Review*, 12, 5–55.

Bäbler, B. (1998) *Fleißige Thrakerinnen und wehrhafte Skythen. Nichtgriechen im klassischen Athen und ihre archäologische Hinterlassenschaft*. Stuttgart and Leipzig.

Backhuys, T. (2017) "Ammenvertrag aus der Zeit des Tiberius und unbestimmter Text in Buchschrift: *P.Sorb.* inv. 2129 + *P.Lips.* inv. 162. Mit einer Neuedition von *P.Rein.* II 103 = *C.Pap.Gr.* I 14. 201," *ZPE*, 201, 219–31.

Bagnall, R. (1993) "Slavery and society in Late Roman Egypt," in B. Halpern and D. Hobson (eds.), *Law, Politics and Society in the Ancient Mediterranean World*, Sheffield, 220–40.

Bathrellou, E. (2012) "Slave networks in Menander," in A. El-Nahas (ed.), *Festschrift in Honour of Prof. Ahmed Etman*, Cairo, 141–58.

Bathrellou, E. (2014) "Relationships among slaves in Menander," in A. H. Sommerstein (ed.), *Menander in Contexts*, New York and London, 40–57.

Beavis, M. A. (2020) "Six years a slave: The *Confessio* of St Patrick as early Christian slave narrative", *Irish Theological Quarterly*, 85, 339–51.

Bellemore, J. (1995) "Cato the Younger in the East in 66 BC," *Historia*, 44, 376–9.

Bellen, H. (1971) *Studien zur Sklavenflucht im römischen Kaiserreich*. Stuttgart.

Bellen, H. (1982) "Antike Staatsräson. Die Hinrichtung der 400 Sklaven des römischen Stadtpräfekten L. Pedanius Secundus im Jahre 61 n. Chr.," *Gymnasium*, 89, 449–67.

Bellen, H. and Heinen, H. (eds.) (2001) *Fünfzig Jahre Forschungen zur antiken Sklaverei an der Mainzer Akademie 1950–2000: Miscellanea zum Jubiläum*. Stuttgart.

Berlin, I. and Morgan, P. D. (eds.) (1991) *The Slaves' Economy: Independent Production by Slaves in the Americas*. London.

Bieżuńska-Małowist, I. (1974) *L'esclavage dans l'Égypte gréco-romaine. Première partie: période ptolémaïque*. Wroclaw.

Bieżuńska-Małowist, I. (1977) *L'esclavage dans l'Égypte gréco-romaine. Seconde partie: période romaine*. Wroclaw.

Billault, A. (2019) "Achilles Tatius, slaves and masters," in Panayotakis and Paschalis (2019), 95–106.

Binsfeld, A. and Ghetta, M. (eds.) (2019) *Ubi servi erant? Die Ikonographie von Sklaven und Freigelassenen in der römischen Kunst*. Stuttgart.

Biraud, M. and Zucker, A. (eds.) (2018) *The Letters of Alciphron: A Unified Literary Work?* Leiden and Boston, MA.

Birley, A. R. (1980) *The People of Roman Britain*. Berkeley and Los Angeles, CA.

Blanchard, A. (2013) *Ménandre: Le Héros, L'Arbitrage, La Tondue, La Fabula Incerta du Caire*. Paris.

Blake, S. (2013) "Now you see them: slaves and other objects as elements of the Roman master," *Helios*, 39, 193–211.

Bodel, J. (2004) "The organization of the funerary trade at Puteoli and Cumae," in *Libitina e dintorni: Atti dell'XI Rencontre franco-italienne sur l'epigraphie*, Rome, 147–72.

Bodel, J. (2005) "*Caveat emptor*: towards a study of Roman slave-traders," *JRA*, 18, 181–95.

Bodel, J. (2017) "Death and social death in ancient Rome," in Bodel and Scheidel (2017), 81–108.

Bodel, J. and Scheidel, W. (eds.) (2017) *On Human Bondage: After Slavery and Social Death*. Chichester.

Bömer, F. (1990) *Untersuchungen über die Religion der Sklaven in Griechenland und Rom. 3: Die wichtigsten Kulte der griechischen Welt*. 2nd edition. Wiesbaden.

Borbonus, D. (2014) *Columbarium Tombs and Collective Identity in Augustan Rome*. New York.

Bowersock, G. W. (2012) *Empires in Collision in Late Antiquity*. Waltham, MA.

Bowie, E. (2019) "Animals, slaves and masters in Longus' *Daphnis and Chloe*," in Panayotakis and Paschalis (2019), 107–26.

Bowman, A. and Thomas, J. D. (1994) *The Vindolanda Tablets*. London.

Boyce, B. (1991) *The Language of the Freedmen in Petronius' Cena Trimalchionis*. Leiden and New York.

Boyxen, B. (2018) *Fremde in der hellenistischen Polis Rhodos: zwischen Nähe und Distanz*. Berlin and Boston, MA.

Bradley, K. R. (1979) "Holidays for slaves," *Symbolae Osloenses*, 54, 111–18.

Bradley, K. R. (1984) *Slaves and Masters in the Roman Empire: A Study in Social Control*. New York.

Bradley, K. R. (1985) "The early development of slavery at Rome," *Historical Reflections / Réflexions Historiques*, 12, 1–8.

Bradley, K. R. (1989) *Slavery and Rebellion in the Roman World, 140 BC-70 BC*. Bloomington, IN.

Bradley, K. R. (1991) "'The regular, daily traffic in slaves': Roman history and contemporary history," *CJ*, 87, 125–38.

Bradley, K. R. (1994) *Slavery and Society at Rome*. Cambridge.

Bradley, K. R. (2000) "Animalizing the slave: the truth of fiction," *JRS*, 90, 110–25.

Bradley, K. R. (2004) "On captives under the Principate," *Phoenix*, 58, 298–318.

Bradley, K. R. (2008) "Seneca and slavery," in J. G. Fitch (ed.), *Seneca*, Oxford, 335–47.

Bradley, K. R. (2012) *Apuleius and Antonine Rome: Historical Essays*. Toronto.

Bradley, K. and Cartledge, P. (eds.) (2011) *The Cambridge World History of Slavery 1: The Ancient Mediterranean World*. Cambridge.

Bravo, B. (1980) "Sulan. Représailles et justice privée contre des étrangers dans les cités grecques," *Annali della Scuola normale superiore di Pisa: Classe di lettere e filosofia, série III*, 10, 675–987.

Brock, R. (2007) "Figurative slavery in Greek thought," in Serghidou (2007), 217–24.

Brooten, B. J. (1996) *Love between Women: Early Christian Responses to Female Homoeroticism*. Chicago, IL and London.

Brunt, P. A. (1975) "Two great Roman landowners," *Latomus*, 34, 619–35.

Bruun, C. (2013) "Greek or Latin? The owner's choice of names for *vernae* in Rome," in George (2013), 19–42.

Bruun, C. (2014) "Slaves and freed slaves," in C. Bruun and J. Edmondson (eds.), *The Oxford Handbook of Roman Epigraphy*, Oxford, 605–26.

Buckland, W. W. (1908) *The Roman Law of Slavery: The Condition of the Slave in Private Law from Augustus to Justinian*. Cambridge.

Buonocore, M. (1991) "Tradizione ed evoluzione grafico formale dell'epigrafia greca di età romana nell'area di Regium-Locri," *Bollettino della Badia Greca di Grottaferrata*, 45, 229–54.

Bushala, E. W. (1969) "The *pallake* of Philoneus," *AJP*, 90, 65–72.

Butrica, J. (2005) "Some myths and anomalies in the study of early Roman sexuality," *Journal of Homosexuality*, 49, 209–69.

Cabanes, P. (1974) "Les inscriptions du théâtre de Bouthrôtos," in *Actes du colloque 1972 sur l'esclavage*, Besançon, 105–209.

Caldelli, M. L. and Ricci, C. (1999) *Monumentum familiae Statiliorum: un riesame*. Rome.

Camodeca, G. (2006) "Cura secunda della tabula cerata londinese con la compravendita della puella Fortunata," *ZPE*, 157, 225–30.

Caneva, S. and Delli Pizzi, A. (2015) "Given to a deity? Religious and social reappraisal of human consecrations in the Hellenistic and Roman East," *CQ*, 65, 167–91.

Canevaro, M. (2018) "The public charge for *hubris* against slaves: the honour of the victim and the honour of the *hubristēs*," *JHS*, 138, 100–26.

Canevaro, M. (forthcoming) "Social mobility vs. societal stability. Once again on the aims and meaning of Solon's reforms," in M. Canevaro and J. Bernhardt (eds.), *From Homer to Solon: Continuity and Change in Archaic Greece*, Leiden.

Capozza, M. (ed.) (1979) *Schiavitù, manomissione e classi dipendenti nel mondo antico*. Rome.

Carlsen, J. (1995) *Vilici and Roman Estate Managers until AD 284*. Rome.

Carlsen, J. (2013) *Land and Labour: Studies in Roman Social and Economic History*. Rome.

Cartledge, P. (1985) "Rebels and *Sambos* in classical Greece: a comparative view," in P. Cartledge and F. D. Harvey (eds.), *Crux: Essays in Greek History Presented to G. E. M. de Ste. Croix on His 75th Birthday*, London, 16–46.

Caruso, A. (2018) "Atleti e tombe a tegole ricurve nella chora metapontina di IV sec. AC," in S. Bonomi and C. Malacrino (eds.), *Ollus leto datus est: architettura, topografia e rituali funerari nelle necropoli dell'Italia meridionale e della Sicilia tra antichità e Medioevo*, Reggio, 61–70.

Cataldi, S. (2000) "*Akolasia* e *isegoria* di meteci e schiavi nell'Atene dello Pseudo-Senofonte: una riflessione socio-economica," in M. Sordi (ed.), *L'opposizione nel mondo antico*, Milan, 75–101.

Cavallini, E. (1994) "Legge di natura e condizione dello schiavo," *Labeo: rassegna di diritto romano*, 40, 72–86.

Cecconi, G. A. (2002) *Commento storico al libro II dell'epistolario di Q. Aurelio Simmaco*. Pisa.

Champlin, E. (2005) "Phaedrus the fabulous," *JRS*, 95, 97–123.

Chaniotis, A. (2009) "Ritual performances of divine justice: the epigraphy of confession, atonement and exaltation in Roman Asia Minor," in Cotton et al. (2009), 115–53.

Chaniotis, A. (2017) "Violence in the dark: emotional impact, representation, response," in M. Champion and L. O'Sullivan (eds.), *Cultural Perceptions of Violence in the Hellenistic World*, London and New York, 100–15.

Chaniotis, A. (2018) "Epigraphic evidence," in Hodkinson, Kleijwegt and Vlassopoulos (2016–present), published online, DOI: 10.1093/oxfordhb/9780199575251.013.3.

Cheesman, C. (2009) "Names in *-por* and slave naming in republican Rome," *CQ*, 59, 511–31.

Christes, J. (1979) *Sklaven und Freigelassene als Grammatiker und Philologen im antiken Rom*. Stuttgart.

Clarke, J. R. (2003) *Roman Sex, 100 BC – AD 250*. New York.

Coarelli, F. (2005) "L''Agora des Italiens': lo *statarion* di Delo?" *JRA*, 18, 196–212.

Cobb, C. (2017) "Hidden truth in the body of Euclia: Page duBois' *Torture and Truth* and *Acts of Andrew*," *Biblical Interpretation*, 25, 19–38.

Cockle, H. (1981) "Pottery manufacture in Roman Egypt: a new papyrus," *JRS*, 71, 87–97.

Cohen, E. E. (1992) *Athenian Economy and Society: A Banking Perspective*. Princeton, NJ.

Cohen, E. E. (2013) "Sexual abuse and sexual rights: slaves' erotic experience at Athens and Rome," in T. K. Hubbard (ed.), *A Companion to Greek and Roman Sexualities*, Chichester, 184–98.

Cohen, E. E. (2015) *Athenian Prostitution: The Business of Sex*. New York.

Cohen, E. E. (2018) "Slaves operating businesses: legal ramifications for ancient Athens – and for modern scholarship," in P. Perlman (ed.), *Ancient Greek Law in the 21st Century*, Austin, TX, 54–69.

Collon, C. (2012) "Secondary characters furthering characterization: the depiction of slaves in the *Acts of Peter*," *JBL*, 131, 797–818.

Cotton, H. M., Hoyland, R. G., Price, J. J. and Wasserstein, D. J. (eds.) (2009) *From Hellenism to Islam: Cultural and Linguistic Change in the Roman near East*. Cambridge.

Courtney, E. (1995) *Musa Lapidaria: A Selection of Latin Verse Inscriptions*. Atlanta, GA.

Cox, C. (2013) "Coping with punishment: the social networking of slaves in Menander," in Akrigg and Tordoff (2013), 159–72.

Crawford, M. H. (2010) "From Alcibiades to Diocletian: slavery and the economy in the *longue durée*," in Roth (2010a), 61–73.

Crowther, N. B. (1992) "Slaves and Greek athletics," *Quaderni Urbinati di Cultura Classica*, 40, 35–42.

Culasso Gastaldi, E. (2000) "L'iscrizione trilingue del Museo di Antichità di Torino (dedicante greco, cultura punica, età romana)," *Epigraphica*, 62, 11–28.

Cunningham, I. C. (2002) "Herodas: Mimes," in *Theophrastus: Characters. Herodas: Mimes. Sophron and Other Mime Fragments*. Cambridge, MA.

Czajkowski, K. and Eckhardt, B. (2018) "Law, status and agency in the Roman provinces," *P&P*, 241, 3–31.

D'Ambra, E. and Métraux, G. P. (eds.) (2006) *The Art of Citizens, Soldiers and Freedmen in the Roman World*. Oxford.

D'Arms, J. H. (1991) "Slaves at Roman *convivia*," in W. Slater (ed.), *Dining in a Classical Context*, Ann Arbor, MI, 171–83.

Dal Lago, E. and Katsari, C. (eds.) (2008) *Slave Systems Ancient and Modern*. Cambridge.

Daoust, A. B. (2019) "*Philonicus Demetriusque*: craft specialization in the funerary relief of two freedmen," *Mouseion*, 16, 227–48.

Davidson, J. (1997) *Courtesans and Fishcakes: The Consuming Passions of Classical Athens*. New York.

de Churruca, J. (1982) "L'anathème du Concile de Gangres contre ceux qui sous prétexte de christianisme incitent les esclaves à quitter leurs maîtres," *Revue historique de droit français et étranger*, 60, 261–78.

de Melo, W. (2011) *Plautus: The Merchant. The Braggart Soldier. The Ghost. The Persian.* Cambridge, MA.

de Souza, P. (2011) "War, slavery and empire in Roman imperial iconography," *BICS*, 54, 31–62.

de Ste. Croix, G. E. M. (1981) *The Class Struggle in the Ancient Greek World, from the Archaic Period to the Arab Conquest*. London.

de Wet, C. L. (2015) *Preaching Bondage: John Chrysostom and the Discourse of Slavery in Early Christianity*. Auckland, CA.

de Wet, C. L. (2018) *The Unbound God: Slavery and the Formation of Early Christian Thought*. London and New York.

de Zulueta, F. (1946) *The Institutes of Gaius. Part I: Text with Critical Notes and Translation*. Oxford.

Demont, P. (2007) "La peur et le rire: la perception de l'esclavage dans les *Grenouilles* d'Aristophane," in Serghidou (2007), 179–92.

Derlien, J. (2003) *Asyl: die religiöse und rechtliche Begründung der Flucht zu sakralen Orten in der griechisch-römischen Antike*. Marburg.

Desbiens, J. (2017) *Les esclaves dans les lamelles de Dodone*. PhD dissertation, University of Montreal.

Descat, R. (2006) "*Argyrōnetos*: les transformations de l'échange dans la Grèce archaïque," in P. G. van Alfen (ed.), *Agoranomia: Studies in Money and Exchange Presented to John H. Kroll*, New York, 21–36.

Dickey, E. (2015) *The Colloquia of the Hermeneumata Pseudodositheana, Volume II*. Cambridge.

Diggle, J. (2004) *Theophrastus: Characters*. Cambridge.

Dilts, M. R. (1974) *Claudii Aeliani Varia Historia*. Leipzig.

Dionisotti, A. C. (1982) "From Ausonius' schooldays? A schoolbook and its relatives," *JRS*, 72, 83–125.

Döhler, M. (2018) *Acta Petri: Text, Übersetzung und Kommentar zu den Actus Vercellenses*. Berlin.

Donderer, M. and Spiliopoulou-Donderer, I. (1993) "Spätrepublikanische und kaiserzeitliche Grabmonumente von Sklavenhändlern," *Gymnasium*, 100, 254–66.

Dondin-Payre, M. and Tran, N. (eds.) (2016) *Esclaves et maîtres dans le monde romain: expressions épigraphiques de leurs relations*. Rome.

Drew-Bear, T. (1999) *Phrygian Votive Steles*. Ankara.

Droß-Krüpe, K. (2020) "How (not) to organise Roman textile production. Some considerations on merchant-entrepreneurs in Roman Egypt and the ἱστωνάρχης," in M. Mossakowska-Gaubert (ed.), *Egyptian Textiles and Their Production: 'Word' and 'Object' (Hellenistic, Roman and Byzantine Periods)*, Lincoln, NE, 128–38.

Duchêne, H. (1986) "Sur la stèle d'Aulus Caprilius Timotheos, *sômatemporos*," *BCH*, 110, 513–30.

Duncan-Jones, R. (2016) *Power and Privilege in Roman Society*. Cambridge.

Eck, W. and Heinrichs, J. (1993) *Sklaven und Freigelassene in der Gesellschaft der römischen Kaiserzeit*. Darmstadt.

Edmondson, J. (2011) "Slavery and the Roman family," in Bradley and Cartledge (2011), 337–61.

Eidinow, E. (2012) "'What will happen to me if I leave?' Ancient Greek oracles, slaves and slave owners," in Hodkinson and Geary (2012), 244–78.

Eidinow, E. and Taylor, C. (2010) "Lead-letter days: writing, communication and crisis in the ancient Greek world," *CQ*, 60, 30–62.

Epstein, S. (2008) "Why did Attic building projects employ free laborers rather than slaves?" *ZPE*, 166, 108–12.

Evans-Grubbs, J. (2010) "Hidden in plain sight: *expositi* in the community," in V. Dasen and T. Späth (eds.), *Children, Memory, and Family Identity in Roman Culture*, Oxford, 293–310.

Evans-Grubbs, J. (2013) "Between slavery and freedom: disputes over status and the Codex Justinianus," *Roman Legal Tradition*, 9, 31–93.

Fentress, E. (2005) "On the block: *catastae, chalcidica* and *cryptae* in early Imperial Italy," *JRA*, 18, 220–34.

Fentress, E. (2011) "Slavers on chariots," in A. Dowler and E. R. Galvin (eds.), *Money, Trade and Trade Routes in Pre-Islamic North Africa*, London, 65–71.

Fentress, E., Goodson, C. and Maiuro, M. (eds.) (2016) *Villa Magna: An Imperial Estate and Its Legacies*. London.

Fentress, E. and Maiuro, M. (2011) "Villa Magna near Anagni: the emperor, his winery and the wine of Signia," *JRA*, 24, 333–69.

Ferrari, F. (1997) *Romanzo di Esopo*. Milan.

Figueira, T. (ed.) (2004) *Spartan Society*. Swansea.

Finley, M. I. (1975) "Utopianism ancient and modern," in idem (ed.), *The Use and Abuse of History*, London, 178–92.

Finley, M. I. (1977) "Aulos Kapreilios Timotheos, slave trader," in idem (ed.), *Aspects of Antiquity: Discoveries and Controversies*, 2nd edition, New York, 154–66.

Finley, M. I. (1980) *Ancient Slavery and Modern Ideology*. London.

Finley, M. I. (ed.) (1987) *Classical Slavery*. London.

Fischer, J. (2010) "Unfreiheit und Sexualität im klassischen Athen," in J. Fischer and M. Ulz (eds.), *Unfreiheit und Sexualität von der Antike bis zur Gegenwart*, Zurich and New York, 58–82.

Fischer, J. (2017) "Sklaverei und Religion im klassischen Griechenland," in idem (ed.), *Studien zu antiken Religionsgeschichte*, Cracow, 67–107.

Fisher, N. R. E. (1995) "*Hybris*, status and slavery," in Powell (1995), 58–98.

Fisher, N. R. E. (2001) *Aeschines: Against Timarchus*. Oxford.

Fisher, N. R. E. (2008) "'Independent' slaves in classical Athens and the ideology of slavery," in C. Katsari and E. Dal Lago (eds.), *From Captivity to Freedom: Themes in Ancient and Modern Slavery*, Leicester, 123–46.

Fitzgerald, W. (2000) *Slavery and the Roman Literary Imagination*. Cambridge.

Fleming, R. (1999) "*Quae corpore quaestum facit*: the sexual economy of female prostitution in the Roman Empire," *JRS*, 89, 38–61.

Flexsenhar, M. (2019) *Christians in Caesar's Household: The Emperors' Slaves in the Makings of Christianity*. Philadelphia, PA.

Flory, M. B. (1978) "Family in 'familia': kinship and community in slavery," *American Journal of Ancient History*, 3, 78–95.

Flower, H. I. (2017) *The Dancing Lares and the Serpent in the Garden: Religion at the Roman Street Corner*. Princeton, NJ.

Forbes, C. A. (1955) "The education and training of slaves in antiquity," *TAPA*, 86, 321–60.

Forsdyke, S. (2012) *Slaves Tell Tales: And Other Episodes in the Politics of Popular Culture in Ancient Greece*. Princeton, NJ.

Fortacín Piedrafita, J. (1983) "La donación del diácono Vicente al monasterio de Asán y su posterior testamento como obispo de Huesca en el siglo VI: Precisiones críticas para la fijación del texto," *Cuadernos de Historia Jerónimo Zurita*, 47–8, 59–64.

Fountoulakis, A. (2007) "Punishing the lecherous slave: desire and power in Herondas 5," in Serghidou (2007), 251–64.

Fuhrmann, C. J. (2012) *Policing the Roman Empire: Soldiers, Administration and Public Order*. New York.

Fuks, A. (1984) *Social Conflict in Ancient Greece*. Jerusalem and Leiden.

Fynn-Paul, J. (2009) "Empire, monotheism and slavery in the greater Mediterranean region from antiquity to the early modern era," *P&P*, 205, 3–40.

Fynn-Paul, J. and Pargas, D. (eds.) (2018) *Slaving Zones: Cultural Identities, Ideologies and Institutions in the Evolution of Global Slavery*. Leiden.

Gabrielsen, V. (2003) "Piracy and the slave-trade," in A. Erskine (ed.), *A Companion to the Hellenistic World*, Malden, MA, 389–404.

Gaca, K. L. (2010) "The andrapodizing of war captives in Greek historical memory," *TAPA*, 140, 117–61.

Gagarin, M. and Perlman, P. (2016) *The Laws of Ancient Crete, c. 650-400 BCE*. Oxford.

Gallimore, S. (2010) "Amphora production in the Roman world: a view from the papyri," *BASP*, 47, 155–84.

Galvao-Sobrinho, C. R. (2012) "Feasting the dead together: household burials and the social strategies of slaves and freed persons in the early Principate," in S. Bell and T. Ramsby (eds.), *Free at Last! The Impact of Freed Slaves on the Roman Empire*, London and New York, 130–76.

Gamauf, R. (2009) "Slaves doing business: the role of Roman law in the economy of a Roman household," *ERH*, 16, 331–46.

Gardner, J. F. (1989) "The adoption of Roman freedmen," *Phoenix*, 43, 236–57.

Gardner, J. F. (1993) *Being a Roman Citizen*. London and New York.

Garlan, Y. (1987) "War, piracy and slavery in the Greek world," in Finley (1987), 7–21.

Garlan, Y. (1988) *Slavery in Ancient Greece*. Ithaca, NY.

Garland, A. (1992) "Cicero's *familia urbana*," *G&R*, 39, 163–72.

Garnsey, P. (1996) *Ideas of Slavery from Aristotle to Augustine*. Cambridge.

Garrido-Hory, M. (1997) "'Puer' et 'minister' chez Martial et Juvénal," in M. Moggi and G. Cordiano (eds.), *Schiavi e dipendenti nell'ambito dell' "oikos" e della "familia"*, Pisa, 307–27.

Garrido-Hory, M. (1998) *Juvénal. Esclaves et affranchis à Rome*. Besançon.

Gauthier, P. and Hatzopoulos, M. B. (1993) *La loi gymnasiarchique de Beroia*. Athens.

Gawlinski, L. (2011) *The Sacred Law of Andania: A New Text with Commentary*. Berlin and Boston, MA.

George, M. (2002) "Slave disguise in ancient Rome," *Slavery & Abolition*, 23.2, 41–54.

George, M. (2006) "Social identity and the dignity of work on freedmen's reliefs," in d'Ambra and Métraux (2006), 19–29.

George, M. (2011) "Slavery and Roman material culture," in Bradley and Cartledge (2011), 385–413.

George, M. (ed.) (2013) *Roman Slavery and Roman Material Culture*. Toronto.

Gernet, L. (1923) *Antiphon: Discours*. Paris.

Giannella, N. J. (2014) *The Mind of the Slave: The Limits of Knowledge and Power in Roman Law and Society*. PhD dissertation, University of Southern California.

Giannella, N. J. (2019) "The freedom to give: the legal basis of Seneca's treatment of slaves in *De beneficiis*," *CP*, 114, 79–99.

Glancy, J. A. (2000) "Slaves and slavery in the Matthean parables," *JBL*, 119, 67–90.

Glancy, J. A. (2002a) *Slavery in Early Christianity*. Oxford and New York.

Glancy, J. A. (2002b) "Family plots: burying slaves deep in historical ground," *Biblical Interpretation*, 10, 57–75.

Glancy, J. A. (2012) "Slavery in *Acts of Thomas*," *Journal of Early Christian History*, 2.2, 3–21.

Glancy, J. A. (2018) "'To serve them all the more': Christian slaveholders and Christian slaves in antiquity," in Fynn-Paul and Pargas (2018), 23–49.

Glazebrook, A. (2011) "*Porneion*: prostitution in Athenian civic space," in Glazebrook and Henry (2011), 34–59.

Glazebrook, A. (2014) "The erotics of manumission: prostitutes and the πρᾶσις ἐπ' ἐλευθερίᾳ," *Eugesta*, 4, 53–80.

Glazebrook, A. and Henry, M. M. (eds.) (2011) *Greek Prostitutes in the Ancient Mediterranean, 800 BCE–200 CE*. Madison, WI.

Gnoli, T. (2005-8) "C. Iulius Mygdonius: un Parto a Ravenna," *Felix Ravenna*, 161.4, 141–56.

Goette, H. R. (1986) "Die Bulla," *Bonner Jahrbucher*, 186, 133–64.

Golden, G. K. (2013) *Crisis Management during the Roman Republic*. Cambridge.

Golden, M. (1985) "*Pais*, 'child' and 'slave,'" *L'antiquité classique*, 54, 91–104.

Golden, M. (2008) *Greek Sport and Social Status*. Austin, TX.

Golden, M. (2011) "Slavery and the Greek family," in Bradley and Cartledge (2011), 134–52.

Gonzales, A. (2003) *Pline le jeune: esclaves et affranchis à Rome*. Paris.

Grawehr, M. (2019) "Of toddlers and donkeys: Roman lamps with slaves and self-representations of slaves," in Binsfeld and Ghetta (2019), 91–119.

Gray, C. (2015) *Jerome, Vita Malchi: Introduction, Text, Translation, and Commentary*. Oxford.

Green, F. M. (2015) "Witnesses and participants in the shadows: the sexual lives of enslaved women and boys," *Helios*, 42, 143–62.

Grieser, H. (2001) "Asketische Bewegungen in Kleinasien im 4. Jahrhundert und ihre Haltung zur Sklaverei," in Bellen and Heinen (2001), 381–400.

Groen-Vallinga, M. J. and Tacoma, L. E. (2015) "Contextualising condemnation to hard labour in the Roman Empire," in C. G. de Vito and A. Lichtenstein (eds.), *Global Convict Labour*, Leiden and Boston, MA, 49–78.

Groen-Vallinga, M. J. and Tacoma, L. E. (2017) "The value of labour: Diocletian's Prices Edict," in C. Verboven and C. Laes (eds.), *Work, Labour, and Professions in the Roman World*, Boston, MA and Leiden, 104–32.

Guyot, P. (1980) *Eunuchen als Sklaven und Freigelassene in der griechisch-römischen Antike*. Stuttgart.

Hanson, V. D. (1992) "Thucydides and the desertion of Attic slaves during the Decelean war," *CA*, 11, 210–28.

Harper, K. (2008) "The Greek census inscriptions of late antiquity," *JRS*, 98, 83–119.

Harper, K. (2010a) "Slave prices in late antiquity (and in the very long term)," *Historia*, 59, 206–38.

Harper, K. (2010b) "The *SC Claudianum* in the *Codex Theodosianus*: social history and legal texts," *CQ*, 60, 610–38.

Harper, K. (2011) *Slavery in the Late Roman World AD 275–425*. Cambridge.

Harper, K. (2013) *From Shame to Sin: The Christian Transformation of Sexual Morality in Late Antiquity*. Cambridge, MA and London.

Harper, K. (2017) "Freedom, slavery, and female sexual honor in antiquity," in Bodel and Scheidel (2017), 109–21.

Harries, J. and du Plessis, P. J. (2013) "The *senatus consultum Silanianum*: court decisions and judicial severity in the early Roman empire," in P. J. du Plessis (ed.), *New Frontiers: Law and Society in the Roman World*, Edinburgh, 51–70.

Harrill, J. A. (1993) "Ignatius, *Ad Polycarp*. 4.3 and the corporate manumission of Christian slaves," *Journal of Early Christian Studies*, 1, 107–42.

Harris, E. M. (2002) "Did Solon abolish debt-bondage?" *CQ*, 52, 415–30.

Harris, E. M. (2004) "Notes on a lead letter from the Athenian agora," *Harvard Studies in Classical Philology*, 102, 157–70.

Harris, E. M. (2012) "Homer, Hesiod and the 'origins' of Greek slavery," *Revue des Études Anciennes*, 114, 345–66.

Harris, W. V. (1994) "Child-exposure in the Roman Empire," *JRS*, 84, 1–22.

Harris, W. V. (1999) "Demography, geography and the sources of Roman slaves," *JRS*, 89, 62–75.

Harris, W. V. (2001) *Restraining Rage: The Ideology of Anger Control in Classical Antiquity*. Cambridge, MA.

Harris, W. V. (2015) "Prolegomena to a study of the economics of Roman art," *AJA*, 119, 395–417.

Harrison, T. (2019) "Classical Greek ethnography and the slave trade," *CA*, 38, 36–57.

Härtel, G. (1977) "Einige Bemerkungen zur rechtlichen Stellung der Sklaven und zur Beschränkung der Willkür des Herren gegenüber dem Sklaven bei der Bestrafung im 2./3. Jh. u. Z. anhand der *Digesten*," *Klio*, 59, 337–47.

Harvey, D. (2004) "The clandestine massacre of the Helots (Thucydides 4.80)," in Figueira (2004), 199–217.

Harvey, F. D. (1988) "Herodotus and the man-footed creature," in L. J. Archer (ed.), *Slavery and Other Forms of Unfree Labour*, London, 42–52.

Hasegawa, K. (2005) *The Familia Urbana during the Early Empire: A Study of Columbaria Inscriptions*. Oxford.

Hasenohr, C. (2003) "Les *Compitalia* à Délos," *BCH*, 127, 167–249.

Hasenohr, C. (2007) "Les Italiens à Délos: entre romanité et hellénisme," *Pallas*, 73, 221–32.

Hasenohr, C. (2017) "L'*emporion* de Délos, creuset de mobilité sociale? Le cas des esclaves affranchis italiens," in A. Rizakis, F. Camia and S. Zoumbaki (eds.), *Social Dynamics under Roman Rule. Mobility Status Change in the Provinces of Achaia and Macedonia*, Athens, 119–31.

Hawkins, C. (2016) *Roman Artisans and the Urban Economy*. Cambridge.

Heinen, H. (2006) "Amtsärztliche Untersuchung eines toten Sklaven. Überlegungen zu P. Oxy. III 475," in Marcone (2006), 194–202.

Hengstl, J. (1983) "Einige juristische Bemerkungen zu drei 'Töpferei-Mieturkunden,'" in F. Pastori (ed.), *Studi in onore di Arnaldo Biscardi. IV*, Milan, 663–73.

Henry, M. M. (2011) "The traffic in women: from Homer to Hipponax, from war to commerce," in Glazebrook and Henry (2011), 14–33.

Herrmann-Otto, E. (1994) *Ex ancilla natus: Untersuchungen zu den "hausgeborenen" Sklaven und Sklavinnen im Westen des römischen Kaiserreiches*. Stuttgart.

Herschbell, J. P. (1995) "Epictetus: a freedman on slavery," *AS*, 26, 185–204.

Heubner, H. (1994) *P. Cornelii Taciti libri qui supersunt*, vol. 1, corrected edition. Stuttgart and Leipzig.

Hillner, J. (2001) "Die Berufsangaben und Adressen auf den stadtrömischen Sklavenhals-bändern," *Historia*, 50, 193–216.

Hilton, J. (2019) "The role of gender and sexuality in the enslavement and liberation of female slaves in the ancient Greek romances," in Panayotakis and Paschalis (2019), 1–18.

Himmelmann, N. (1971) *Archäologisches zum Problem der griechischen Sklaverei*. Mainz.

Hodkinson, S. (2008) "Spartiates, helots and the direction of the agrarian economy: toward an understanding of helotage in comparative perspective," in Dal Lago and Katsari (2008), 285–320.

Hodkinson, S. and Geary, D. (eds.) (2012) *Slaves and Religions in Graeco-Roman Antiquity and Modern Brazil*. Newcastle upon Tyne.

Hodkinson, S., Kleijwegt, M. and Vlassopoulos, K. (eds.) (2016–) *The Oxford Handbook of Greek and Roman Slaveries*, published online, DOI: 10.1093/oxfordhb/9780199575251.001.0001.

Holleran, C. (2013) "Women and retail in Roman Italy," in E. A. Hemelrijk and G. Woolf (eds.), *Women and the Roman City in the Latin West*, Leiden, 313–30.

Hopkins, K. (1978) *Conquerors and Slaves: Sociological Studies in Roman History, Volume I*. Cambridge.

Hopkins, K. (1993) "Novel evidence for Roman slavery," *P&P*, 138, 3–27.

Horsley, G. H. R. (1983) *New Documents Illustrating Early Christianity, 3: A Review of the Greek Inscriptions and Papyri Published in 1978*. North Ryde NSW.

Horsley, G. H. R. (1987) *New Documents Illustrating Early Christianity, 4: A Review of the Greek Inscriptions and Papyri Published in 1979*. North Ryde NSW.

Huemoeller, K. P. (2020) "Freedom in marriage? Manumission for marriage in the Roman world," *JRS*, 110, 123–39.

Huemoeller, K. P. (2021) "Captivity for all? Slave status and prisoners of war in the Roman Republic," *TAPA*, 151, 101–25.

Hülsen, K. (2008) *"Tempelsklaverei" in Kleinasien: Ein Beitrag zum Tempeldienst in hellenistischer und römischer Zeit*. PhD dissertation, Universität Trier.

Hunt, P. (1998) *Slaves, Warfare and Ideology in the Greek Historians*. Cambridge.

Hunt, P. (2001) "The slaves and the generals of Arginusae," *AJP*, 122, 359–80.

Hunt, P. (2011) "Slaves in Greek literary culture," in Bradley and Cartledge (2011), 22–47.

Hunt, P. (2015) "Trojan slaves in classical Athens: ethnic identity among Athenian slaves," in Taylor and Vlassopoulos (2015), 128–54.

Hunt, P. (2016) "Violence against slaves in classical Greece," in Riess and Fagan (2016), 136–61.

Hunt, P. (2018) *Ancient Greek and Roman Slavery*. Malden, MA.

Hunter, V. (2006) "Pittalacus and Eucles: slaves in the public service of Athens," *Mouseion*, 6, 1–13.

Hunter, V. J. (1994) *Policing Athens: Social Control in the Attic Lawsuits, 420–320 BC*. Princeton, NJ.

Husby, T. (2017) *Recognizing Freedom: Manumission in the Roman Republic*. PhD dissertation, City University of New York.

Incelli, E. (2016) "Le rapport maître-esclave et les modalités de manumission dans l'empire romain," in Dondin-Payre and Tran (2016), 30–40.

Ireland, S. (2010) *Menander: The Shield and the Arbitration*. Oxford.

Ismard, P. (2017) *Democracy's Slaves: A Political History of Ancient Greece*. Cambridge, MA and London.

Ismard, P. (2019) *La cité et ses esclaves: institution, fictions, expériences*. Paris.

Ito, T. (2004) "Did the *hektemoroi* exist?" *PdP*, 59, 241–7.

Jacques, J.-M. (1996) "La figure de l'étranger dans la Comédie Nouvelle: à propos du *Bouclier de Ménandre*," *Littératures Classiques*, 27, 323–32.

Johnston, I. and Horsley, J. H. R. (2011) *Galen: Method of Medicine*. Cambridge, MA.

Jones, W. H. S. (1933) *Pausanias. Description of Greece, Volume III: Books 6–8.21 (Elis 2, Achaia, Arcadia)*. Cambridge, MA.

Jongman, W. (2003) "Slavery and the growth of Rome. The transformation of Italy in the second and first centuries BCE," in C. Edwards and G. Woolf (eds.), *Rome the Cosmopolis*, Cambridge, 100–22.

Jordan, B. (1990) "The ceremony of the helots in Thucydides, IV, 80," *L'Antiquité Classique*, 59, 37–69.

Jordan, D. R. (2000) "A personal letter found in the Athenian Agora," *Hesperia*, 69, 91–103.

Joshel, S. R. (1992) *Work, Identity and Legal Status at Rome: A Study of the Occupational Inscriptions*. Norman, OK and London.

Joshel, S. R. (2010) *Slavery in the Roman World*. New York.

Joshel, S. R. (2011) "Slaves in Roman literary culture," in Bradley and Cartledge (2011), 214–40.

Joshel, S. R. and Murnaghan, S. (eds.) (1998) *Women and Slaves in Greco-Roman Culture*. London.

Joshel, S. R. and Petersen, L. H. (2014) *The Material Life of Roman Slaves*. New York.

Kamen, D. (2009) "Servile invective in classical Athens," *SCI*, 28, 43–56.

Kamen, D. (2013) *Status in Classical Athens*. Princeton, NJ.

Kamen, D. (2016) "Manumission and slave-allowances in classical Athens," *Historia*, 65, 413–26.

Kamen, D. and Marshall, C. W. (eds.) (2021) *Slavery and Sexuality in Classical Antiquity*. Madison, WI.

Kampen, N. B. (2013) "Slaves and *liberti* in the Roman army," in George (2013), 180–97.

Kaster, R. A. (1988) *Guardians of Language: The Grammarian and Society in Late Antiquity*. Berkeley, Los Angeles, CA and London.

Keenan, J. G., Manning, J. G. and Yiftach-Firanko, U. (eds.) (2014) *Law and Legal Practice in Egypt from Alexander to the Arab Conquest: A Selection of Papyrological Sources in Translation, with Introductions and Commentary*. Cambridge.

Kirbihler, F. (2007) "P. Vedius Rufus, père de P. Vedius Pollio," *ZPE*, 160, 261–71.

Klees, H. (1975) *Herren und Sklaven: die Sklaverei im oikonomischen und politischen Schrifttum der Griechen in klassischer Zeit*. Frankfurt.

Klees, H. (1990) "Griechisches und Römisches in den Traumdeutungen Artemidors für Herren und Sklaven," in C. Boerker and M. Donderer (eds.), *Das antike Rom und der Osten: Festschrift für K. Parlasca*, Erlangen, 53–76.

Klees, H. (1998) *Sklavenleben im klassischen Griechenland*. Stuttgart.

Klees, H. (2005) "Untersuchungen zur Sklaverei bei Plutarch," *Laverna*, 16, 15–65.

Kleijwegt, M. (ed.) (2006a) *The Faces of Freedom: The Manumission and Emancipation of Slaves in Old World and New World Slavery*. Leiden and Boston, MA.

Kleijwegt, M. (2006b) "Freedpeople: a brief cross-cultural history," in Kleijwegt (2006a), 3–68.

Kleijwegt, M. (2006c) "Freed slaves, self-presentation and corporate identity in the Roman world," in Kleijwegt (2006a), 89–116.

Kleijwegt, M. (2013) "Debt bondage and chattel slavery in early Rome," in G. Campbell and A. Stanziani (eds.), *Debt and Slavery in the Mediterranean and Atlantic Worlds*, London, 43–52.

Klein, R. (1982) "Die Sklavenfrage bei Theodoret von Kyrrhos: die 7. Rede des Bischofs über die Vorsehung'," in G. Wirth et al. (eds.), *Romanitas, Christianitas: Untersuchungen zur Geschichte und Literatur der römischen Kaiserzeit*, Berlin and New York, 586–633.

Klein, R. (2000) *Die Haltung der kappadokischen Bischöfe Basilius von Caesarea, Gregor von Nazianz und Gregor von Nyssa zur Sklaverei*. Stuttgart.

Knoch, S. (2017) *Sklavenfürsorge im Römischen Reich: Formen und Motive zwischen humanitas und utilitas*. Zurich and New York.

Kolendo, J. (1978) "Les esclaves dans l'art antique. La stèle funéraire d'un marchand d'esclaves thraces découverte à Amphipolis," *Archeologia*, 29, 24–34.

Kolendo, J. (1979) "Éléments pour une enquête sur l'iconographie des esclaves dans l'art hellénistique et romain," in Capozza (1979), 161–74.

Konstan, D. (2012) "A world without slaves: Crates' *Thêria*," in C. W. Marshall and G. Kovacs (eds.), *No Laughing Matter: Studies in Athenian Comedy*, London, 13–18.

Konstan, D. (2013) "Menander's slaves: the banality of violence," in Akrigg and Tordoff (2013), 144–58.

Koortbojian, M. (2006) "The freedman's voice: the funerary monument of Aurelius Hermia and Aurelia Philematio," in d'Ambra and Métraux (2006), 91–9.

Köpstein, H. (1993) "Sklaven in der *Peira*," *Fontes Minores*, 9, 1–33.

Korporowicz, Ł. J. (2011) "Buying a slave in Roman Britain: the evidence from the *Tabulae*," *Revue Internationale des Droits de l'Antiquité*, 58, 211–24.

Kriger, D. (2011) *Sex Rewarded, Sex Punished: A Study of the Status "Female Slave" in Early Jewish Law*. Boston, MA.

Kudlien, F. (1986) *Die Stellung des Arztes in der römischen Gesellschaft. Freigeborene Römer, Eingebürgerte, Peregrine, Sklaven, Freigelassene als Ärzte*. Stuttgart.

Kudlien, F. (1991) *Sklavenmentalität im Spiegel antiker Wahrsagerei*. Stuttgart.

Kyle, D. G. (1998) *Spectacles of Death in Ancient Rome*. London and New York.

Ladjimi-Sebaï, L. (1988) "À propos du collier d'esclave trouvé à Bulla Regia," *Africa*, 10, 212–9.

Laes, C. (2008) "Child slaves at work in Roman antiquity," *AS*, 38, 235–83.

Laes, C. and Vuolanto, V. (2017) "Household and family dynamics in late-antique southern Gaul," in S. R. Huebner and G. Nathan (eds.), *Mediterranean Families in Antiquity: Households, Extended Families and Domestic Space*, Oxford, 258–82.

Laird, M. L. (2015) *Civic Monuments and the Augustales in Roman Italy*. New York.

Łajtar, A. (2010) "From Egypt to Palestine: two notes on published texts," *JJP*, 40, 145–52.

Lambertini, R. (1984) "L'etimologia di *servus* secondo i giuristi romani," in V. Giuffrè (ed.), *Sodalitas: Scritti in onore di Antonio Guarino 5*, Naples, 2385–94.

Landrea, C. (2016) "La familia méconnue des Valerii Messallae (Ier s. av. – Ier s. ap. J.-C.)," in Dondin-Payre and Tran (2016), 87–100.

Lattanzi, E., Lazzarini, L. and Mosino, F. (1989) "La tegola di Pellaro," *PdP*, 44, 286–310.

Laubenheimer, F. (2013) "Amphoras and shipwrecks: wine from the Tyrrhenian Coast at the end of the Republic and its distribution in Gaul," in J. DeRose Evans (ed.), *A Companion to the Archaeology of the Roman Republic*, Malden, MA and Oxford, 97–109.

Laubry, N. (2016) "La désignation de la postérité. Autour de la formule *libertis libertabusque posterisque eorum* dans les inscriptions funéraires romaines," in Dondin-Payre and Tran (2016), 59–72.

Lauffer, S. (1956) *Die Bergwerkssklaven von Laureion, I-II.* Wiesbaden.

Launaro, A. (2011) *Peasants and Slaves: The Rural Population of Roman Italy (200 BC to AD 100).* Cambridge.

Lenski, N. (1995) "The Gothic civil war and the date of the Gothic conversion," *Greek, Roman & Byzantine Studies,* 36, 51–87.

Lenski, N. (2008) "Captivity, slavery and cultural exchange between Rome and the Germans from the first to the seventh century CE," in C. M. Cameron (ed.), *Invisible Citizens: Captives and Their Consequences,* Salt Lake City, UT, 80–109.

Lenski, N. (2009) "Schiavi armati e formazione di eserciti privati nel mondo tardoantico," in G. Urso (ed.), *Ordine e sovversione nel mondo greco e romano,* Pisa, 146–75.

Lenski, N. (2011a) "Captivity and slavery among the Saracens in Late Antiquity (ca. 250-630 CE)," *AT,* 19, 237–66.

Lenski, N. (2011b) "Captivity and Romano-Barbarian interchange," in R. W. Mathisen and D. Shanzer (eds.), *Romans, Barbarians and the Transformation of the Roman World,* Farnham, 185–98.

Lenski, N. (2016) "Violence and the Roman slave," in Riess and Fagan (2016), 275–98.

Lenski, N. (2017) "Peasant and slave in late antique North Africa, c. 100-600 CE," in R. Lizzi Testa (ed.), *Late Antiquity in Contemporary Debate,* Cambridge, 113–55.

Lenski, N. (2018) "Framing the question: what is a slave society?" in Lenski and Cameron (2018), 15–57.

Lenski, N. and Cameron, C. M. (eds.) (2018) *What Is a Slave Society? The Practice of Slavery in Global Perspective.* Cambridge.

Leone, A. (1996) "Un'*adultera meretrix* a Bulla Regia: alcuni aspetti della città tardoantica," in M. Khanoussi, P. Ruggeri and C. Vismara (eds.), *L'Africa romana: Atti dell'XI Convegno di studio,* Ozieri, 1371–83.

Lepelley, C. (1981) "La crise de l'Afrique romaine au début du Ve siècle, d'après les lettres nouvellement découvertes de Saint Augustin," *Comptes rendus de l'Académie des Inscriptions et Belles-Lettres,* 125, 445–63.

Lewis, D. M. (1957) "The first Greek Jew," *Journal of Semitic Studies,* 2, 264–6.

Lewis, D. M. (2013) "Slave marriages in the laws of Gortyn: a matter of rights?" *Historia,* 62, 390–416.

Lewis, D. M. (2017) "Notes on slave names, ethnicity, and identity in classical and Hellenistic Greece," *U schyłku starożytności-Studia źródłoznawcze,* 16, 183–213.

Lewis, D. M. (2018) *Greek Slave Systems in Their Eastern Mediterranean Context, c. 800-146 BC.* Oxford.

Lewis, D. M. (2019) "Piracy and slave trading in action in classical and Hellenistic Greece," *Mare Nostrum,* 10.2, 79–108.

Lewis, D. M. (forthcoming) "The local slave systems of ancient Greece," in D. W. Tandy and S. D. Gartland (eds.), *Voiceless, Invisible, and Countless: The Experience of Subordinates in Greece, 800–300 BC,* Oxford.

Lewis, J. P. (2013) "Did Varro think that slaves were talking tools?" *Mnemosyne,* 66, 634–48.

Liebeschuetz, J. H. W. G. (1972) *Antioch: City and Imperial Administration in the Later Roman Empire.* Oxford.

Link, S. (2001) "*Dolos* und *woikeus* im Recht von Gortyn," *Dike,* 4, 87–112.

Lintott, A. (2002) "Freedmen and slaves in the light of legal documents from first-century AD Campania," *CQ,* 52, 555–65.

Liverani, M. (2000) "The Garamantes: a fresh approach," *Libyan Studies,* 31, 17–28.

Llewellyn-Jones, L. (2002) "Eunuchs and the royal harem in Achaemenid Persia (559–331 BC)," in S. Tougher (ed.), *Eunuchs in Antiquity and Beyond,* Swansea and London, 19–49.

Llewelyn, S. R. (1992) *New Documents Illustrating Early Christianity, 6: A Review of the Greek Inscriptions and Papyri Published in 1980–81.* North Ryde NSW.

Llewelyn, S. R. (1997) *New Documents Illustrating Early Christianity, 8: A Review of the Greek Inscriptions and Papyri Published in 1984–85*. Grand Rapids, MI and Cambridge.

Lombardo, M. (1987) "I *Peridinoi* di Platone (*Leg.*, 6, 777c) e l'etnogenesi brettia," *Annali della Scuola normale superiore di Pisa: Classe di lettere e filosofia*, 17, 611–48.

López Barja de Quiroga, P. (2006) "How (not) to sell a son – *Twelve Tables* 4, 2," *ZSS*, 123, 297–308.

López Barja de Quiroga, P. (2010) "Empire sociology: Italian freedmen, from success to oblivion," *Historia*, 59, 321–41.

López Barja de Quiroga, P. (2020) "Patronage and slavery in the Roman world: the circle of power," in Hodkinson, Kleijwegt and Vlassopoulos (2016–), published online, DOI: 10.1093/oxfordhb/9780199575251.013.31.

Lotze, D. (1959) Μεταξὺ ἐλευθέρων καὶ δούλων. *Studien zur Rechtsstellung unfreier Landbevölkerungen in Griechenland bis zum 4. Jh. v. Chr.* Berlin.

Lovén, L. L. (2012) "Roman family reliefs and the commemoration of work: text, images and ideals," in M. Harlow and L. L. Lovén (eds.), *Families in the Roman and Late Antique World*, London and New York, 141–56.

Luraghi, N. (2002) "Helotic slavery reconsidered," in A. Powell and S. Hodkinson (eds.), *Sparta: Beyond the Mirage*, Swansea, 227–48.

Luraghi, N. (2009) "The helots: comparative approaches, ancient and modern," in S. Hodkinson (ed.), *Sparta: Comparative Approaches*, Swansea, 261–304.

Luraghi, N. and Alcock, S. E. (eds.) (2003) *Helots and Their Masters in Laconia and Messenia: Histories, Ideologies, Structures*. Cambridge, MA and London.

Ma, J. (2004) "You can't go home again: displacement and identity in Xenophon's *Anabasis*," in R. Lane Fox (ed.), *The Long March: Xenophon and the Ten Thousand*, New Haven, CT and London, 330–45.

MacLean, R. (2018) *Freed Slaves and Roman Imperial Culture: Social Integration and the Transformation of Values*. Cambridge.

MacLean, R. (2020) "The absence of slavery in the Golden Age: Cynic and Stoic perspectives," *AJP*, 141, 147–77.

MacMullen, R. (1986) "Personal power in the Roman Empire," *AJP*, 107, 512–24.

MacMullen, R. (1987) "Late Roman slavery," *Historia*, 36, 359–82.

Mactoux, M. M. (1988) "Lois de Solon sur les esclaves et formation d'une société esclavagiste," in T. Yuge and M. Doi (eds.), *Forms of Control and Subordination in Antiquity*, Leiden, 331–54.

Madigan, B. (2013) *The Ceremonial Statues of the Roman Gods*. Leiden and Boston, MA.

Maffi, A. (2014) "Identificare gli schiavi nei documenti greci," in M. De Pauw and S. Coussement (eds.), *Identifiers and Identification Methods in the Ancient World: Legal Documents in Ancient Societies*, Leuven, 197–206.

Magdalene, F. R. and Wunsch, C. (2011) "Slavery between Judah and Babylon: the exilic experience," in L. Culbertson (ed.), *Slaves and Households in the near East*, Chicago, IL and London, 113–34.

Maillot, S. (forthcoming) "Freedom to curse: Theogenes the slave and the Syrian Therapeutai of Delos," in S. Kravaritou and M. Stamatopoulou (eds.), *Religious Interactions in the Hellenistic World*, Leiden and Boston, MA.

Manganaro, G. (1982) "Monete e ghiande inscritte degli schiavi ribelli in Sicilia," *Chiron*, 12, 237–44.

Manning, C. E. (1989) "Stoicism and slavery in the Roman Empire," *Aufstieg und Niedergang der Römischen Welt II*, 36.3, 1518–43.

Marcone, A. (ed.) (2006) *Medicina e società nel mondo antico*. Florence.

Marr, J. L. and Rhodes, P. J. (2008) *The "Old Oligarch": The Constitution of the Athenians Attributed to Xenophon*. Oxford.

Martin, D. B. (1993) "Slavery and the ancient Jewish family," in S. J. D. Cohen (ed.), *The Jewish Family in Antiquity*, Atlanta, GA, 113–29.

Martin, D. B. (2003) "Slave families and slaves in families," in D. L. Balch and C. Osiek (eds.), *Early Christian Families in Context: An Interdisciplinary Dialogue*, Grand Rapids, MI and Cambridge, 207–30.

Martin, R. (1971) *Recherches sur les agronomes latins et leurs conceptions économiques et sociales.* Paris.

Marzi, M. (1977) *Oratori attici minori: Iperide, Eschine, Licurgo.* Turin.

Massaro, M. (2007) "Una coppia affiatata: *CLE* 959," in P. Kruschwitz (ed.), *Die metrischen Inschriften der römischen Republik*, Berlin, 271–97.

Mavrojannis, T. (2018) "Le commerce des esclaves syriens (143–88 av. J.-C.)," *Syria: Archéologie, Art et Histoire*, 85, 245–74.

Mavrojannis, T. (2019) *Il commercio degli schiavi in Siria e nel Mediterraneo Orientale. Il quadro politico dall'inizio della pirateria cilicia sino a Pompeo.* Rome.

Mayerson, P. (2000) "The economic status of potters in P. Oxy. L 3595–3597 & XVI 1911, 1913," *BASP*, 37, 97–100.

McCarthy, K. (2000) *Slaves, Masters and the Art of Authority in Plautine Comedy.* Princeton, NJ.

McGinn, T. A. J. (1990) "*Ne serva prostituatur*: restrictive covenants in the sale of slaves," *ZSS*, 107, 315–53.

McKeown, N. (2007) "The sound of John Henderson laughing: Pliny 3.14 and Roman slaveowners' fear of their slaves," in Serghidou (2007), 265–79.

McKeown, N. (2012) "Magic, religion, and the Roman slave: resistance, control and community," in Hodkinson and Geary (2012), 279–308.

McLuhan, E. (2001) "*Ministerium seruitutis meae*: the metaphor and reality of slavery in Saint Patrick's *Epistola* and *Confessio*," in J. Carey, M. Herbert and P. Ó. Riain (eds.), *Studies in Irish Hagiography: Saints and Scholars*, Dublin, 63–71.

Mele, A. (1994) "Rites d'initiation des jeunes et processus de libération: le cas des Brettii," in Annequin and Garrido-Hory (1994), 37–58.

Mihăilescu-Bîrliba, L. (2006) *Les affranchis dans les provinces romaines de l'Illyricum.* Wiesbaden.

Millar, F. (1984) "Condemnation to hard labour in the Roman Empire, from the Julio-Claudians to Constantine," *PBSR*, 52, 124–47.

Millett, P. (2007) "Aristotle and slavery in Athens," *G&R*, 54, 178–209.

Moatti, C. (2015) *The Birth of Critical Thinking in Republican Rome.* Cambridge.

Morley, N. (2011) "Slavery under the Principate," in Bradley and Cartledge (2011), 265–86.

Morris, I. (1998) "Remaining invisible: the archaeology of the excluded in classical Athens," in Joshel and Murnaghan (1998), 193–220.

Morris, I. (2011) "Archaeology and Greek slavery," in Bradley and Cartledge (2011), 176–93.

Morton, P. (2012) *Refiguring the Sicilian Slave Wars: From Servile Unrest to Civic Disquiet and Social Disorder.* PhD dissertation, University of Edinburgh.

Morton, P. (2013) "Eunus: the cowardly king," *CQ*, 63, 237–52.

Morton, P. (2014) "The geography of rebellion: strategy and supply in the two 'Sicilian slave wars,'" *BICS*, 57, 20–38.

Mouritsen, H. (2011) *The Freedman in the Roman World.* Cambridge.

Mouritsen, H. (2013) "Slavery and manumission in the Roman elite: a study of the columbaria of the Volusii and the Statilii," in George (2013), 43–68.

Ndoye, M. (2010) *Groupes sociaux et idéologie de travail dans les mondes homérique et hésiodique.* Besançon.

Neutel, K. B. (2015) *A Cosmopolitan Ideal: Paul's Declaration "Neither Jew Nor Greek, Neither Slave Nor Free, Nor Male and Female" in the Context of First-Century Thought.* London and New York.

Nicholson, E. (2018) "Polybios, the laws of war, and Philip V of Macedon," *Historia*, 67, 434–53.

North, J. (2012) "The ritual activity of Roman slaves," in Hodkinson and Geary (2012), 67–93.

Noy, D. (2000) *Foreigners at Rome: Citizens and Strangers.* London.

Noy, D., Panayotov, A. and Bloedhorn, H. (2004) *Inscriptiones Judaicae Orientis, vol. I: Eastern Europe.* Tübingen.

Nutton, V. (1977) "*Archiatri* and the medical profession in antiquity," *PBSR*, 45, 191–226.

O'Sullivan, T. M. (2011) *Walking in Roman Culture*. New York.

Oakley, S. (1993) "The Roman conquest of Italy," in J. Rich and G. Shipley (eds.), *War and Society in the Roman World*, London and New York, 9–37.

Occhipinti, E. (2015) "Athenaeus' Sixth Book on Greek and Roman slavery," *SCI*, 34, 115–27.

Oost, S. I. (1958) "The career of M. Antonius Pallas," *AJP*, 79, 113–39.

Osborne, R. (2017) "Visual evidence – of what?" in Hodkinson, Kleijwegt and Vlassopoulos (2016–), published online, DOI: 10.1093/oxfordhb/9780199575251.013.27.

Osgood, J. (2006) *Caesar's Legacy: Civil War and the Emergence of the Roman Empire*. Cambridge.

Padilla Peralta, D.-E. (2017) "Slave religiosity in the Roman Middle Republic," *CA*, 36, 317–69.

Panayotakis, S. and Paschalis, M. (eds.) (2019) *Slaves and Masters in the Ancient Novel*. Groningen.

Panzeri, A. (2011) *Dione di Prusa: Su libertà e schiavitù. Sugli schiavi. Discorsi 14 e 15*. Pisa and Rome.

Paradiso, A. (1991) *Forme di dipendenza nel mondo greco. Ricerche sul VI libro di Ateneo*. Bari.

Paradiso, A. (2004) "The logic of terror: Thucydides, Spartan duplicity and an improbable massacre," in Figueira (2004), 179–98.

Paradiso, A. (2007) "Sur la servitude volontaire des Mariandyniens d'Héraclée du Pont," in Serghidou (2007), 23–33.

Paradiso, A. (2008) "Politiques de l'affranchissement chez Thucydide," in A. Gonzales (ed.), *La fin du statut servile (affranchissement, libération, abolition)? Hommage à Jacques Annequin Volume 1*, Besançon, 65–76.

Parker, H. (1989) "Crucially funny, or Tranio on the couch: the *servus callidus* and jokes about torture," *TAPA*, 119, 233–46.

Parker, H. N. (2007) "Free women and male slaves, or Mandingo meets the Roman empire," in Serghidou (2007), 281–98.

Parmenter, C. S. (2020) "Journeys into slavery along the Black Sea coast, c. 550–450 BCE," *CA*, 39, 57–94.

Paschalis, M. (2019) "Masters and slaves in pseudo-Lucian's *Onos* and Apuleius' *Metamorphoses*," in Panayotakis and Paschalis (2019), 222–35.

Patterson, C. (1985) "'Not worth the rearing': the causes of infant exposure in ancient Greece," *TAPA*, 115, 103–23.

Patterson, O. (1982) *Slavery and Social Death: A Comparative Study*. Cambridge, MA.

Pearse, L. (1975) "A forgotten altar of the *collegium fabrum tignariorum* of Rome," *Epigraphica*, 37, 100–23.

Pennacchietti, F. (2002) "Un termine latino nell'iscrizione punica *CIS* no. 143? Una nuova congettura," in B. G. Luigi and M. Carla (eds.), *La parola al testo. Scritti per Bice Mortara Garavelli*, Alessandria, 304–12.

Penner, L. (2012) "Gender, household structure and slavery: re-interpreting the aristocratic columbaria of early imperial Rome," in R. Laurence and A. Strömberg (eds.), *Families in the Greco-Roman World*, London, 143–58.

Perry, B. E. (1965) *Babrius, Phaedrus: Fables*. Cambridge, MA.

Perry, M. J. (2013) *Gender, Manumission and the Roman Freedwoman*. New York.

Perry, M. J. (2015) "Sexual damage to slaves in Roman law," *Journal of Ancient History*, 3, 55–75.

Petersen, L. H. (2006) *The Freedman in Roman Art and Art History*. New York.

Pomeroy, A. J. (1991) "Status and status-concern in the Greco-Roman dream-books," *AS*, 22, 51–74.

Porter, J. D. (2019) "Slavery and Athens' economic efflorescence," *Mare Nostrum*, 10.2, 25–50.

Powell, A. (ed.) (1995) *The Greek World*. London.

Prieur, J.-M. (1989) *Acta Andreae: Textus*. Turnhout.

Rackham, H., et al (1938–63) *Pliny. Natural History*. 10 vols. Cambridge, MA.

Rahlfs, A. and Hanhart, R. (2006) *Septuaginta*. Stuttgart.

Ramelli, I. (2016) *Social Justice and the Legitimacy of Slavery: The Role of Philosophical Asceticism from Ancient Judaism to Late Antiquity*. Oxford.

Ramin, J. and Veyne, P. (1981) "Droit romain et société: les hommes libres qui passent pour esclaves et l'esclavage volontaire," *Historia*, 30, 472–97.

Randall, R. H. (1953) "The Erechtheum workmen," *AJA*, 57, 199–210.

Rauh, N. K. (1997) "Who were the Cilician pirates?" in S. Swiny et al. (eds.), *Res Maritimae: Cyprus and the Eastern Mediterranean from Prehistory to Late Antiquity*, Atlanta, GA, 263–83.

Rauh, N. K., Dillon, M. J. and McClain, T. D. (2008) "*Ochlos nautikos*: leisure culture and underclass discontent in the Roman maritime world," *Memoirs of the American Academy in Rome*, supplementary volume 6, 197–242.

Rawson, E. (1985) *Intellectual Life in the Late Roman Republic*. London.

Reduzzi-Merola, F. (1990) *"Servo parere". Studi sulla condizione giuridica degli schiavi vicari e dei sottoposti a schiavi nell'esperienza greca e romana*. Naples.

Reeve, M. D. (1982) *Longus, Daphnis et Chloe*. Leipzig.

Rei, A. (1998) "Villains, wives, and slaves in the comedies of Plautus," in Joshel and Murnaghan (1998), 92–108.

Reilly, J. (1989) "Many brides: 'mistress and maid' on Athenian lekythoi," *Hesperia*, 58, 411–44.

Reynolds, J. (1982) *Aphrodisias and Rome*. London.

Richlin, A. (2014) "Talking to slaves in the Plautine audience," *CA*, 33, 174–226.

Richlin, A. (2017) *Slave Theater in the Roman Republic: Plautus and Popular Comedy*. Cambridge.

Ricl, M. (2009) "Legal and social status of *threptoi* and related categories in narrative and documentary sources," in Cotton et al. (2009), 93–114.

Riess, W. and Fagan, G. G. (eds.) (2016) *The Topography of Violence in the Greco-Roman World*. Ann Arbor, MI.

Rihll, T. (1996) "The origin and establishment of ancient Greek slavery," in M. L. Bush (ed.), *Serfdom and Slavery: Studies in Legal Bondage*, London and New York, 89–111.

Rihll, T. (2008) "Slavery and technology in pre-industrial contexts," in Dal Lago and Katsari (2008), 127–47.

Rihll, T. (2010) "Skilled slaves and the economy: the silver mines of the Laurion," in H. Heinen (ed.), *Antike Sklaverei, Rückblick und Ausblick: Neue Beiträge zur Forschungsgeschichte und zur Erschließung der archäologischen Zeugnisse*, Stuttgart, 203–22.

Ringrose, K. M. (2003) *The Perfect Servant: Eunuchs and the Social Construction of Gender in Byzantium*. Chicago, IL.

Rio, A. (2012) "Self-sale and voluntary entry into unfreedom, 300–1100," *Journal of Social History*, 45, 661–85.

Rio, A. (2017) *Slavery after Rome, 500–1100*. Oxford.

Rizakis, A. D. (2002) "L'émigration romaine en Macédoine et la communauté marchande de Thessalonique: perspectives économiques et sociales," in C. Müller and C. Hasenohr (eds.), *Les Italiens dans le monde grec: IIe siècle av. J.-C.-Ier siècle ap. J.-C.: circulation, activités, intégration*, Paris, 109–32.

Robert, L. (1955) *Hellenica: Recueil d'épigraphie, de numismatique et d'antiquités grecques, Volume X*. Paris.

Robinson, O. F. (2005) "Some peripheral aspects of the speech *Pro Cluentio*," *Fundamina*, 11, 265–74.

Rose, K. F. (1967) "Trimalchio's accountant," *CP*, 62, 258–9.

Rosivach, V. J. (1999) "Enslaving *barbaroi* and the Athenian ideology of slavery," *Historia*, 48, 129–57.

Roth, U. (2005) "Food, status, and the *peculium* of agricultural slaves," *JRA*, 18, 278–92.

Roth, U. (2007) *Thinking Tools: Agricultural Slavery between Evidence and Models*. London.

Roth, U. (ed.) (2010a) *By the Sweat of Your Brow: Roman Slavery in Its Socio-Economic Setting*. London.

Roth, U. (2010b) *"Peculium*, freedom, citizenship: golden triangle or vicious circle? An act in two parts," in Roth (2010a), 91–120.

Roth, U. (2011) "Men without hope," *PBSR*, 79, 71–94.

Roth, U. (2016) "Slavery and the Church in Visigothic Spain: the donation and will of Vincent of Huesca," *AT*, 24, 433–52.

Rothwell, K. S. (1995) "Aristophanes' *Wasps* and the sociopolitics of Aesop's fables," *CJ*, 90, 233–54.

Roubineau, J.-M. (2018) "Exclus du gymnase, exclus au gymnase. Note sur la loi gymnasiarchique de Béroia," in C. Moatti and C. Müller (eds.), *Statuts personnels et espaces sociaux: questions grecques et romaines*, Paris, 177–85.

Rouge, J. (1983) "Escroquerie et brigandage en Afrique romaine au temps de Saint Augustin (*Ep.* 8* et 10*)," in *Les lettres de Saint Augustin découvertes par Johannes Divjak*, Paris, 177–88.

Roy, J. (2012) "Cittadini ridotti in schiavitù: il consolidarsi della schiavitù nella Grecia classica," in A. Di Nardo and G. A. Lucchetta (eds.), *Nuove e antiche schiavitú*, Naples, 53–66.

Salerno, E. (2016-7) "The *taurobolium* in Gallia: a link between the centre and the periphery," *Talanta*, 48–9, 215–43.

Saller, R. P. (1994) *Patriarchy, Property and Death in the Roman Family.* Cambridge.

Salway, B. (2010) "*Mancipium rusticum sive urbanum*: the slave chapter of Diocletian's edict on maximum prices," in Roth (2010a), 1–20.

Samson, R. (2002) "Slavery, the Roman legacy," in J. Drinkwater and H. Elton (eds.), *Fifth-Century Gaul: A Crisis of Identity?*, Cambridge, 218–27.

Sandbach, F. H. (1990) *Menandri reliquiae selectae.* Revised edn with new Appendix, Oxford.

Santangelo, F. (2007) *Sulla, the Elites and the Empire: A Study of Roman Policies in Italy and the Greek East.* Leiden and Boston, MA.

Scheidel, W. (1990) "Free-born and manumitted bailiffs in the Graeco-Roman world," *CQ*, 40, 591–3.

Scheidel, W. (1996) "Reflections on the differential valuation of slaves in Diocletian's Price Edict and in the United States," *MBAH*, 15, 67–79.

Scheidel, W. (2002) "The hireling and the slave: a transatlantic perspective," in P. Cartledge, E. E. Cohen and L. Foxhall (eds.), *Money, Labour and Land: Approaches to the Economics of Ancient Greece*, London and New York, 193–202.

Scheidel, W. (2005) "Real slave prices and the relative cost of slave labor in the Greco-Roman world," *AS*, 35, 1–17.

Schepers, M. A. (1905) *Alciphronis rhetoris epistularum libri iv.* Leipzig.

Schlange-Schöningen, H. (2003) *Die römische Gesellschaft bei Galen. Biographie und Sozialgeschichte.* Berlin and New York.

Schlange-Schöningen, H. (2006) "Galen on slavery," in Marcone (2005), 180–93.

Scholl, R. (1990) *Corpus der ptolemäischen Sklaventexte, I-III.* Stuttgart.

Schumacher, L. (2001) *Sklaverei in der Antike: Alltag und Schicksal der Unfreien.* Munich.

Schumacher, L. (2006) *Corpus der Römischen Rechtsquellen zur Antiken Sklaverei. Teil VI: Stellung des Sklaven im Sakralrecht.* Stuttgart.

Segal, E. (1968) *Roman Laughter: The Comedy of Plautus.* Cambridge, MA.

Sells, D. (2013) "Slaves in the fragments of Old Comedy," in Akrigg and Tordoff (2013), 91–110.

Serghidou, A. (ed.) (2007) *Fear of Slaves, Fear of Enslavement in the Ancient Mediterranean = Peur de l'esclave, peur de l'esclavage en Méditerranée ancienne (discours, représentations, pratiques).* Besançon.

Severyns, A. (1927) "Deux «graffiti» de Délos," *BCH*, 51, 234–43.

Shaner, K. A. (2018) *Enslaved Leadership in Early Christianity.* Oxford.

Shaw, B. D. (1984) "Bandits in the Roman empire," *P&P*, 105, 3–52.

Shaw, B. D. (2001) *Spartacus and the Slave Wars: A Brief History with Documents.* Boston, MA.

Shaw, B. D. (2014) "The great transformation: slavery and the free Republic," in H. I. Flower (ed.), *The Cambridge Companion to the Roman Republic*, Cambridge, 187–212.

Sherk, R. K. (1970) "Daos and Spinther in Menander's *Aspis*," *AJP*, 91, 341–3.

Silver, M. (2011) "Contractual slavery in the Roman economy," *Ancient History Bulletin*, 25, 73–132.

Sosin, J. D. (2015) "Manumission with *paramone*: conditional freedom?" *TAPA*, 145, 325–81.

Sosin, J. D. (2017) "Ransom at Athens ([Dem.] 53.11)," *Historia*, 66, 130–46.

Stewart, R. (2012) *Plautus and Roman Slavery*. Malden, MA and Oxford.

Straus, J. A. (1977) "Quelques activités exercées par les esclaves d'après les papyrus de l'Egypte romaine," *Historia*, 26, 74–88.

Straus, J. A. (2004a) *L'Égypte gréco-romaine révélée par les papyrus: L'esclave*. Liege.

Straus, J. A. (2004b) *L'achat et la vente des esclaves dans l'Égypte romaine. Contribution papyrologique à l'étude de l'esclavage dans une province orientale de l'Empire romain*. Munich and Leipzig.

Straus, J. A. (2016) "Papyrological evidence," in Hodkinson, Kleijwegt and Vlassopoulos (2016–), published online, DOI: 10.1093/oxfordhb/9780199575251.013.35.

Strobel, K. (1987) "Einige Bemerkungen zu den historisch-archäologischen Grundlagen einer Neuformulierung der Sigillatenchronologie für Germanien und Rätien und zu wirtschafts-geschichtlichen Aspekten der römischen Keramikindustrie," *MBAH*, 6.2, 75–115.

Stupperich, R. (1983) "Zur *dextrarum iunctio* auf frühen römischen Grabreliefs," *Boreas*, 6, 143–50.

Syme, R. (1961) "Who was Vedius Pollio?" *JRS*, 51, 23–30.

Szidat, J. (1985) "Zum Sklavenhandel in der Spätantike (Aug. *Epist.* 10*)," *Historia*, 34, 362–71.

Taylor, C. and Vlassopoulos, K. (eds.) (2015) *Communities and Networks in the Ancient Greek World*. Oxford.

Tchernia, A. (2016) *The Romans and Trade*. Oxford.

Tedeschi, G. (1986) "Il canto di Hybrias il cretese, un esempio di poesia conviviale," *Quaderni di filologia classica*, 5, 53–74.

Texier, J. G. (1979) "Les esclaves et l'esclavage dans l'œuvre de Polybe," in Capozza (1979), 115–42.

Thalmann, W. G. (1996) "Versions of slavery in the *Captivi* of Plautus," *Ramus*, 25, 112–45.

Thierfelder, A. (1968) *Philogelos: Der Lachfreund, von Hierokles und Philagrios*. Munich.

Thomas, Y. (1999) "L' 'usage' et les 'fruits' de l'esclave. Opérations juridiques romaines sur le travail," *Enquête: Anthropologie, Histoire, Sociologie*, 7, 203–30.

Thompson, E. A. (1957) "Slavery in early Germany," *Hermathena*, 89, 17–29.

Thompson, E. A. (1985) *Who Was Saint Patrick?* Rochester, NY.

Thompson, F. H. (2003) *The Archaeology of Greek and Roman Slavery*. London.

Thonemann, P. (2020) *An Ancient Dream Manual: Artemidorus' The Interpretation of Dreams*. Oxford.

Thurmond, D. L. (1994) "Some Roman slave collars in *CIL*," *Athenaeum*, 82, 459–93.

Todd, S. C. (2013) "Male slave sexuality and the absence of moral panic in classical Athens," *BICS*, 56.2, 37–53.

Tomlin, R. S. O. (2003) "'The girl in question': a new text from Roman London," *Britannia*, 34, 41–51.

Tomlin, R. S. O. (2008) "'*Paedagogium* and *septizonium*': two Roman lead tablets from Leicester," *ZPE*, 167, 207–18.

Tomlin, R. S. O. (2010) "Cursing a thief in Iberia and Britain," in F. Marco Simón and R. L. Gordon (eds.), *Magical Practice in the Latin West*, Leiden and Boston, MA, 245–74.

Traglia, A. (1974) *Opere di Marco Terenzio Varrone*. Turin.

Tran, N. (2013) "The work statuses of slaves and freedmen in the great ports of the Roman world (first century BCE–second century CE)," *Annales. Histoire, Sciences Sociales: English Edition*, 68, 659–84.

Tran, N. (2014) "Esclaves et ministres des Lares dans la société de l'Arles antique," *Gallia*, 71, 103–20.

Treggiari, S. (1969) *Roman Freedmen during the Late Republic*. Oxford.

Trevett, J. (1992) *Apollodoros, the Son of Pasion*. Oxford.

Trimble, J. (2016) "The Zoninus collar and the archaeology of Roman slavery," *AJA*, 120, 447–72.

Trümper, M. (2009) *Graeco-Roman Slave Markets: Fact or Fiction?* Oxford.

Tucker, C. W. (1982) "Women in the manumission inscriptions at Delphi," *TAPA*, 112, 225–36.

Urbainczyk, T. (2008) *Slave Revolts in Antiquity*. Berkeley, CA.

van Minnen, P. (2000) "Prisoners of war and hostages in Graeco-Roman Egypt," *JJP*, 30, 155–63.

van Seters, J. (2007) "Law of the Hebrew slave: a continuing debate," *Zeitschrift für die alttestamentliche Wissenschaft*, 119, 169–83.

van Wees, H. (2003) "Conquerors and serfs: wars of conquest and forced labour in archaic Greece," in Luraghi and Alcock (2003), 33–80.

van Wees, H. (2013) "Farmers and hoplites: models of historical development," in D. Kagan and G. F. Viggiano (eds.), *Men of Bronze: Hoplite Warfare in Ancient Greece*, Princeton, NJ and Oxford, 222–55.

Vaucher, D. (2018) "Glaubensbekenntnis oder Sklavengehorsam? Petrus von Alexandrien zu einem christlichen Dilemma," *Vigiliae Christianae*, 72, 533–60.

Vermote, K. (2016) "The *macula servitutis* of Roman freedmen. *Neque enim aboletur turpitudo, quae postea intermissa est?*" *Revue belge de Philologie et d'Histoire*, 94, 131–64.

Vester, C. (2013) "Tokens of identity in Menander's *Epitrepontes*: slaves, citizens and in-betweens," in Akrigg and Tordoff (2013), 209–27.

Veyne, P. (1981) "Le dossier des esclaves-colons romains," *Revue historique*, 265, 3–25.

Vidal-Naquet, P. (1986) "Reflections on Greek historical writing about slavery," in idem (ed.), *The Black Hunter: Forms of Thought and Forms of Society in the Greek World*, Baltimore, MD, 168–88.

Vlassopoulos, K. (2007) "Free spaces: identity, experience and democracy in classical Athens," *CQ*, 57, 33–52.

Vlassopoulos, K. (2009) "Slavery, freedom and citizenship in classical Athens: beyond a legalistic approach," *ERH*, 16, 347–63.

Vlassopoulos, K. (2010) "Athenian slave names and Athenian social history," *ZPE*, 175, 113–44.

Vlassopoulos, K. (2011a) "Greek slavery: from domination to property and back again," *JHS*, 131, 115–30.

Vlassopoulos, K. (2011b) "Two images of ancient slavery: the 'living tool' and the 'koinônia,'" in E. Herrmann-Otto (ed.), *Sklaverei und Zwangsarbeit zwischen Akzeptanz und Widerstand*, Hildesheim, Zurich and New York, 467–77.

Vlassopoulos, K. (2015) "Plotting strategies, networks and communities in classical Athens: the evidence of slave names," in Taylor and Vlassopoulos (2015), 101–27.

Vlassopoulos, K. (2018a) "Hope and slavery," in D. Spatharas and G. Kazantzidis (eds.), *Hope in Ancient Literature, History and Art*, Berlin and Boston, MA, 239–62.

Vlassopoulos, K. (2018b) "Historicising the closed city," in M. Dana and I. Savalli-Lestrade (eds.), *La cité interconnectée: transferts et réseaux institutionnels, religieux et culturels aux époques hellénistique et impériale*, Bordeaux, 43–57.

Vlassopoulos, K. (2019) "The end of enslavement, Greek style," in Hodkinson, Kleijwegt and Vlassopoulos (2016–), published online, DOI: 10.1093/oxfordhb/9780199575251.013.39.

Vlassopoulos, K. (2021a) *Historicising Ancient Slavery*. Edinburgh.

Vlassopoulos, K. (2021b) "Christianity and slavery: Towards an entangled history?" *Post Augustum*, 5, 62–103.

Vlassopoulos, K. (forthcoming) "An entangled history of the Peloponnesian War," in R. Osborne and S. Gartland (eds.), *Rethinking the Peloponnesian War*.

Vogt, J. (1974) *Ancient Slavery and the Ideal of Man*. Oxford.

Volkmann, H. (1961) *Die Massenversklavungen der Einwohner eroberter Städte in der hellenistisch-römischen Zeit*. Mainz.

von Arnim, J. (1893–96) *Dionis Prusaensis quem vocant Chrysostomum quae exstant omnia*. 2 vols. 2nd edn, Berlin.

von Behren, C. (2009) *Sklaven und Freigelassene auf den Grabdenkmälern des nördlichen Schwarzmeerraumes*. PhD dissertation, Universität Trier.

Vuolanto, V. (2003) "Selling a freeborn child: rhetoric and social realities in the late Roman world," *AS*, 33, 169–207.

Wacke, A. (2001) "*Manumissio matrimonii causa*. Die Freilassung zwecks Heirat nach den Ehegesetzen des Augustus," in Bellen and Heinen (2001), 133–58.

Wallace-Hadrill, A. (2008) *Rome's Cultural Revolution*. Cambridge and New York.

Weaver, P. (2004) "P.Oxy. 3312 and joining the household of Caesar," *ZPE*, 149, 196–204.

Weaver, P. R. C. (1964) "*Vicarius* and *vicarianus* in the *familia Caesaris*," *JRS*, 54, 117–28.

Weaver, P. R. C. (1972) *Familia Caesaris: A Social Study of the Emperor's Freedmen and Slaves*. London.

Welwei, K.-W. (1977) *Unfreie im antiken Kriegsdienst. II: Die kleineren und mittleren griechischen Staaten und die Hellenistischen Reiche*. Wiesbaden.

Welwei, K.-W. (2000) *Sub corona vendere: Quellenkritische Studien zu Kriegsgefangenschaft und Sklaverei in Rom bis zum Ende des Hannibalkrieges*. Stuttgart.

Wendt, H. (2016) *At the Temple Gates: The Religion of Freelance Experts in the Roman Empire*. Oxford.

Wiedemann, T. (1981) *Greek and Roman Slavery: A Sourcebook*. London.

Wiedemann, T. (1992) *Emperors and Gladiators*. London and New York.

Wieling, H. (1999) *Corpus der Römischen Rechtsquellen zur Antiken Sklaverei. Teil I: Die Begründung des Sklavenstatus nach ius gentium und ius civile*. Stuttgart.

Wijma, S. M. (2014) *Embracing the Immigrant: The Participation of Metics in Athenian Polis Religion (5th–4th Century BC)*. Stuttgart.

Williams, B. (1993) *Shame and Necessity*. Berkeley, CA and Oxford.

Williams, C. A. (1995) "Greek love at Rome," *CQ*, 45, 517–39.

Williams, D. (2006) *The Warren Cup*. London.

Williams, K. F. (2006) "Pliny and the murder of Larcius Macedo," *CJ*, 101, 409–24.

Wipszycka, E. (1965) *L'industrie textile dans l'Égypte romaine*. Wroclaw, Warsaw and Cracow.

Wolff, H. J. (1966) "Neue juristische Urkunden: III. Beaufsichtigung des Sklavenhandels im römischen Ägypten: die Anakrisis," *ZSS*, 83, 340–9.

Wunsch, C. (2013) "Glimpses on the lives of deportees in rural Babylonia," in A. Berlejung and M. P. Streck (eds.), *Arameans, Chaldeans, and Arabs in Babylonia and Palestine in the First Millennium BC*, Wiesbaden, 247–60.

Zanker, P. (1975) "Grabreliefs römischer Freigelassener," *Jahrbuch des Deutschen Archäologischen Instituts*, 90, 267–315.

Zanker, P. (1993) "The Hellenistic grave stelai from Smyrna: identity and self-image in the polis," in A. Bulloch et al. (eds.), *Images and Ideologies: Self-Definition in the Hellenistic World*, Berkeley and Los Angeles, CA, 212–30.

Zanovello, S. L. (2018) "Some remarks on manumission and consecration in Hellenistic Chaeronea," *Journal of Global Slavery*, 3, 129–51.

Zarmakoupi, M. (2016) "The spatial environment of inscriptions and graffiti in domestic spaces: the case of Delos," in R. Benefiel and P. Keegan (eds.), *Inscriptions in the Private Sphere in the Greco-Roman World*, Leiden and Boston, MA, 50–79.

Zelnick-Abramovitz, R. (2005) *Not Wholly Free: The Concept of Manumission and the Status of Manumitted Slaves in the Ancient Greek World*. Leiden.

Zelnick-Abramovitz, R. (2012) "Slaves and role reversal in ancient Greek cults," in Hodkinson and Geary (2012), 96–132.

Zelnick-Abramovitz, R. (2013) *Taxing Freedom in Thessalian Manumission Inscriptions*. Leiden and Boston, MA.

Zelnick-Abramovitz, R. (2018) "Greek and Roman terminologies of slavery," in Hodkinson, Kleijwegt and Vlassopoulos (2016–), published online, doi: 10.1093/oxfor dhb/9780199575251.013.41.

Zelnick-Abramowitz, R. (2019) "The status of slaves manumitted under *paramonê*," in G. Thür, U. Yiftach and R. Zelnick-Abramowitz (eds.), *Symposion 2017: Vorträge zur griechischen und hellenistischen Rechtsgeschichte*, Vienna, 377–401.

Zoumbaki, S. (2005) "The collective definition of slaves and the limits to their activities," in Anastasiadis and Doukellis (2005), 217–31.

Index of Passages Cited

I. Literary and legal sources[1]

Achilles Tatius, *Leukippe and Kleitophon*
    6.20–2: 167–8
Acts of Andrew 17–22: 188–90
Acts of Peter 14: 136–7
Acts of the Apostles 16:16–19: 95–6
    20:34: 67
Acts of Thomas 2: 83
Aelian, *Various history* 2.7: 229
Aeschines, *Against Timarchos* 54–64: 35–7
    97: 111
Aesop, *Fables* (Hausrath–Hunger) 14: 102
    209: 128
    218: 170
    261: 186–7
Agathias, *Histories* 2.7.1–5: 300–1
Alciphron, *Letters* 1.2: 47
    2.23: 187
    2.24–25: 48
*Alfenus, *Digest* book 7: 86
Ammianus Marcellinus 14.6.16–17: 101
    19.11.1: 290
    28.1.49: 13–14
    31.4.9–11: 291

    31.6.5: 291–2
*Anaxandrides, fr. 4 K–A: 80–1
Antipater of Thessalonica,
    82 Gow–Page: 76–7
Antiphon, *Against the Stepmother* 14–20:
    132–3
Appian, *Civil Wars* 1.1.7: 284–5
    1.11.100: 156–7
    4.4.24: 133
    4.10.81: 157
Apuleius, *Apology* 17: 64–5
Apuleius, *Metamorphoses* 9.12: 92
Aristophanes, *Clouds* 1–7: 24
Aristophanes, *Frogs* 31–4: 288
    948–52: 153
Aristophanes, *Wealth* 510–26: 75–6
Aristotle, *Constitution of the Athenians*
    2, 4–6: 283–4
Aristotle, *Politics* 1253b23–1254a17: 5–6
    1264a17–22: 10–11
    1269a34–b12: 211
Aristotle, *fr. 8.44.472 Rose (Athen. 272c):
    308
Artemidorus, *The interpretation of dreams*
    1.45: 329–30

---

[1] Passages or works marked with an asterisk (*) are cited by the ancient author of a source. References to the fragments of ancient historians and philosophers cited by the ancient authors of sources are consistently offered here, in the index.

III. Papyrological sources

Index of Places and Peoples

Greek and Roman Slaveries, First Edition. Eftychia Bathrellou and Kostas Vlassopoulos.
© 2022 John Wiley & Sons, Inc. Published 2022 by John Wiley & Sons, Inc.

Index of Names[1]

Abbanes, 83
Abel, 83
Abienus, 13–14
Abramos, 293
Achaios, 247
Achillas, 96
Achillodoros, 223
Acilia Lamyra, 181
Adea, 253
Adultera, 131
Aebutius, 272
Aegeates, 188–90
Aelius Barbarus, 159
Aelius Marcianus, 22
Aelius Myron, 159–60
Aemilius Lepidus, 175
Aemilius Paullus, 199
Aesop, 105–6, 122–3, 173–4
Agathokles, 334
Agathon, 312
Agathopous, 315
Agileius, 95
Agis, 9, 287
Agoraste, 172
Agrippina, 331
Aigialos, 15

Aimos, 234
Aineas, 233
Aischylos, 254
Alaric, 292
Albicianus, 233
Albina, 59
Alcman, 10
Alexander Polyhistor, 219
Alexandros, 15, 311, 328, 334
Alexous, 142
Aline, 78–9
Alfia Flora, 181
Alfius Primio, 191
Alke, 324–5
Allenia Salvia, 181
Alocus, 188
Alypius, 207
Alypos, 32
Amandus, 104
Amerimnos, 15
Ammianus, 312
Ammias, 312
Ammonia, 196
Ammonilla, 34
Amphio, 331
Ampudius Philomusus, 270–1

---

[1] In the case of Roman names we have omitted the praenomen, except when it is the single attested name.

Greek and Roman Slaveries, First Edition. Eftychia Bathrellou and Kostas Vlassopoulos.
© 2022 John Wiley & Sons, Inc. Published 2022 by John Wiley & Sons, Inc.

Thematic Index

251–76, 301–2, 306, 316, 319, 324–7, 328, 329, 330, 333–4

Funerary commemoration: 15–6, 32, 37, 38–41, 43–4, 52, 94, 102, 104, 128, 130, 164, 171, 172, 175–7, 180, 193, 196, 225, 255, 256, 262, 267, 269–76, 315–6, 326–7, 330, 335

Gambling: 36, 318, 332
Gender: 16, 17–18, 67–8, 111–2, 167–8, 316, 328
Geopolitics: 210–3
Gymnasion: 10, 27, 87, 146, 154
Gymnêtes: 7

Health: 19, 70, 93, 96, 124, 145, 149, 170
Helots: 4, 7, 9, 10, 11, 79, 120, 211, 282, 286–7, 319
Hiring: 33, 49, 79, 91, 94, 95, 96, 99, 202, 237, 261, 279
Holidays: 96, 119, 297
Homoerotic relations: 35–6, 42, 97, 108, 134, 143, 244, 275–6, 329
Honor: 4, 14, 15, 16, 25, 26, 39, 55, 65, 126, 128, 136, 137, 139, 150, 154, 160–1, 171, 179, 185, 236, 237, 264, 265–6, 269–70, 278, 296, 318, 331, 335, 336
House-born slaves: 28, 52, 58, 70, 97, 144, 153–4, 165, 176, 177, 179, 181, 186, 232, 262–3
Households: 58, 61–2, 69–70, 72, 142, 192, 334–5
Hybris: 152

Identification: 30–4, 37, 141
Imperial freedmen: 106, 159, 160, 161, 177, 181, 229, 265–6, 269, 316
Imperial slaves: 118, 181, 233, 299, 315–6
Independent slaves: 11, 77, 106–7, 112–5, 318–9
Informers: 14, 157, 166, 167, 189–90, 205
Inheritance: 12, 28, 35, 102, 109, 111, 144, 166, 198, 214, 232, 253, 264, 324–6, 328
Initiative: 90, 122, 123, 126, 187
Instrumentality: 5, 65–6, 72, 108
Insult: 22, 65, 131, 137, 191–2, 262
Intercultural exchange: 217–21

Junian Latins: 258–9, 299
Justice: 20, 21, 23, 66, 120, 143, 203, 243, 295, 323

Kinship: 4, 14, 15, 27, 32, 33, 126, 162, 172, 214, 225, 251–2, 295, 299–300, 328
Klarôtai: 7

Korynêphoroi: 7

Law: 12, 34, 57, 86, 89, 99, 143–4, 146, 149–50, 152, 156, 173, 186, 206, 207–8, 214, 224, 229, 231, 237, 252, 253, 256, 257, 264, 281, 283, 298–300, 303, 324–5, 328, 333
Law, civil: 12, 22, 298
Law, natural: 12, 295
Law of nations: 6, 22, 298
Law of persons: 6
Leisure: 9, 211
Legal status: 13, 27–9, 34, 145, 146–7, 152, 154, 178, 204–7, 231–2, 234–5, 237, 298–300, 301–2, 303, 317, 324–5, 328, 329
Lex Aelia Sentia: 89, 256
Lex Cornelia: 264
Lex Fufia Caninia: 57
Liberation: 10, 163–4, 207–9, 212–3, 283
Love: 50–1, 70, 72, 97, 128, 132, 133, 137, 143, 162, 167–8, 181, 244, 263, 325–6
Luxury: 11, 63, 74, 314

Magistri, -ae: 181, 182, 306
Manumission: 9, 24–5, 28, 33, 42, 49–50, 57, 59, 64, 69–70, 89, 112–3, 125, 127, 134, 135, 140, 143, 152, 153, 155–6, 159, 175, 177, 179, 183, 184, 189, 193, 212, 218, 219, 225, 231–2, 250, 251–61, 263, 279–80, 286–7, 288, 301–2, 303, 308, 317, 323, 325–6, 328, 329, 330
Manumission laws: 156, 252–3, 256, 258–9
Mariandynoi: 7, 79, 81
Maroons: 243–4
Marriage: 12, 14, 15, 25–6, 50–1, 71, 133, 137, 142, 169, 170, 172, 173, 174, 175, 181, 202, 247, 268, 272, 303, 324, 336
Masculinity: 49, 93
Masters: 5–6, 10, 13, 16, 19, 22, 23, 34, 38–41, 47, 48, 52, 53, 56–84, 86, 95–6, 97, 142, 254, 295, 309
Masters, elite: 14, 16, 21, 23, 57, 59, 63–4, 66–8, 68–9, 73–4, 93, 94, 98, 99–100, 101, 103, 107–8, 117, 118, 121, 129, 130–1, 133, 136, 138, 140, 143–4, 148, 172, 175, 188–90, 218, 219, 220, 237, 273–4, 300, 331, 336
Masters, enslaved: 60, 233, 279, 315–6
Masters, female: 14, 16, 17–18, 22, 23, 59, 101, 118, 163–4, 235, 251, 260, 261, 262–3, 270, 273–4, 275